Integrated Series in Information Systems

Volume 22

Series Editors
Ramesh Sharda
Oklahoma State University, Stillwater, USA

Stefan Voß
University of Hamburg, Hamburg, Germany

For further volumes:
http://www.springer.com/series/6157

Alan Hevner · Samir Chatterjee

Design Research in Information Systems

Theory and Practice

Forewords by Paul Gray and Carliss Y. Baldwin

 Springer

Alan Hevner
University of South Florida
College of Business
4202 East Fowler Avenue
Tampa FL 33620
USA
ahevner@usf.edu

Samir Chatterjee
Claremont Graduate University
School of Information Systems and
    Technology
130 East 9th Street
Claremont CA 91711
USA
samir.chatterjee@cgu.edu

ISSN 1571-0270
ISBN 978-1-4419-5652-1   e-ISBN 978-1-4419-5653-8
DOI 10.1007/978-1-4419-5653-8
Springer New York Dordrecht Heidelberg London

Library of Congress Control Number: 2010924526

Printed on acid-free paper

Springer is part of Springer Science+Business Media (www.springer.com)

Critical Praise for Design Science Research Book

Well designed systems enable productivity and successful adoption. Poor design is the greatest barrier to both. I highly recommend this book as a guideline to understanding where we have come from and where we are headed in design science.

Kristin M. Tolle, Ph.D., Microsoft External Research, Director, Health and Wellness Team

This enlightening book wonderfully captures the vibrant energy in design science research that Hevner and Chatterjee have been able to mobilize in the information systems design community in the past five years through their work and the successful DESRIST annual conferences. It brings together the contributions of some of the best academic minds from Europe and North America in this growing area, and is the only book of its kind. It is both a foundation and a springboard for enabling the further advancement of design research in information systems.

Omar A. El Sawy, Professor of Information Systems, Marshall School of Business, University of Southern California

This important book provides valuable guidance for design-oriented IS researchers. With an increased demand for more relevant design-oriented research on real-world business problems, this new book on design research in IS has been waited for by many.

Prof. Dr. Robert Winter, Director, Institute of Information Management, University of St. Gallen, Switzerland

Creating and using information systems in business, organizational and consumer settings are both essential and complicated. Most people involved with these information systems initiatives deal with the enormous breadth and depth of complexity by selectively focusing on either the technology aspects, or the managerial, organizational and people impacts. This book on Design Research in Information Systems by Hevner and Chatterjee is an important effort to build bridges across the technology perspective and the managerial and behavioral perspectives of information systems. This important book will help anyone appreciate how those who are building IT systems can contribute to IS research.

Steven Miller, Professor of Information
Systems Practice, Dean, School of Information
Systems, Singapore Management University

This work is timely, crisp, and comprehensive. Hevner and Chatterjee skillfully lead their readers through the central ideas of information systems design science in a way that is not only authoritative and methodical, but also clear and readable. It provides us with a work that serves design researchers both as a complete tutorial and an excellent desk reference.

Richard Baskerville, Professor of CIS
Department, J Mack Robinson College of
Business, Georgia State University

I dedicate this book to all my Georgia State University design colleagues who started the important dialogue when no one else understood our research method. I also dedicate this book to my family, my loving wife Madhumita, and my son Mickey for their support. Finally my gratitude is to my parents for always believing in me. Dad and Mom, you are the greatest generation!

– Samir

I dedicate this book to my fabulous wife, Cindy.

– Alan

Foreword

It is 5 years since the publication of the seminal paper on "Design Science in Information Systems Research" by Hevner, March, Park, and Ram in *MIS Quarterly* and the initiation of the *Information Technology and Systems* department of the *Communications of AIS*. These events in 2004 are markers in the move of design science to the forefront of information systems research. A sufficient interval has elapsed since then to allow assessment of from where the field has come and where it should go.

Design science research and behavioral science research started as dual tracks when IS was a young field. By the 1990s, the influx of behavioral scientists started to dominate the number of design scientists and the field moved in that direction. By the early 2000s, design people were having difficulty publishing in mainline IS journals and in being tenured in many universities. Yes, an annual Workshop on Information Technology and Systems (WITS) was established in 1991 in conjunction with the International Conference on Information Systems (ICIS) and grew each year. But that was the extent of design science recognition. Fortunately, a revival is underway. By 2009, when this foreword was written, the fourth DESRIST conference has been held and plans are afoot for the 2010 meeting. Design scientists regained respect and recognition in many venues where they previously had little. Some behavioral scientists now understand, as this book points out (in Fig. 2.1), that the two disciplinary approaches are tied to one another. Design scientists create IS artifacts that create utility and behavioral scientists create IS theories based on these research results that provide truth. We are not there yet in getting the relationships between the designers and behavioralists completely right. But we can be confident that the link between design science and behavioral science will become complimentary and ever stronger in the years ahead.

Design science is a relatively new field. It traces its roots to the 1969 book "Science of the Artificial" by the late, great Herbert Simon. The artificial refers to the idea that phenomena and entities can depend on choices by the designer rather than being true only because they occur in nature. Much of the world of computing is the result of human design choices. Physical phenomena, such as the speed of light or visual acuity, act as constraints on the design choice. Design science focuses on the relevance of IT artifacts in applications. It involves problems characterized by unstable requirements and constraints and complex interactions among problem components solved by using malleable processes and artifacts, creativity, and team-work. That's quite an order to fulfill for problems that are at heart wicked. Yet it is being done and being done well.

Design science researchers work on understanding, explaining, and improving information systems. They study artifacts such as algorithms, human/computer interfaces, languages, and system design methodologies. Understanding leads to knowledge for predicting how some aspect of a phenomenon behaves. Design uses that knowledge plus innovation to create new improved artifacts that surpass what was available previously. In practice, design itself involves considerations of the internal, the external, and the interface between the internal and the external. That is, design is the know–how for implementing an artifact that satisfies a set of functional requirements. I could go on to explain design research at ever deeper levels. But that would defeat the purpose of your reading this excellent book.

This volume is the first major book on design science I know of. It is authored by two people, Alan Hevner and Samir Chatterjee, who are experienced leaders and experts in the field. They organize and distill its current extent. You will find the book is a much needed contribution for practitioners, students, and faculty in a rapidly evolving area. I found that it broadened my understanding of design science research and believe it will also broaden yours.

Paul Gray
Professor Emeritus, Information Science
Founding Editor, *Communications of AIS*
Irvine, CA

Foreword

In his pathbreaking book, *The Sciences of the Artificial*, Herbert Simon observed that the natural sciences enjoyed a privileged position among academic disciplines. By the opposite token, man-made things were not seen as worthy of true scientific inquiry. Simon disagreed. He argued for the establishment of a set of sciences focused on man-made things and unified by an overarching science of design.

One reason, Simon believed, the sciences of the artificial lagged behind the natural sciences was that interesting man-made systems quickly become very complex. Science prizes simplicity and so is preferentially aimed at simple phenomena and broad generalizations.

Researchers in information technology and information systems (IT/IS) of necessity study complex, man-made systems. Moreover, as computers and communication become cheaper, people are inevitably building new IT/IS systems that push the limits of what is possible. Such systems confront us with "wicked problems" where social, technical, economic, and political constraints interact, and solutions cannot be deduced from scientific principles alone. This is the world of IT/IS research. To quote the fearful words of early scientific cartographers: "Here be dragons."

In domains characterized by complexity, natural science methods can only carry us so far. Such methods leave out the important element of design: the construction of new ways to solve a problem or address a need. Natural science methods take the world as given and do not allow for novelty.

As researchers, how can we allow novel solutions to appear, and then study them in a systematic way? How can we build up scientific knowledge about new designs, in particular, what works and what fails and why? Without such knowledge, we will not be able to understand the large-scale systems we are creating today. The wicked problems will grow evermore wicked. The dragons will win.

Leaving hard-won knowledge about novel solutions scattered about, uncorrelated and unanalyzed, will not make us masters of our own designs. Thus there is a need to build knowledge about designs systematically, to test it rigorously, to share it openly, and to pass it on. Only in this way can we take advantage of what Karl Popper called the "ratchet" of the scientific method: the iterative process by which erroneous conjectures are eliminated through a process of hypothesis formulation, testing and reformulation. (Simon called this the "generate-test cycle," and placed it at the center of his science of design.) It is through this scientific method of learning, Popper argued, that knowledge becomes cumulative. Designs get better. Progress is real.

As Newell and Simon said, every artifact asks a question of the world. Put another way, every new design embodies a set of hypotheses about how the world works. The artifact based on the design tests those hypotheses, confirming some and contradicting others. How can we leverage this innate property of artifacts and designs to build up our stores of scientific knowledge?

Hevner and Chatterjee and the other contributors to this volume explain in a practical and systematic way how to do this. They provide a roadmap that will allow *you* to do first-rate design science research. They explain how to pose good research questions, how to frame your questions in relation to prior work, and how and why you must rigorously evaluate and report your results. They do not tell you how to design, but they will help you to situate your designs in the broader discipline of design science.

Designing will never be made entirely systematic, but the knowledge gleaned in the process can be systematized and tested until it reaches the standard of science. This book explains how. By following its precepts, the knowledge gained from your own design experience can become part of the great body of scientific knowledge that enriches us all.

Carliss Y. Baldwin
Harvard Business School
Baker Library 355
Boston, Massachusetts

Preface

"The proper study of mankind is the science of design."

Herbert Simon

"Engineering, medicine, business, architecture and painting are concerned not with the necessary but with the contingent – not with how things are but with how they might be – in short, with design."

Herbert Simon

Purpose and Motivation of This Book

The creative human activity of design changes the world in which we live for the better. As academic researchers in the field of information systems (IS), the co-authors have observed, studied, and taught design in the development of software-intensive systems for business. We have experienced the difficulties and wicked nature of designing useful systems. More importantly, we have faced classrooms of students with the challenges of how teach the underlying theories and everyday practices of software system design. These experiences and challenges have motivated us to perform research in the science of design, or design science research (DSR), and to write this book.

We believe that the study of information systems design, both its theory and practice, has become an essential part of the education of IS students and professionals. More and more IS graduate and doctoral programs are beginning to offer graduate-level seminars on design science research. The purpose of this book is to fill a void: the lack of a good reference book on design science research. Most current seminars study a collection of research papers from many sources. Often, these papers are written with differing terminology and research perspectives leading to confusion and misunderstandings for students. Here we provide a consistent approach for performing and understanding design science research while maintaining a diversity of opinions from many thought leaders in the IS design community.

Having worked in the information technology and software design fields as academics and industry consultants, the authors of this book have written from their extensive experience as educators of design science research. Many chapters of this book are based on a series of seminars that Dr. Chatterjee has taught at Claremont Graduate University. Dr. Hevner's seminal 2004 article in *Management Information Systems Quarterly* journal has had huge impact in the IS field. (Appendix A is a reprint of the Hevner et al. 2004 article in *MISQ*.) It has raised consciousness toward design science as a rigorous and relevant research paradigm and his evangelistic efforts to promote DSR throughout the world has resulted in a heightened awareness of the urgent need for good design research to improve business processes and systems.

In 2006, Drs. Chatterjee and Hevner founded the Design Science Research in Information Systems and Technology (DESRIST) conference which has become a platform for all leading design IS researchers to present their work and a forum to debate the important issues facing the community. We have selected a handful of the best papers that have appeared in this conference over the past 4 years to be included as chapters of the book. In Appendix B, we have provided a list of exemplar research papers in design science as an aid to students for further reading.

It has been our goal to make this book easy-to-read, easy-to-understand, and easy-to-apply. From frameworks to theory to application design, this book provides a comprehensive coverage of the most salient design science research knowledge that is available at the time of this book's publication.

Intended Audience

The material is suitable for graduate courses in information systems, computer science, software engineering, engineering design, and other design-oriented fields. The book is intended to be used as a core text or reference book for doctoral seminars in design science research. The book does not require an extensive background in design and can be appreciated by any practitioner as well who is working in the field of information systems and technology design. IS faculty and industrial researchers who want to further develop their knowledge and skills in the design science research methodology will find it valuable. Each chapter is self-contained with references.

Alan Hevner   Samir Chatterjee
Tampa, Florida   Claremont, California

Acknowledgments

Writing a book is no small task. It is with great pleasure that we acknowledge the efforts of many people who have contributed either directly or indirectly to the development of this book. The ideas presented in this book have been shaped and influenced by the students who have taken the design science research seminars at Claremont and all those doctoral students that we have graduated. In particular we would like to thank the contributors who despite busy schedules have worked hard to write chapters in this book:

Juhani Iivari

Monica Chiarini Tremblay

Donald Berndt

Robert Judge

Matti Rossi

Maung Sein

Sandeep Purao

Salvatore T. March

Timothy J. Vogus

Sven A. Carlsson

Kevin Williams

We acknowledge the love and support of our families toward this endeavor. Without their sacrifices, this book would not have been possible.

Finally we are grateful to the Springer publishing team for their eager assistance and expert advice. In particular we thank Ramesh Sharda who encouraged us to write this book and the Springer editorial team of Gary Folven, Carolyn Ford, and Neil Levine.

We express our gratitude to Leah Paul, of Integra Software Services and Christine Ricketts of Springer for carefully editing our entire textbook for any errors or incorrect facts.

Contents

Contributors

Donald J. Berndt College of Business at the University of South Florida, Tampa, FL, USA, dberndt@coba.usf.edu

Sven A. Carlsson School of Economics and Management, Lund University, Lund, Sweden, sven_carlsson@hermes.ics.lu.se

Juhani Iivari University of Oulu, Oulu, Finland, juhani.iivari@oulu.fi

Robert Judge, San Diego State University, San Diego, CA, USA, rjudge@mail.sdsu.edu

Salvatore T. March Owen Graduate School of Management, Vanderbilt University , Nashville, TN, USA sal.march@owen.vanderbilt.edu

Sandeep Purao Information Sciences and Technology at Penn State , McKeesport, PA, USA spurao@ist.psu.edu

Matti Rossi Helsinki School of Economics, Helssinki, Finland, matti.rossi@iki.fi

Maung K. Sein University of Agder, Grimstad, Norway, maung.k.sein@uia.no

Monica Chiarini Tremblay Florida International University, Miami, FL, USA, mtremblay68@gmail.com

Timothy J. Vogus Vanderbilt Owen Graduate School of Management, Nashville, TN, USA, timothy.vogus@owen.vanderbilt.edu

Kevin Williams School of Information Systems and Technology, Claremont Graduate University, Claremont, CA, USA kevin.williams@cgu.edu

About the Authors

Alan Hevner (ahevner@usf.edu) is an eminent scholar and professor in the Information Systems and Decision Sciences Department in the College of Business at the University of South Florida. He holds the Citigroup/Hidden River Chair of distributed technology. Dr. Hevner's areas of research expertise include information systems development, software engineering, distributed database systems, health-care information systems and service-oriented systems. He has published more than 150 research papers on these topics and has consulted for several Fortune 500 companies. Dr. Hevner has a Ph.D. in computer science from Purdue University. He has held faculty positions at the University of Maryland and the University of Minnesota. Dr. Hevner is a member of ACM, IEEE, AIS, and INFORMS. He recently completed an assignment as a program manager in the Computer and Information Science and Engineering Directorate at the U.S. National Science Foundation.

Samir Chatterjee (samir.chatterjee@cgu.edu) is a professor in the School of Information Systems & Technology and Founding Director of the Network Convergence Laboratory at Claremont Graduate University, California. Prior to that, he taught at the CIS Department of J Mack Robinson College of Business, Georgia State University, in Atlanta. He holds a B.E (Hons.) in Electronics & Telecommunications Engineering from Jadavpur University, India, and an M.S and Ph.D. from the School of Computer Science, University of Central

Florida. He is widely recognized as an expert in the areas of next-generation networking, voice and video over IP, and e-health technologies. His current research includes the design and implementation of persuasive technologies that can alter human behavior, telemedicine systems, stress management software, and context-aware intervention technologies for managing obesity.

He has published over *100 articles* in refereed conferences and scholarly journals including *IEEE Network, IEEE Journal on Selected Areas in Communications, Communications of the ACM, Journal of MIS, Computer Networks, International Journal of Healthcare Technology & Management, Telemedicine & e-Health Journal, Information Systems Frontiers, JMIS, Information Systems, Computer Communication, IEEE IT Professional, JAMIA, ACM CCR, Communications of AIS, Journal of Internet Technology*, etc. He is principal investigator on several NSF grants and has received funding from private corporations such as BellSouth, Northrop Grumman, and Hitachi for his research. He is the founding program chair for the International Conference on Design Science Research in IS&T (DESRIST 2006, 2007). He is the program chair for persuasive 2009 conference. Dr. Chatterjee is a senior IEEE member and member of ACM, AIS, and AMIA. He has been an entrepreneur and successfully co-founded a start-up company VoiceCore Technologies Inc. in 2000.

Chapter 1
Introduction to Design Science Research

"In the same way that industrial designers have shaped our everyday life through objects that they design for our offices and for our homes, software interaction design is shaping our life with interactive technologies – computers, telecommunications, mobile phones and virtual worlds. If I were to sum up this in one sentence, I would say that it's about shaping our everyday life through digital artifacts – for work, for play, and for entertainment."

–Gillian Crampton Smith (Moggridge 2007)

Since the dawn of the digital revolution, information technologies have changed the way we live, work, play, and entertain. Designers of IT-based digital technology products play a critical role in ensuring that their designed artifacts are not just beautiful but provide value to their users. Users are increasingly interacting with a digital world. Designing interactions in this new world is a challenging task. The experiences we have when we browse the web, or visit amazon.com, sell/buy stuff on eBay or play amusing games on our mobile cell phones do have a tremendous impact on how we live our lives. Designing information systems is even more challenging.

1.1 What Is Design? – Different Perspectives

You know when you see a good design but it is often hard to define it. Charles Eames offered the following: "A plan for arranging elements in such a way as to best accomplish a particular purpose." Design is the instructions based on knowledge that turns things into value that people use. It embodies the instruction for making the things. However, design is not the thing. For example, we can say that source code is design while compiled code is the thing itself.

A number of disciplines have all made design a central element in what they do. This includes architecture, engineering, computer science, software engineering,

A. Hevner, S. Chatterjee, *Design Research in Information Systems*, Integrated Series in Information Systems 22, DOI 10.1007/978-1-4419-5653-8_1,
© Springer Science+Business Media, LLC 2010

media, and art design and information systems. They all have slightly different views on what they call design.

Engineering design is the systematic intelligent generation and evaluation of specifications for artifacts whose form and function achieve stated objectives and satisfy specified constraints (Dym and Little 2000).

Software (engineering) design is a "thing" as well as a "process" which is conscious, keeps human concerns in the center, is a conversation with materials, is creative, has social consequences, and is a social activity (Winograd 1996).

When it comes to design, we are best familiar with beautiful architectures that capture our imagination. Mitch Kapor actually wrote that good software should be like well-designed buildings. They exhibit three characteristics:

- *Firmness*: A program should not have any bugs that inhibit its function.
- *Commodity*: A program should be suitable for the purposes for which it was intended.
- *Delight*: The experience of using the program should be a pleasurable one.

Our interest in this book is to understand design and its role in both the academic discipline and practice we call the information systems. Design in information systems is both an iterative process (set of activities) and a resulting product (artifact) – a verb and a noun (Walls et al. 1992). Very simply stated, design in information systems deals with building software artifacts which solve a human problem. The designed artifact must be evaluated to show that not only does it solve the problem but also does it in an efficient manner by providing utility to its user. But how does one conduct design research? Is design a research methodology? Is design even a scientific paradigm?

1.2 What Is Research?

To explain fully what is research or how to do research is beyond the scope of this book. However, the thesis we are explaining is a type of research method we call design science research. Hence in that context, it is important to know a little bit about research.

Research can be very generally defined as an activity that contributes to the *understanding* of a *phenomenon* (Kuhn 1970; Lakatos 1978). *Phenomenon* is typically a set of behaviors of some entity that is found *interesting* by the researcher or by a group – a research community. *Understanding* is knowledge that allows prediction of the behavior of some aspects of the phenomenon. Everywhere, our knowledge is incomplete and problems are waiting to be solved. We address the void in our knowledge and those unresolved problems by asking relevant questions and seeking answers to them. The role of research is to provide a method for obtaining those answers by inquiringly studying the evidence within the parameters of the scientific method.

Research is a process through which we attempt to achieve systematically and with the support of data the answer to a question, the resolution of a problem, or a greater understanding of a phenomenon. This process, frequently called *research methodology*, has eight distinct characteristics:

- Research originates with a question or problem
- Research requires a clear articulation of a goal
- Research follows a specific plan of procedure
- Research usually divides the principal problem into more manageable subproblems
- Research is guided by the specific research problem, question, or hypothesis
- Research accepts certain critical assumptions
- Research requires collection and interpretation of data or creation of artifacts
- Research is by its nature cyclical, iterative, or more exactly helical

1.3 Is Design a Science?

There is considerable debate in the community whether design is a science or a practice. What constitutes a science is a big question that is perhaps outside the scope of this book. But we would like to understand the elements of how science is structured? Vannevar Bush (1945) had said that science has two end points on a scale: *Basic* fundamental research (typically funded by federal agencies such as NSF) and *applied* research (typically funded by corporations). Any science develops and evolves over time and proceeds through various stages. A useful tool that is often used to analyze the development of science is the Stokes matrix (see Fig. 1.1).

Science can be structured in two axes. On the vertical axis, it represents how fundamental the knowledge is. On the horizontal axis, it represents how useful that

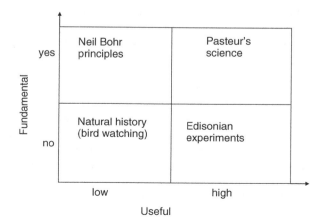

Fig. 1.1 The Stokes matrix quadrants

knowledge is to solve everyday problems. Most science begins at the lower left quadrant referred to as "natural history." This is similar to bird watching, where scientists observe what is happening. Then they capture that basic observation and codify it as knowledge. We do not understand fully why things behave the way they do but we can describe what we see. This is an important quadrant and with respect to design, we have a lot of captured tacit and codified knowledge of design, design process, and product outputs. But note that this knowledge is rather of low usefulness.

The lower right corner represents the "Edisonian experiments" quadrant where the knowledge is not that fundamental but experiments are proving to be quite useful. Hands-on experiments and playing with design are critical in this phase. It is more useful when you actually build designs. The "Neil's Bohr" quadrant on the upper left corner is when science becomes more fundamental but its usefulness is still restricted. We think that the present understanding of design science research is currently located at this quadrant (in the present moment). Lots of the pioneering work done by Herb Simon, Chris Alexander, Fred Brooks, David Parnas, and others belong here. This is fundamental knowledge that designers can put to use. The upper right quadrant termed "Pasteur's quadrant" is where we would like to go: fundamental design knowledge that is extremely useful. That is where a science of design will emerge. Carliss Baldwin at a recent keynote talk at an NSF workshop summarized it well:

> There are theories and design principles in individual design domains such as architecture, engineering design, and software engineering. But a science of design will not emerge from core domains. It has to come from an overarching disciplinary scientific field. The science of design and its theories should be generalizable and applicable across a wide variety of domains and specialties (NSF 2007, PI Workshop on Science of Design, Arlington, Virginia).

In the context of the present discussions, one can ponder on what is good science? It is widely accepted that the basic goal of good science is to develop a theory, paradigm, or model that provides a basis for research to understand the phenomenon being studied. This model is useful only in so far as it helps to explain the observations. To this end, science develops by a formal procedure, usually termed "the scientific method."

In a brilliant essay, Kirschenmann (2002) laments on how traditional scientific economy of prestige and the generous funding that follows it has distorted the entire "scientific process" which was once a "purely academic pursuit" but has now "been commercialized to an astonishing degree by researchers themselves." How has this happened? Evelyn Fox Keller posits "Scientists, she says, "are language-speaking actors" and "the words they use play a crucial role in motivating them to act, in directing their attention, in framing their questions, and in guiding their experimental efforts." Today we are in a world where we do not see science that questions established dogmas but rather science that is directed by commercial and monetary interests.

1.4 What Is Design Science Research?

Based on the notions and discussions above, we can now define design science research (DSR) as follows:

Design science research is a research paradigm in which a designer answers questions relevant to human problems via the creation of innovative artifacts, thereby contributing new knowledge to the body of scientific evidence. The designed artifacts are both useful and fundamental in understanding that problem.

We hereby lay down the first principle of DSR:

The fundamental principle of design science research is that knowledge and understanding of a design problem and its solution are acquired in the building and application of an artifact.

1.5 Placing DSR in Context

Our community of practice is information technology and information systems. Information is "data that has been processed into a form that is meaningful to the recipient and is of real or perceived value in current or prospective actions or decisions." Technology has been defined as "practical implementations of intelligence." Technology is practical, or useful, rather than being an end in itself. It is embodied, as in implementations or artifacts, rather than being solely conceptual (March and Smith 1995; Hevner et al. 2004). Technology includes the many tools, techniques, materials, and sources of power that humans have developed to achieve their goals. Technologies are often developed in response to specific task requirements using practical reasoning and experiential knowledge. IT then is technology used to acquire and process information in support of human purposes. It is typically instantiated as IT systems – complex organizations of hardware, software, procedures, data, and people, developed to address tasks faced by individuals and groups, typically within some organizational setting.

IS is a unique discipline concerned with how IT intersects with organizations and how it is managed. IS research to date has produced knowledge by two complementary but distinct paradigms, *behavioral sciences* and *design sciences* (Hevner et al. 2004). Behavioral science which draws its origins from natural science paradigm seeks to find the truth. It starts with a hypothesis, then researchers collect data, and either prove or disprove the hypothesis. Eventually a theory develops. Design science on the other hand is fundamentally a problem-solving paradigm whose end goal is to produce an artifact which must be built and then evaluated. Working with the technology and going through the process of construction and understanding the salient issues with the artifact is central to this paradigm. Architects, engineers, and computer scientists have always conducted such type of work. The knowledge generated by this research informs us how an artifact can be improved, is better than existing solutions, and can more efficiently solve the problem being addressed. It is important to note that artifacts are not exempt from theories. They rely on kernel theories that are applied, tested, modified, and extended (Walls et al. 1992). But there is considerable debate around the issue of whether there is a design theory or whether a science of design is even possible (NSF 2003; Hooker 2004).

1.6 The Spectrum of IS DSR

In all the definitions above, one can note that design is often a complex process and designing useful artifacts is hard due to the need for creative advances in domain areas in which existing theory is often insufficient. For our discipline, we are concerned with designing artifacts that use information technology (IT) and are applied to organizations and society in general. As Lee (2001) points out the characteristic that distinguishes IS from the other fields is as follows:

> Research in the information systems field examines more than just the technological system, or just the social system, or even the two side by side; in addition, it investigates the phenomenon that emerges when the two interact.

The term *artifact* is used to describe something that is artificial, or constructed by humans, as opposed to something that occurs naturally (Simon 1996). Such artifacts must improve upon existing solutions to a problem or perhaps provide a first solution to an important problem. IT artifacts, which are the end-goal of any design science research project, are broadly defined as follows:

- Constructs (vocabulary and symbols)
- Models (abstractions and representations)
- Methods (algorithms and practices)
- Instantiations (implemented and prototype systems)
- Better design theories

In both Herbert Simon's seminal work *The Sciences of the Artificial (1996)* and Nigel Cross' *Developing a Discipline of Design/Science/Research (2001),* we clearly see the importance they place on doing (construction). Simon believed that design is concerned with how things ought to be in order to attain goals (Gregor and Jones 2007). He saw the design process as generally concerned with finding a satisfactory design, rather than an optimum design. He believed "both the shape of the design and the shape and organization of the design process are essential components of a theory of design" (pp. 130–131). Cross on the other hand gives less importance to theory but stresses on knowledge that is acquired through the building process:

> We must not forget that design knowledge resides in products themselves; in the forms and materials and finishes which embody design attributes. Much everyday design work entails the use of precedents or previous exemplars – not because of laziness by the designer but because the exemplars actually contain knowledge of what the product should be (Cross 2001).

A research paradigm is the set of activities a research community considers appropriate to the production of understanding (knowledge) in its research methods or techniques. Historically, some communities have a nearly universal agreement on the phenomenon of interest and the research methods for investigating it. They are termed paradigmatic communities. There are other communities, however, where a number of different methods are appropriate. These are termed multi-paradigmatic communities. Information systems is an excellent example of a multi-paradigmatic community (Vaishnavi and Kuechler 2007).

Figure 1.2 shows the balance in scope of focus for three related disciplines: information systems (IS), software engineering (SE), and computer science (CS). CS researchers are much closer to actual working code. SE researchers are dealing with software at production and operational levels and they do have to face some organizational issues. IS researchers are closer to deployment of information technology in an organization. Hence besides working code, they face management and organizational challenges as well. The scope of focus also dictates the genesis of problems. This organizational focus bears on the specifications and eventual evaluation conducted. This would be discussed in more detail in Chapter 3.

Fig. 1.2 Discipline balance and scope of work scale

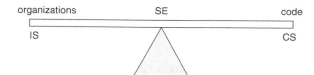

1.7 Difference Between Routine Design Practice and DSR

One source of confusion to novice design science researchers is to understand the subtle difference between conducting DSR versus practicing routine design. Is the iPod a good design or is it an example of design science research? If you break open the iPod and lay out its fundamental components, you will typically find memory, hard disk, CPU, some code, some audio input/output interfaces, and a song selection dial. None of these are new. They have existed for quite some time. But what the iPod did is to integrate them in a rather innovative way and produce an artifact that has tremendous value to music listeners. Is any new knowledge created in the process? Perhaps yes or perhaps no. It depends on whether the designers at Apple had actually invented something new with the compact design, the easy-to-use dial interface, or produced better sound clarity. They may have. In that case, if the team documents that their new "artifact" is better, faster, or more optimal through rigorous evaluation methods and comparison with similar artifacts, then new knowledge is indeed created and this would be considered DSR. But if no new knowledge is created, then this would be considered applying best practices and conducting routine design.

1.8 Conclusions

The information systems field has been energized by a flurry of recent activity that centers on the use of design research as an important research paradigm. We acknowledge that design research has broader appeal and knowledge has been created by several design fields. However, our community and the context of this book are information systems. Our goal is partly to legitimize design science as a valid method of doing research in the field. The other goal is to learn from related design disciplines and adopt successful design principles that can be appropriated for information systems research. In this book, we will explore the origins of DSR, its history, foundation, techniques, exemplars, and its future. Various techniques and methods will be discussed. Understanding the principles, theories, and foundations is the first step to ensure that you know when you are doing great design science research work.

References

Bush, V. (1945) *Science: The Endless Frontier.* A Report to the President by Vannevar Bush, July 1945. Accessed at URL http://www.nsf.gov/od/lpa/nsf50/vbush1945.htm

Cross, N. (2001) Design/science/research: developing a discipline, in *Fifth Asian Design Conference: International Symposium of Design Science*, Su Jeong Dang Printing Company, Seoul Korea.

Dym, C. L. and P. Little (2000) *Engineering Design: A Project-Based Introduction*, J. Wiley & Sons, Inc., Hoboken, NJ.

Gregor, S. and D. Jones (2007) The anatomy of a design theory, *Journal of AIS* 8 (5), pp. 312–335.

Hevner, A., S. March, J. Park, and S. Ram (2004) Design science in information systems research. *MIS Quarterly* 28 (1), pp. 75–105.

Hooker, J. N. (2004) Is design theory possible? *Journal of Information Technology Theory and Application* 6 (2), pp. 73–83.

Kirschenmann, F. (2002) What constitutes sound science? *Annual Sigma Xi Lecture*, Iowa State University, Ames, IA.

Kuhn, T. (1970) *The Structure of Scientific Revolutions,* University of Chicago Press, Chicago.

Lakatos, I. (1978) *The Methodology of Scientific Research Programmes*, Cambridge University Press, Cambridge.

Lee, A. S. (2001) Editorial, *MIS Quarterly* 25 (1), pp. iii–vii.

March, S. T. and G. F. Smith (1995) Design and natural science research on information technology, *Decision Support Systems* 15, pp. 251–266.

Moggridge, B. (2007) *Designing Interactions,* The MIT Press, Cambridge, MA.

NSF (2003) *Science of Design: Software-Intensive Systems,* National Science Foundation, Washington, DC.

Simon, H. (1996) *The Sciences of Artificial*, 3rd edn., MIT Press, Cambridge, MA.

Vaishnavi, V. K. and W. Kuechler Jr. (2007) *Design Science Research methods and Patterns: Innovating Information and Communication Technology,* Auerbach Publications, Taylor & Francis Group, Boca Raton, FL, New York, NY.

Walls, J. G., G. R. Widmeyer et al. (1992) Building an Information System Design Theory for Vigilant EIS, *Information Systems Research* 3 (1), pp. 36–59.

Winograd, T. (1996). *Bringing Design to Software*, Addison-Wesley, Reading, MA.

Chapter 2
Design Science Research in Information Systems

Good design is a renaissance attitude that combines
technology, cognitive science, human need, and beauty to
produce something that the world didn't know it was missing.
– Paola Antonelli
Design is where science and art break even.
– Robin Mathew

2.1 Information Systems Research

Design activities are central to most applied disciplines. Research in design has a long history in many fields including architecture, engineering, education, psychology, and the fine arts (Cross 2001). The computing and information technology (CIT) field since its advent in the late 1940s has appropriated many of the ideas, concepts, and methods of design science that have originated in these other disciplines. However, information systems (IS) as composed of inherently mutable and adaptable hardware, software, and human interfaces provide many unique and challenging design problems that call for new and creative ideas.

The design science research paradigm is highly relevant to information systems (IS) research because it directly addresses two of the key issues of the discipline: the central, albeit controversial, role of the IT artifact in IS research (Weber 1987; Orlikowski and Iacono 2001; Benbasat and Zmud 2003) and the perceived lack of professional relevance of IS research (Benbasat and Zmud 1999; Hirschheim and Klein 2003). Design science, as conceptualized by Simon (1996), supports a pragmatic research paradigm that calls for the creation of innovative artifacts to solve real-world problems. Thus, design science research combines a focus on the IT artifact with a high priority on relevance in the application domain.

A tradition of design science research in the IS field has been slow to coalesce. Research in IS has been dominated by studies of the impacts of IT artifacts on organizations, teams, and individuals. Design research was considered the province of more technical disciplines such as computer science and electrical engineering. However, in the early 1990s the IS community recognized the importance of design science research to improve the effectiveness and utility of the

A. Hevner, S. Chatterjee, *Design Research in Information Systems*, Integrated Series in Information Systems 22, DOI 10.1007/978-1-4419-5653-8_2,
© Springer Science+Business Media, LLC 2010

IT artifact in the context of solving real-world business problems. Evidence of this awakening came in the 1991 formation of the Workshop on Information Technology and Systems (WITS), ground-breaking research by Nunamaker and his Electronic Group Decision Support Systems (GDSS) team at the University of Arizona (Nunamaker et al. 1991) and new thinking on how design science is defined, theorized, and actualized in the IS field (e.g., Iivari 1991; Walls et al. 1992; March and Smith 1995).

With encouragement from many leaders of the IS community, the author team of Alan Hevner, Salvatore March, Jinsoo Park, and Sudha Ram thought deeply about what constitutes good design science research in IS. They adapted the design research traditions of other fields to the unique contexts of IS design research. In particular, the seminal thinking of Herbert Simon in *Sciences of the Artificial* (Simon 1996) supported their ideas. After a number of review cycles and benefiting from many insightful reviewer comments, their research essay appeared in *Management Information Systems Quarterly* (*MISQ*) in March 2004 (Hevner et al. 2004). This paper is included in an appendix to this book. The following section provides a concise overview of the paper. The remainder of this chapter discusses the impacts of the 2004 *MISQ* paper and expands on its content.

2.2 Summary of Hevner, March, Park, and Ram 2004 *MISQ* Paper

Information systems are implemented within an organization for the purpose of improving the effectiveness and efficiency of that organization. The utility of the information system and characteristics of the organization, its work systems, its people, and its development and implementation methodologies together determine the extent to which that purpose is achieved. It is incumbent upon researchers in the Information Systems (IS) discipline to further knowledge that aids in the productive application of information technology to human organizations and their management and to develop and communicate "knowledge concerning both the management of information technology and the use of information technology for managerial and organizational purposes" (Zmud 1997).

Acquiring such knowledge involves two complementary but distinct paradigms, natural (or behavioral) science and design science (March and Smith 1995). The behavioral science paradigm has its roots in natural science research methods. It seeks to develop and justify theories (i.e., principles and laws) that explain or predict organizational and human phenomena surrounding the analysis, design, implementation, and use of information systems. Such theories ultimately inform researchers and practitioners of the interactions among people, technology, and organizations that must be managed if an information system is to achieve its stated purpose, namely improving the effectiveness and efficiency of an organization. These theories impact and are impacted by design decisions made with respect to the system development methodology used and the functional capabilities, information contents, and human interfaces implemented within the information system.

The design science paradigm has its roots in engineering and the sciences of the artificial (Simon 1996). It is fundamentally a problem-solving paradigm. It seeks to create innovations that define the ideas, practices, technical capabilities, and products through which the analysis, design, implementation, and use of information systems can be effectively and efficiently accomplished. Design science research in IS addresses what are considered to be *wicked problems* (Rittel and Webber 1984; Brooks 1987). That is, those problems characterized by

- unstable requirements and constraints based on ill-defined environmental contexts,
- complex interactions among subcomponents of the problem,
- inherent flexibility to change design processes as well as design artifacts (i.e., malleable processes and artifacts),
- a critical dependence upon human cognitive abilities (e.g., creativity) to produce effective solutions, and
- a critical dependence upon human social abilities (e.g., teamwork) to produce effective solutions.

Technological advances are the result of innovative, creative design science processes. If not "capricious," they are at least "arbitrary" (Brooks 1987) with respect to business needs and existing knowledge. Innovations, such as database management systems, high-level languages, personal computers, software components, intelligent agents, object technology, the Internet, and the World Wide Web, have had dramatic and at times unintended impacts on the way in which information systems are conceived, designed, implemented, and managed.

A key insight here is that there is a complementary research cycle between design science and behavioral science to address fundamental problems faced in the productive application of information technology (see Fig. 2.1). Technology and

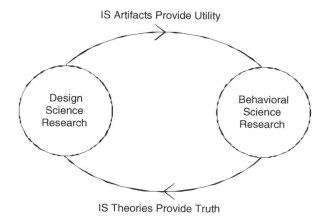

Fig. 2.1 Complementary nature of design science and behavioral science research

behavior are not dichotomous in an information system. They are inseparable. They are similarly inseparable in IS research. Philosophically these arguments draw from a pragmatist philosophy that argues that truth (justified theory) and utility (artifacts that are effective) are two sides of the same coin and that scientific research should be evaluated in light of its practical implications. In other words, the practical relevance of the research result should be valued equally with the rigor of the research performed to achieve the result.

The primary goal of the *MISQ* paper is to provide an understanding of how to conduct, evaluate, and present design science research to IS researchers and practicing business managers. The research activities of design science within the IS discipline are described via a conceptual framework for understanding information systems research and a clear set of guidelines or principles are proscribed for conducting and evaluating good design science research (see Table 2.1). A detailed discussion of each of the seven guidelines is presented in the 2004 *MISQ* paper. The proposed guidelines are applied to assess recent exemplar papers published in the IS literature in order to illustrate how authors, reviewers, and editors can apply the guidelines consistently. The paper concludes with an analysis of the challenges of performing high-quality design science research and a call for greater synergistic efforts between behavioral science and design science researchers.

Table 2.1 Design Science Research Guidelines

Guideline	Description
Guideline 1: Design as an Artifact	Design science research must produce a viable artifact in the form of a construct, a model, a method, or an instantiation
Guideline 2: Problem relevance	The objective of design science research is to develop technology-based solutions to important and relevant business problems
Guideline 3: Design evaluation	The utility, quality, and efficacy of a design artifact must be rigorously demonstrated via well-executed evaluation methods
Guideline 4: Research contributions	Effective design science research must provide clear and verifiable contributions in the areas of the design artifact, design foundations, and/or design methodologies
Guideline 5: Research rigor	Design science research relies upon the application of rigorous methods in both the construction and evaluation of the design artifact
Guideline 6: Design as a search process	The search for an effective artifact requires utilizing available means to reach desired ends while satisfying laws in the problem environment
Guideline 7: Communication of research	Design science research must be presented effectively to both technology-oriented and management-oriented audiences

2.3 Impacts of 2004 *MISQ* Paper on Design Science Research

The 2004 *MISQ* paper has had a strong impact on the field as Information Systems researchers recognize the values the design science paradigm brings to a research project. It is the natural desire of researchers to improve things. For some it is not enough to study and understand why nature is as it is, but they want to know how they can improve the way it is. Design science research attempts to focus human creativity into the design and construction of artifacts that have utility in application environments.

Design science offers an effective means of addressing the relevancy gap that has plagued academic research, particularly in the management and information systems disciplines. Natural science research methods are appropriate for the study of existing and emergent phenomena; however, they are insufficient for the study of "wicked organizational problems," the type of problems that require creative, novel, and innovative solutions. Such problems are more effectively addressed using type of paradigm shift offered by design science.

Design science research in the IS field is now better positioned as an equal, complementary partner to the more prevalent behavioral science research paradigm. The key contribution is a new way of thinking about what makes IS research relevant to its various audiences of managers, practitioners, and peer researchers in related fields. Design must still be informed by appropriate theories that explain or predict human behavior; however, these may be insufficient to enable the development and adaptation of new and more effective organizational artifacts. Scientific theories may explain existing or emergent organizational phenomena related to extant organizational forms and artifacts but they cannot account for the qualitative novelty achieved by human intention, creativity, and innovation in the design and appropriation of such artifacts. That is, science, the process of understanding "what is," may be insufficient for design, the process of understanding "what can be."

Researchers in application domains as disparate as health care, E-commerce, biology, transportation, and the fine arts identify the key role of designed artifacts in improving domain-specific systems and processes. The models and guidelines of the 2004 *MISQ* paper support researchers to bring a rigorous design science research process into projects that heretofore had not clearly described how new ideas become embedded in purposeful artifacts and then how those artifacts are field tested in real-world environments.

Since the 2004 publication of the Hevner, March, Park, and Ram paper, the broadening recognition of design science research in the IS field has led to a number of important new activities and research directions:

– A new, multi-disciplinary research conference, Design Science Research in Information Systems & Technology (DESRIST), has been established and four offerings of the conference have been held from 2006 to 2009. An important characteristic of DESRIST has been its multi-disciplinary attendance and agenda. This environment has allowed the IS community to interact more closely with other design-focused disciplines, such as engineering and architecture.

- A special issue of MISQ on Design Science Research appeared in 2008 (MISQ 2008).
- The design science guidelines described in this paper have provided a structured path for doctoral students interested in using this methodology in their research, structuring and legitimizing their research. Most IS doctoral programs in major universities now provide a research seminar dedicated to design science research methods and projects.
- Leading international scholars in IS are actively extending the research ideas found in the 2004 MISQ paper. Examples include research by Gregor and Jones (2007), Iivari (2007), and Peffers, Tuunanen, Rothenberger, and Chatterjee (2008).
- Leading journals in the IS field have expanded their boards to include more senior editors and associate editors who have used and who now understand the design science approach. This will ultimately pave the way for more design science research papers to get published and thus benefit the whole field by enhancing the relevance of IS research.

It is exciting to see the ongoing discussions and increased interest in design science research projects in the IS field. Information systems and organizational routines are among the key components of organizational design as they are extensions of human cognitive capabilities. They are the tools of knowledge work enabling new organizational forms and providing management and decision-making support. For example, incentive structures related to job performance such as achieving sales, product quality, or customer satisfaction goals require information gathering and analysis capabilities. Management of outsourcing and inter-organizational partnerships requires secure information sharing. Identification of problems and opportunities requires the gathering and analysis of business intelligence. More and more frequently business decisions are made relying on information from the computer-based analysis and recommendations. Similarly, organizational routines are intended to provide guidance to human action within prescribed organizational contexts. Yet even such artifacts are appropriated and adapted by humans in ways and for purposes that the designers may not have envisioned. With the renewed interest in design science research in the information systems and organizational science disciplines, future research will focus on the co-design of information processing capabilities and organizational structures.

2.4 Extending the Reach of Design Science Research in IS

The critical reactions (both positive and negative) from the IS community toward the 2004 *MISQ* paper and the design science guidelines have led to several important extensions for the application of design science ideas to IS research. To conclude this chapter, a number of key issues are addressed.

2.4.1 *Design Science Research vs. Professional Design*

One issue that must be clearly addressed in design science research is differentiating high-quality professional design or system building from design science research. The difference is in the nature of the problems and solutions. Professional design is the application of existing knowledge to organizational problems, such as constructing a financial or marketing information system using "best practice" artifacts (constructs, models, methods, and instantiations) existing in the knowledge base. On the other hand, design science research addresses important unsolved problems in unique or innovative ways or solved problems in more effective or efficient ways. The key differentiator between professional design and design research is the clear identification of a contribution to the archival knowledge base of foundations and methodologies and the communication of the contribution to the stakeholder communities.

In the early stages of a discipline or with significant changes in the environment, each new artifact created for that discipline or changed environment is "an experiment" that "poses a question to nature" (Newell and Simon 1976). Existing knowledge is used where appropriate; however, often the requisite knowledge is nonexistent. In other words the knowledge base is inadequate. Reliance on creativity and trial and error search are characteristic of such research efforts. As design science research results are codified in the knowledge base, they become "best practices." Professional design and system building then become the routine application of the knowledge base to known problems.

2.4.2 *Design as Research vs. Researching Design*

Design science research has been interpreted as including two distinctly different classes of research – 'design as research' and 'researching design.' While the 2004 *MISQ* paper focuses on the former class of research, it is important to recognize the existence and importance of both types of research.

Design as Research encompasses the idea that doing innovative design that results in clear contributions to the knowledge base constitutes research. Knowledge generated via design can take several forms including constructs, models, methods, and instantiations (March and Smith 1995). Design research projects are often performed in a specific application context and the resulting designs and design research contributions may be clearly influenced by the opportunities and constraints of the application domain. Additional research may be needed to generalize the research results to broader domains. Design as research, thus, provides an important strand of research that values research outcomes that focus on improvement of an artifact in a specific domain as the primary research concern and, then, seeks a broader, more general understanding of theories and phenomena surrounding the artifact as an extended outcome.

Researching Design shifts the focus to a study of designs, designers, and design processes. The community of researchers engaged in this mode of research was organized under the umbrella of the design research society starting as early as the mid-1960s. Because of their focus on methods of designing, they have been able to articulate and follow the goal of generating domain-independent understanding of design processes, although their investigations have been focused largely in the fields of architecture, engineering, and product design. Although it is difficult to provide unambiguous and universally accepted definitions of design processes, working definitions suggest designing is an iterative process of planning, generating alternatives, and selecting a satisfactory design. Examples of work from this stream, therefore, include use of representations and languages (Oxman 1997), use of cognitive schemas (Goldschmidt 1994), and theoretical explorations (Love 2002).

Although similarities are many, the two fields of design study have been different in their focus and trajectory. Of the differences, three are most visible. First, design as research emphasizes the domain in which the design activity will take place, placing a premium on innovativeness within a specific context. In contrast, researching design emphasizes increased understanding of design methods often independent of the domain. Second, the domains of study for the first subfield have typically been the information and computing technologies as opposed to architecture and engineering for the second. Finally, the closest alliances from the design as research have been formed with disciplines such as computer science, software engineering, and organization science. Researching design is more closely allied with cognitive science and professional fields such as architecture and engineering.

2.4.3 Design Science Research Cycles

The 2004 *MISQ* paper presents design science as a research paradigm to be employed in IS research projects. As such, the discussion does not propose a detailed process for performing design science research. However, a key insight can be gained by identifying and understanding the existence of three design science research cycles in any design research project as shown in Fig. 2.2 (Hevner 2007).

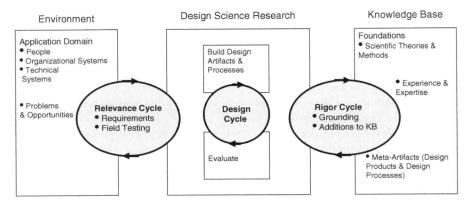

Fig. 2.2 Design science research cycles

Figure 2.2 borrows the IS research framework found in (Hevner et al. 2004) and overlays a focus on three inherent research cycles. The *Relevance Cycle* bridges the contextual environment of the research project with the design science activities. The *Rigor Cycle* connects the design science activities with the knowledge base of scientific foundations, experience, and expertise that informs the research project. The central *Design Cycle* iterates between the core activities of building and evaluating the design artifacts and processes of the research. These three cycles must be present and clearly identifiable in a design science research project. The following sections briefly expand on the definitions and meanings of each cycle.

2.4.3.1   The Relevance Cycle

Design science research is motivated by the desire to improve the environment by the introduction of new and innovative artifacts and the processes for building these artifacts (Simon 1996). An application domain consists of the people, organizational systems, and technical systems that interact to work toward a goal. Good design science research often begins by identifying and representing opportunities and problems in an actual application environment.

Thus, the relevance cycle initiates design science research with an application context that not only provides the requirements for the research (e.g., the opportunity/problem to be addressed) as inputs but also defines acceptance criteria for the ultimate evaluation of the research results. Does the design artifact improve the environment and how can this improvement be measured? The output from the design science research must be returned into the environment for study and evaluation in the application domain. The field study of the artifact can be executed by means of appropriate technology transfer methods such as action research (Cole et al. 2005; Jarvinen 2007).

The results of the field testing will determine whether additional iterations of the relevance cycle are needed in this design science research project. The new artifact may have deficiencies in functionality or in its inherent qualities (e.g., performance, usability) that may limit its utility in practice. Another result of field testing may be that the requirements input to the design science research were incorrect or incomplete with the resulting artifact satisfying the requirements but still inadequate to the opportunity or problem presented. Another iteration of the relevance cycle will commence with feedback from the environment from field testing and a restatement of the research requirements as discovered from actual experience.

2.4.3.2   The Rigor Cycle

Design science draws from a vast knowledge base of scientific theories and engineering methods that provides the foundations for rigorous design science research. As importantly, the knowledge base also contains two types of additional knowledge:

- The experiences and expertise that define the state of the art in the application domain of the research.
- The existing artifacts and processes (or meta-artifacts (Iivari 2007)) found in the application domain.

The rigor cycle provides past knowledge to the research project to ensure its innovation. It is contingent on the researchers to thoroughly research and reference the knowledge base in order to guarantee that the designs produced are research contributions and not routine designs based on the application of known design processes and the appropriation of known design artifacts.

While rigorous advances in design are what separate a research project from the practice of routine design, we need to be careful to identify the sources and types of rigor appropriate for design research. The risk comes when experts in other research paradigms attempt to apply their standards of rigor to design research projects in which creative inspiration or gut instinct may lead to design decisions. To insist that all design decisions and design processes be based on grounded behavioral or mathematical theories may not be appropriate or even feasible for a truly cutting-edge design artifact. Such theories may as yet be undiscovered or incomplete and the research activities of design and evaluation of the artifact may advance the development and study of such theories.

Consideration of rigor in design research is based on the researcher's skilled selection and application of the appropriate theories and methods for constructing and evaluating the artifact. Design science research is grounded on existing ideas drawn from the domain knowledge base. Inspiration for creative design activity can be drawn from many different sources to include rich opportunities/problems from the application environment, existing artifacts, analogies/metaphors, and theories (Iivari 2007). This list of design inspiration can be expanded to include additional sources of creative insights (Csikszentmihalyi 1996).

Additions to the knowledge base as results of design research will include any additions or extensions to the original theories and methods made during the research, the new artifacts (design products and processes), and all experiences gained from performing the iterative design cycles and field testing the artifact in the application environment. It is imperative that a design research project makes a compelling case for its rigorous bases and contributions lest the research be dismissed as a case of routine design. Definitive research contributions to the knowledge base are essential to selling the research to an academic audience just as useful contributions to the environment are the key selling points to a practitioner audience.

2.4.3.3 The Design Cycle

The internal design cycle is the heart of any design science research project. This cycle of research activities iterates more rapidly between the construction of an artifact, its evaluation, and subsequent feedback to refine the design further. Simon (1996) describes the nature of this cycle as generating design alternatives and evaluating the alternatives against requirements until a satisfactory design is achieved. As discussed above, the requirements are input from the relevance cycle and the design and evaluation theories and methods are drawn from the rigor cycle. However, the design cycle is where the hard work of design science research is done. It is important to understand the dependencies of the design cycle on the other two cycles while appreciating its relative independence during the actual execution of the research.

During the performance of the design cycle a balance must be maintained between the efforts spent in constructing and evaluating the evolving design artifact. Both activities must be convincingly based on relevance and rigor. Having a strong grounded argument for the construction of the artifact, as discussed above, is insufficient if the subsequent evaluation is weak. Juhani (2007) states, "The essence of Information Systems as design science lies in the scientific evaluation of artifacts." Artifacts must be rigorously and thoroughly tested in laboratory and experimental situations before releasing them into field testing along the relevance cycle. This calls for multiple iterations of the design cycle in design science research before contributions are output into the relevance cycle and the rigor cycle.

2.4.4 A Checklist for Design Science Research

While the seven guidelines in the 2004 *MISQ* paper have been largely accepted as integral to top quality design science research, requests have been made for a more specific checklist of questions to evaluate a design research project. The questions in Table 2.2 provide such a checklist that has been used to assess progress on design research projects. In practice, design researchers have found these questions to form a useful checklist to ensure that their projects address the key aspects of design science research. To demonstrate the relationship of these questions with the three research cycles discussed in the previous section, Fig. 2.3 maps the eight questions to the appropriate research cycle.

2.4.5 Publication of Design Science Research

Guideline 7 (see Table 2.1) addresses the dissemination of design science research results in appropriate journal outlets. Much feedback to the 2004 *MISQ* paper has centered on the willingness of top-ranked journals in the IS and computer science (CS) fields to publish design science results. Any discussion of top-quality publication outlets must draw a distinction between journals with technology-focused audiences and management-focused audiences. Good design science research produces results of interest for both audiences. Technology audiences need sufficient detail to enable the described artifact to be constructed (implemented) and used within an appropriate context. It is important for such audiences to understand the processes by which the artifact was constructed and evaluated. This establishes repeatability of the research project and builds the knowledge base for further research extensions by future design science researchers.

Table 2.2 Design science research checklist

Questions	Answers
1. What is the research question (design requirements)?	
2. What is the artifact? How is the artifact represented?	
3. What design processes (search heuristics) will be used to build the artifact?	
4. How are the artifact and the design processes grounded by the knowledge base? What, if any, theories support the artifact design and the design process?	
5. What evaluations are performed during the internal design cycles? What design improvements are identified during each design cycle?	
6. How is the artifact introduced into the application environment and how is it field tested? What metrics are used to demonstrate artifact utility and improvement over previous artifacts?	
7. What new knowledge is added to the knowledge base and in what form (e.g., peer-reviewed literature, meta-artifacts, new theory, new method)?	
8. Has the research question been satisfactorily addressed?	

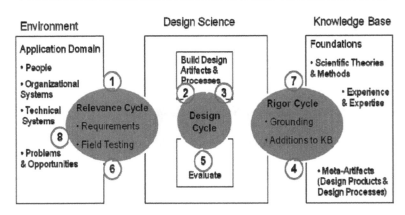

Fig. 2.3 Questions mapped to three design research cycles

On the other hand, management audiences need sufficient detail to determine if organizational resources should be committed to constructing (or purchasing) and using the artifact within their specific organizational context. The rigor of the artifact design process must be complemented by a thorough presentation of the experimental design of the artifact's field test in a realistic organizational environment. The emphasis must be on the importance of the problem and the novelty and utility of the solution approach realized in the artifact.

References

Benbasat, I. and R. Zmud (1999) Empirical research in information systems: the question of relevance, *MIS Quarterly* 23 (1), pp. 3–16.

Benbasat, I. and R. Zmud (2003) The identity crisis within the IS discipline: defining and communicating the discipline's core properties, *MIS Quarterly* 27 (2), pp. 183–194.

Brooks, F., Jr. (1987) No silver bullet: essence and accidents of software engineering, *IEEE Computer* 20 (4), pp. 10–19.

Cole, R., S. Purao, M. Rossi, and M. Sein (2005), Being proactive: where action research meets design research, in *Proceedings of the Twenty-Sixth International Conference on Information Systems*, Las Vegas, pp. 325–336.

Cross, N. (2001) Designerly Ways of Knowing: Design Discipline vs. Design Science, *Design Issues* 17 (3), pp. 49–55.

Csikszentmihalyi, M. (1996) *Creativity: Flow and Psychology of Discovery and Invention*, HarperCollins, New York.

Goldschmidt, G. (1994) On visual thinking: the vis kids of architecture, *Design Studies* 15 (2), pp. 158–174.

Gregor, S. and D. Jones (2007) The anatomy of a design theory, *Journal of the AIS* 8 (5), Article 2, pp. 312–335.

Hevner, A., S. March, J. Park, and S. Ram (2004) Design science in information systems research, *MIS Quarterly* 28 (1), pp. 75–105.

Hevner, A. (2007) A three-cycle view of design science research, *Scandinavian Journal of Information Systems* 19 (2), pp. 87–92.

Hirschheim, R. and H. Klein (2003) Crisis in the IS field? A critical reflection on the state of the discipline, *Journal of the AIS* 4 (5), pp. 237–293.

Iivari, J. (1991) A paradigmatic analysis of contemporary schools of IS development, *European Journal of Information Systems* 1 (4), pp. 249–272.

Iivari, J. (2007) A paradigmatic analysis of information systems as a design science, *Scandinavian Journal of IS* 19 (2), pp. 39–64.

Jarvinen, P. (2007) Action research is similar to design science, *Quality & Quantity* 41, pp. 37–54.

Love, T. (2002) Constructing a coherent cross-disciplinary body of theory about designing and designs: some philosophical issues, *International Journal of Design Studies* 23 (3), pp. 345–361.

March, S. and G. Smith (1995) Design and natural science research on information technology, *Decision Support Systems* 15, pp. 251–266.

MISQ (2008) Special issue on design science research, *MIS Quarterly* 32 (4), pp. 725–868.

Newell, A. and H. Simon (1976) Computer science as empirical inquiry: symbols and search, *Communications of the ACM* 19 (3), pp. 113–126.

Nunamaker, J., M. Chen, and T. D. M. Purdin (1991) Systems development in information systems research, *Journal of Management Information Systems* 7 (3), pp. 89–106.

Orlikowski, W. and C. Iacono (2001) Research commentary: desperately seeking the 'IT' in IT research: a call for theorizing the IT artifact, *Information Systems Research* 12, pp. 121–134.

Oxman, R. (1997) Design by re-representation: a model of visual reasoning in design, *Design Studies* 18 (4), pp. 329–347.

Peffers, K., T. Tuunanen, M. Rothenberger, and S. Chatterjee (2008) A design science research methodology for information systems research, *Journal of Management Information Systems* 24 (3), pp. 45–77.

Rittel, H. and M. Webber (1984) Planning problems are wicked problems, in *Developments in Design Methodology*, N. Cross (ed.), John Wiley & Sons, New York, pp. 135–144.

Simon, H. (1996) *The Sciences of Artificial*, 3rd edn., MIT Press, Cambridge, MA.

Walls, J., G. Widmeyer, and O. El Sawy (1992) Building an information system design theory for vigilant EIS, *Information Systems Research* 3 (1), pp. 36–59.

Weber, R. (1997) Towards a theory of artifacts: a paradigmatic base for information systems research, *Journal of Information Systems* 1 (1), pp. 3–20.

Zmud, R. (1997) Editor's comments, *MIS Quarterly* 21 (2), pp. xxi–xxii.

Chapter 3
Design Science Research Frameworks

People sometimes ask me what they should read to find out about artificial intelligence. Herbert Simon's book Sciences of the Artificial *is always on the list I give them. Every page issues a challenge to conventional thinking, and the layman who digests it well will certainly understand what the field of artificial intelligence hopes to accomplish. I recommend it in the same spirit that I recommend Freud to people who ask about psychoanalysis, or Piaget to those who ask about child psychology: If you want to learn about a subject, start by reading its founding fathers.*

– George A. Miller, Complex Information Processing

3.1 Understanding the Natural and Artificial Worlds

The founding father of design science was Herbert E. Simon. Well known for his work on AI, decision making, and economics, Simon wrote a thought-provoking book called *Sciences of the Artificial* in the 1960s (Simon 1996). His profound insight was that certain phenomena or entities are "artificial" in the sense that they are contingent to the goals or purposes of their designer. In other words, they could have been different had the goals been different (as opposed to natural phenomena which are necessarily evolved given natural laws). He further posits: Since artifacts are contingent, how is a science of the artificial possible? How to study artifacts empirically? On the other hand, Simon also deals with the notion of complexity. This is necessary because artificiality and complexity are inextricably interwoven.

We are all familiar with natural science (especially physics and biology) but the world around us is mostly man-made, i.e., artificial. It evolves with mankind's goals. So science must encompass both natural and goal-dependent (artificial) phenomena. Simon in his book discusses how to relate these two. There are two perspectives on

A. Hevner, S. Chatterjee, *Design Research in Information Systems*, Integrated Series in Information Systems 22, DOI 10.1007/978-1-4419-5653-8_3,
© Springer Science+Business Media, LLC 2010

artifacts, synthetic vs. analytic. The *science of the artificial* is really the science (analytic or descriptive) of engineering (synthetic or prescriptive).

Artifacts

- are synthesized,
- may imitate appearances of natural things,
- can be characterized in terms of functions, goals, adaptation, and
- are often discussed in terms of both imperatives and descriptives.

3.2 Toward a Theory of Complex Systems

Simon's seminal work gives us first clues toward understanding what he called "complex systems." Fulfillment of purpose involves a relation between the artifact, its environment, and a purpose or goal. Alternatively, one can view it as the interaction of an inner environment (internal mechanism), an outer environment (conditions for goal attainment), and the interface between the two. In this view, the real nature of the artifact is the interface. Both the inner and outer environments are abstracted away. The science of the artificial should focus on the interface, the same way design focuses on the "functioning."

Simulation is the imitation of the interface and is implied by the notion of artificiality. Simulation can also be viewed as adaptation to the same goal. It can be used to better understand the original (simulated) entity because simulation can help predict behavior by making explicit "new" knowledge, i.e., knowledge that is indeed derivable but only with great effort. Simulation is even possible for poorly understood systems by abstraction of organizational properties.

Computers are organizations of elementary components whose function only matters. They are a special class of artifacts that can be used to perform simulations (in particular of human cognition). They can be studied in the abstract, namely using mathematics. Yet, they can and must also be studied empirically. Their study as an empirical phenomenon requires simulation (example of time-sharing systems). In conclusion, the behavior of computers will turn out to be governed by simple laws, the apparent complexity resulting from that of the environment they are trying to adapt to.

In his book, Simon notices that complexity is a general property of systems that are made of different parts and that the emergent behavior is hard to characterize.

In the first part of his book he argues that complexity takes the form of hierarchy and that hierarchical systems evolve faster than nonhierarchical ones. Very generally, a hierarchy is a recursive partition of a system into subsystems. Examples of hierarchies are common in social, biological, physical, and symbolic (e.g., books) systems. In biological systems, it is argued that hierarchical systems evolve faster because the many subsystems form as many intermediate stable stages in the process. Similarly in the problem-solving activity, mainly a selective trial-and-error process, intermediate results constitute stable subassemblies that indicate progress.

The second part of his argument is that hierarchies have the property of *near decomposability*, namely that (1) the short-term (high-frequency) behavior of each subsystem is approximately independent of the other components and (2) in the long run, the (low-frequency) behavior of a subsystem depends on that of other components in only an aggregate way. The example of cubicle and room temperature in a building is provided. Other examples are common in natural and social systems.

The last part of the thesis deals with system *descriptions*. It is argued that the description of a system need not be as complex as the system due to the redundancy present in the latter. Redundancy results from the fact that there are only a limited number of distinct elementary components. Complex systems are obtained by varying their combination. Also, the near-decomposability property can be generalized to the "empty world hypothesis" that states that most things are only weakly connected with most other things. Therefore, descriptions may contain only a fraction of the connections. There are two main types of descriptions. State descriptions and process descriptions deal with the world as sensed and as acted upon, respectively. The behavior of any adaptive organism results from trying to establish correlations between goals and actions.

In conclusion, a general theory of complex systems must refer to a theory of hierarchy. And the near-decomposability property simplifies both the behavior of a complex system and its description. In the study of DSR, one repeatedly stumbles upon such complex systems and their behavior. Even to this date, Herbert Simon's work remains the most influential thinking that guides this field of design and artificial sciences.

3.3 Systems Development in Information Systems Research

One of the earliest contribution of design science to IS is the seminal work done by Nunamaker et al. (1990–91). They claim that the central nature of systems development leads to a multi-methodological approach to IS research that consists of four research strategies: theory building, experimentation, observation, and systems development. Theory building includes development of new ideas and concepts and construction of conceptual frameworks, new methods, or models (e.g., mathematical models, simulation models, and data models) (Nunamaker et al. 1990–91). Theories (particularly mathematical models) are usually concerned with generic system behaviors and are subject to rigorous analysis. Experimentation on the other hand includes research strategies such as laboratory and field experiments, as well as computer and experimental simulations. It straddles the gulf between theory building and observation in that experimentation may concern itself with either the validation of the underlying theories or the issues of acceptance or technology transfer. Observation includes methods such as case studies, field studies, and sample surveys that are unobtrusive research operations.

Systems development framework consists of five stages: conceptual design, constructing the architecture of the system, analyzing the design, prototyping (may include product development), and evaluation. The framework is shown in Fig. 3.1.

Fig. 3.1 System development research model (adopted from Nunamaker et al. (1990–91))

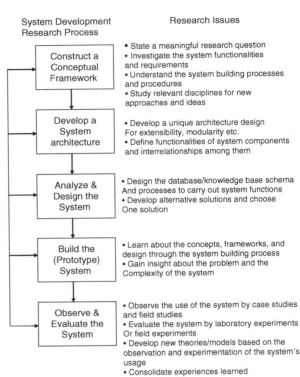

3.4 The General Design Cycle

Takeda et al. (1990) have analyzed the reasoning that occurs in the course of a general design cycle (GDC). Vaishnavi and Kuechler (2004) have extended this analysis to explicate the knowledge generated in a design effort and apply the cycle specifically to design science research (Vaishnavi and Kuechler 2007) as illustrated in Fig. 3.2.

In this model, all design begins with awareness of problem. The problem genesis can be from many places (we discuss this later in the book). Here you not only identify the problem but also define it. The next stage is a preliminary suggestion for a problem solution that is abductively drawn from the existing knowledge or theory based on the problem area or developed using an appropriate research methodology.

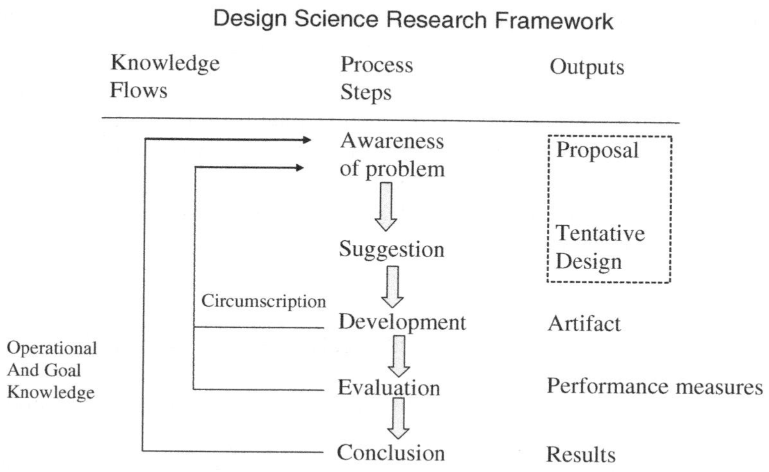

Design Science Research Framework

Knowledge Flows	Process Steps	Outputs

Fig. 3.2   Reasoning in the general design cycle (adopted from Vaishnavi and Kuechler (2007))

Once a tentative design is settled on, the next stage is actual development. This is a creative stage where the design is further refined and an actual artifact is produced through many iterations. This is the only phase of GDC that requires a constructivist methodology (Vaishnavi and Kuechler 2007).

Once an implementation (or prototype) is ready, it isevaluated according to functional specification implicit or explicit in the suggestion. Empirical methods are often used in evaluation. It is important to determine how well an artifact works (Hevner et al. 2004), and researchers should use methods and techniques similar to theory testing (March and Smith 1995) including action research, controlled experiments, simulation, or scenarios. There are iterations and feedback involved in these stages cited as circumscription. Finally a project is terminated and concluded.

3.5   Action Research Framework

Action research is an established research method in use in the social and medical sciences since the mid-twentieth century (Baskerville 1999). Action researchers are among those who assume that complex social systems cannot be reduced for meaningful study. The fundamental contention of the action researcher is that complex social processes can be studied best by introducing changes into these processes and observing the effects of these changes (Baskerville 1999).

In its origins, the essence of action research is a simple two-stage process:

- First, the diagnostic stage involves a collaborative analysis of the social situation by the researcher and the subjects of the research. Theories are formulated concerning the nature of the research domain.

- Second, the therapeutic stage involves collaborative change experiments. In this stage changes are introduced and the effects are studied.

Baskerville (1999) in his tutorial presents the five phases of action research process: (1) diagnosing, (2) action planning, (3) action taking, (4) evaluating, and (5) specifying learning. There are cyclical iterations between these stages and as one can see, there are synergies with GDC and other DSR frameworks. We discuss action design in   chapter 13   of this book.

3.6 The Design Science Research Methodology (DSRM)

Peffers et al. (2008) propose and develop a design science research methodology (DSRM) for the production and presentation of DS research in IS. This effort contributes to IS research by providing a commonly accepted framework for successfully carrying out DS research and a mental model for its presentation. It may also help with the recognition and legitimization of DS research and its objectives, processes, and outputs and it should help researchers to present research with reference to a commonly understood framework, rather than justifying the research paradigm on an ad hoc basis with each new paper.

The final objective of a DSRM process is to provide a mental model for the characteristics of research outputs. "A mental model is a "small-scale [model]" of reality . . .[that] can be constructed from perception, imagination, or the comprehension of discourse. [Mental models] are akin to architects' models or to physicists' diagrams in that their structure is analogous to the structure of the situation that they represent, unlike, say, the structure of logical forms used in formal rule theories (Johnson-Laird and Byrne 2007)." Outcomes from DS research are clearly expected to differ from those of theory testing or interpretative research and a process model should provide us with some guidance, as reviewers, editors, and consumers, about what to expect from DS research outputs. March and Smith (1995) contributed to this expectation with their ideas about research outputs. Hevner et al. (2004) further elaborated on this expectation by describing DS research's essential elements. A mental model for the conduct and presentation of DS research will help researchers to conduct it effectively.

The DS process includes six steps: problem identification and motivation; definition of the objectives for a solution, design, and development; demonstration; evaluation; and communication.

Activity 1. *Problem identification and motivation.* Define the specific research problem and justify the value of a solution. Since the problem definition will be used to develop an artifact that can effectively provide a solution, it may be useful to atomize the problem conceptually so that the solution can capture its complexity. Justifying the value of a solution accomplishes two things: it motivates the researcher and the audience of the research to pursue the solution and to accept the results and it helps to understand the reasoning associated with the researcher's understanding of the problem. Resources required for this activity include knowledge of the state of the problem and the importance of its solution.

Some of the researchers explicitly incorporate efforts to transform the problem into system objectives, also called meta-requirements (Walls et al. 1992) or requirements (Eekels and Roozenburg 1991), while for the others this effort is implicit, e.g., part of programming and data collection (Archer 1984), or implicit in the search for a relevant and important problem. Identified problems do not necessarily translate directly into objectives for the artifact because the process of design is necessarily one of partial and incremental solutions. Consequently, after the problem is identified, there remains the step of determining the performance objectives for a solution.

Activity 2. *Define the objectives for a solution.* Infer the objectives of a solution from the problem definition and knowledge of what is possible and feasible. The objectives can be quantitative, e.g., terms in which a desirable solution would be better than current ones, or qualitative, e.g., a description of how a new artifact is expected to support solutions to problems not hitherto addressed. The objectives should be inferred rationally from the problem specification. Resources required for this include knowledge of the state of problems and current solutions, if any, and their efficacy.

All of the researchers focus on the core of design science across disciplines: *design and development.* In some of the research, e.g., Eekels and Roozenburg (1991), the design and development activities are further subdivided into more discrete activities whereas other researchers focus more on the nature of the iterative search process (Hevner et al. 2004).

Activity 3. *Design and development.* Create the artifact. Such artifacts are potentially constructs, models, methods, or instantiations (each defined broadly) (Hevner et al. 2004) or "new properties of technical, social, and/or informational resources (Jarvinen 2007)". Conceptually, a design research artifact can be any designed object in which a research contribution is embedded in the design. This activity includes determining the artifact's desired functionality and its architecture and then creating the actual artifact. Resources required moving from objectives to design and development include knowledge of theory that can be brought to bear in a solution.

Next, the solutions vary from a single act of *demonstration* (Walls et al. 1992) to prove that the idea works to a more formal *evaluation* (Nunamaker et al. 1990–91; Eekels and Roozenburg 1991; Hevner et al. 2004; Vaishnavi and Kuechler 2007) of the developed artifact. Eekels and Roozenburg (1991) and Nunamaker et al. (1990–91) include both of these phases.

Activity 4. *Demonstration.* Demonstrate the use of the artifact to solve one or more instances of the problem. This could involve its use in experimentation, simulation, case study, proof, or other appropriate activity. Resources required for the demonstration include effective knowledge of how to use the artifact to solve the problem.

Activity 5. *Evaluation.* Observe and measure how well the artifact supports a solution to the problem. This activity involves comparing the objectives of a solution to actual observed results from use of the artifact in the demonstration. It requires knowledge of relevant metrics and analysis techniques. Depending on the nature of the problem venue and the artifact, evaluation could take many forms. It could include such items as a comparison of the artifact's functionality with the solution objectives from activity two above, objective quantitative performance measures, such as budgets or items produced, the results of satisfaction surveys, client feedback, or simulations. It could include quantifiable measures of system performance, such as response time or availability. Conceptually, such evaluation could include any appropriate empirical evidence or logical proof. At the end of this activity the researchers can decide whether to iterate back to step three to try to improve the effectiveness of the artifact or to continue on to communication and leave further improvement to subsequent projects. The nature of the research venue may dictate whether such iteration is feasible or not.

Finally, Archer (1984) and Hevner et al. (2004) propose the need for *communication* to diffuse the resulting knowledge.

Activity 6. *Communication.* Communicate the problem and its importance, the artifact, its utility and novelty, the rigor of its design, and its effectiveness to researchers and other relevant audiences, such as practicing professionals, when appropriate. In scholarly research publications, researchers might use the structure of this process to structure the paper, just as the nominal structure of an empirical research process (problem definition, literature review, hypothesis development, data collection, analysis, results, discussion, and conclusion) is a common structure for empirical research papers. Communication requires knowledge of the disciplinary culture.

3.7 Concluding Thoughts

A number of different design science research frameworks and methodology are presented in this chapter. The purpose is to provide valuable guidelines that design researchers may consider. But we caution the researcher that these steps or methods are useful only when you are able to apply it to your design situation and problem context. It is important to keep in mind that every design science project requires a certain level of creativity.

References

Archer, L. B. (1984) *Systematic Method for Designers,* John Wiley, London.

Baskerville, R. L. (1999) Investigating information systems with action research, *Communications of the Association for Information Systems* 2 (19). Available at: http://aisel.aisnet.org/cais/vol2/iss1/19

Eekels, J. and N. F. M. Roozenburg (1991) A methodological comparison of the structures of scientific research and engineering design: their similarities and differences. *Design Studies* 12 (4), pp. 197–203.

Hevner, A., S. March, J. Park, and S. Ram (2004) Design science in information systems research, *MIS Quarterly* 28 (1), pp. 75–105.

Jarvinen, P. (2007) Action research is similar to design science, *Quality & Quantity* 41 (1), pp. 37–54.

Johnson-Laird, P. and R. Byrne (2000) A gentle introduction, Mental Models Website, School of Psychology, Trinity College, Dublin (available at www.tcd.ie/Psychology/Ruth_Byrne/mental_models/).

March, S. T. and G. F. Smith (1995) Design and natural science research on information technology, *Decision Support Systems* 15, pp. 251–266.

Nunamaker, J. F., M. Chen et al. (1990–91) Systems development in information systems research, *Journal of Management Information Systems* 7 (3), pp. 89–106.

Peffers, K., T. Tuunanen, M. A. Rothenberger, and S. Chatterjee (2008) A design science research methodology for information systems research. *Journal of Management Information Systems (JMIS)* 24 (3), pp. 45–77.

Simon, H. A. (1996) *Sciences of the Artificial*, MIT Press, Cambridge, MA.

Takeda, H., P. Veerkamp, T. Tomiyama, and H. Yoshikawam (1990) Modeling design processes, *AI Magazine*, Winter, pp. 37–48.

Vaishnavi, V. and W. Kuechler (2004) Design Research in Information Systems, January 20, 2004. URL: http://desrist.org/design-research-in-information-systems/

Vaishnavi, V. K. and W. Kuechler Jr. (2007) *Design Science Research methods and Patterns: Innovating Information and Communication Technology,* Auerbach Publications, Taylor & Francis Group, Boca Raton, FL, New York.

Walls, J. G., G. R. Widmeyer et al. (1992) Building an information system design theory for vigilant EIS, *Information Systems Research* 3 (1), pp. 36–59.

Chapter 4
On Design Theory

Theory thus become instruments, not answers to enigmas, in which we can rest.
We don't lie back upon them, we move forward, and, on occasion, make nature over again by their aid.

– William James (1907)

4.1 What Is Theory?

Science progresses because of advancement in theories. Dictionary definitions show that the word theory can take on many meanings, including "a mental view" or "contemplation," "a concept or mental scheme of something to be done, or the method of doing it; a systematic statement of rules or principles to be followed," a "system of ideas or statements held as an explanation or account of a group of facts or phenomena; a hypothesis that has been confirmed or established by observation or experiment and is propounded or accepted as accounting for the known facts; statements of what are held to be the general laws, principles, or causes of something known or observed," a "mere hypothesis, speculation, conjecture" (Gregor 2006).

Shirley Gregor (2006) in her recent essay examines the structural nature of theory in Information Systems. Many people argue that theory is not even an end goal for design research (March and Smith 1995). But within the business school environment where most IS programs reside, management and IS scholars spend lot of energy defending various research methods. Debates about *deductive* versus *inductive* theory building or field observation versus large-sample numerical data affect our lives. Yet respected members of our community (Simon, Solow, Staw, Sutton, Hayes) have continued to express concerns that collective efforts of business academics have produced a paucity of theory that is intellectually rigorous, practically useful, and able to stand the tests of time and changing circumstances (Carlile and Christensen 2005). Hence it becomes important to understand how theories are built. We begin by looking at the cycle of theory building.

A. Hevner, S. Chatterjee, *Design Research in Information Systems*, Integrated Series in Information Systems 22, DOI 10.1007/978-1-4419-5653-8_4,
© Springer Science+Business Media, LLC 2010

4.2 Cycle of Theory Building

Carlile and Christensen outline a process of theory building that links questions
about data, methods, and theory (Carlile and Christensen 2005). The building of
theory occurs in two major stages – the *descriptive stage* and the *normative stage*.

Within each of these stages, theory builders proceed through three steps: *observation, categorization, and association*. The theory-building process iterates through
these stages again and again (see Fig. 4.1).

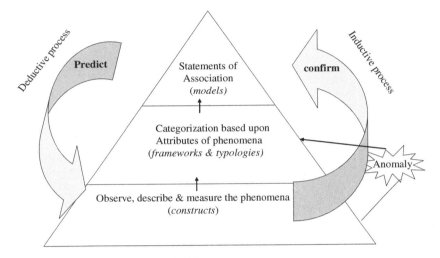

Fig. 4.1 Stages of descriptive theory building

In the past management researchers have quite carelessly applied the term theory
to research activities that are conducted within one of these steps.

Terms such as "utility theory" in economics and "contingency theory" in organization design actually refer only to an individual stage in the theory-building process
in their respective fields.

4.2.1 Observation

We start at the bottom of the pyramid. As first step researchers **observe** phenomena
and carefully describe and measure what they see. Documenting what one sees and
measurement of the phenomena in words and numbers are important. This is the
foundation work, the base of the pyramid. The phenomena being explored in this
stage includes not just things such as people, organizations, and technologies, but
processes as well. Researchers in this step often develop abstractions from the messy
detail of phenomena that we term *constructs*. Constructs help us understand and
visualize what the phenomena are, how they operate. It is necessary to identify the
correct constructs.

As an example, for years, scholars of inventory policy and supply chain system used the tools of operations research to derive evermore-sophisticated optimizing algorithms for inventory replenishment. Most were based on the assumption that managers know what their levels of inventory are. Ananth Raman's (Narayanan and Raman 2004) path-breaking research of the phenomena, however, obviated much of this research when he showed that most firms' computerized inventory records were broadly inaccurate – even when they used state-of-the-art automated tracking systems. Bower (1970) created constructs of *impetus* and *context* in resource allocation process, explaining how momentum builds behind certain investment proposals and fails to coalesce behind others.

4.2.2 Classification

With the phenomena observed and described researchers move up the pyramid to the second stage in which they classify the phenomena into categories. In the descriptive stage of theory building, the classification schemes that scholars propose typically are defined by the attributes of the phenomena. Examples from management phenomena include diversified vs. focused firms, vertically integrated vs. specialist firms, or publicly traded vs. privately held companies (Carlile and Christensen 2005).

Such categorization schemes attempt to simplify and organize the world in ways that highlight possibly consequential relationships between the phenomena and outcomes of interest. These schemes are often referred to as *frameworks or typologies*.

4.2.3 Defining Relationships

In the third step, researchers explore the association between the category-defining attributes and the outcomes observed. Researchers recognize and make explicit what differences in attributes, and differences in the magnitude of those attributes, correlate most strongly with the patterns in the outcomes of interest.

Techniques such as regression analysis typically are useful in defining these correlations. Often we refer to the output of studies at this step as *models*. Descriptive theory that quantifies the degree of correlation between the category-defining attributes of the phenomena and the outcomes of interest is generally only able to make probabilistic statements of association representing average tendencies (Carlile and Christensen 2005). The model helps us to understand which variables actually impact the dependent variable (outcome) of interest through averages. No causality can be inferred yet.

As an example, Hutton et al. (2003) have studied how stock prices have responded to earnings announcements that were phrased or couched in various terms. They coded types of words and phrases in the statements as explanatory variables in a regression equation, with the ensuing change in equity price as the dependent variable. Research results such as this is important descriptive theory; however, at this point it can only assert on average what attributes are associated with the best results. A specific manager of a specific company cannot know if following those same codes of words for company announcement will lead to a similar gain in stock price. The ability to predict such things awaits the development of normative theory in this field.

4.2.4 Anomaly – Improving Descriptive Theory

The inductive portion of the theory building moves researchers from the bottom to the top of the pyramid using three steps: observation, categorization, association. Theory begins to improve when researchers cycle from the top back to the bottom of this pyramid in the deductive portion of the cycle – seeking to "test" the hypothesis that had been inductively formulated. This is mostly done to see if the correlations between attributes also hold in other data sets than the ones that were used for the original inductive steps. If it correlates in a new data set, this "test" confirms that the theory is of use under the conditions or circumstances observed. The researcher returns the model to its place atop the pyramid tested but unimproved. It is only when an anomaly is identified, an outcome for which the theory cannot account that an opportunity to improve theory occurs. Once an anomaly is found, researchers look for new attributes or further categorization that explains the observed anomaly in the new data set.

4.3 Transition to Normative Theory

It is important to move beyond statements of correlation to define what *causes* the outcome of interest. This is typically achieved by careful detailed empirical and ethnographic observation. It is necessary to leap across to the top of the pyramid of *causal theory*. With their understanding of causality, researchers then work to improve theory by following the same three steps that were used in the descriptive stage.

Hypothesizing that their statement of causality is correct, they cycle deductively to the bottom of the pyramid to test the causal statement. If an anomaly is encountered, they delve into categorization stage. By cycling up and down the pyramid of normative theory, researchers will ultimately define the set of situations or circumstances in which managers might find themselves when pursuing the outcomes of interest. This allows researchers to make contingent statements of causality, i.e., to show how and why the causal mechanisms result in a different outcome in different situations (Carlile and Christensen 2005).

As described above, theory building is a time-consuming and laborious effort that often is a result of several researchers in the community working together to put different parts of the puzzle. It is only through recursive cycling up (inductive) and down (deductive) that we test and prove (or disprove) theories over time.

Now that we understand the basic process of theory building, we turn our attention to design theory in information systems.

4.4 Taxonomy of Theory Types in Information Systems

Gregor, in her essay "The Nature of Theory in Information Systems" (Gregor 2006) provides a comprehensive look at various theories proposed in IS discipline and explores the structural nature or ontological character of those theory. Gregor summarizes and shows theories as abstract entities that aim to *describe, explain,* and *enhance understanding* of the world. In some cases, it provides *predictions* of what will happen in the future and to give a basis for intervention and action.

Some theories are statements that say how something should be done in practice. Others are statements providing a lens for viewing or explaining the world. Then there are theories that are statements of relationships among constructs that can be tested. By combining the goals of theory, Gregor classifies IS theories into the five types (see Table 4.1) and the distinguishing features of each theory type are shown in the right-hand column. It is important to note that allocating theories to classes is not trivial. A theory that is primarily analytic, describing a classification system, can have implications of causality (Gregor 2006).

Table 4.1 Different types of theory in IS (adopted from Gregor (2006))

Theory type	Distinguishing attributes
I. Analysis	Says what is The theory does not extend beyond analysis and description. No causal relationships among phenomena are specified and no predictions are made
II. Explanation	Says what is how, why, when, and where The theory provides explanations but does not aim to predict with any precision. There are no testable propositions
III. Prediction	Says what is and what will be The theory provides predictions and has testable propositions but does not have well-developed justificatory causal explanations
IV. Explanation and prediction (EP)	Says what is, how, why, when, where, and what will be Provides predictions and has both testable propositions and causal explanations
V. Design and action	Says how to do something The theory gives explicit prescriptions (e.g., methods, techniques, principles of form and function) for constructing an artifact

Table 4.2 shows the components of theories across the taxonomy. This specification allows IS researchers (1) to identify what theory is composed of in general and (2) to analyze the components of their own theory and the theory of others. This is a useful framework as more new theories are developed in the IS community.

Table 4.2 Structural components of theory (adopted from Gregor (2006))

Theory component (components common to all theory)	Definition
Means of representation	The theory must be represented physically in some way: in words, mathematical terms, symbolic logic, diagrams, tables, or graphically. Additional aids for representation could include pictures, models, or prototype systems
Constructs	These refer to the phenomena of interest in the theory (Dubin's "units"). All of the primary constructs in the theory should be well defined. Many different types of constructs are possible: for example, observational (real) terms, theoretical (nominal) terms, and collective terms
Statements of relationship	These show relationships among the constructs. Again, these may be of many types: associative, compositional, unidirectional, bidirectional, conditional, or causal. The nature of the relationship specified depends on the purpose of the theory. Very simple relationships can be specified: for example. "x is a member of class A"
Scope	The scope is specified by the degree of generality of the statements of relationships (signified by modal qualifiers such as "some," "many," "all," and "never") and statements of boundaries showing the limits of generalizations
Theory component (components contingent on theory purpose)	
Causal explanations	The theory gives statements of relationships among phenomena that show causal reasoning (not covering law or probabilistic reasoning alone)
Testable propositions (hypotheses)	Statements of relationships between constructs are stated in such a form that they can be tested empirically
Prescriptive statements	Statements in the theory specify how people can accomplish something in practice (e.g., construct an artifact or develop a strategy)

4.5 Is Design Theory Possible?

The scientific design community is split on this topic. One camp says that there can be a design theory while other camp does not believe that there can be such a theory. In this section, we discuss three views. First, we present the Information

Systems Design Theory (ISDT) (Walls et al. 1992) as an example of an early design theory that exists and have been cited by the IS community. Then we present John Hooker's (Hooker 2004) contrasting perspective of why such a theory cannot exist (yet)? Finally we briefly discuss Gregor and Jones (2007) in which they list what the anatomy of a IS design theory should have if one has to have a design theory.

4.5.1 Information Systems Design Theory

In 1992, Walls, Widmeyer, and El-Sawy formally specified design theory in IS adapting Simon's ideas for the IS context. They specified the components of an ISDT as shown in Fig. 4.2. They are the following:

1. Meta-requirements, the class of goals to which the theory applies.
2. Meta-design, the class of artifacts hypothesized to meet the meta-requirements.
3. Kernel design product theories, theories from natural and social sciences that govern design requirements.
4. Testable design product hypotheses, statements required to test whether the meta-design satisfies meta-requirements.
5. Design method, a description of the procedures for constructing the artifact.
6. Kernel-design process theories, theories from natural or social sciences that inform the design process.
7. Testable design process hypotheses, statements required to test whether the design method leads to an artifact that is consistent with meta-design.

Design product		
1.	Meta-requirements	Describes the class of goals to which the theory applies
2.	Meta-design	Describes a class of artifacts hypothesized to meet the meta-requirements
3.	Kernel theories	Theories from natural or social sciences governing design requirements
4.	Testable design product hypotheses	Used to test whether the meta-design hypotheses satisfies the meta-requirements
Design process		
1.	Design method	A description of procedure(s) for artifact construction
2.	Kernel theories	Theories from natural or social sciences governing design process itself
3.	Testable design process hypotheses	Used to verify whether the design hypotheses method results in an artifact which is consistent with the meta-design

Fig. 4.2 An ISDT (adapted from Walls et al. (1992))

In assessing the extent of use of ISDT the authors again conducted a study in 2004. They found that 26 articles have referenced ISDT and they were able to identify four different levels of usage (Walls et al. 2004):

Level 1: ISDT is used as a *cloak of theoretical legitimacy* to describe the design features and requirements of a new class of information systems.

Level 2: ISDT is used as a *common language and framework* for determining the meta-requirements for a new class of information systems and how its instances should be designed.

Level 3: ISDT is used as a *way of generating new insights* about the characteristics of a new class of information systems.

Level 4: The *richness of ISDT itself is enhanced* through usage as scholars discover gaps and omissions and improvements that can be made to ISDT that are revealed by working through it in their own context.

While Walls' et al. ISDT may be the first formal specification of a design theory in IS, its limited use to date points toward certain shortcomings. The specification as presented does not lend to immediate use as a theory. Rather more people have found it useful as a framework, which is one step toward a larger theory. Another difficulty with this seems to be the unnecessary separation of theory components for a "design process" on top of a "design product" and the lack of a clear definition as to what comprises a "product" and what comprises a "process." Furthermore, the exact nature of the things that are addressed by the "class of goals to which the theory applies" is not clear.

4.5.2 Hooker's View on Design Theory

Hooker (2004) argues that the notion of a theory of design is problematic because design, like medicine or management, is a practice. "In a sense design is pre-theory. Whereas chemistry or physics is defined by a set of phenomenon it is assigned to study, design is defined by a task it is assigned to do. It is not to dispute that one can theorize about design practice, in the sense that one can theoretically understand the socio-psychological phenomenon of design. But that is not design theory" (Hooker 2004).

> Knowledge of how to design cannot be reduced to theory, for reasons that grow out of philosophy of science.

We know that a number of practical sciences are centered on design: physical artifacts, software, organizations, or information systems. This raises the issue of whether there can be in fact a science of design with a theoretical basis. Hooker (2004) maintains that there cannot be a theory of design in the same sense that there is a theory of physics or chemistry. He argues that design is a practice (the process view of IS) that cannot be reduced to theory because practice is essentially pretheoretical. Quinn's indeterminacy of translation thesis (Quinne 1961) implies the following: without pretheoretical discourse to supply the concepts explained by theories, there would be no way to understand what it means for competing theories to offer different explanations of the same phenomenon.

Design theory should provide knowledge of how to design. Much of this exists within the creative mind, is highly problem and scenario dependent, and is extremely dynamic to be generalizable. Hooker points out that there can be a supporting theory that is uniquely associated with a practice, even though it does not completely explain the practice itself. Design theory must organize our knowledge of design practice. However, this "knowledge of design practice" has two very different meanings and implications. It can refer to knowledge about socio-physiological theory of what designers do (our supporting theory) or knowledge one must have in order to practice design. The latter is much harder.

4.5.3 Toward the Anatomy of an IS Design Theory

One can argue that the goal of design science is all about efficacy and utility. There is no truth that we seek. Hence theory is unimportant. Gregor and Jones on the other hand argue that we can begin to lay out the anatomy of what constitutes a good IS design theory (Gregor and Jones 2007). They state the following:

> Our argument is that any design theory should include as a minimum: (1) the purpose and scope, (2) the constructs, (3) the principles of form and function, (4) the artifact mutability, (5) testable propositions, and (6) justificatory knowledge.

Figure 4.3 explains these core components.

The above is a useful first step toward building a design theory. However, we claim that this in itself is not a theory. A design theory or a science of design is a noble goal that remains elusive as of yet.

Component	description
Core components	
1. Purpose and Scope	"What the system is for", the set of meta-requirements or goals that specifies the type of artifact to which theory applies
2. Constructs	Representation of the entities of interest in the theory.
3. Principle of form And function	The abstract "blueprint" or architecture that describes an IS artifact, either product or method/intervention.
4. Artifact mutability	The changes in state of the artifact anticipated in the theory, that is, what degree of artifact change is encompassed by the theory
5. Testable propositions	Truth statements about design theory
6. Justificatory knowledge	The underlying knowledge or theory from the natural or social or design sciences that gives a basis and explanation for the design (kernel theories)

Fig. 4.3 Six components of an information systems design theory

4.6 Conclusions

Design work and design knowledge in information systems are very important for both research and practice. There has been little effort paid to date to the problem of specifying design theory so that it can be communicated, justified, and developed. In this chapter, we presented what theory is and how theories should be developed. We then presented the two sides of the argument in which one side claims that there can be such a thing as design theory while the other argues against it. We would like to leave the reader with the understanding that an IS design theory is still a work in progress and Gregor and Jones' anatomy of the IS design theory is a very good starting point to conduct further research.

References

Bower, J. (1970) *Managing the Resource Allocation process,* Prentice Hall, Englewood Cliffs, NJ.

Carlile, P. R. and C. M. Christensen (2005) The cycles of theory building in management research, Working Paper Publication, HBS Working Paper Number: 05-057.

Gregor, S. (2006) The nature of theory in information systems, *MIS Quarterly* 30 (3), pp. 611–642.

Gregor, S. and D. Jones (2007) The anatomy of a design theory, *Journal of AIS* 8 (5), pp. 312–335.

Hooker, J. N. (2004) Is design theory possible? *Journal of Information Technology Theory and Application* 6 (2), pp. 73–83.

Hutton, A., G. Miller et al. (2003) The role of supplementary statements in the disclosure of management earnings forecasts, *Journal of Accounting Research* 41, pp. 867–890.

March, S. T. and G. F. Smith (1995) Design and natural science research on information technology, *Decision Support Systems,* 15, pp. 251–266.

Narayanan, V. G. and A. Raman (2004) Aligning incentives in supply chains, *Harvard Business Review* 82 (11).

Quinne, W. V. (1961) *Two Dogmas of Empericism: In From a Logical Point of View: Nine Logico-philosophical Essays,* Harper and Row, New York.

Walls, J. G., G. R. Widmeyer et al. (1992) Building an information system design theory for vigilant EIS, *Information Systems Research* 3 (1), 36–59.

Walls, J. G., G. R. Widmeyer, and O. A. El Sawy (2004) Assessing information system design theory in perspective: how useful was our 1992 initial rendition?, *JITTA: Journal of Information Technology Theory and Application* 6 (2), pp. 43–58.

Chapter 5
Twelve Theses on Design Science Research in Information Systems

Some problems have such complex social, economic, or organizational interactions that they can't be solved fully. They've become popularly known as "wicked problems".

Robert W. Lucky, IEEE Spectrum, July 2009

This essay discusses 12 theses for guiding design science research. They are aimed at strengthening the design science orientation of Information Systems, clarifying future discourses on design science research aspects of the discipline, and giving some further guidelines for design science research in Information Systems.

5.1 Introduction

Although the current interest in design science research (DSR) (Nunamaker et al. 1990–1991; Walls et al. 1992; March and Smith 1995; Hevner et al. 2004; Gregor and Jones 2007) has been marked by an attempt to make it legitimate to do DSR in Information Systems (IS), DSR is still a sidetrack of IS research. Recognizing that IS ultimately is a practical discipline (Avison and Wood-Harper 1991), the message of the present chapter is that DSR should be its dominant research orientation. It is also important that the above articles have turned our attention to how to do rigorous DSR. Most notably, Hevner et al. (2004) propose seven guidelines for DSR and Gregor and Jones (2007) analyze the components of IS design theory.

Unfortunately, but understandably, the rapidly increased interest in DSR has led to uncertainty about what DSR is or should be (Baskerville 2008, Kuechler and Vaishnavi 2008, Winter 2008). In particular, its relation to "scientific design," "design science," and the "science of design" in the sense of Cross (1993, 2001) seems to be a source of continued confusion (McKay and Marshall 2007). The relationships between these and DSR will be elaborated at the end of the present chapter.

Juhani Iivari

A. Hevner, S. Chatterjee, *Design Research in Information Systems*, Integrated Series in Information Systems 22, DOI 10.1007/978-1-4419-5653-8_5,
© Springer Science+Business Media, LLC 2010

The primary purpose of this chapter is to discuss 12 theses suggested in Iivari (2007) to summarize the disciplinary, ontological, epistemological and methodological analysis of IS as a design science. The 12 theses are as follows:

1 IS is ultimately an applied or practical discipline (discipline).
2 Prescriptive research is an essential part of IS as an applied or practical discipline (discipline).
3 The design science activity of building IT artifacts is an important part of prescriptive research in IS (discipline).
4 The primary interest of IS lies in IT applications, and therefore IS as a design science should be based on a sound ontology of IT artifacts and especially of IT applications (ontology).
5 IS as a design science builds IT meta-artifacts that support the development of concrete IT applications (ontology).
6 Prescriptive knowledge of IT artifacts forms a knowledge area of its own and cannot be reduced to the descriptive knowledge of theories and empirical regularities (epistemology).
7 The resulting IT meta-artifacts essentially entail design product and design process knowledge (epistemology).
8 The term "design theory" should be used only when it is based on a sound kernel theory (epistemology).
9 Constructive research methods should make the process of building IT meta-artifacts disciplined, rigorous, and transparent (methodology).
10 Explication of the practical problems to be solved, the existing artifacts to be improved, the analogies and metaphors to be used, and/or the kernel theories to be applied is significant in making the building process disciplined, rigorous, and transparent (methodology).
11 IS as a design science cannot be value-free, but it may reflect means-end, interpretive, or critical orientation (ethics).
12 The values of design science research should be made as explicit as possible (ethics).

These theses were not discussed in detail in Iivari (2007). The hope is that the following discussion will clarify the nature and role of DSR in IS and will give some further guidelines for such research.

5.2 Thesis 1: IS Is an Applied or Practical Discipline

There seems to be a certain reluctance in IS to characterize it as an applied discipline. One can identify two reasons for this. The first is that applied science may be deemed inferior to more "pure" science (Pitt 2000), and the second may be the conceptual confusion related to "applied science," "applied research," "pure science," and "basic research."[1] Referring to Strasser (1985), Gregor (2008) prefers the term "practical science," and Avison and Wood-Harper (1991) characterize IS as a "practical discipline."

It may be that terms such as "practical science" or "practical discipline" are more neutral than "applied discipline" for expressing the overall orientation of IS.[2] More essential than terminology, however, is the question of what implications this view has for IS research. Benbasat and Zmud (2003), for example, implicitly include the idea of IS as an applied or practical discipline in their statement of its aims:

> "our focus should be on how *to best design IT artifacts and IS systems* to increase their compatibility, usefulness, and ease of use or on how to best manage and support IT or IT-enabled business initiatives" [*italics* added by the author],

They nevertheless prefer to define the core of the field only in terms of a nomological net. As they do not recognize IS as a design science, their nomological net treats it as if it were only natural/behavioral research in which artifacts just happen to be part of the nomological net.

The characterization of IS as an applied or practical discipline strengthens its practical orientation: its general interest is in how to change the world and not only in how the world is. IS as an applied or practical discipline means that DSR is not a sidetrack, as is currently the situation, but should be its central orientation.

5.3 Thesis 2: Prescriptive Research Is an Essential Part of IS as an Applied or Practical Discipline

The idea of IS as an applied or practical discipline (Thesis 1) does not mean that it should include only "applied research." Most disciplines comprise both "basic research" and "applied research." When speaking about various types of research within a discipline, I find the distinction between descriptive and prescriptive research clearer than that between "basic research" and "applied research."

Bazerman (2005) recommends that social sciences should have more prescriptive implications for organizations and for society at large, claiming that economics has been more successful in deriving theoretical implications than the other social sciences. Indeed, economics provides a good example of descriptive and prescriptive research. Adapting Chmielewicz (1970), Lehtovuori (1973) proposes that one can identify four levels in economics as a discipline: the conceptual level, the descriptive level of economic theory, the prescriptive level of economic policy, and the normative level of economic philosophy. The research goal at the conceptual level

---

[1] Referring to the first reason, the "anxiety discourse" (King and Lyytinen 2004) regarding the academic legitimacy and credibility of the discipline has been an amazingly significant issue in information systems, guiding far too much of the evolution of the discipline.

[2] Hassan (2006) points out that it is more appropriate to speak about Information Systems as a field than as a discipline. The reasons are its lack of theory development and its weak boundaries. Despite this inaccuracy, I will speak below about the "IS discipline".

is essentialist: concepts and conceptual frameworks do not have any truth value or "truthlikeness" (Niiniluoto 1999), but simply attempt to capture the essence of the phenomena. The research goal at the level of economic theory is theoretical, to find causal relationships, and that at the level of economic policy is pragmatic, to find means-end relationships. Both causal and means-end relationships have a truth value. The level of economic philosophy has a normative research goal, being concerned with values that do not have any truth value.

The resultant structure when applied to IS is illustrated in Fig. 5.1.[3] Concepts and conceptual frameworks at the conceptual level aim at identifying essences in the research territory and their relationships. They may be more or less useful when developing theories at the descriptive level, which aim at describing, understanding and explaining how things are.

Stated briefly, the conceptual level is interested in "what things are out there," descriptive research in "how things are out there," and prescriptive research in "how things could be out there" and "how one can effectively achieve specified ends". The prescriptive level covers both recommendations and artifacts as outcomes of DSR. These do not have any truth or truth-like value as such, but statements about their efficiency and effectiveness do.

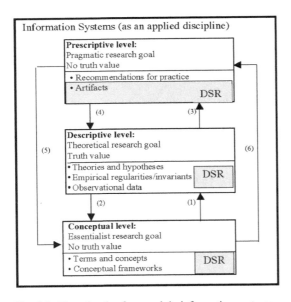

Fig. 5.1 Three levels of research in information systems

---

[3]Figure 5.1 drops the normative level of the original framework of Chmielewicz (1970) and Lehtovuori (1973). The normative level is interested in "how ought things to be?" Normative statements express "You ought to want A and to achieve this you should do X if you believe that you are in a situation B." The reason for the exclusion is that it is still a controversial question whether one can reach "ought-to" conclusions based on "what is."

The hierarchy of Fig. 5.1 can be mapped to the types of "theories" suggested by Gregor (2006). "Theories for analyzing and describing" lie at the conceptual level, "theories for predicting" are empirical regularities, "theories for explaining and predicting" refer to theories at the descriptive level, and "theories for design and action" represent the prescriptive level. Only "theories of explaining," when interpreted as grand theories such as critical social theory, structuration theory, actor-network theory, activity theory, do not have any representation in Fig. 5.1.

5.4 Thesis 3: The Design Science Activity of Building IT Artifacts Is an Important Part of Prescriptive Research in Information Systems

Figure 5.1 also illustrates the position of DSR in the framework, indicating that it may be conceptual, descriptive or prescriptive. [4] Philosophical treatments of prescriptive research (Bunge 1967b; Niiniluoto 1993) tend to interpret the prescriptive level as comprising only prescriptions based on practical implications of descriptive research and do not recognize complex artifacts as research outcomes. Niiniluoto (1993), for example, suggests that the typical knowledge claims of descriptive science are deterministic or probabilistic causal laws such as

(1) X causes A in situation B
(2) X tends to cause A in situation B with probability p

One can also derive predictions from these descriptive laws:

(3) X causes A in situation B
    X occurred in situation b
    The situation b is of type B
    Hence, A will occur in b

and also technical norms such as

(4) If you want A and you believe that you are in a situation B, then

   – you should do X (if X is a necessary cause of A)
   – it is rational for you to do X (if X is a sufficient cause of A)
   – it is profitable for you to do X (if X is a probabilistic cause of A)

---

[4] Interestingly, Winter (2008) applies the tenets of a 1990 edition of Chmielewicz's book (underlying Fig. 5.1) to structure DSR. His mapping of models, methods, constructs, and theories is quite consistent with Fig. 5.1, but he associates instantiations with the normative level. This differs from my interpretation of Chmielewicz (1970) based on Lehtovuori (1974).

Niiniluoto (1993) gives some examples of X, such as medical treatments, fertilizers, and materials used in aeroplanes, but fails to explicitly recognize X's as results of DSR or design product knowledge of X's as a separate category of knowledge at the prescriptive level.

The claim of thesis 3 is that the DSR activity of building IT artifacts is an important part of prescriptive research in IS. Evaluation as a DSR activity lies at the descriptive level. It studies how effective and efficient the artifacts are compared with existing artifacts. As illustrated by Hevner et al. (2004), evaluation applies the very same research methods as does descriptive research more generally. As such, descriptive DSR (i.e., evaluation) does not differ much from other descriptive research. In fact, if the plea of Orlikowski and Iacono (2001) to take the IT artifact seriously in IS research is to be heeded, much of it could be descriptive DSR, making the borderline between evaluation as a DSR activity and more general descriptive research increasingly diffuse.

As pointed out by March and Smith (1995), many artifacts are primarily concepts (constructs) or conceptual frameworks (models and methods). Therefore the building of constructs, models, and methods is indicated in Fig. 5.1 as both prescriptive and conceptual research at the same time.

5.5 Thesis 4: The Primary Interest of IS Lies in IT Applications, and Therefore IS as a Design Science Should Be Based on a Sound Ontology of IT Artifacts and Especially of IT Applications

The three worlds of Popper (1978) provide a good starting point for such an ontology (Iivari 2007). World 1 is about material nature, World 2 about consciousness and mental states, and World 3 about products of human social action. World 3 clearly includes human artifacts, and it also covers institutions and theories, where institutions are social constructions that have been objectified (Berger and Luckman 1967).

If we conceive of IS as a design science that also builds IT artifacts, a natural question is what sort of artifacts we build, especially if we wish to distinguish IS from its sister disciplines, computer science and software engineering, which also focus on IT artifacts. I would suggest that the primary interest of IS lies in IT applications, and therefore IS as a design science should be based on a sound ontology of IT artifacts and especially of IT applications.

The typology for IT applications proposed in Iivari (2007) distinguishes seven archetypes of IT applications based on the function/role that the application serves: automating, augmenting, mediating, informing, entertaining, artisticizing, and accompanying. One could add fantasizing applications to this list. The first four functions are close to "technology as a labor substitution tool," "technology as a productivity tool," "technology as a social relations tool," and "technology as an information processing tool" in Orlikowski and Iacono (2001). Thus the typology essentially extends these four categories by incorporating four additional ones. Computer games illustrate the capability of IT applications to entertain. IT applications may also attempt to arouse artistic experience, and one can easily imagine a new sort of art that is essentially built on the interactive character of computer technology. IT artifacts such as digital pets can accompany human users. Finally, virtual fantasy worlds such as Second Life allow fantasizing applications.

A sound typology of IT artifacts, and especially of IT applications, is significant for a number of reasons. First, it is obvious that IT artifacts differ in design. A compiler design, for example, is quite different from the design of a specific information system, and the designing of an information system differs from game design. Second, as Swanson (1994) and Lyytinen and Rose (2003) suggest, IT artifacts differ in their diffusion. Third, it is my conjecture that IT application archetypes also differ in their acceptance, so that the Technology Acceptance Model (Davis et al. 1989; Venkatesh et al. 2003) is valid only in the case of certain IT application artifacts.

5.6   Thesis 5: IS as a Design Science Builds IT Meta-artifacts That Support the Development of Concrete IT Applications

One should note, however, that IS as a design science does not attempt to develop concrete IT applications, but rather meta-artifacts that help develop the concrete IT applications. van Aken (2004) makes a similar distinction between general solution concepts (meta-IT artifacts) and specific solution concepts (concrete IT applications).

Making a similar distinction, Walls et al. (1992) speak about meta-requirements and meta-design. Meta-artifacts can further be divided into *meta-artifacts for the IT product* and *meta-artifacts for the systems development process*. In the case of information systems, the former comprise technical implementation resources such as application domain-specific software components, application frameworks, application packages, ERP systems, development environments, IS generators, or their prototypes, which can be used in the technical implementation of an IS artifact, and also more abstract models and principles such as IS meta-models, various architectural models, analysis and design patterns and application-dependent design principles for use in the design and implementation of the IS product, while the latter correspond to the "design process" in the information system design theory of Walls et al. (1992) and comprise systems development approaches, methods, techniques and tools, for example.

Kuechler and Vaishnavi (2008) criticize the constructivist view of DSR adopted in Thesis 5 that emphasizes artifacts as research outputs of DSR. One should note, however, that the distinction between DSR and descriptive (behavioral) research is first of all epistemological. Descriptive research attempts to produce empirical regularities and theoretical understanding that can be assessed in terms of truth or "truthlikeness," whereas artifacts as outputs of DSR are only useful to varying extents. Hevner et al. (2004) clearly recognize this epistemological difference when they state that the goal of behavioral science research is truth and the goal of DSR is utility (p. 80).

5.7 Thesis 6: Prescriptive Knowledge of IT Artifacts Forms a Knowledge Area of Its Own and Cannot Be Reduced to the Descriptive Knowledge of Theories and Empirical Regularities

Niiniluoto's (1993) technical norms (see Thesis 3) give an impression that design science knowledge (technical norms) is largely reducible to descriptive knowledge (causal laws). The relationship between science and technology has been of considerable interest (Gardner 1994, 1995), leading to the conclusion that descriptive science and technology are separate, even though mutually interacting, bodies of thought, and that prescriptive knowledge cannot be reduced to descriptive knowledge of theories and empirical regularities (Layton 1974). [5]

The link between descriptive research and prescriptive research seems to be particularly weak in IS, where IT artifacts are relatively independent of descriptive theories concerning nature, human beings, organizations and other institutions, although quite recently IT has enabled new organizational forms to be developed based on networking and virtuality. Even though technical implementability is a significant issue, the dependence of IT artifacts on the laws of nature is mainly latent, and IS designers do not need to be constantly considering them. One can expect that the need for theories of human beings is the most obvious in the context of human–computer interaction (HCI), but the theoretical foundation of HCI is unclear and fragmented (Clemmensen 2006). It is also uncertain to what extent existing theories inform HCI design either directly or indirectly through design methods, standards, guidelines, etc.

The situation in IS is very similar. It has a diversity of reference disciplines from which it has adopted a number of theories (Benbasat and Weber 1996), but these theories are weakly linked to IT artifacts and their design. Even so, people design reasonably successful IT artifacts. This makes one to wonder whether the IS research community tends to exaggerate the significance of descriptive theoretical knowledge for prescriptive knowledge regarding how to design successful IT artifacts.

---

[5] Lyytinen and King (2004) also touch upon this issue when criticizing the linear science -> technology -> society model. One should note, however, that they do not go very far in their criticism when discussing the cyclical society -> science -> technology -> society model as an alternative.

5.8 Thesis 7: The Resulting IT Meta-artifacts Essentially Entail Design Product and Design Process Knowledge

Bunge (1967a) notes that the primary target of any scientific research, whether pure or applied, is to advance knowledge. Pure science has a purely cognitive aim, whereas applied science (technology) also has practical, utilitarian aims. If we accept Bunge's view and take IT meta-artifacts seriously as major outputs of DSR, this will imply that meta-artifacts for design product and systems development process (see Thesis 5) essentially entail knowledge. This is in line with Walls et al. (1992), who conceptualize meta-artifacts as design theories, and Hevner et al. (2004), who include IT artifacts (constructs, models, methods, and even instantiations) in the knowledge base.

van Aken (2004) claims that "the mission of a design science is to produce knowledge for the design and realization of artifacts, i.e. to solve construction problems, or to be used in the improvement of the performance of existing entities, i.e. to solve improvement problems." He also suggests three types of design science knowledge: object knowledge of the characteristics of artifacts and their materials, realization knowledge of the physical processes to be used to realize the designed artifacts, and process knowledge, of characteristics of the design process (van Aken 2005). In addition, he links the three types of design knowledge to technical norms of the form "if you wish to achieve A in situation B, then do something like X."[6] X in technical norms may refer to object design, realization design, or process design.

The distinction between design product knowledge, technological rules, and technical norms in prescriptive design science knowledge is set out in Table 5.1. The design product knowledge embedded in artifacts is a relatively weakly understood form of knowledge. The first three aspects of design product knowledge in Table 5.1 are close to the three criteria for artifacts identified by Beckman (2002): intentional, operational, and structural. Beckman illustrates these in the case of "knifehood." The intentional criterion implies that a thing is a knife because it is used as a knife, the operational criterion means that a thing is a knife because it works like a knife, and the structural criterion suggests that a thing is a knife because it has the shape and fabric of a knife. Beckman (2002) also includes a fourth criterion, the conventional one, which implies that a thing is a knife because it fits the reference of the common concept of "knife." In the DSR context, the conventional criterion is a significant goal in the sense that the artifact (e.g., a new systems development method OO+++) will be accepted as a valid instance of a given class concept (e.g., object-oriented methods) by a relevant community (e.g., practitioners). Despite this, I do not think that it is an inherent aspect of the artifact, since the artifact may achieve

---

[6]van Aken is referring here to technological rules (Bunge 1967b) of the following type: in order to achieve A do acts 1–*n* in a given order. One can interpret technological rules in the sense of Bunge (1967b) as expressing design process knowledge, but van Aken interprets them as technical norms in the sense of Niiniluoto (1993).

Table 5.1 Prescriptive design science knowledge

Design product knowledge	The artifact
	– idea, concept, style
	– functionality, behavior
	– architecture, structure
	– possible instantiation
Design process knowledge	In order to achieve A
Technological rules (Bunge 1967b)	– do $(act_1, act_2, \ldots, act_n)$
Technical norms (Niiniluoto 1993)	If you want A and you believe
	that you are in a situation B, then
	– you should do X
	– it is rational for you to do X
	– it is profitable for you to do X

general community acceptance years after its invention and construction. Therefore, the conventional criterion is not explicitly listed in Table 5.1, but following March and Smith (1995), instantiation is included as a fourth aspect.

It should be noted that some DSR literature tends to emphasize the significance of instantiations as research outcomes of DSR. Instantiations are, of course, significant as "proofs of a concept" (Nunamaker et al. 1990–1991). They may also increase the practical utility of the ideas, but from the research point of view they are secondary. The essential thing is the design product knowledge they entail.

5.9 Thesis 8: The Term "Design Theory" Should Be Used Only When It Is Based on a Sound Kernel Theory

Walls et al. (1992) pioneered the idea that design science should be rooted in theories. Ideally, theories should serve as sources of ideas in DSR, and they suggested that an "IS design theory" for a product should consist of meta-requirements (the class of goals to which the theory applies), meta-design (the class of artifacts hypothesized to meet the meta-requirements), kernel theories (theories from the natural and social sciences governing design), and testable design product hypotheses (used to test whether the meta-design satisfies the meta-requirements). An "IS design theory" for a process would comprise a design method (a description of the procedures for artifact construction), kernel theories, and testable design process hypotheses (used to verify whether the design method results in an artifact which is consistent with the meta-design).

Although I am afraid that the strong theory orientation of the leading IS journals may exaggerate the dependence of prescriptive knowledge on descriptive knowledge (see Thesis 6), I would consider the existence of a kernel theory to be a defining characteristic of a "design theory." Since Walls et al. (1992) point out that kernel theories are derived from the natural and social sciences and from mathematics, I wish to point out that it is not necessary for a kernel to be from some reference discipline external to IS. A kernel theory can be a theory specific to IS. As stated by Gregor (2006), a kernel theory may be a descriptive IS-specific "theory for predicting" or "explaining and predicting," an IS-specific theory "for analyzing and describing," or even another IS design theory or "theory for design and action," provided that the kernel theory is considered sound enough by the relevant scientific community.

Essentially, the claim is that without a sound kernel theory it is not justified to speak about "design theory." This is quite an ambitious requirement, because it is difficult, as Walls et al. (1992) demonstrate, to find convincing examples of IT meta-artifacts with well-defined kernel theories. As a result there seems to be some tendency to soften the requirements for a kernel theory. Markus et al. (2002), for example, allow any practitioner theory-in-use to serve as a kernel theory. This implies that a design theory is not necessarily based on any scientifically validated knowledge. Taking a cynical viewpoint, if kernel theory is forgotten, there is a danger that the idea of a "design theory" will be (mis)used just to make our field sound more scientific without any serious attempt to strengthen the scientific foundation of the meta-artifacts proposed. [7]

5.10 Thesis 9: Constructive Research Methods Should Make the Process of Building IT Meta-artifacts Disciplined, Rigorous, and Transparent

Recognizing that much of the research in computer science and software engineering in particular has consisted of constructing artifacts, the term "constructive research" was suggested in Iivari (1991) to denote the specific research methods required for constructing artifacts. [8] Although well-recognized in the design science literature, the building of artifacts is relatively poorly understood as a design science research activity, especially as compared with evaluation. [9] March and Smith (1995) do not have much to say about the activity of constructing artifacts, although they do point out the novelty of an artifact (construct, model, method, or instantiation) and the persuasiveness of the claims that the new artifact should be effective. They also emphasize that instantiations that apply known constructs, models, and methods to

---

[7] In fact, I think that Walls et al. (1992) fall into this trap when they suggest that the information systems development life cycle is a design theory. I am not aware of any kernel theory on which it is based.

[8] Note that well-known classifications of IS research methods such as those of Benbasat (1985), Jenkins (1985), and Galliers and Land (1987) do not recognize anything resembling constructive research methods nor, even, does a recent review of research methods in the IS literature (Chen and Hirschheim, 2004).

[9] The article of Hevner et al. (2004) illustrates this. They suggest a detailed list of methods for evaluation, but nothing corresponding to the building of artifacts. There is also a rich body of literature on evaluation that can be applied in the design science context (Verschuren and Hartog 2005).

novel tasks may be of little significance if there is not sufficient uncertainty about their applicability.

The seven design science research guidelines suggested by Hevner et al. (2004) do not directly address the question of how artifacts are built, although many of them touch upon the topic. Guideline 1 suggests artifacts as products of design science research, Guideline 2 emphasizes that design science research should develop technology-based solutions to important and relevant problems, and Guideline 4 discusses the contributions of design science research, emphasizing that the artifact must be innovative, solving a heretofore unsolved problem or solving a known problem in a more effective or efficient manner (p. 82). The novelty of artifacts makes it possible to distinguish IS from the ordinary practice of developing IT artifacts. Guideline 5, concerning research rigor, imposes a requirement that design science research must apply rigorous methods for both the construction and evaluation of artifacts. This rigor, according to Hevner et al. (2004), should be derived from the effective use of *prior* research (the existing knowledge base). Guideline 6 suggests that design is essentially a search process for discovering an effective solution to a problem, largely following Simon (1969/1981/1996) in this respect. I find this idea of the building of artifacts as problem solving somewhat problematic, for two reasons. First, what the problem is is often a problem. The problem is not necessarily given, but instead the researcher has considerable discretion in deciding what the problem is. Thus the constructing of a design science artifact is as much problem setting as problem solving. Second, design as a search process implies an idea that alternatives are there to be discovered. In reality they are not, but rather they must be constructed in some way. [10]

To my knowledge, treatment of how to build artifacts in DSR provided by Nunamaker et al. (1990–1991) is still the most refined of its type. They propose that systems development could serve as a specific research method for constructing artifacts, introducing a model of four interacting research activities, theory building, experimentation, observation, and systems development, where systems development lies at the center. The process that they propose for systems development is quite a conventional software development model. In as far as the artifacts to be built are systems, systems development is a natural candidate for methods of constructive research. The method seems particularly relevant when the purpose is to validate the concept by implementing (instantiating) the system. One should note, however, that not all artifacts developed in DSR within computer science, information systems, and software engineering are information or software systems (e.g., systems development methods), and it is an open question as to what extent systems development methods work as research methods. If systems development methods really are applicable, this should put an end to the regression of meta-levels between artifacts, since systems development methods, as meta-artifacts for the IS development process, could be employed for developing other meta-artifacts.

---

[10] Despite of these critical comments, I see problem solving as a useful heuristic metaphor to be used when considering alternative solutions, especially for different components of the artifact.

It is widely understood that the building of artifacts in DSR is at least ideally a creative process (Nunamaker et al., 1990–1991; March and Smith 1995; Hevner et al. 2004). One could maintain that it has a lot in common with theory building, which has been of interest in the methodology of science (e.g., Dubin 1969). One can speculate, however, that artifacts in particular leave much more space for creative imagination, since they are not assumed to describe or explain any existing reality. IT artifacts may create their own virtual world (e.g., computer games, computer art, computer pets, and virtual fantasy world applications) in which the laws of nature, for example, are not valid. Because of the creative element, it is difficult to define an appropriate method for the design science activity of artifact building.

Despite the above difficulty, I see the existence of constructive research methods as highly essential to the identity of IS as a design science. It is the rigor of constructing IT artifacts that distinguishes IS as a design science from the practice of building IT artifacts. One should note here that the construction of innovative IT artifacts (or IT meta-artifacts) is not a monopoly of the research community, but practitioners may also do it. Acknowledging this, there are two options for demarcating IS as a design science from inventions made by practitioners. The first is to accept that there is no constructive research method that distinguishes the two, but that the difference lies in the evaluation: the essence of IS as a design science lies in the scientific evaluation of artifacts. This is one option, but it easily leads to reactive research in which IS as a design science focuses on the evaluation of existing IT artifacts rather than on the building of new ones.

The second option is to try to specify a reasonably rigorous constructive research method for building IT artifacts. It would then be this method that differentiated the design science construction of IT artifacts from the Gyro Gearloose style of invention in practice. [11] If a practitioner applies the same rigor as an IS researcher, he/she is essentially a researcher. I would expect that this would make IS as a design science more proactive, attempting to guide the evolution of IT and not merely react to it.

5.11 Thesis 10: Explication of the Practical Problems to Be Solved, the Existing Artifacts to Be Improved, the Analogies and Metaphors to Be Used, and/or the Kernel Theories to Be Applied Is Significant in Making the Building Process Disciplined, Rigorous, and Transparent

Should an artifact as an outcome of DSR always be based on recognizable theory? March and Smith (1995) point out that design science artifacts are often invented without any clear descriptive theory. The possibility of an IT artifact not having any

---

[11] Gyro Gearloose is a fictional character created by Carl Barks for the Walt Disney Company. The purpose of using this figure to symbolize inventors in the field is not to ridicule them, but quite the contrary.

kernel theory raises the question of the criteria governing whether an artifact can be considered a scientific contribution and publishable in IS journals. The requirement of an underlying descriptive theory may considerably limit DSR, possibly excluding the most innovative design science outcomes from major IS journals. [12] As noted above, Guideline 4 in Hevner et al. (2004), that the artifact must be innovative, solving a heretofore unsolved problem or solving a known problem in a more effective or efficient manner leads to an additional question of whether complete evaluation of the proposed artifact is required. The situation is analogous to theory building: if the building of a theory is accepted as a scientific contribution without complete testing, why cannot the building of a novel IT meta-artifact also be accepted without complete evaluation, provided that the IT meta-artifact is novel and well-argued? The idea of an IT meta-artifact being well-argued means that it cannot come "out of the blue," but must be rigorously constructed from specific origins.

Hevner et al. (2004) propose that the rigor of DSR should be derived from the effective use of *prior* research (an existing knowledge base). I would claim that the construction process should also be made as transparent as possible if it is to be considered a design science activity. Knowing that these proposals are preliminary, I suggest four major sources of ideas for DSR to make the building process more disciplined, rigorous, and transparent:

1 Practical problems and opportunities
2 Existing artifacts
3 Analogies and metaphors
4 Theories

The first of these emphasizes the practical relevance of research. Furthermore, it is well known in innovation diffusion research (Rogers 1995) that customers serve as a significant source of innovations (von Hippel 1988), especially in the case of IT innovations (von Hippel 2005). I do not claim that researchers should attempt to solve practical problems exactly as they appear in practice. A practical problem may be a conglomerate of different problems, and a piece of research may not attempt to address the whole conglomerate but may focus only on a specific subproblem. A practical problem may also be abstracted to make it more general and easier to link to theories. One should note, however, that design science is also about potentiality. A new idea or artifact may provide totally new opportunities to improve practice long before practitioners recognize any problem. There are many significant innovations in our field that illustrate this, such as the relational data model and the first ideas of object orientation.

Most DSR consists of incremental improvements to existing artifacts, as illustrated by research into conceptual information modeling in the 1970s and into

---

[12] Could Berners-Lee, for example, have published his ideas on WWW in a top IS journal?

object-oriented systems development in the 1990s. Typically, the marginal value of additional improvements decreases until the research gradually fades out. [13]

It is also well known that analogies and metaphors stimulate creativity (Couger et al. 1993). In the case of IT artifacts, for instance, cognitive and biological theories have provided useful metaphors for computing, such as neural networks and genetic algorithms. The desktop metaphor led to the graphical user interfaces which predominate nowadays, and the spreadsheet metaphor led to spreadsheet software, which forms one of the most widely applied personal productivity tools.

5.12 Thesis 11: IS as a Design Science Cannot Be Value-Free, but It May Reflect Means-End, Interpretive, or Critical Orientation

DSR in itself implies an ethical change from describing and explaining the existing world to shaping it. The ethics of research concern the responsibility of a scientist for the consequences of his research and its results. Even though it may be questionable whether any research can be value-free, it is absolutely clear that DSR cannot be. Consequently, the basic values of research should be expressed as explicitly as possible.

Adapting Chua (1986), Iivari (1991) distinguished three potential roles for IS as an applied discipline: (1) means-end oriented, (2) interpretive, and (3) critical. In the first case the scientist aims at providing knowledge as a means for achieving given ends (goals), without questioning the legitimacy of those ends. According to Chua (1986), the aim of an "interpretivist scientist is to enrich people's understanding of their action", "how social order is produced and reproduced" (p. 615). The goals (ends) of action are often not so clear, and one should also focus on unintended consequences. A critical scientist will see that research has "a critical imperative: the identification and removal of domination and ideological practice" (p. 622). Goals (ends) can be subjected to critical analysis. [14]

Much DSR is naturally means-end oriented. This concerns especially constructive research involved with the building of artifacts. But constructive research can also be critical, as exemplified by the Scandinavian trade-unionist systems development approach (Bjerknes et al. 1987). Evaluation studies can be means-end oriented, interpretive, and/or critical, where a means-end-oriented evaluation is only interested in how effectively the artifact helps achieve the given goals or ends, an interpretive piece of evaluation research may attempt to achieve a rich understanding

---

[13] One can, of course, observe a similar phenomenon in descriptive research, as illustrated by the extensions of the Technology Acceptance Model (Davis et al. 1989).

[14] Note that Iivari (1991) applied the above distinction as an ethical dimension, whereas Orlikowski and Baroudi (1991) applied a very similar distinction as an epistemological dimension. The critical perspective clearly illustrates the problem with the epistemological dimension. Critical research may apply either a positivistic or an anti-positivistic epistemology.

of how an IT artifact is really appropriated and used and what its effects are, without confining the focus on the given ends of its initial construction; and a critical study is interested in how an IT artifact enforces or removes unjustified domination or ideological practices.

5.13 Thesis 12: The Values of Design Science Research Should Be Made as Explicit as Possible

More concretely, one can also question the values of IS research, i.e., whose values and what values dominate it, emphasizing that research may openly or latently serve the interests of particular dominant groups. The interests served may be those of the host organization as perceived by its top management, those of IS users, those of IS professionals, or potentially those of other stakeholder groups in society.

5.14 Conclusions and Final Comments

The aim of this chapter is to strengthen the design science orientation of IS. If fully adopted, this orientation would mean profound changes in the disciplinary identity of IS, in its ontology, epistemology, methodology, and ethics. It will not necessarily be easy to get these changes understood and accepted in the IS research community. In addition to natural resistance to change, there is a certain ambiguity in the idea of design science research.

The idea of DSR in IS is still in its formative stage. As new members join the DSR community, each of them may bring in his or her own interpretation of what DSR is. While the plurality of ideas is definitely beneficial, especially at this early stage, it is also good for people to understand what they are talking about. Individual keywords in DSR such as "design" and "artifact" can easily be misleading, since IS development in practice is essentially design, and the concept of "artifact" can be interpreted very broadly to cover all World 3 objects and phenomena in the ontology of Popper (1978). The phrase "design science" is also problematic, since it is used in a quite different meaning in the design studies community (Cross 1993, 2001) from that used by Walls et al. (1992), March and Smith (1995), and Hevner et al. (2004), where the focus is clearly on DSR.

Regarding the attempt to clarify the relationship between DSR and related research areas as set out in Fig. 5.2, one should note that articles such as Nunamaker et al. (1990–1991), March and Smith (1995), Hevner et al. (2004), and the present chapter represent research into DSR in IS. In addition to advocating the need for DSR research in IS, they attempt to provide concepts (March and Smith 1995), principles (Hevner et al. 2004), theses (the present work), and research methods (Nunamaker et al. 1990–1991) for DSR in an IS context.

Essentially following Walls et al. (1992), DSR in IS is divided in Fig. 5.2 into DSR focused on IT products and DSR focused on the systems development process.

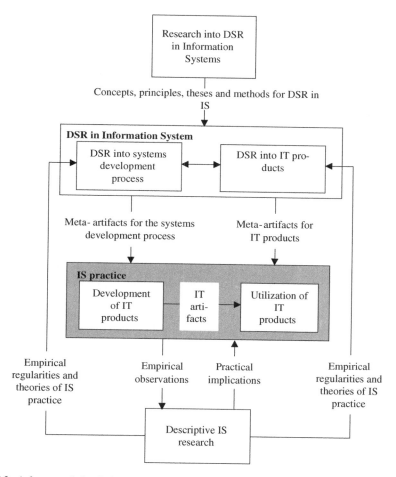

Fig. 5.2 A framework for design-related research areas in information systems

These are assumed to produce meta-artifacts for IT products and meta-artifacts for the systems development process for use in IS practice (see Thesis 5 above), where IS practice is taken to comprise the development of IT products (especially concrete IT applications) to be utilized in practice.

The IS practice of developing and utilizing IT products forms a central phenomenon to be investigated and understood by descriptive IS research. This descriptive research may provide a scientifically founded understanding of IS practice that may support DSR in IS, and it may also convert the observed empirical regularities and validated theories into prescriptive practical implications (recommendations).

Figure 5.2 makes it possible to understand the relationships between DSR and "scientific design," "design science," and the "science of design" as characterized by Cross (1993, 2001). According to Cross (2001, p. 53), "scientific design" means that design products should be based on scientific knowledge, "design science" means that the design process is based on "an explicitly, organized, rational, and wholly systematic approach to design", as if the design process was "a scientific activity in itself", and the "science of design" means the scientific study of design activity itself. If confined to IT products, "scientific design" resembles DSR into IT products in Fig. 5.2, although the latter does not necessarily share the idea that design products should be based on scientific knowledge (cf. Thesis 6 above). Similarly, "design science" resembles DSR into the systems development process, although not all DSR into the systems development process shares the idea that the design process should be based on an explicitly, organized, rational, and wholly systematic approach to design. Descriptive IS research includes the "science of design" when the focus of the latter lies in the design of IT artifacts. Note also that DSR includes design, which may also be the focus of "science of design." [15]

As pointed out above, the work of Hevner et al. (2004) does not represent DSR in Information Systems, but is research into DSR in Information Systems. Although their work has been criticized for adopting a biased and narrow view of information systems and IS design (McKay et al. 2008), its greatest weakness in my view is its generality. If the IS/IT-specific examples are deleted and the IS/IT-specific terms are translated into more neutral ones such as "design" and "artifact," their framework for DSR is a very general one and not particularly specific to Information Systems. One challenge for future research, to my mind, will be to refine Hevner et al. (2004) toward a more IS/IT-specific version.

References

Avison, D. E. and A. T. Wood-Harper (1991) Information systems development research: an exploration of ideas in practice, *The Computer Journal* 34 (2), pp. 98–112.

Baskerville, R. (2008) What design science is not, *European Journal of Information Systems* 17, pp. 441–443.

Bazerman, M. H. (2005) Conducting influential research: the need for prescriptive implications, *Academy of Management Review* 30 (1), pp. 25–31.

Beckman, S. (2002) The nature of artifacts, in Dahlbom, B., Beckman, S. and Nilsson, G. B., *Artifacts and Artificial Science*, Almqvist & Wiksell International, Stockholm, pp. 45–92.

Benbasat, I. (1985) An analysis of research methodologies, in *The Information Systems Research Challenge*, McFarlan, F. W. ed., Harvard Business School Press, Boston, MA, pp. 47–85.

Benbasat, I. and R. Weber (1996) Rethinking diversity in information systems research, *Information Systems Research* 7 (4), pp. 389–399.

Benbasat, I. and R. W. Zmud (2003) The identity crisis within the discipline: defining and communicating the discipline's core properties, *MIS Quarterly* 27 (2), pp. 183–194.

Berger, P. and T. Luckman (1967) *The Social Construction of Reality: A Treatise on Sociology of Knowledge*, Doubleday, New York, NY.

Bjerknes, G., P. Ehn, and M. Kyng (eds.) (1987) *Computers and Democracy*, Avebury, Aldershot.

---

[15] Hevner et al. (2004) characterize the difference between design activities by stating that design in IS practice is routine and design as part of DSR is more innovative. This is a slightly unfortunate characterization, since design in IS practice is frequently anything but routine.

Bunge, M. (1967a) *Scientific Research I, The Search for System*, Springer-Verlag, New York.

Bunge, M. (1967b) *Scientific Research II. The Search for Truth*, Springer-Verlag, New York.

Chen, W. and R. Hirschheim (2004) A paradigmatic and methodological examination of information systems research from 1991 to 2001, *Information Systems Journal* 14 (3), pp. 197–235.

Chmielewicz, K. (1970) *Forschungskonzeptionen der Wirtschaftswissenschaft*, Stuttgart.

Chua, W. F. (1986) Radical developments in accounting thought, *The Accounting Review*, LXI (5), pp. 583–598.

Clemmensen, T. (2006) Whatever happened to the psychology of human–computer interaction? A biography of the life of a psychological framework within a HCI journal, *Information Technology & People* 19 (2), pp. 121–151.

Couger, J. D., L. F. Higgins, and S. C. Mcintyre (1993) (Un)structured creativity in information systems organizations, *MIS Quarterly* 17 (4), pp. 375–397.

Cross, N. (1993) Science and design methodology, *Research in Engineering Design* 5, pp. 63–69.

Cross, N. (2001) Designerly ways of knowing: design discipline versus design science, *Design Issues* 17 (3), pp. 49–55.

Davis, F. D., R. P. Bagozzi, and P. R. Warshaw (1989) User acceptance of computer technology: a comparison of two theoretical models, *Management Science* 35 (8), pp. 982–1003.

Dubin, R. (1969) *Theory Building*, The Free Press, New York.

Galliers, R. D. and F. F. Land (1987) Choosing appropriate information systems research methodologies, *Communications of the ACM* 30 (11), pp. 900–902.

Gardner, P. L. (1994) The relationship between technology and science: some historical and philosophical reflections. Part I, *International Journal of Technology and Design Education* 4 (2), pp. 123–153.

Gardner, P. L. (1995) The relationship between technology and science: some historical and philosophical reflections. Part II, *International Journal of Technology and Design Education* 5 (1), pp. 1–33.

Gregor, S. (2006) The nature of theory in information systems, *MIS Quarterly* 30 (3), pp. 611–642.

Gregor, S. (2008) Building theory in a practical science, in *Information Systems Foundations: Answering the Unanswered Questions About Design Research, The 4th ANU Workshop on Information Systems Foundations*, Australian National University, Canberra, Australia.

Gregor, S. and D. Jones (2007) The anatomy of a design theory, *Journal of the AIS* 8 (5), pp. 312–335.

Hassan, N. R. (2006) Is information systems a discipline? A Foucauldian and Toulminian analysis, in *Proceedings of the Twenty-Seventh International Conference on Information Systems*, Milwaukee, pp. 425–440.

Hevner, A. R., S. T. March, J. Park, and S. Ram (2004) Design science in information systems research, *MIS Quarterly* 28 (1), pp. 75–105.

Iivari, J. (1991) A paradigmatic analysis of contemporary schools of IS development, *European Journal of Information Systems* 1 (4), pp. 249–272.

Iivari, J. (2007) Paradigmatic analysis of information systems as a design science, *Scandinavian Journal of Information Systems* 19 (2), pp. 39–63.

Jenkins, A. M. (1985) Research methodologies and MIS research, in Mumford, E., Hirschheim, R., Fitzgerald, G. and Wood-Harper, A.T. (eds.), *Research Methods in Information Systems*, North-Holland, Amsterdam, pp. 103–117.

King, J. L. and K. Lyytinen (2004) Reach and grasp, *MIS Quarterly* 28 (4), pp. 539–551.

Kuechler, W. and V. Viashnavi (2008) The emergence of design research in information systems in North America, *Journal of Design Research* 7 (1), pp. 1–16.

Layton, E. T. Jr. (1974) Technology as knowledge, *Technology and Culture* 15, pp. 31–41.

Lehtovuori, J. (1973) *Liiketaloustieteen metodologista taustaa*, Turun kauppakorkeakoulun julkaisuja, AI-6.

Lyytinen K. and J. L. King (2004) Nothing at the center? Academic legitimacy in the information systems field, *Journal of the AIS* 5 (6), pp. 220–246.

Lyytinen, K. and G. M. Rose (2003) The disruptive nature of information technology innovations: the case of Internet computing in systems development organizations, *MIS Quarterly* 27 (4), pp. 557–595.

March, S. T. and G. F. Smith (1995) Design and natural science research on information technology, *Decision Support Systems* 15, pp. 251–266.

Markus, M. L., A. Majchrzak, and L. Gasser (2002) A design theory for systems that support emergent knowledge processes, *MIS Quarterly* 26 (3), pp. 179–212.

McKay, J. and P. Marshall, P. (2007) Science, design, and design science: seeking clarity to move design science research forward in information systems, in *Proceedings of the Eighteenth Autsralasian Conference on Information Systems*, pp. 604–614.

McKay, J., P. Marshall, and G. Heath (2008) An exploration of the concept of design in information systems, in *Information Systems Foundations: Answering the Unanswered Questions About Design Research, The 4th ANU Workshop on Information Systems Foundations*, Australian National University, Canberra, Australia.

Niiniluoto, I. (1993) The aim and structure of applied research, *Erkenntnis* 38, pp. 1–21.

Niiniluoto, I. (1999) *Critical Scientific Realism*, Oxford University Press, Oxford.

Nunamaker, J. F., M. Chen, and T. D. M. Purdin (1990–1991) System development in information systems research, *Journal of Management Information Systems* 7 (3), pp. 99–106.

Orlikowski, W. J. and C. S. Iacono (2001) Research commentary: desperately seeking the "IT" in IT research – a call theorizing the IT artifact, *Information Systems Research* 12 (2), pp. 121–134.

Pitt, J. C. (2000) *Thinking about Technology, Foundations of the Philosophy of Technology*, Seven Bridges Press, New York, NY.

Popper, K. (1978) *Three Worlds*, The Tanner Lectures on Human Values, Delivered at the University of Michigan, Ann Arbor, MI.

Rogers, E. M. (1995) *Diffusion of Innovations*, 4th edn., The Free Press, New York.

Simon, H. (1969/1981/1996) *The Sciences of Artificial*, MIT Press, Cambridge, MA.

Strasser, S. (1985) *Understanding and Explanation Basic Ideas Concerning the Humanity of the Human Sciences*, Duquesne University Press, Pittsburg, PA.

Swanson, B. (1994) Information systems innovation among organizations, *Management Science* 40 (9), pp. 1069–1092.

van Aken, J. E. (2004) Management research based on the paradigm of design sciences: the quest for field-tested and grounded technological rules, *Journal of Management Studies* 41 (2), pp. 219–246.

van Aken, J. E. (2005) Valid knowledge for the professional design of of large and complex design processes, *Design Studies* 26, pp. 379–404.

Venkatesh, V., M. G. Morris, G. B. Davis, and F. D. Davis (2003) User acceptance of information technology: toward a unified view, *MIS Quarterly*, 27 (3), pp. 425–478.

Verschuren, P. and R. Hartog (2005) Evaluation in design-oriented research, *Quality & Quantity* 39, pp. 733–762.

von Hippel, E. (1988) *The Sources of Innovation*, Oxford University Press, Oxford.

von Hippel, E. (2005) *Democratizing Innovation*, The MIT Press, Cambridge, MA.

Walls, J., G. R. Widmeyer, and O. A. El Sawy (1992) Building an information system design theory for vigilant EIS, *Information Systems Research* 3 (1), pp. 36–59.

Winter, R. (2008) Design science research in Europe, *European Journal of Information Systems* 17, pp. 470–475.

Chapter 6
A Science of Design for Software-Intensive Systems

> *There is something fascinating about science. One gets such wholesale returns of conjecture out of such a trifling investment of fact.*
>
> Mark Twain, Life on the Mississippi, 1883

6.1 Science of Design Challenges

Future complex software-intensive systems (SIS) will be vastly different from the software systems that run today's world. Revolutionary advances in hardware, networking, information, and human interface technologies will require entirely new ways of thinking about how software-intensive systems are conceptualized, built, and evaluated. As we envision the future of tera[1]-computing and even peta[2]-computing environments, new science of design principles are needed to provide the foundations for managing issues of complexity, composition, quality, cost, and control of software-intensive systems.

Evidence suggests that software-intensive systems development has already reached the limits of technologies developed in the first 60 years of computing. New, innovative principles, practices, and tools will be needed to move software development into the next generation of computing environments. Manual methods of software and systems engineering must be replaced by computational automation that will transform the field into a true scientific and engineering discipline. Other science/engineering fields have made this transformation to their everlasting benefit. Computational theories, models, and tools of subject matter dominate mature disciplines, such as electrical engineering and aeronautical engineering. Analogous

---

[1]Tera = 10^{12} or 1 trillion. Tera-computing environments support trillion-line software programs running on networks connecting trillions of computers at terahertz bandwidth speeds.
[2]Peta = 10^{15} or 1000 trillion.

A. Hevner, S. Chatterjee, *Design Research in Information Systems*, Integrated Series in Information Systems 22, DOI 10.1007/978-1-4419-5653-8_6,
© Springer Science+Business Media, LLC 2010

computational models for software are now just emerging and must be incubated with focused research and development (R&D) and supportive demonstration environments. While much of the research focus during first 60 years of computing was on correct syntax-directed computation of details for computer execution, the focus of the next 60 years will shift to semantics-directed computation of correct abstractions for human understanding and manipulation.

The challenges of building large-scale software-intensive systems are unique and very different from the challenges of building large physical systems. Wulf (2006) identifies three principal reasons for the unique challenges of software-intensive systems:

1. Software-intensive systems are more complex than physical systems. Emergent properties are difficult to predict. We do not understand the science and first-class properties of software design.
2. Software has fewer constraints than physical systems. Thus, there are many more design options. The design space is enormous. It is very difficult to understand, model, and make effective design trade-offs for software-intensive systems.
3. The mathematics describing software-intensive systems lacks continuity. Discrete mathematics does not support efficient testing and analysis of software. It is impossible to exhaustively test a software-intensive system based on the discontinuities of the underlying mathematics.

A new vision of science of design research for SIS must achieve the following essential objectives:

- Intellectual amplification: Research must extend the human capabilities (cognitive and social) of designers to imagine and realize large-scale, complex software-intensive systems.
- Span of control: Research must revolutionize techniques for the management and control of complex software-intensive systems through development, operations, and adaptation.
- Value generation: Research must create value and have broad impacts for human society via the science and engineering of complex software-intensive systems and technologies.

The goal of this chapter is to present a vision of science of design research directions and to propose a framework for achieving this vision. The content of this chapter has benefitted greatly from my experiences at the National Science Foundation (NSF) during 2006–2008 and draws from many discussions with colleagues at NSF which I gratefully acknowledge here.

6.2 Software-Intensive Systems

A difficulty faced when discussing research in the field of software-intensive systems is the lack of common terminology for key concepts. The field is teeming with terms that are overloaded with meanings (e.g., system, design) or varied terms for the same basic concept (e.g., object, component, module). The goal of the following discussion is not to propose a new ontology but to simply define the terms used in this chapter.

A *system* can be defined generally as a collection of elements that work together to form a coherent whole. *Software-intensive systems (SIS)*, then, are systems in which some, but not necessarily all, of the component elements are realized in software. Figure 6.1 illustrates three layers of any software-intensive system – the human layer, the software layer, and the platform layer. Two critical interfaces are shown – the human–software interface and the software–platform interface.

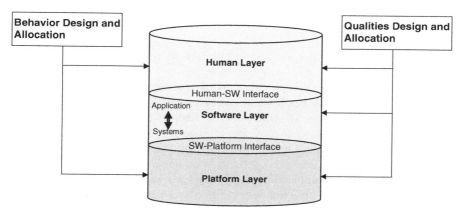

Fig. 6.1 Software-intensive system layers

The development of a SIS entails many important decisions such as the design and allocation of system behaviors (e.g., functions, actions) and system qualities (e.g., performance, security, reliability) to the different layers. For example, a particular system activity could be realized in hardware (platform), via a service call (software), by human behavior (human), or some combination of activities across all three layers. Likewise, a performance requirement (e.g., response time) for a SIS transaction could be divided and allocated as performance requirements in each of the layers.

Figure 6.2 shows the growth of the software layer, in size and percentage of the overall system, as a future trend. The role of software will become dominant in nearly all complex systems. Thus, research and development in SIS must actively address the challenges of using software as the primary building material in future complex systems.

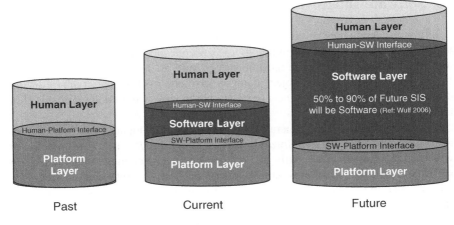

Fig. 6.2 Software-intensive system trends

Beyond individual, self-contained SIS, nearly all future systems will be connected to environmental resources and other systems via network connections. These connections lead to complex systems-of-systems architectures for providing behaviors and qualities. Figure 6.3 demonstrates that there are identifiable networks across all three SIS layers. Physical networks support the transmission of digital and analog data among system platforms. Software networks provide the middleware layers and protocols that transform the transmitted data into information that is shared among the information processing systems. Social networks provide a means of interaction and community among the human participants of the complex system (Fiadeiro 2007). Humans use the system information to make decisions, execute actions on the environment, and build application domain knowledge bases.

Figure 6.4 zooms in on the software layer to show its makeup of software code, information, and control within the context of an application domain. The overlaps among these three concepts support varying methods and techniques of understanding and building the software layer of systems. For example, software architectures define structures for integrating the concepts of code, information, and control for a particular application domain system. The message is that the software layer in a SIS is a challenging and fertile field of research opportunities.

6.3 Science of Design Principles

The science that provides foundations for the engineering of complex software-intensive system must be predicated on a set of fundamental principles. A principle is a clear statement of truth that guides or constraints action. A principle can also be formed as a rule or a standard of conduct. It is this search and discovery of fundamental principles that underlie the research agenda of a SIS research program.

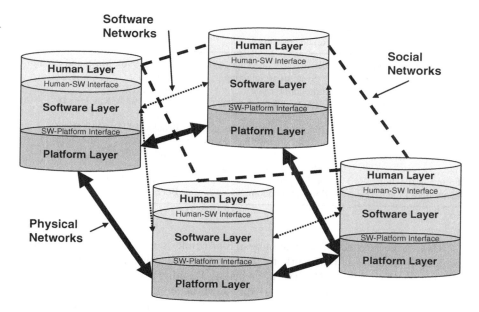

Fig. 6.3 Physical, software, and social networks of software-intensive systems

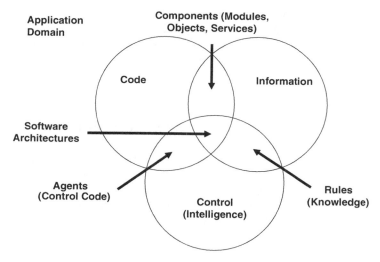

Fig. 6.4 Concepts in the software layer

Table 6.1 Current CSIS development principles

Principle	Related practices	References
System Abstraction	Hierarchical decomposition Systems architecting	Simon (1996); Maier and Rechtin (2000)
Levels	Protocol layering	Dijkstra (1968)
Information hiding	Objects Object-oriented languages	Parnas (1972); Kay (1984)
Intellectual control	Computer architectures Chief programmer teams	Brooks (1995); Mills (1983)
Computational thinking	Relational database Systems and languages	Codd (1970)
Form and function	Design patterns	Alexander (1979)
Economics of systems	Software economics	Boehm (1981)

This vision for a set of science of design principles aligns with Peter Denning's project to identify a framework for the fundamental principles for the field of computing (Denning 2003, 2005).[3] Whereas Denning's goal is to demonstrate the central role of computing as a true scientific field in relationship to other sciences; the goal of a SIS research program will be to discover, articulate, and use these principles to guide the effective and efficient development of future complex software-intensive systems.

A quick look back at the computer science field shows only a handful of truly fundamental principles that have guided the current development of complex software-intensive systems over the past 60 years. Table 6.1 summarizes several of these key principles.

The research and development projects that led to the principles and related practices found in Table 6.1 were transformative in providing breakthrough ideas for developing complex software-intensive systems. New transformative ideas are needed to move the field forward to build and manage SIS for the 21st century.

6.4 Categories of Software-Intensive Systems Principles

The future challenge is to bring researchers from multiple disciplines to discover and define fundamental principles and practices upon which future complex software-intensive systems will be imagined, architected, designed, built, and operated. As exemplars of critically important categories of fundamental principles that should be addressed in science of design research, we propose the following:

---

[3]Great Principles of Computing web site: http://cs.gmu.edu/cne/pjd/GP

- Computational principles: Computational thinking underlies true scientific and engineering fields (Wing 2006; Denning 2007). The field must better identify its rigorous mathematical and computational foundations to support the more effective and efficient SIS representations, models, analyses/manipulations, development methods/tools, and system instantiations
- Scalability principles: Scalability of system concepts is absolutely essential in order to build ultra-large-scale systems (Northrop et al. 2006). Effective ideas must apply equally well to the development and operations of small systems and of massive, complex systems.
- Creative principles: We solicit fundamental principles that enhance human cognitive abilities and support the creative process in the development of complex software-intensive systems. Effective human–computer interfaces for both development environments and application systems will embody these principles.
- Adaptability principles: In the development of future SIS, it will be impossible to specify or predict a priori all of the behaviors or qualities of the system. Runtime composition of system components will result in unknown, emergent behaviors and qualities during operation. Thus, key principles of adaptability must be discovered and applied to manage the evolution of the system as it adapts to its environment and transaction load.
- Ethical principles: The development of a SIS implies an ethical responsibility of how the system shapes its environment. The consequences of the system are formed by the ethical principles on which it was designed and built. Ethical principles would help us understand what values inform the development of the SIS and whose interests are served by the system.
- Economic principles: Cost goes hand-in-hand with complexity. Complex systems cost significantly more to develop, produce, and operate. Under current economics, the coordination costs of SIS rise exponentially with increases in size and complexity. A deeper understanding of the economic principles of complex systems is required in order to evaluate the feasibility and market impacts of SIS.
- Decidability principles: Consideration of a wide range of fundamental principles must eventually lead to decisions on how to imagine, architect, design, build, and operate a desired complex software-intensive system. What are the decidability principles that underlie the construction of such SIS decision models? How, for example, would we evaluate trade-offs among ethical principles and economic principles in a SIS decision model?

Among others, these are several of the key categories of principles that must be studied in a comprehensive science of design research agenda.

6.5 A Proposed Research Vision

A research vision for the science of design of software-intensive systems is presented in Figs. 6.5 and 6.6. As seen in Fig. 6.5, the intellectual merit of this research must be drawn from scientific theories originating from several disciplines

Science of Design in Software-Intensive Systems
Research Vision

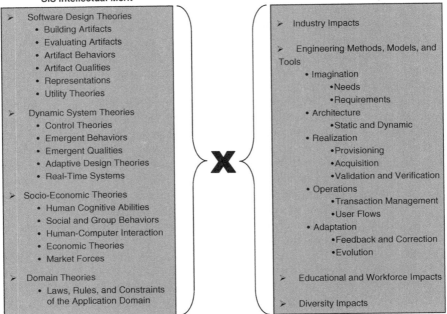

Fig. 6.5 Science of design in SIS research vision

including computer science, software engineering, systems engineering, socio-economic fields, and the application domain. The broader impacts of the research must be felt in the scientific community, industry, government, academia, and human society.

6.6 SIS Scientific Theories

The scientific theories for fundamental science of design research in SIS are identified in the following categories and briefly discussed. A full description of all these grounding theories is beyond the scope of this chapter but can be readily found via a literature review on the listed topics.

6.6.1 Software Design Theories

- Building artifacts
- Evaluating artifacts

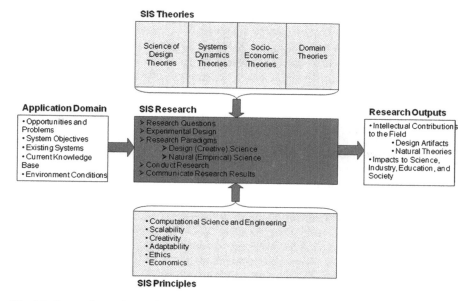

Fig. 6.6 Research on science of design in software-intensive systems

- Artifact behaviors
- Artifact qualities
- Representations
- Utility theories

New ideas in software design research will necessarily draw from the classic works of software theory by Simon (1996), Mills (1983), Parnas (1972), Dijkstra (1968), Brooks (1995), Freeman (1987), Boehm (1981), and many other thought leaders in the software field. These time-tested software principles are weighed alongside the latest ideas in the field to find the right balance of pure and applied research directions.

6.6.2 Dynamic System Theories

- Control theories
- Emergent behaviors
- Emergent qualities
- Adaptive design theories
- Real-time systems

Dynamic system theories provide the bases for understanding the dynamic behaviors of complex systems (Forrester 1961; Randers 1980). The essence is the recognition that the structure of any system — the circular, interlocking, temporal, spatial, and sometimes non-deterministic relationships among its components — is often just as important in determining its behavior as the individual components themselves. There are often properties-of-the-whole which result in dynamic, emergent behaviors and qualities which cannot be explained in terms of the behaviors and qualities of the parts.

6.6.3 Socio-economic Theories

- Human cognitive abilities
- Social and group behaviors
- Human–computer interaction
- Economic theories
- Market forces

Socio-economic theories will play a major role toward understanding the factors leading to success or failure in the development and use of software-intensive systems. For example, the design of software system architectures and software components must support economic business cases for utility, marketability, usability, and other system features important for successful deployment. Initial research on economic models for software design, such as Baldwin and Clark's (2000) study of design in the computing industry, is an important first step in this research area. Another research area of great interest is the open-source models of software development, operations, and evolution.

6.6.4 Domain Theories

Each and every software-intensive system is embedded within an application domain from which it draws its relevance and utility. Domain theories provide essential laws, rules, and constraints that ground the development and use of all systems in that domain. For example, complex software-intensive systems for airplanes must be developed in full awareness of the science and engineering of aeronautics. Similarly, a banking system must be grounded in the regulations and policies of the international and national financial systems.

6.7 SIS Engineering Activities

The effective engineering of software-intensive systems of any size and complexity consists of five primary activities as performed by skilled development teams:

1. Imagination: All system stakeholders participate in imagining the needs and requirements of a desired system. New and better methods and models for capturing and specifying system requirements are greatly needed. In particular, the search for rigorous specification models that are efficiently usable by software developers and effectively understandable by system stakeholders remains an important research effort.

2. Architecture: The need to architect complex systems has been recognized by the scientific and engineering communities in all domain fields of design. Theories of systems architecture are commonplace in fields ranging from buildings and landscaping (Alexander 1979) to nanotechnologies and even to an evolving understanding of the architecture of the human brain and body. Research on software architectures is relatively new (Shaw and Garlan 1996; Bass et al. 2003) and many of the underlying principles and theories are yet to be discovered (Maier and Rechtin 2000). Architecting involves both the art and science of designing and building systems. The architecture of a software system can be envisioned as the structures, protocols, standards, and aesthetics that provide the required system behaviors, state, qualities, and, even beauty (Gelernter 1998).

3. Realization: The actual construction of the system can be realized in many different ways. Software components are composed in an integrated application system. A software component provides a unit of behavior in the software system (Brown 2000). The component can be realized in forms such as software modules, services, objects, routines, and functions depending on the development environment. Artifacts of component development include behavioral specifications, designs, program code, test cases for unit, integration, and system testing, and documentation for system operators and system users. The state of a software component is represented in its data structures – variables, files, and databases. The designs for service behavior and state go hand-in-hand to achieve the greatest service utility and quality.

4. Operations: The deployment and effective operation of a system in the application environment are key engineering challenges. The interactions of software components and key user and environmental interfaces during system execution make up the real-time behaviors of the software system as a whole. The goals of management and control of software dynamics leads to a number of interesting research topics. User transactions can be described and formalized as flows of control, data, and qualities among software components. As an example of this line of thinking, consider a user transaction in a software system as an identifiable flow with requested behaviors and qualities. This flow is presented to the software architecture in a dynamic environment which can determine at that point in time whether the software system can provide the behaviors and qualities requested. If the flow is allowed to execute on the architecture, its instantiation will draw behaviors and qualities from a dynamic composition of components in the software system. While some research and development has been performed in the areas of workflows and business process flows (e.g., Aalst and Hee, 2002), more work is needed on the analysis and design of complex, network-centric systems to support and optimize user flows.

5. Adaptation: It is impossible to specify or predict a priori all of the behaviors or dynamic properties of a complex system while it is operating in unpredictable, possibly adverse, dynamic environments. Runtime composition of systems will result in unknown, emergent behaviors and qualities during operation. Thus, dynamic composition methods and key principles of adaptability must be discovered and applied to manage the evolution of the system as it adapts to its environment and transaction load. Complex systems often operate in complex environments on which they have little control and to which they must react quickly and reliably. The flexible nature of software and its inherent malleability provide the potential for systems to adapt autonomously to environmental conditions.

6.8 SIS Research Project Framework

A science of design research project, as shown in Fig. 6.5, is a cross-product of the grounding scientific theories and broader impacts of the research to include the new contributions to an engineering phase of the software-intensive system life cycle. Figure 6.6 provides a SIS research project framework. The inputs to the research are the SIS theories, principles, and application domain and the output of the research is the contributions to the application environment (relevance) and the scientific knowledge base (rigor).

Examples of challenging science of design for SIS research questions include the following:

- How can we design and evaluate SIS architectures for future computing environments to achieve the greatest understandability, utility, and quality?
- Knowing that designs of complex systems emerge throughout the development process and operations, how do we build flexibility into processes, methods, and models?
- How do we analyze and perform trade-offs between information design, control design, and software design?
- How can complex systems be designed in environments where the component parts are developed and controlled by multiple, independent entities?
- How will new physical platforms (hardware, communications) be integrated most effectively into SIS? What new interfaces and systems software are needed?
- What economic and social trade-offs are needed to best describe and understand the dynamics of SIS and the impacts of those systems on industrial, governmental, and societal infrastructures?
- How do we produce software system designs leading to systems that have the capacity to respond to surprise in operational environments?
- How do we best achieve human in the loop for SIS to enable and enhance human capabilities and values? What new human–computer interfaces are needed?

6.9 Intellectual Drivers for Science of Design in SIS Research

To conclude this chapter, we will focus on three key intellectual drivers for science of design research in software-intensive systems. One potentially radical approach for rethinking SIS foundations is to start from a small set of intellectual drivers of systems thinking and then apply an in-depth understanding of these drivers to real-world problems via science of design SIS research. The following three system concepts provide the most basic challenges and opportunities for transformative research: complexity, composition, and control.

Managing *complexity* (technical, human, and societal) in the development, operation, and evolution of software-intensive systems is an overriding challenge. Research to rethink IS complexity can be inspired by models in other scientific fields, both physical sciences and social sciences. For example, consider the development of IS artifacts that have the same robustness in the presence of complexity as biological organisms. Designing models and methods for managing complexity will require creative ideas for new information technology (IT) abstractions, representations, and languages.

Rethinking complexity will necessarily lead to changes in the way the *qualities* of IT artifacts are viewed. Current thinking assumes that if an accurate system specification can be produced up front then a system that fits stakeholder needs will naturally follow. Such an assumption is wrong when systems become complex enough to result in unexpected, emergent behaviors and properties in unstable operational environments. Software-intensive IS are subject to multiple stakeholders' inconsistent, contradictory, and partially understood objectives for behaviors and properties, such as performance, reliability, security, usability, and sustainability. While model-checking technologies have provided some useful forms of systems assurance, new ways of understanding and conceptualizing how IS qualities can be measured and evaluated are desired.

The essence of SIS design and evolution is *composition* of the system from component parts that may be developed by different parties in different languages and to different specifications. Mashups are examples of innovative approaches for composing disparate components of software and information. A composed system must interact properly with complex, uncertain environments, and the aggregate must be trusted. This concept requires that IS implementations respect the concerns of the domain, the intended usage, and the technology substrate (hardware and software) upon which systems execute. Successful identification of useful properties of IS must draw upon the relevant disciplines. We need new theories of abstraction, structuring, behavior and configuration as well as new logics for representing and reasoning about large systems in support of efficient and sustainable component-oriented engineering approaches. New theories of complexity and composition are needed to predict and reason about scalability in ways that can be empirically verified. A key challenge will be to identify perspicuous, useful, end-to-end properties and models that span hardware and software technology platforms, the problem domain, user interaction, and context of use.

Control of SIS has become increasingly challenging in situations of diverse software and data provenance, such as open-source communities and dynamic supply chains. In such settings, requirements for dynamic composition have both human and automation aspects. Human cognition imposes limits on our abilities to design complex artifacts. New techniques to augment human intellectual control and coordination of the design, development, and use of complex software-intensive systems are desired. For example, autonomic control of large-scale, distributed software-intensive systems can reduce or remove the requirement for human attention during runtime while still satisfying the needs of human users. Concepts of software system self-awareness and human–computer partnerships can lead to optimum system performance, negotiated access to resources, and novel IS configurations suitable to a particular situation. Research projects in this field might be inspired by emerging ideas in collective intelligence (e.g., wisdom of the crowds), virtual organizations (e.g., open-source user communities), and cognitive theories of abstraction, decomposition, and synthesis.

As we enter a future world of pervasive computing and ubiquitous cyber-physical devices it is essential that IT artifacts and the integrated systems containing these artifacts are reliable, adaptable, and sustainable. Science of design for SIS research must draw its foundations from multiple research disciplines and paradigms in order to effectively address a wide range of system challenges. Three of the most important intellectual drivers of future science of design in SIS research will be dealing with complexity, composition, and control. Consideration of these drivers must be the basis for the design of innovative artifacts and the development of rigorous theories to rethink the development, evolution, and adaptation of future information systems.

References

van der Aalst, W. and K. van Hee (2002) *Workflow Management: Models, Methods, and Systems*, The MIT Press, Cambridge, MA.

Alexander, C. (1979) *The Timeless Way of Building*, Oxford University Press, Oxford.

Baldwin, C. and K. Clark (2000) *Design Rules: The Power of Modularity*, The MIT Press, Cambridge, MA.

Bass, L., P. Clements, and R. Kazman (2003) *Software Architecture in Practice*, 2nd edn, Addison-Wesley, Boston, MA.

Boehm, B. (1981) *Software Engineering Economics*, Prentice-Hall, Upper Saddle River, NJ.

Brooks, F. (1995) *The Mythical Man-Month: Essays on Software Engineering*, 2nd edn, Addison-Wesley, Reading, MA.

Brown, A. (2000) *Large-Scale Component Based Development*, Prentice-Hall, Upper Saddle River, NJ.

Codd, E. (1970) A relational model of data for large shared databanks, *Communications of the ACM* 13 (6), pp. 380–387.

Denning, P. (2003) Great principles of computing, *Communications of the ACM* 46 (11), pp. 15–20.

Denning, P. (2005) Is computer science science? *Communications of the ACM* 48 (4), pp. 27–31.

Denning, P. (2007) Computing is a natural science, *Communications of the ACM* 50 (7), pp. 13–18.

Dijkstra, E. (1968) The structure of the 'T.H.E.' multiprogramming system, *Communications of the ACM* 11 (5), pp. 341–346.

Fiadeiro, J. (2007) Designing for software's social complexity," *IEEE Computer*, 40 (1), pp. 34–39.

Forrester, J. (1961) *Industrial Dynamics*. Pegasus Communications, Waltham, MA.

Freeman, P. (1987) *Software Perspectives: The System is the Message*, Addison-Wesley, Reading, MA.

Gelernter, D. (1998) *Machine Beauty: Elegance and the Heart of Technology*, Basic Books, New York.

Kay, A. (1984) Computer software, *Scientific American*, 250, pp. 41–47.

Maier M. and E. Rechtin (2000) *The Art of Systems Architecting*, 2nd edn, CRC Press, Boca Raton, FL.

Mills, H. (1983) *Software Productivity*, Little, Brown, and Co., Boston, MA.

Northrop, L. et al. (2006) *Ultra-Large-Scale Systems: The Software Challenges of the Future*, Software Engineering Institute Report at http://www.sei.cmu.edu/uls/files/ULS_Book2006.pdf, Carnegie-Mellon University.

Parnas, D. (1972) On the criteria for decomposing systems into modules, *Communications of the ACM* 15 (12), pp. 1053–1058.

Randers, J. (1980) *Elements of the System Dynamics Method*, MIT Press, Cambridge, MA.

Shaw, M. and D. Garlan (1996) *Software Architecture: Perspectives on an Emerging Discipline*, Prentice-Hall, Englewood Cliffs, NJ.

Simon, H. (1996) *The Sciences of the Artificial*, 3rd edn, The MIT Press, Cambridge, MA.

Wing, J. (2006) Computational thinking, *Communications of the ACM* 49 (3), pp. 33–35.

Wulf, W. (2006) Keynote Presentation to USC Center for Software & Systems Engineering Symposium, Los Angeles, CA.

Chapter 7
People and Design

What is design? It's where you stand with a foot in two worlds –
the world of technology and the world of people and human
purposes – and you try to bring the two together.

– (Mitch Kapor, A Software Design Manifesto, 1990).

Information technology design is by no means simple. Most real-world problems are not simple and they often have no correct solution. The challenges that everyday designers' face is to handle trade-offs. It is the conscious choice among many alternatives each of which places constraints on utility and resources. As Mitch Kapor suggests above, a designer stands with one foot in the technology and one foot in the domain of human concerns, and these two worlds are not easily commensurable (Winograd 1996).

David Liddle who was head of Xerox PARC's Star project says *"Software design is the act of determining the user's experience with a piece of software. It has nothing to do with how the code works inside, or how big or small the code is. The designer's task is to specify completely and unambiguously the user's whole experience. The most important thing to design properly is the user's conceptual model. Everything else should be subordinated to making that model clear, obvious, and substantial."*

Software design is a social process in which people design things to be used by people and the entire process (should) use people. While design is primarily a result of the qualities and activities of the creative individual, the designer operates in a larger social setting. Interaction with other people and things, the organization and workplace aspects often lead to complex and controversial design considerations. In this chapter, we start by looking at designing for consumers. That is then followed by a brief discussion of the practice of ethnographic principles in design involving people, community, and society. We then discuss Schon's ideas on reflective stance in design. We finally end this chapter with a look at how to design for scale, with Google as an example.

A. Hevner, S. Chatterjee, *Design Research in Information Systems*, Integrated Series
in Information Systems 22, DOI 10.1007/978-1-4419-5653-8_7,
© Springer Science+Business Media, LLC 2010

7.1 Designing for Consumers

In the last 30 years or so, we have learned a great deal about how software artifacts are created in the labs and how eventually they find their way to the marketplace and become consumer goods. But the evolution and adaptability are subtle. David Liddle, lead designer of Xerox Star, gives the best example of how technology is adopted in three phases – the *enthusiast* phase, the *professional* phase, and the *consumer* phase. "The maturity of a technology has profound implications for designing interactions, as the nature of design process changes as each phase is reached" (Moggridge 2007).

The first phase is the enthusiast phase in which the early adopters use the technology for its newness and aesthetic appeal. The geeks and the nerds enjoy the fact that it is rather difficult to use. The enthusiasts push the capabilities and limits of the artifact much beyond the wildest expectations of its original inventors or designers. A classic example is the creation of the World Wide Web by Tim Berners Lee and much of the excitement in the mid-1990s with dot com technologies. The web had been transformed to many things beyond Lee's original intended scope and use.

The second phase is when professionals bring the technology into the work place and professionals find clever ways of using it to do something practical. The focus immediately is on value, reliability, and how much should it cost? With time, there is standardization of controls, making it reliable and reasonably priced becomes important.

The last stage is success with consumers. In some way it is the measure of ultimate success. We humans are a frighteningly adaptable species. A good tool should adjust itself to the user, but good tools are hard to find, and so we have learned to adapt ourselves to the plethora of gadgets and gizmos that are thrown our way. Of course, sometimes we are frustrated and throw in the towel when the computer expects us to do things to which we are reluctant. We are slowly but surely expecting user-friendliness to convert to user experience. "We use tools to accomplish tasks, and we abandon tools when the efforts required to make the tool deliver exceeds our threshold of indignation" (Winograd 1996). Consumer level products must have an element of delight and enjoyment. That is something every designer must strive for.

If designers want to attract and delight consumers (or customers) for their work, they need to fully understand the people for whom they design. It was much easier in the past when the USA was a mass market. One design fits all. They bought similar things, liked similar food, and enjoyed similar activities and goods. But the USA today is a highly fragmented market with diverse people of many ethnic background and the growth trend is toward diversity (Laurel 2003). Today people spend their time and money on their individual beliefs, their personal desires, and their specific needs (Laurel 2003). People now control big business. The power has shifted and with the rapid emergence of e-commerce and the Internet-based retail, big business is scrambling to understand what consumers need and how they can serve them. Businesses across the globe are vying for people's attention and their pocket books. "How these customers choose can make or break a company, an institution or an individual artisan" (Laurel 2003).

7.2 Practice of Ethnography in Design

To design products that consumers want, it is important to deeply understand them through their values, cultures, and environment. A research technique called ethnography that originated in anthropology has become a central practice in design research. Anthropology is the study of human behavior, how people experience and make sense of what they themselves and others do. Culture involves the practices, artifacts, sensibilities, and ideas that constitute and inform our everyday lives. Tim Plowman (Laurel 2003) describes "As a working concept, culture includes phenomena ranging from how we tie our shoes to religious beliefs, flirting, the categories we use to parse the world, body piercing, and how we navigate an interface. Typically, we don't realize how and to what extent we are participating in and therefore shaping culture." Whether we are using a PC with the latest operating system or surfing the web over the Internet, these designed artifacts engage humans through their utility as well as their cultural location – the "situatedness" through which design artifacts recursively derive their meaning and are simultaneously the object of interpretation (Laurel 2003).

Social scientists have typically used ethnographic method for studying and learning about a person or small group of people in order to theorize about culture at a more general level. In order to understand how design influences us and the relationship between design research and social science, we must study a research method called ethnography – a practice increasingly central to design research. Ethnography is scientifically descriptive and interpretive. It requires analytic rigor and process as well as inductive analysis (applies to inductive step for theory).

The key idea embodied in ethnographic studies draws from the seminal work of Bronislaw Malinowski whose famous term "the imponderabilia of actual life" revealed that one could truly understand a culture or its people by being one of them, living with indigenous people for long periods of time (Young 2004). Instead of drawing conclusions from second-hand information, use first-hand data as much as possible. Since that time, many different types of ethnographic techniques have surfaced.

Designers have adopted qualitative design research methods in order to understand customers. It is all about learning about them from listening, watching them, or experiencing their lives first hand. While focus groups have received traditional attention, it has morphed into a family of related methods.

Traditional focus group is a gathering of 10–12 consumers who are led in a tightly scripted discussion by a trained moderator, usually for about two hours.

It can be for any topic or purpose, but are recommended primarily when you want to generate ideas and/or expand understanding without needing to reach consensus. Also popular are *mini-focus groups* that typically have six to eight consumers. *1-on-1 interviews* are very helpful also in which one person is interviewed by researcher who is following either a tightly scripted guide or a loose outline. Typical duration can be from half an hour to more hours if necessary. *Dyads* include two friends interviewed as a pair by a moderator following an outline or lightly scripted guide for at least one hour. *Super groups* have 50–100 people gathered in a large auditorium to view products, designs, or other exhibits presented on a large screen. *Triads* have three or more people. They may run the risk of group influence. *Party groups* spend two or three hours in one person's home in a more informal setting and casual stress-free environment.

A newer technique is *online discussion groups* which are still in its infancy. A huge advantage of this technique is the easy access to diverse customers who may be located anywhere in the world through the use of the Internet.

Much early work done at Xerox Parc (GUI, HCI, CSCW, and networking) in the early 1980s used ethnography in the design process. Xerox had hired a number of anthropologists. The same spirit has been continued by several Silicon Valley design firms such as IDEO, Apple, Microsoft, Google, Intel, Herman Miller, and others. These commercial firms also conduct ethnography studies of their consumers. Like academic studies, these businesses also require a well-defined set of hypothesis and research objectives to test those hypotheses. But in academia these research objectives tend to be complex and grounded in a body of previous research. It often takes years or a career to address them. Designers and developers on the other hand have to do things fast. Research objectives that designers have to deal with typically need to be defined in a matter of weeks or days (Laurel 2003). Hence commercial ethnographers quickly summarize relevant information, synthesize data, and draw conclusions. Experience definitely matters.

Designers unknowingly create the future. But it is not easy. Technology designers and consumer product designers face the daunting challenge of "crossing the chasm" by creating things that do not exist today and ensuring that there will be an eventual market and need for these products. This is a hard thing to do. Most companies (start-ups) fail and fall through the chasm (Moore 1991). But today's designers have a number of potential different methods to work with that include focus groups, expert interviews, surveys, ethnographic techniques, field research, storyboarding and use of prototypes. These techniques can not only help them create better designs but also leap through Moore's chasm. Further, designers can pursue Eric Dishman's ideas of a simple *asking, observing, and performing* cycle through different phases of a project. Asking is getting as much information about the people who will likely use a product. This may require understanding of their culture. Observing actual people in real-world setting helps to determine extreme behaviors and unusual patterns. Performing is about designers acting/testing out the future lives of their imagined end-users as well as getting those users to critique plausible future scenarios.

7.3 Reflection in Action (Schon's View)

Donald Schon has studied professionals and designers. His subject interests range from psychiatrists and social workers to architects and jazz musicians. His book *The Reflective Practitioner* (Schon 1983) explains what it means to apply expertise. Software designers can learn quite a bit from other design disciplines and in particular the notion of reflection in action as explained by Donald Schon.

In our everyday life, we go about doing things, activities that exhibit knowledge in a special way. Although we often cannot say what it is we know, we do know how to take action. We carry out many recognitions and judgments without thinking about them. Basic activities such as walking fall in this category. These actions seem normal and we do not even remember how we learned them.

Reflection in action is different in the sense that it is closely tied to the experience of surprise. Sometimes we think about what we are doing in the midst of performing an act. The surprise may be pleasant or unpleasant but based on that, we take some more action as we continue to perform. We think about what it is we are doing and in turn influence that doing. A great example is to watch a group of jazz musicians. They perform together and yet they continue to improvise and innovate on the piece. When one musician does some note combinations, it may be peculiar but it is a pleasant surprise. Another musician picks up on that event, and improvises to create more action and the whole result may come out to be beautiful. "The players keep on playing while, on occasion, noting and responding to the surprises produced by other players" (Winograd 1996).

Schon explains that this innovate, reflect, and further innovate method is germane to designers and their design process. It is rare that the designer has the entire design in her head in advance and then merely translates it. Most of the time, she makes progress incrementally. As she goes along, she is making judgments and decisions. Sometimes, the designer's judgments have the intimacy of a conversational relationship, where she is getting some response back from the medium, she is seeing what is happening – what it is that she has created – and she is making judgments about it at that level. As a designer works with a problem, she is continually in the process of developing a path into it, forming new appreciations and understandings as she makes new moves. The designer evaluates a move by asking a variety of questions, such as "Are the consequences desirable?" "Does the current state of the design conform to implications set up by earlier moves?" "What new problems or potentials have been created?" These new ideas and findings lead to new actions. Figure 7.1 shows Schon's view of the design process.

7.4 Designing for Scale – Google and People

So far in this chapter we have seen how people design things for people by studying their culture, habits, and behavior. A key property of most software application design today is scalability, i.e., the application performs well with many users. As

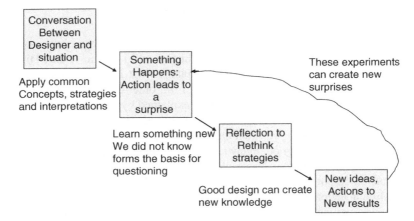

Fig. 7.1 Schon's view of the design process

the user base grows, the application remains stable and performs efficiently. One classic example is the search engine site known as Google.

The 1990s saw a period of madness often referred to as the "dot com" days. The creation of Mosaic (later Netscape) gave rise to a tremendous period of excitement in which the IT community witnessed a revolution. This revolution brought in the information age. Entrepreneurs with ideas received unlimited venture fund; start-ups were ubiquitous and the stock market rewarded those companies that had very little actual revenue. The business models did not matter as long as banner ads were there. The infrastructure people built new networks, routers, and switches hoping that traffic would never cease. Looking back upon that time, we all wonder now why the euphoria lasted as long as it did. It lasted partly because there were some true innovation and revolution going on. Life truly was different because of the Internet.

At last the bubble burst and the crash came. Investors lost billions. Start-ups that were promising dreams folded and real estate once again became affordable in Silicon Valley. People lost their jobs, homes and the downturn was quite brutal. Amidst all these changes was born a small start-up called Google. Sergey Brin and Larry Page met as graduate students at Stanford University's Computer Science Department in fall of 1995. They collaborated to develop technology that would eventually become the foundation for the Google search engine. Googles' evolution and history is an interesting example of experimentation by trial and error for designers.

Brin was interested in data mining, finding patterns, and relationships among large data sets. Larry was interested to gather all the links on the web and together they found an interesting problem to solve. Their technique was called PageRank (US Patent 6285999). It is a tool to compare one web page with another. PageRank helps you determine the importance of pages based on the links to them. PageRank does not count the links; it uses the vast link structure of the web as an organizational tool:

PageRank is a link analysis algorithm, named after Larry Page, used by the Google Internet search engine that assigns a numerical weighting to each element of a hyperlinked set of documents, such as the World Wide Web, with the purpose of "measuring" its relative importance within the set. The algorithm may be applied to any collection of entities with reciprocal quotations and references. The numerical weight that it assigns to any given element E is also called the PageRank of E and denoted by PR(E).

With little experiments, Larry and Brin figured out that PageRank could be used as an effective search tool.

Terry Winograd who had been an advisor to Larry at Stanford sums it up quite well: "I think they have been successful for a number of reasons, but largely because they have respected what it is they think users can do and what users want. I think that's a big lesson from Google. They don't say, "Here's what we are going to force on you, here's what we think we can sell you". They really started from a point of view of, "Here's what we hope will be useful". Let's find out. Let's try it (Moggridge 2007)."

We will conclude this chapter with a brief discussion of Google's philosophy that can be found from their web site.

1. Focus on the user and all else will follow
2. It is best to do one thing really, really well
3. Fast is better than slow
4. Democracy works on the web
5. You do not need to be at your desk to need an answer
6. You can make money without doing evil
7. There is always more information out there
8. The need for information crosses all borders
9. You can be serious without a suit
10. Great is not just good enough

While the above 10 points apply directly to Google, we believe that they are excellent guidelines for researchers doing design work.

As anyone who has used Google web site for search realizes that their interface is clear and simple. They have one bar to type in what you are looking for. People come to Google to search. There is no need to clutter that page with anything else that can distract the user. This simple and yet very effective design principle has gone a long way to the success of Google. Their revenue has been through clicks and advertisement. But advertizing on the site must offer relevant content and not be a distraction. Doing one thing really well makes it fast and efficient. Hence Google has always been about the best user experience and nothing else. As of April 2006, there are 91 million searches per day on Google within the USA. That number worldwide is close to 200 million searches per day. This is a true testimony to their scalability.

References

Laurel, B. (ed.) (2003) *Design Research: Methods and Perspectives*, The MIT Press, Cambridge, MA.

Moggridge, B. (2007) *Designing Interactions*, The MIT Press, Cambridge, MA.

Moore, G. A. (1991) *Crossing the Chasm: Marketing and Selling High-Tech Products to Mainstream Customers*, Harper Business Essentials, New York.

Schon, D. (1983) *The Reflective Practitioner: How Professionals Think in Action*, Basic Books, New York.

US Patent 6285999. URL at http://patft.uspto.gov/netacgi/nph-Parser?Sect2= PTO1 &Sect2= HITOFF&p=1&u=%2Fnetahtml%2FPTO%2Fsearch-bool.html&r=1&f= G&l=50 &d= PALL & RefSrch=yes&Query=PN%2F6285999, Accessed July 2009.

Winograd, T (1996) *Bringing Design to Software*, Addison-Wesley, Reading, MA.

Young, M. (2004) *Malinowski: Odyssey of an Anthropologist, 1884–1920*, Yale University Press, New Have, CT.

Chapter 8
Software Design: Past and Present

A fact in itself is nothing. It is valuable only for the idea attached to it, or for the proof which it furnishes.

– Claude Bernard

8.1 A Software Design Framework

The design of software has been one of the greatest challenges in the development of information systems. From its fairly primitive beginnings in the form of toggling on/off switches and punching holes in paper tapes, software has come to dominate the cost of all forms of information systems. Yet, instead of gaining increasing mastery over the processes of software design, we continue to be challenged by new software technologies, greater quality expectations, and higher complexities of integrated systems. Thus, software design remains an essentially wicked problem that is typically crafted to each software-intensive system developed.

This chapter presents a brief overview of the progress made in software design over the past 60 years. The presentation is structured on the software design framework found in Fig. 8.1. We view software as composed of four basic design elements – an architecture; the algorithmic procedure in a programming language; the data in a structured format; and the human–computer interaction with enabling human–computer interfaces. Bringing these design elements together into an effective software design requires well-defined software development processes and development methods as shown at the center of the framework.

Our goal in this chapter is to present a brief historical retrospective of software design challenges and successful design solutions (Campbell-Kelly and Aspray 1996; Hevner and Berndt 2000). Learning from the lessons of the past we can hope to build improved software designs for present and future software-intensive systems.

A. Hevner, S. Chatterjee, *Design Research in Information Systems*, Integrated Series in Information Systems 22, DOI 10.1007/978-1-4419-5653-8_8,
© Springer Science+Business Media, LLC 2010

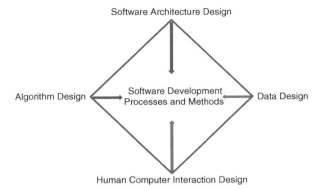

Fig. 8.1 Software design framework

8.2 Software Architecture

The three technology components of a computing environment – computing platform, communication networks, and software – are integrated via system architecture into a functional, effective information system. A classic paper by Zachman (1987) presents an information systems architecture framework made up of the elements of *data*, *process*, and *networking*. The Zachman IS architecture combines representations of these elements into an architectural blueprint for a business application. The framework of this chapter differs by including the computing platform (hardware and OS) as a fundamental systems element and combining algorithmic procedure (i.e., process) and data into the software architecture element.

We focus our discussion here on the software architecture component of the overall systems architecture. The goal of software architecture is to provide a mapping or "blueprint" to integrate all required functionalities and qualities of the desired information system provided by software. The objectives of all system stakeholders must be considered and represented in the design of the software architecture. Design trade-offs are key decision points in the development of an effective architecture.

The importance of software architectures for the development of complex systems has been clearly recognized in the software engineering literature (Shaw and Garlan 1996; Bass et al. 2003; Taylor et al. 2009). Architectural styles are identified based on their organization of software components and connectors for the transmission of data and control among components. The following discussion of software architectures is organized chronologically. Information systems have evolved and become more complex due to the requirements for meeting many, sometimes conflicting, functional, and quality objectives. We will see how over time the architectural solutions attempt to satisfy these multiple objectives.

8.2.1 Manual Business Processes

In the centuries leading up to the invention of the computer, businesses focused their creative energies on the development of effective business processes for production, personnel management, accounting, marketing, and sales. Standard operating procedures (SOPs) and workflow processes were widely used throughout business history. The concept of a "general systems theory" guided the structure and application of these business processes.

Even before the advent of computers, intellectual leaders, such as Herbert Simon and C. West Churchman, were extending the ideas of systems thinking into business organizations (Kast and Rosenzweig 1972). Such systemic business processes were performed manually up to around 1950. However, the business focus of getting the critical business processes right before automation remains an underlying tenet of all successful organizations today and for the foreseeable future.

8.2.2 Mainframe Architectures

The automation of business processes with the original large mainframe computer systems occurred slowly at first. The 1950s and early 1960s saw a vast majority of business application programs written in COBOL based on basic *data-flow architectures*. During this era computer systems consisted primarily of the computational platform (e.g., mainframe and operating system) and early application software systems. In a data-flow architecture, data in the form of variables, records, or files move from one computer system application to the next until the required business process is completed. The simplest form of a data-flow architecture is known as a *batch sequential architecture*. Data is batched into large files and the application programs are batched for sequential runs on the data files. The classic master file–transaction file applications are based on batch sequential processing. The *pipe and filter architecture* is a more general model of dataflow. Pipes carry data from one filter to the next in a network dataflow. A filter accepts streams of data as input, performs some processing on the data, and produces streams of data as output. The filter performs local transformations of an input into an output on a continuing basis. Each filter is independent of all other filters in the data-flow architecture. The pipe and filter structure provided the underlying computational model for the UNIX operating system (Bach 1987).

8.2.3 Online, Real-Time Architectures

During the time from 1965 to 1974, businesses began to realize the competitive advantages of online, real-time processing. The evolving technologies of databases, data communications, and the computational platform (e.g., minicomputers and real-time operating systems) enabled sophisticated real-time business and scientific applications to be developed. Online processing required important new advances in data communications (e.g., remote job entry, real-time data queries, and updates), database repositories (e.g., hierarchical and network databases), and operating systems (e.g., multiprogramming, real-time interrupts, resource allocation). The critical need was to align these new technologies and the software architecture with sufficient performance to meet rigorous response time and data capacity requirements.

The principal architecture used to meet these requirements was a *repository architecture*. A central repository of operational data in file and database formats represents the current state of the application system. Multiple sources of independent transactions (i.e., agents) perform operations on the repository. The interactions between the central repository and the external agents can vary in complexity, but in the early days of online applications they consisted mostly of simple queries or updates against the repository. The real-time operating system provides integrity and concurrency control as multiple transactions attempt to access the data in real time. The data-centric nature of most business applications has made the repository architecture with real-time requirements a staple of application development.

8.2.4 Distributed, Client–Server Architectures

Around 1975 decentralization of control became a key business and information systems strategy. The ability to decentralize the organization and move processing closer to the customer brought about major changes in thinking about work processes and the supporting computer systems. The technology components to support true distributed processing were available during this era to support these decentralized business strategies. Networks of communicating computers consisted of mainframes, minicomputers, and increasingly popular microcomputers. *Distributed architectures* became the norm for building new business computer systems (Peebles and Manning 1978; Scherr 1978).

Distributed computing provided a number of important advantages for computing systems. Partitioning the workload among several processors at different locations enhanced performance. System availability was increased due to redundancy of hardware, software, and data in the system. Response time to customer requests was improved since customer information was located closer to the customer site. The ability to integrate minicomputers and microcomputers into the distributed architecture provided significant price-performance advantages. The potential disadvantages of the distributed system were loss of centralized control of data and applications and performance costs of updating redundant data across the network.

An important variant of the distributed architecture is the *client–server architecture*. A server process, typically installed in a larger computer, provides services to client processes, typically distributed on a network. A server can be independent of the number and type of its clients, while a client must know the identity of the server and the correct calling sequence to obtain service. Examples of services include database systems and specialized front-end and back-end components.

8.2.5 Component-Based Architectures

During the latter decades of the 20th century, an important focus was on the alignment of business strategy with information technology (IT) strategy in the organization. A *strategic alignment model* proposed by Henderson and Venkatraman (1993) posits four basic alignment perspectives:

1. Strategy execution: The organization's business strategy is well defined and determines the organizational infrastructure and the IT infrastructure. This is the most common alignment perspective.
2. Technology transformation: The business strategy is again well defined, but in this perspective it drives the organization's IT strategy. Thus, the strategies are in alignment before the IT infrastructure is implemented.
3. Competitive potential: The organization's IT strategy is well defined based upon innovative IT usage to gain competitive advantage in the marketplace. The IT strategy drives the business strategy which in turn determines the organizational infrastructure. The strategies are aligned to take advantage of the IT strengths of the organization.
4. Service level: The IT strategy is well defined and drives the implementation of the IT infrastructure. The organizational infrastructure is formed around the IT infrastructure. The business strategy does not directly impact the IT strategy.

While all four perspectives have distinct pros and cons, the alignment of the business strategy and the IT strategy before the development of the organizational and IT infrastructures in perspectives 2 and 3 provides a consistent vision to the organization's business objectives. This vision was translated into the system and software architectures of the organization's IT systems.

This time period saw the traditional business strategy of "make and sell" transformed into a strategy of "sense and respond" (Haeckel and Nolan 1996). Two new software architectures were devised to meet these changing environmental demands.

Event-driven architectures have become prevalent in business systems that must react to events that occur in the business environment (Barrett et al. 1996). When an important event occurs a signal is broadcast by the originating component. Other components in the system that have registered an interest in the event are notified and perform appropriate actions. This architecture clearly performs well in a "sense and respond" business environment. Note that announcers of events are unaware of which other components are notified and what actions are generated by the event. Thus, this architecture supports implicit invocation of activity in the system. This architecture provides great flexibility in that actions can be added, deleted, or changed easily for a given event.

The important new development ideas of component-based development have led naturally to the design and implementation of *component-based architectures* (Brown 2000). Business systems are composed of functional components glued together by middleware standards such as CORBA, DCOM, and Enterprise JavaBeans. In many cases the components are commercial off-the-shelf (COTS) products. Thus, organizations are able to build complex, high-performance systems by integrating COTS components via industry standard middleware protocols. This minimizes development risk while allowing the business organization to effectively align its IT strategy with its business strategy via judicious selection of best practice functional components. Enterprise resource planning (ERP) business systems from vendors like SAP, Baan, and Oracle utilize component-based architectures to allow clients to customize their business systems to their organization's requirements.

8.2.6 Service-Oriented Architectures

The influence of the World Wide Web has required businesses to rethink their business and IT strategies to take greatest advantage of its revolutionary impact. This current era of Internet and ubiquitous computing will generate new web-based *service-oriented architectures* (SOA) for integrating the capabilities of the Internet into business functions of marketing, sales, distribution, and funds transfer (Erl 2005). Service orientation provides a loose coupling of services glued together in business flows to support end-user goals of functionalities and qualities. SOA separates these functions and qualities into distinct units, or services, which developers make accessible over a network in order that users can combine and reuse them in the production of applications. These services communicate with each other by passing data from one service to another or by coordinating an activity between two or more services.

The implications of service-oriented architectures are just now being studied. The rapid exchange of information via push and pull technologies to any point of the globe will eliminate most boundaries and constraints on international commerce. However, critical issues of security, privacy, cultural differences (e.g., language), intellectual property, and political sensitivities will take many years to be resolved.

8.3 Algorithmic Design

Solving a scientific or business problem first requires the creation of an algorithm that provides a step-by-step procedure for accepting inputs, processing data, and producing outputs. Algorithms are typically represented in natural language or some form of structured format like pseudocode or flowcharts. The objective of computer programming is to code this algorithm in a form such that an important problem can be solved via the use of a computer system. The history of computer programming languages has been documented in several excellent sources (Wexelblat 1981; Bergin and Gibson 1996) and will not be addressed here.

8.3.1 Early Program Design

Programming in the early days of computing involved wiring plugboards, setting toggle switches on the side of the computer, or punching holes in paper tape. The wiring, switch settings, and holes represented instructions that were interpreted and executed by the computer. Each time a program was run the boards had to be re-wired, switches had to be reset, or the paper tape re-punched. The stored program computer changed this onerous task by storing the program in internal memory and executing it upon command.

The 1960s brought major advances in program compilers and assemblers. The role of a compiler is to translate a high-level language in which humans can write algorithms into a computer's internal set of instructions. The assembler then translates the computer instructions into binary machine code for placement in the computer's memory. The research and development of compilers and assemblers led rapidly to the creation of the first computer programming languages.

IBM developed FORTRAN (FORmula TRANslation) for the 704 computer in early 1957, contributing to the popularity of the product line. John Backus and his team defined the language to support engineering applications that required fast execution of mathematical algorithms (Backus 1979). FORTRAN has gone through many generations and remains popular even today for engineering applications.

Business computing had different requirements. Efficient data handling was critical and business programmers had the need for a more user-friendly, English-like language. In 1959, a team of Department of Defense developers, including Grace Murray Hopper, defined a business-oriented programming language COBOL (common business-oriented language). COBOL is a highly structured, verbose language with well-defined file handling facilities. The English-like syntax makes programs more readable and self-documenting. It was also the first language to be standardized, so its programs could run on different hardware platforms.

8.3.2 Structured Program Design

As application software systems grew in size a crisis in software development was created. Large programs (e.g., 50,000–100,000 lines of code) were being developed. These programs were very difficult to read, debug, and maintain. Software routinely failed and repairs were difficult and time-consuming. The worldwide nature of the software problem was reflected in the NATO software engineering conferences held in 1968 (Garmisch, Germany) and 1969 (Rome) (Naur and Randell 1969; Buxton and Randell 1970). The term "software engineering" was coined to generate discussion as to whether the development of software was truly an engineering discipline.

The issues of software development and how to solve the software crisis debated at these early conferences remain relevant even today.

Edsger Dijkstra's influential 1968 paper, "Go-To Statement Considered Harmful," (Dijkstra 1968) addressed a major problem in existing programming languages. Flow of logical control through a program was often haphazard leading to "spaghetti code" programs. Software researchers, like Dijkstra and Harlan Mills, proposed structured programming as the answer to out-of-control program flow (Mills 1986). The use of only three simple structures – sequence, selection, and iteration – can express the control flow of any algorithm (Boehm and Jacopini 1966). This understanding led to the development of new structured programming languages.

The languages Pascal and ALGOL-68 initiated some of the principal structured programming concepts. However, they had little commercial impact. Meanwhile, new versions of FORTRAN-IV and COBOL integrated new structured features.

8.3.3 Recent Algorithm Design Paradigms

Object-oriented (OO) design originated in simulation languages, such as Simula, during the 1960s. An object-oriented design of an algorithm models a collection of cooperating *objects*. Each object bounds a coherent set of activities (methods) and information (data structures). An object can be viewed as an independent entity in the application world with capabilities of interacting with other objects via the receiving and sending of messages. Object-oriented design highlights the design principles information hiding, data abstraction, encapsulation, modularity, polymorphism, and inheritance (Booch, Maksimchuk, Engel, Young, Conallen, and Houston 2007). Many current programming languages support OO design and coding.

Aspect-oriented (AO) design extends the OO paradigm by identifying cross-cutting concerns (e.g., aspects) in an application design (Jacobson and Ng 2005). By separating distinct concerns, design modularity is improved and satisfaction of the cross-cutting aspect can be more effectively designed, implemented, tested, and monitored in operation. Examples of aspects are security, logging, and transactions. Research and development on aspect-oriented design and programming is still in early stages.

8.3.4 Widely Used Programming Languages

In the early 1970s, Ken Thompson and Dennis Ritchie developed a new systems programming language called C, using the language to implement UNIX. By allowing access to low-level machine operations, this language defied many of the tenets of structured programming. Regardless, C has become a very popular programming language, particularly within the last two decades of programming as personal computers have dominated the desktops. The language C++ evolved from C for the programming of object-oriented business applications (Ritchie and Thompson 1974). Variations of the C language proliferate in today's programming environments.

Visual programming languages, such as Visual Basic (VB), incorporate facilities to develop graphic user interfaces (GUIs) for business applications. Such languages are particularly effective in the development of client–server distributed applications where the end-user at the client site needs an efficient, friendly interface.

The advent of the Internet and service-oriented architectures has provided the impetus for efficient, platform independent programs that can be distributed rapidly to Internet sites and executed. The Java programming language was developed at Sun Microsystems to fit this need (Gosling et al. 2005).

8.4 Data Design

The management of data in systems predates recorded history. The first known writing was done on Sumerian stone tablets and consisted of a collection of data on royal assets and taxes. Writing on papyrus and eventually on paper was the predominate manner of manual data management up to the beginning of the 20th century. First mechanical and then electronic machinery rapidly changed the ways in which data is managed.

8.4.1 Punched Card Data Management

Although automated looms and player pianos used punched cards to hold information, the first true automated data manager was the punched card system designed by Herman Hollerith to produce the 1890 census. Automated equipment for handling and storing punched cards was the primary means of managing business data until the era of automation. An entire data management industry, whose leader was IBM, grew up around punched cards.

8.4.2 Computerized File Management

The use of the UNIVAC I computer system for the 1950 census heralded the era of automation in business computing. To replace punched cards, magnetic drums and tapes were developed to store data records. Without the constraints of an 80-column card format, new, innovative data structures were devised to organize information for fast retrieval and processing. Common business applications for general-ledger, payroll, banking, inventory, accounts receivable, shipping invoices, contact management, human resources, etc., were developed in COBOL. All of these programs were centered on the handling of large files of data records. The prevailing system architecture during this era was that of batch-oriented processing of individual transactions. Files of transactions were run against a master file of data records, usually once a day or once a week. The problems with this architecture were the inherent delays of finding and correcting errors in the transactions and the lack of up-to-date information in the master file at any point in time (Gray 1996).

8.4.3 Online Data Processing

Direct access to data in magnetic storage led to improved structures for rapidly locating a desired data record in a large data file while still allowing efficient sequential processing of all records. *Hierarchical data models* presented data in hierarchies of one-to-many relationships. For example, a department record is related to many employee records and an employee record is related to many project records. Sophisticated indexing techniques provided efficient access to individual data records in the file structure. Popular commercial file systems, such as IBM's indexed sequential access mechanism (ISAM) and virtual sequential access mechanism (VSAM), provided very effective support for complex business applications based on large data sets.

Hierarchical data models lacked a desired flexibility for querying data in different ways. In the above example, the hierarchy as designed would not efficiently support the production of a report listing all employees working on a given project. A more general method of modeling data was needed. An industrial consortium formed the Data Base Task Group (DBTG) to develop a standard data model. Led by Charles Bachman, who had performed research and development of data models at General Electric, the group proposed a *network data model*. The DBTG network model was based on the insightful concepts of data independence and three levels of data schemas:

- External subschema: Each business application had its own subset view of the complete database schema. The application subschema was optimized for efficient processing.
- Conceptual schema: The global database schema represented the logical design of all data entities and the relationships among the entities.
- Physical schema: This schema described the mapping of the conceptual schema onto the physical storage devices. File organizations and indexes were constructed to support application processing requirements.

Data independence between the schema levels allowed a developer to work at a higher level while remaining independent of the details at lower levels. This was a major intellectual advance that allowed many different applications, with different subschemas, to run on a single common database platform.

8.4.4 Relational Databases

E.F. Codd, working at IBM Research Laboratory, proposed a simpler way of viewing data based on relational mathematics (Codd 1970). Two-dimensional relations are used to model both data entities and the relationships among entities based upon the matching of common attribute values. The mathematical underpinnings of the *relational data model* provided formal methods of relational calculus and relational algebra for the manipulation and querying of the relations. A standard data definition and query language, structured query language (SQL), was developed from these foundations.

Commercialization of the relational model was a painstaking process. Issues of performance and scalability offset the advantages of easier conceptual modeling and standard SQL programming. Advances in query optimization led to relational systems that could meet reasonable performance goals. The relational model fit nicely with new client–server architectures. The move of processing power to distributed client sites called for more user-friendly graphical user interfaces and end-user query capabilities. At the same time, more powerful processors for the servers boosted performance for relational processing.

8.4.5 Current Trends in Data Management

Data design and the effective management of data have always been and will remain the center of most computing systems. The digital revolution has drastically expanded our definition and understanding of knowledge, information, and data. Multimedia data includes audio, pictures, video, documents, touch (e.g., virtual reality), and, maybe even, smell. New applications are finding effective ways of managing and using multimedia data.

Object-oriented methods of software development attempt to break the boundary between algorithmic procedures and data (Stonebraker 1996). Two main themes characterize the use of object technology in database management systems: object-relational technology integrates the relational model and support for objects, while object-oriented systems take a more purist approach.

A major challenge for the future of data management will be how to manage the huge amounts of information flowing over the World Wide Web. It is estimated that a majority of business (e.g., marketing, sales, distribution, and service) will be conducted over the Internet in the near future. New structures for web databases must support real-time data capture, ongoing analyses of data trends and anomalies (e.g., data mining), multimedia data, real-time data streaming, and high levels of security. In addition, web-enabled business will require very large databases, huge numbers of simultaneous users, and new ways to manage transactions.

8.5 Human–Computer Interaction (HCI) Design

The effectiveness of any computer application is determined by the quality of its interactions and interfaces with the external world. This area of research and development has been termed human–computer interaction (HCI).

8.5.1 Early Computer Interactions

The first computer interactions were via toggle switches, blinking lights, paper tape punches, and primitive cathode-ray tubes. Quickly the need for more effective input/output devices brought about the use of card readers/punches and teletype printers. Up to 1950, however, interaction with the computer was the domain of computer specialists who were trained to handle these arcane and unwieldy interfaces.

The use of computers in effective systems required more usable, standard human–computer interfaces. Early on, the standard input medium was the Hollerith card. Both the program and data were keypunched on cards in standardized formats. The cards were organized into card decks, batched with other card decks, and read into the computer memory for execution. Output was printed on oversized, fan-fold computer paper. Businesses were required to hire computer operations staff to maintain the computer systems and to control access to the computer interfaces. End-user computing was rare during this era.

8.5.2 Text-Based Command Interfaces

As computer use grew during the 1970s, the demand from end-users for more effective, direct interaction with the applications grew correspondingly. Moving from batch computer architectures to online distributed architectures necessitated new terminal-based interfaces for the application users. Computer terminals were designed to combine a typewriter input interface with a cathode-ray tube output interface. Terminals were connected to the mainframe computer via direct communication lines. The design of the computer terminal was amazingly successful and remains with us today as the primary HCI device. HCI interfaces for online applications were either based on scrolling lines of text or on predefined bit-mapped forms with fields for text or data entry.

Standard applications began to proliferate in the environment of online computing, for example

- Text editing and word processing: The creation, storage, and manipulation of textual documents rapidly became a dominant use of business computers. Early text editors were developed at Stanford, MIT, and Xerox PARC. Commercial WYSIWYG (what you see is what you get) word processing packages came along in the early 1980s with LisaWrite, a predecessor to MacWrite, and WordStar.

- Spreadsheets: Accounting applications are cornerstone business activities. Commercial accounting packages have been available for computers since the 1950s. The spreadsheet package VisiCalc became a breakthrough product for business computing when it was introduced in 1979. Lotus 1-2-3 and Microsoft Excel followed as successful spreadsheet packages.
- Computer-aided design: The use of computers for computer-aided design (CAD) and computer-aided manufacturing (CAM) began during the 1960s and continues today with sophisticated application packages.
- Presentation and graphics: Research and development on drawing programs began with the sketchpad system of Ivan Sutherland in 1963. Computer graphics and paint programs have been integrated into business applications via presentation packages, such as Microsoft's PowerPoint.

Text-based command languages were the principal forms of HCI during the 1970s and 1980s for the majority of operating systems, such as UNIX, IBM's MVS and CICS, and DEC's VAX VMS. The users of these systems required a thorough knowledge of many system commands and formats. This type of text-based command language carried over to the first operating systems for personal computers. CPM and MS-DOS constrained users to a small set of pre-defined commands that frustrated end-users and limited widespread use of personal computers.

8.5.3 The WIMP Interface

Many years of research and development on computer graphical user interfaces (GUIs) have led to today's WIMP (windows, icons, mouse, and pull-down menus) HCI standards. Seminal research and development by J. Licklider at ARPA, Douglas Englebart at Stanford, and the renowned group at Xerox PARC led to the many innovative ideas found in the WIMP interface (Myers 1998). The first commercial computer systems popularizing WIMP features were the Xerox Star, the Apple Lisa, and the Apple Macintosh. The X Window system and the Microsoft Windows versions made the WIMP interface a standard for current computing systems.

More than any other technology, the WIMP interface and its ease of use brought the personal computer into the home and made computing accessible to everyone. Advantages to businesses included an increase in computer literate employees, standard application interfaces across the organization, decreased training time for new applications, and a more productive workforce.

8.5.4 Current Trends in HCI

As with all computer technologies the Internet has brought many changes and new challenges to HCI. The World Wide Web is based on the concept of hypertext whereby documents are linked to related documents in efficient ways. Documents on the Internet use a standard coding scheme (HTML and URLs) to identify the locations of the linked documents. Specialized web browsers provide the interfaces for viewing documents on the web. Mosaic from the University of Illinois was the first popular web browser. Currently, open source Apache and Microsoft Internet Exchange (IE) provide the most widely used web browsers. New information exchange standards, such as the Extensible Markup Language (XML), will support improved methods for moving both data and metadata (e.g., semantics) on the WWW.

There are numerous important new directions in the field of HCI, for example

- Gesture recognition: The recognition of human gestures began with light pens and touch-sensitive screens. Hand writing recording and recognition is a subject of ongoing research.
- Three-dimensional graphics: Research and development on three-dimensional interfaces has been an active area, particularly in CAD-CAM systems. Three-dimensional visualization of the human body has the potential to revolutionize surgery and health care.
- Virtual reality: Scientific and business uses of virtual reality are just now being explored. Head-mounted displays and data gloves will become commercially viable in the near future for marketing demonstrations and virtual design walkthroughs.
- Voice recognition and speech: audio interfaces to computer systems have been available for the past decade. However, the limited vocabulary and requirements for specific voice pattern recognition remain problems to overcome before widespread use.
- Mobile devices: HCI and effective interfaces for mobile devices call for a full understanding of the challenges (e.g., battery power, small screen size) and opportunities (e.g., connectivity, computing power) found in handheld and wearable devices.

8.6 Software Development Processes and Methods

The four software design components of software architecture, algorithmic programming, data, and HCI are brought together in the design and implementation of a business application via software development processes and methods. A *software development process* is a pattern of activities, practices, and transformations that support managers and engineers in the use of technology to development and maintain software systems. A *software development method* is a set of principles, models, and techniques for effectively creating software artifacts at different stages of development (e.g., requirements, design, implementation, testing, and deployment). Thus, the process dictates the order of development phases and the transition criteria for transitioning from one phase to the next, while the method defines what is to be done in each phase and how the artifacts of the phase are represented. The history of software design and development has seen important advances in both software processes and software methods. We briefly track the evolution of these advances in this section.

8.6.1 Software Development Processes

In early software development projects very little attention was paid to organizing the development of software systems into stages. Programmers were given a problem to solve and were expected to program the solution for computer execution. The process was essentially "code and fix." As problems became more complex and the software grew in size this approach was no longer feasible.

The basic "waterfall process" was defined around 1970 (Royce 1970). A well-defined set of successive development stages (e.g., requirements analysis, detailed design, coding, testing, implementation, and operations) provided enhanced management control of the software development project. Each stage had strict entrance and exit criteria. Although it had several conceptual weaknesses, such as limited feedback loops and overly demanding documentation requirements, the waterfall process model served the industry well for over 20 years into the 1990s. The principal department of defense process standard for the development of system software systems during this period, DOD-STD-2167A, was based on the waterfall approach.

Innovative ideas for modeling software development processes include the *spiral model* (Boehm 1988) and *incremental development* (Trammell et al. 1996). The spiral model shows the development project as a series of spiraling activity loops. Each loop contains steps of objective setting, risk management, development/verification, and planning. Incremental development emphasizes the importance of building the software system in well-defined and well-planned increments. Each increment is implemented and certified correct before the next increment is started. The system is thus grown in increments under intellectual and management control.

A standard, flexible software development process is essential for management control of development projects. Recent efforts to evaluate the quality of software development organizations have focused on the software development process. The Software Engineering Institute (SEI) proposed the capability maturity model (CMM) to assess the maturity of an organization based on how well key process areas are performed (Paulk 1994). The CMM rates five levels of process maturity:

- Initial: Ad hoc process
- Repeatable: Stable process with a repeatable level of control
- Defined: Effective process with a foundation for major and continuing progress
- Managed: Mature process containing substantial quality improvements
- Optimized: Optimized process customized for each development project

The principal goal of the CMM was for organizations to understand their current process maturity and to work toward continuous process improvement. The international ISO-9000 standards contain similar provisions to evaluate the effectiveness of the process in software development organizations.

8.6.2 Early Development Methods

Early methods of program design were essentially ad hoc sketches of logic flow leading to the primary task of writing machine code. These design sketches evolved into flowcharting methods for designing program logic. Basic techniques also evolved for the development activities of requirements analysis, software design, and program testing.

The creation of software was initially considered more of a creative art than a science. As computing systems and software requirements became more complex into the 1960s, development organizations quickly lost the ability to manage software development in a predictable way. Defined development processes and methods brought some controls to software construction. Structured methods for the analysis and design of software systems appeared during the late 1960s and early 1970s. Two primary approaches were defined – *procedure-oriented methods* and *data-oriented methods*.

The development of procedure-oriented methods was strongly influenced by the sequential flow of computation supported by the dominant programming languages, COBOL and FORTRAN. The focus of software development under this paradigm is to identify the principal functions (i.e., procedures) of the business system and the dataflows among these functions. The system functions are hierarchically decomposed into more detailed descriptions of subfunctions and dataflows. After sufficient description and analysis, the resulting functions and data stores are designed and implemented as software modules with input–output interfaces. Primary examples of procedure-oriented system development methods include structured analysis and structured design methods (Stevens et al. 1974; Yourdon 1989).

Data-oriented system development places the focus on the required data. The data-centric paradigm is based on the importance of data files and databases in large business applications. System data models are developed and analyzed. System procedures are designed to support the data processing needs of the application. The design and implementation of the application software is constructed around the database and file systems. Primary data-oriented methods included the Warnier–Orr methods (Orr 1977) and information engineering (Martin 1989).

8.6.3 Object-Oriented Methods

In the early 1980s, object-oriented (OO) methods of software development were proposed for building complex software systems. Object orientation is a fundamentally different view of a system as a set of perceptible objects and the relationships among the objects. Each object in the application domain has a *state*, a set of *behaviors*, and an *identity*. A business enterprise can be viewed as a set of persistent objects. Business applications are developed by designing the relationships and interactions among the objects. Advocates point out several significant advantages of OO system development, including increased control of enterprise data, support for reuse, and enhanced adaptability to system change. Risks of OO development include the potential for degraded system performance and the startup costs of training and gaining OO experience. A plethora of OO development methods in the 1980s have converged into the unified modeling language (UML) standards (Fowler 2003).

8.6.4 Formal Development Methods

The requirement for highly reliable, safety-critical systems in business, industry, and the public sector has increased interest in formal software development methods. Formal methods are based on rigorous, mathematics-based theories of system behavior (Wing 1990; Luqi and Goguen 1997). Formal methods, such as the cleanroom methods (Mills et al. 1986; Prowell et al. 1999), support greater levels of correctness verification on all artifacts in the development process: requirements, design, implementation, and testing. The use of formal methods requires the use of mathematical representations and analysis techniques entailing significant discipline and training in the development team. While anecdotal evidence of the positive effects (e.g., improved quality and increased productivity) of formal methods is often reported (Gerhart et al. 1993) more careful study of the trade-offs in implementing formal methods are needed (Pfleeger and Hatton 1997).

8.6.5 Component-Based Development (CBD) Methods

The current widespread trend for the development of large-scale computing systems is component-based development (CBD). CBD extends the ideas of software reuse into a full-scale development process whereby complete business applications are delivered based upon the interaction and integration of software components (Brown 2000). A component is essentially a software module with well-defined interfaces to the external world. Thus, each component provides a service to the application system. New products and standards for middleware provide the "glue" for building systems from individual components. The technologies of DCOM, CORBA, and Enterprise JavaBeans are a start for enabling CBD processes and methods. Object-oriented concepts, such as encapsulation and class libraries, and emphasis on system architectures, such as *n*-tier client–server, support the realization of CBD in application environments.

8.6.6 Agile Development Methods

Agile software development espouses a philosophy of building software systems where requirements and working software evolve through interactions among self-organizing, cross-functional developer teams. The Agile Manifesto (2001), as developed by a core group of software thinkers, promotes the following set of principles:

"We are uncovering better ways of developing software by doing it and helping others do it. Through this work we have come to value:

- **Individuals and interactions** over processes and tools
- **Working software** over comprehensive documentation
- **Customer collaboration** over contract negotiation
- **Responding to change** over following a plan

That is, while there is value in the items on the right, we value the items on the left more."

A number of popular software development approaches, such as extreme programming (XP) (Beck and Andres 2005) and Scrum (Schwaber 2004), are based on the philosophy and practices of the agile movement.

8.6.7 Controlled-Flexible Development Methods

A central dynamic in software development is the trade-off between control and flexibility. Strong management control is desirable in environments with strict budgetary or schedule constraints and those that require high-quality results, such as safety-critical systems. This control is typically achieved through upfront development of a plan that defines system requirements, architectures, designs, budgets, and schedules with the hope that the development will proceed smoothly based on the pre-determined script. In executing the plan, the developers have limited flexibility to modify their activities within the plan's controls.

A movement to encourage flexibility in software projects has resulted in a number of development approaches, such as rapid prototyping (Baskerville and Stage 1996), synchronize and stabilize (Cusumano and Yoffie 1999), the rational unified process (RUP) (Kruchten 2000), and the agile approaches of XP and Scrum as mentioned in the previous section. The essence of flexibility is the ability to improvise in reaction to changes – changes in requirements, budgets, schedules, risks, etc.

The goal is to find the most effective trade-off between control and flexibility for each specific software development project. Boehm and Turner (2004) propose using project dimensions such as technology sophistication, project size, staffing expertise, diversity of stakeholders, and application domains. While others highlight the need to tailor development methods to projects (Fitzgerald et al. 2003; Fitzgerald et al. 2006). However, there is a scarcity of theory and practical guidance to describe the balance between control and flexibility for a software development project.

Recent work by Harris et al. (2009a, 2009b) proposes the use of emergent controls such as *scope boundaries* and *ongoing feedback* to understand the trade-offs between control and flexibility. Scope boundaries constrain the set of feasible solutions without dictating specific outcomes. These boundaries can be thought of as risk management mechanisms that shape the attention of the software team. Examples of scope boundaries from XP include a shared vision, partial specifications, predefined architectures, fixed APIs, and resource constraints. The intersection of all the scope boundary controls defines the feasible space for exploration.

Ongoing feedback in software development projects provide teams with checkpoints to validate that progress is headed in the right direction based on feedback from multiple stakeholders, including all members of the development team. Teams with few scope boundaries need more feedback.

For example, XP methods have broad boundaries but contain pervasive feedback techniques including pair programming, daily team review meetings, co-location of team members with visible progress indicators, daily software builds, co-location with customer representatives, and very short release cycles to gain broad market exposure. In contrast, the rational unified process (RUP) approach tightly defines development scope and only offers feedback through iteration releases. If scope boundaries are tightened sufficiently to remove all choice from the development team, there is no need for interim feedback and the approach becomes more of a specification-driven approach. Thus, the goal of a controlled-flexible development method is to achieve a trade-off among emergent outcome controls, balancing the restrictiveness of scope boundaries with opportunities for dynamic feedback.

References

Agile Manifesto (2001) *Manifesto for Agile Software Development*, http://agilemanifesto.org.

Bach, M. (1987) *The Design of the UNIX Operating System*, Prentice Hall, Englewood Cliffs, NJ.

Backus, J. (1979) The history of FORTRAN I, II, and III, *IEEE Annuals of the History of Computing* 1 (1), pp. 21–37.

Barrett, D., L. Clarke, P. Tarr, and A. Wise (1996) A framework for event-based software integration, *ACM Transactions on Software Engineering and Methodology* 5 (4), pp. 378–421.

Baskerville, R. and J. Stage (1996) Controlling prototype development through risk analysis, *MIS Quarterly* 20 (4), pp. 481–504.

Bass, L., P. Clements, and R. Kazman (2003) *Software Architecture in Practice*, 2nd edn, Addison-Wesley, Reading, MA.

Beck, K. and C. Andres (2005) *Extreme Programming Explained: Embrace Change, 2nd ed, XP Series*, Addison-Wesley, Inc., Boston, MA.

Bergin, T. and R. Gibson (eds) (1996) *History of Programming Languages II*, ACM Press, Addison-Wesley, Reading, MA.

Boehm, B. (1988) A spiral model of software development and enhancement, *IEEE Computer* 21 (5), pp. 61–72.

Boehm, B. and R. Turner (2004) *Balancing Agility and Discipline: A Guide for the Perplexed*, Addison-Wesley, Inc., Boston, MA.

Boehm, C. and G. Jacopini (1966) Flow diagrams, turing machines, and languages with only two formation rules, *Communications of the ACM* 9 (5), pp. 366–371.

Booch, G., R. Maksimchuk, M. Engel, B. Young, J. Conallen, and K. Houston, (2007) *Object-Oriented Analysis and Design with Applications*, 3rd edn, Addison-Wesley, Inc., Boston, MA.

Brown, A. (2000) *Large Scale Component Based Development*, Prentice-Hall PTR, Upper Saddle River, NJ.

Buxton, J. and B. Randell (1970) *Software Engineering Techniques: Report on a Conference Sponsored by the NATO Science Committee*, Rome, Italy, 1969, NATO.

Campbell-Kelly, M. and W. Aspray (1996) *Computer: A History of the Information Machine*, Basic Books, New York.

Codd, E. (1970) A relational model of data for large shared data banks, *Communications of the ACM* 13 (6), pp. 377–387.

Cusumano, M. and D. Yoffie (1999) Software development on Internet time, *IEEE Computer* 32 (10), pp. 60–69.

Dijkstra, E. (1968) The Go-To statement considered harmful, *Communications of the ACM* 11 (3), pp. 147–148.

Erl, T. (2005) *Service-Oriented Architecture (SOA): Concepts, Technology, and Design*, Prentice-Hall PTR, Upper Saddle River, NJ.

Fitzgerald, B., N. Russo, and T. O'Kane (2003) Software development tailoring at Motorola, *Communications of the ACM* 46 (4), pp. 65–70.

Fitzgerald, B., G. Hartnett, and K. Conboy (2006) Customizing agile methods to software practices at Intel Shannon, *European Journal of Information Systems* 15 (2), pp. 200–213.

Fowler, M. (2003) *UML Distilled: A Brief Guide to the Standard Object Modeling Language*, 3rd edn, Addison-Wesley, Inc., Boston, MA.

Gerhart, S., D. Craigen, and A. Ralston (1993) Observation on industrial practice using formal methods, *Proceedings of the 15th International Conference on Software Engineering*, Computer Society Press, Silver Spring, MD.

Gosling, J., B. Joy, G. Steele, and G. Bracha (2005) *The Java Language Specification*, 3rd edn, Addison-Wesley, Boston, MA.

Gray, J. (1996) Evolution of data management, *IEEE Computer* 29 (10), pp. 38–46.

Haeckel, S. and R. Nolan (1996) Managing by Wire: Using IT to Transform a Business from "Make and Sell" to "Sense and Respond", Chapter 7 in J. Luftman (ed.) *Competing in the Information Age: Strategic Alignment in Practice*, Oxford University Press, Oxford.

Harris, M., A. Hevner, and R. Collins (2009a) Controls in flexible software development, *Communications of the Association for Information Systems* 24 (43), pp. 757–776.

Harris, M., R. Collins, and A. Hevner (2009b) Control of flexible software development under uncertainty, *Information Systems Research: Special Issue on Flexible and Distributed Information Systems Development* 20 (3), pp. 400–419.

Henderson, J. and N. Venkatraman (1993) Strategic alignment: leveraging information technology for transforming organizations," *IBM Systems Journal* 32 (1), pp. 4–16.

Hevner, A. and D. Berndt (2000) Eras of Business Computing, in M. Zelkowitz (ed.) *Advances in Computers, Vol. 52*, Academic Press, Inc., San Diego, CA, pp. 1–90.

Jacobson, I. and P. Ng (2005) *Aspect-Oriented Software Development with Use Cases*, Addison-Wesley, Inc., Boston, MA.

Kast, F. and J. Rosenzweig (1972) General systems theory: applications for organization and management, *Academy of Management Journal* 15 (3), pp. 447–465.

Kruchten, P. (2000) *The Rational Unified Process: An Introduction*, 2nd edn, Addison-Wesley, Inc., Reading, MA.

Luqi and J. Goguen (1997) Formal methods: promises and problems, *IEEE Software* 14 (1), pp. 73–85.

Martin, J. (1989) *Information Engineering: Books 1-3*, Prentice-Hall, Englewood Cliffs, NJ.

Mills, H. (1986) Structured programming: retrospect and prospect, *IEEE Software* 3 (6), pp. 58–66.

Mills, H., R. Linger, and A. Hevner (1986) *Principles of Information Systems Analysis and Design*, Academic Press, Inc., Boston, MA.

Myers, B. (1998) A brief history of human-computer interaction technology, *Interactions* 5 (2), pp. 44–54.

Naur, P. and B. Randell (1969) *Software Engineering: Report on a Conference Sponsored by the NATO Science Committee*, Garmisch, Germany, 1968, NATO.

Orr, K. (1977) *Structured Systems Development*, Yourdon Press, Prentice-Hall, Englewood Cliffs, NJ.

Paulk, M. (ed.) (1994) *The Capability Maturity Model: Guidelines for Improving the Software Process*, Addison-Wesley, Reading, MA.

Peebles, R. and E. Manning (1978) System architecture for distributed data management, *IEEE Computer* 11 (1), pp. 40–47.

Pfleeger, S. and L. Hatton (1997) Investigating the influence of formal methods, *IEEE Computer* 30 (2), pp. 33–43.

Prowell, S., C. Trammell, R. Linger, and J. Poore (1999) *Cleanroom Software Engineering: Technology and Process*, Addison-Wesley, Inc., Reading, MA.

Ritchie, D. and K. Thompson (1974) The UNIX time-sharing system, *Communications of the ACM* 17 (7), pp. 365–375.

Royce, W. (1970) Managing the development of large software systems: concepts and techniques, *Proceedings of IEEE WESTCON*, Los Angeles.

Scherr, A. (1978) Distributed data processing, *IBM Systems Journal* 17 (4), pp. 324–343.

Schwaber, K. (2004) *Agile Project Management with Scrum*, Microsoft Press, Inc, Redmond, WA.

Shaw, M. and D. Garlan (1996) *Software Architecture: Perspectives on an Emerging Discipline*, Prentice-Hall, Englewood Cliffs, NJ.

Stevens, W., G. Myers, and L. Constantine (1974) Structured design, *IBM Systems Journal* 13 (2), pp. 115–139.

Stonebraker, M. (1996) *Object-Relational DBMSs: The Next Great Wave*, Morgan Kaufmann, San Francisco, CA.

Taylor, R., N. Medvidovic, and E. Dashofy (2009) *Software Architecture: Foundations, Theory and Practice*, John Wiley & Sons, Hoboken, NJ.

Trammell, C., M. Pleszkoch, R. Linger, and A. Hevner (1996) The incremental development process in cleanroom software engineering, *Decision Support Systems* 17 (1), pp. 55–71.

Wexelblat, R. (ed.) (1981) *History of Programming Languages I*, Academic Press, Boston, MA.

Wing, J. (1990) A Specifier's introduction to formal methods, *IEEE Computer* 23 (9), pp. 10–23.

Yourdon, E. (1989) *Modern Structured Analysis*, Yourdon Press, Prentice-Hall, Englewood Cliffs, NJ.

Zachman, J. (1987) A framework for information systems architecture," *IBM Systems Journal* 26 (3), pp. 276–292.

Chapter 9
Evaluation

> *I keep six honest serving men. They taught me all I knew. Their names are What and Why and When and How and Where and Who.*

> – Rudyard Kipling

Evaluation is a key element in the design of IT-based artifacts. A designer finds a suitable and interesting problem to solve. Then they come up with design solutions. That is followed by the actual build phase. After they have built the artifact, the next phase is evaluating for efficiency, utility, or performance.

Evaluation is a crucial component in the design science research process. The designed IT artifact is a socio-technical entity that exists within an environment (business or social) which lays out the requirements for its evaluation. Such evaluation of IT artifacts requires definition of appropriate metrics and possibly the gathering and analysis of appropriate data. IT artifacts can be evaluated in terms of functionality, completeness, consistency, accuracy, performance, reliability, usability, fit with the organization, and other relevant quality attributes (Hevner, March et al. 2004).

In this chapter, it is our goal to help the reader understand the different issues, questions, methods, and techniques that arise when one does evaluation. To present a full detailed analysis of various techniques is beyond the scope of this chapter or the book, but we hope that the reader will learn to ask the right questions, know when to apply which technique and be confident to look at the right places for more answers.

9.1 What Is Evaluation?

Evaluation is the systematic determination of merit, worth, and significance of something (information resource, healthcare program) or someone. Evaluation often is used to characterize and appraise subjects of interest in a wide range of human enterprises, including the arts, criminal justice, foundations and nonprofit organizations, government, health care, and other technology services.

A. Hevner, S. Chatterjee, *Design Research in Information Systems*, Integrated Series in Information Systems 22, DOI 10.1007/978-1-4419-5653-8_9,
© Springer Science+Business Media, LLC 2010

Most people understand the term "evaluation" as a means of making decision by measuring something. We all make evaluations in our everyday life. Let us take a simple example. You are planning to go on a holiday to the Greek Islands. But you are not sure which island(s) in Greece you must visit. So you look up information on some travel guide web sites. You may also call your friend and ask "So what did you think of Crete?" In effect what you are doing is collecting information, gathering data, analyzing what you have, and then make a choice – your conclusion and findings.

In information systems field, evaluation is rather difficult and complex. What do you evaluate? Do you evaluate the performance of the system (technical) or its overall usefulness to the end-user (socio-technical) or both? In our field, we study the collection, processing, and dissemination of variety of business information and we "build" IT artifacts – software and hardware – to facilitate such activities. Such information resources and systems exhibit a number of characteristics which could be studied (Friedman and Wyatt 1997). Take the example of a clinical decision support system in a hospital. The technically minded might focus on inherent characteristics, asking such questions as "How many queries can the system answer per second." But physicians who use such a system might ask more pragmatic questions such as "Is the knowledge base that drives this system up to date with current clinical protocols?" A hospital superintendent may have broader questions in mind "Are we seeing improvements in patient outcomes with the use of the CDSS?"

In this chapter, we do not describe exhaustively how each different evaluation method can be used to answer each kind of question. Instead we describe briefly the range of techniques available and focus on those that can be easily applied to various cases.

9.2 Why Do We Perform Evaluations?

There are many reasons for conducting evaluation studies. They are often dictated by stakeholders. Some of the reasons why we need to evaluate information systems include the following:

Promotional: To increase the adoption and use of IS within organizations, we must evaluate systems and show that they not only work but are safe, reliable, and cost-effective. This gives reassurance to CIOs and managers who then feel confident that they know the systems they are purchasing.

Scholarly: As a major scientific discipline, ongoing examination of the structure, function, and impact of information resources must be a primary method for uncovering its principles (Friedman and Wyatt 1997). Most often when reviewers examine new research, they tend to give importance to how well the system or proposed technology has been evaluated and compared against existing similar systems. In a design science conference, a paper with no evaluation is least likely to be accepted for publication.

Practical: Without evaluating their new systems, designers can never know which techniques or methods are more effective, or why certain approaches fail. It is only through evaluation that designers come to understand the nuances of their design and add to the body of knowledge for other future designers to learn from.

9.3 Differing Perspectives of Stakeholders

When an information system (or resource) is being evaluated, different stakeholders often have different perspectives. They all look at the same thing with different viewpoints. Let us take an example. Say that a new startup company has designed and launched a new product for noninvasive blood sugar measurement (see Fig. 9.1). As this product is launched, there are various stakeholders who are interested in its outcome. The stakeholders are patients (who will likely use the new device), doctors (who will likely recommend usage), designers/developers (who are motivated to see it succeed in the marketplace), and finally payers (who have funded the development and would like to get a return).

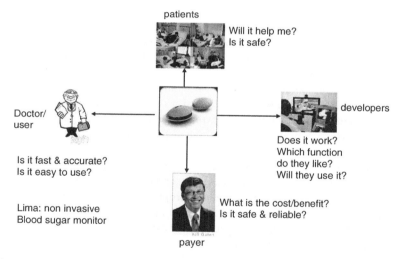

Fig. 9.1 Differing perspectives on a new technology device

For patients, the important questions are (1) will it help me? and (2) is it safe? For doctors, they are interested in (3) is it fast and accurate enough? and (4) is it easy to use for patients?

The developers are interested in a slightly different set of questions: (5) Does it work according to specification? (6) Which function would patients really like to see? and (7) Will they use it? The payers who funded the development are interested in (8) What is the cost/benefit ratio of this device? (9) Is it safe and reliable enough to become a market leader?

9.4 Basic Structure of Evaluation Studies

Irrespective of when, where, and how an evaluation is done, all evaluation studies have certain structure in common. That structure is shown in Fig. 9.2.

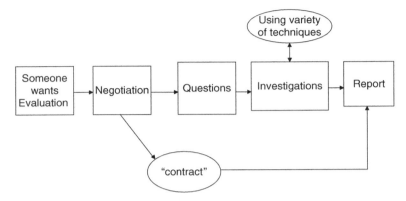

Fig. 9.2 Structure of an evaluation study

All evaluation is initiated by someone who needs to know. That someone could be the designer himself or it could be a funding agency who wants to know how something they have funded actually performs. It could be an individual or a group – but the evaluation must begin with a process of negotiation to identify the questions that will be a starting point for the study (Friedman and Wyatt 1997). The outcome of such negotiation is typically a set of questions and details on how the evaluation is to be conducted and for how long. All these understandings get into a written contract. The contract must be clear on the questions whose answers the evaluation is seeking.

The next step includes the actual investigations, collecting the data to address the questions and conducting experiments. The techniques for performing the evaluation are numerous. The data are analyzed appropriately to answer the questions we are asking. Finally a report is created for those individuals or groups who need to know. The format of the report must be in line with the stipulations of the contract; the content of the report follows from the questions asked and the data collected. Most reports are written documents although sometimes reports can be presented through live demos and presentations.

All evaluations can be broadly classified into two major philosophical groupings: objectivist and subjectivist. "Objectivist" approach is derived from a *logical-positivist* philosophical orientation – the same as in classic experimental sciences. "This position suggests that the merit and worth of an information resource can in principle be measured with all observations yielding the same result. Rational persons can and should agree on what attributes of a resource are important to measure and what results of these measurements would be identified as a most desirable, correct, or positive outcome" (Friedman and Wyatt 1997). Because numerical measurement allows precise statistical analysis of performance over time, it is prima facie superior to a verbal description. Hence primary analysis is conducted using quantitative methods.

"Contrast this to a subjectivist approach based on assumptions that derives from an *intuitionist–pluralist* philosophical position. This approach says that what is observed about a resource depends in fundamental ways on the observer" (Friedman and Wyatt 1997). Different observers of the same phenomenon might legitimately come to different conclusions. Both can be objective in their appraisals even if they do not agree. Merit and worth must be explored in context. The value of a resource emerges through study of the resource as it functions in a particular organizational or enterprise environment. Individuals and groups can legitimately hold different perspectives on what constitutes desirable outcomes. Verbal description can be highly illuminating and hence qualitative data are valuable.

Evaluation should be viewed as an exercise in argument, rather than as a demonstration, because any study appears equivocal when subjected to serious scrutiny.

9.5 The Art of Performance Evaluation

Performance is often a key criterion in the design of software systems and digital artifacts. Evaluation is critical for procurement and use of computer-based systems (Jain 1991). The goal of designers, scientists, analysts, and users is to get the highest performance for a given cost. All design science researchers must develop a basic knowledge of performance evaluation terminology and techniques.

When a designer designs and builds a "system," testing its performance through various techniques can be done for a variety of reasons. Some of them include the following:

- Comparing this system with other similar systems
- Determining the optimal value of a parameter (system tuning)
- Finding performance bottlenecks
- Characterizing the load on the system (workload characterization)
- Determining the number and sizes of components (capacity planning)
- Predicting the performance at future loads (scaling and forecasting).

The three main techniques used for performance evaluation are *analytical modeling, simulation, and measurement*. The term *metrics* refers to the criteria used to evaluate the performance of the system. Typical examples of metrics are response time or throughput. The requests made by the users of the system are called *workloads*. The workload of a database system would consist of queries and other requests it executes of users. A common everyday challenge faced by designers is to select performance metrics that should be used to compare the performance of the different kinds of systems. Take a moment to think what metric you would choose to evaluate the performance of

– two disk drives
– two transaction processing e-commerce systems
– two packet retransmission algorithms

Selecting an *evaluation technique* and *selecting a metric* are two key steps in all performance evaluation projects. There are a number of factors to explore before deciding on which evaluation technique to choose. Table 9.1 shows criteria for selecting an evaluation technique.

Table 9.1 How to select an evaluation technique (adopted from Jain, 1991)

No.	Criterion	Analytical modeling	Simulation	Measurement
1	Stage	Any	Any	Post-prototype
2	Time required	Small	Medium	Varies
3	Tools	Analysts	Software	Instrumentation
4	Accuracy	Low	Moderate	Varies
5	Trade-off evaluation	Easy	Moderate	Difficult
6	Cost	Small	Medium	High
7	Scalability	Low	Medium	High

Analytical modeling is mathematical calculations that can help to observe how variables of interest relate to other factors. Using simple and quick calculations we can find optimal values for variables of interest. We often use analytical modeling as a back-of-the-envelope calculation. Techniques such as queuing theory are examples of analytical modeling. *Simulations* deal with writing software code in a simulation language that mimics the behavior for the proposed system. It gives an easy way to visualize the performance of certain metrics over time. *Measurements* are possible only when a proposed system already exists. Measurement studies must be conducted carefully and are sometimes difficult to duplicate as conditions change. Measurements are the real thing.

As shown in Table 9.1, there are seven criteria in order of importance that can help designers choose an evaluation technique. The first criterion is the life cycle stage of the system. If the design or solution is in an idea stage, analytical and simulation techniques can be quickly applied. Measurement can only be applied at post-prototype stage. The second criterion is time required. This is often critical. Simulation code can take a lot of time to develop and so can actual measurement studies. But analytical models are quick to apply. Criteria 5 refer to trade-off evaluation. It is extremely easy to do that in analytical modeling by appropriately changing the symbols or equation. The cost of trade-off analysis is moderate and more difficult in a simulation which might require one to write new code for new components to be tested. It is extremely hard to do what-if scenarios with real systems. They are not flexible enough for rapid modification and reconfiguration. The other criteria listed in Table 9.1 are self-explanatory.

The goal of every performance study is either to compare different alternative designs or to find the optimal parameter value. Until validated, all evaluation results are suspect:

- Do not trust the results of a simulation model until they have been validated by analytical modeling or measurements
- Do not trust results of an analytical model until they have been validated by a simulation model or measurements
- Do not trust the results of a measurement until they have been validated by simulation or analytical modeling

9.6 Avoiding Common Mistakes in Performance Evaluation

No goals: Any endeavor without goals is bound to fail. The need for a goal may sound obvious, but many performance efforts are started without any clear goals (Jain 1991). A performance analyst and design team starts immediately to model or simulate the design. A common claim is that the model will be flexible enough to be easily modified to solve different problems. Experienced analysts know that there is no such thing as a general-purpose model. Each model must be developed with a particular goal in mind. Setting goals is not a trivial exercise.

Unsystematic approach: Often analysts adopt an unsystematic approach whereby they select system parameters, factors, metrics, and workloads arbitrarily. This leads to inaccurate conclusions. The systematic approach is to identify a complete set of goals, system parameters, factors, metrics, and workloads.

Analysis without understanding the problem: Many analysts feel that nothing is achieved without a model and numerical data in place. A large share of the analysis effort should go in to defining a problem. As they say, a problem well stated is half solved.

Incorrect performance metrics: A common mistake is that analysts choose those metrics that can be easily computed or measured rather than the ones that are relevant.

Wrong evaluation techniques: Analysts often have a preference of one technique over the other. Those proficient in queuing techniques will tend to change every performance problem to a queuing problem even if the system is too complex and easy to measure. The classic cliché "When you have a hammer, everything you see is a nail" applies to this mistake.

A systematic evaluation framework is shown in Fig. 9.3.

9.7 Conducting an Objectivist Comparative Study – A Brief Example

Socio-technical evaluation of the usefulness of IT artifacts designed to solve specific organizational or human problems is an important part of information systems study. In this brief example, we will introduce some key notions that are often utilized in objectivist evaluation studies. This is an example borrowed from the classic text on medical informatics evaluation by Friedman and Wyatt (1997). The domain of our example is medical informatics and hospital systems. Consider a hospital

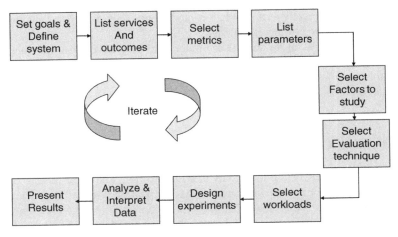

Fig. 9.3 A systematic evaluation process

that performs orthopedic surgery. It has been noticed that postoperative patients are developing a kind of infection. An IT design team is brought in and they develop a reminder system that prompts doctors to order prophylactic antibiotics for orthopedic patients to prevent postoperative infections. The intervention is the installation and commissioning of the reminder system; the subjects are the physicians and the tasks are the patients cared for by the physicians.

In a comparative study, the investigator typically creates a contrasting set of conditions to compare the effects of one with those of another. The researcher identifies a sample of participants. For example, it would be natural to compare a group of patients and their postoperative infection rates before and after the intervention; in this case the electronic reminder system. Some variable of interest is measured for each participant. The *dependent variable* forms a subset of the variables in the study that captures the outcomes of interest to the investigator. The *independent variables* are included in a study to explain the measured values of the dependent variables. Measurement challenges almost always arise in the assessment of the outcome or dependent variable for a study.

These types of studies are often called *before–after* studies. The investigator makes baseline measurements of antibiotic ordering and postoperative infection rates before the information resource is installed, and then makes the same measurements after it is in routine use. Initial hypothetical results are shown in Table 9.2.

Table 9.2 Baseline and post-installation results

	Antibiotic prescribing rate	Postoperative infection rate
Baseline results (before installation)	40%	10%
Post-installation results	60%	5%

Evaluator may claim that the halving of the infection rate can be safely attributed to the alert system, especially because it was accompanied by a 20% improvement in doctors' antibiotic prescribing. There might be many other factors that could have led to the perceived difference in results. If there was a long gap between the baseline and postoperative measurements, then during this gap, new staff may have been hired in the hospital, the case-mix of patients could have altered, new prophylactic antibiotics might have been introduced, or clinical audit meetings might have highlighted the infection problem causing greater clinical awareness. Simply assuming that reminder system caused the benefit is naive. What can we do to improve on this experiment?

One way to address some of the problems in the above conclusions is to use *simultaneous nonrandomized controls*. This calls for outcome measurements on doctors and patients not influenced by the prophylactic antibiotic reminder system but who are subject to the other changes taking place in the environment. If we do the before and after measurements for both groups, it strengthens the design because it gives an estimate of the changes due to the "nonspecific" factors taking place during the study period.

So in this new study design, two parallel groups are compared. One group gets to use the intervention (called the reminder group) and the other group does not get to use it (called the control group). We focus on postoperative infection rate as a single outcome measure or dependent variable. The independent variables are "time" and "group." Hypothetical results from the study are shown in Table 9.3.

Table 9.3 Postoperative infections in reminder and control groups

	Postoperative infection rates	
	Reminder group	Control group
Baseline results	10%	10%
Post-intervention results	5%	11%

There is the same improvement in the group where reminders were available, but no improvement (indeed slight deterioration) where no reminders were available. This finding shows a stronger inference toward the reminder system being the reason for improvement.

Even though the two parallel groups are simultaneous, skeptics may still refute our argument by claiming that there is some systematic, unknown difference between clinicians or patients in the reminder or control groups. One could argue that the control group must be in a specific ward within the hospital which is not very clean and where infection prevention maintenance is not taken seriously. Perhaps the reminder group is in a ward where hospital staffs have taken lots of steps to improve infections. How can we improve this design?

A better strategy is to ensure that the controls are truly comparable by randomizing them. We must remove any systematic differences, whether due to known or unknown factors. This can be done by randomizing. Thus we could randomly allocate half of the doctors on both wards to receive the antibiotic reminders and the remaining doctors to work normally. Table 9.4 shows the hypothesized results of such a study.

Table 9.4   Randomized postoperative infections between reminder and control

	Postoperative infection rates	
	Reminder physicians	Control physicians
Baseline results	11%	10%
Post-intervention results	6%	8%

As we see in the table, the baseline results for the two groups are almost similar as they were allocated to groups randomly. The reduction in infection rate is more in reminder group than that in the control group. The only systematic difference between the two groups of patients is the use of the reminder system by their doctors. If the sample size is large enough for these results to be statistically significant, we might conclude with some confidence that giving doctors the reminder system caused reduction in infection rates.

9.8   Threats to Inference and Validity

In the brief example above, we started with a random sample of population (patients and physicians). In our target sample, we showed through our randomized control experiments that the reminder system was truly responsible for reducing the infection rate. What if that was not true? If the system was truly effective and the study also shows that then we have reached a perfect equilibrium. But if the system was actually not effective but our study says so, then we have a false-positive or a type 1 error. Vice versa, if the system was actually effective but our experiment results showed that it was not then we would get a false-negative or type 2 error. The last quadrant of Fig. 9.4 shows that if the system was not effective and study also revealed that, then we are fair (Schroeder et al., 2007).

	System is truly effective	System is actually ineffective
Study shows It is	√	FP or type I error
Study shows It is not	FN or type II error	√

Fig. 9.4   Errors in evaluation

9.9 Conclusions

As a researcher conducting design science work, one can evaluate the technical aspects of your artifact or you could also evaluate the socio-technical aspects including usefulness and organizational impact. There are a number of different evaluation techniques one has at his/her disposal. If one pursues the technical performance aspect, then you could choose between analytical modeling, simulation, or actual measurements. If one chooses the organizational impact aspect, then you would conduct studies using quantitative surveys or qualitative interviews. It is important to keep in mind that even before design is available, one could evaluate needs and requirements through exploratory focus groups and after design is complete and artifact is in use, one could conduct confirmatory focus group studies (see Chapter 10).

Using *observational* case studies, one could study the designed artifact in depth in a certain business environment. Field studies can also monitor the use of artifact in multiple projects to gain valuable understanding of its value and utility. Several *analytical* techniques can be employed. In static analysis, one examines the structure of artifact for static qualities (e.g., complexity). Architecture analysis studies the fit of the artifact into technical information system architecture. In optimization studies, one can demonstrate inherent optimal properties of the artifact or provide optimality bounds on artifact behavior. Dynamic analysis typically studies artifact in use for dynamic qualities such as performance.

Experimental methods can include controlled experiments in which you study the artifact in controlled environment for qualities (e.g., usability). Using simulation models, one can execute the artifact with artificial data and observe dynamic performance behavior and scalability. *Testing* evaluation strategies can also be employed. Functional (black box) testing helps to discover failures, and defects. Structural (white box) testing usually performs coverage of testing of some metric (e.g., execution paths) in artifact implementation. Finally, *descriptive* evaluation methods may also be employed. One such method is the informed argument. It uses information from knowledge base to build a convincing argument for artifact's utility. Scenarios construction method constructs detailed scenarios around artifact to demonstrate its utility.

References

Friedman, C. P. and J. C. Wyatt (1997) *Evaluation Methods in Medical Informatics*, Springer-Verlag New York, LLC.

Hevner, A., S. March, J. Park, and S. Ram (2004) Design science in information systems research." *MIS Quarterly* 28 (1), pp. 75–105.

Jain, R. (1991) *The Art of Computer Systems Performance Analysis*, J. Wiley & Sons, Inc, New York.

Schroeder, L. D., D. L. Sjoquist, and P. E. Stephan (2007) *Understanding Regression Analysis: An Introductory Guide*. Sage Series: Quantitative Applications in the Social Sciences, No. 07-057.

Chapter 10
The Use of Focus Groups in Design Science Research

> *The only possible conclusion the **social** sciences can draw is: some do, some don't.*
>
> – Ernest Rutherford

Focus groups to investigate new ideas are widely used in many research fields. The use of focus groups in design science research poses interesting opportunities and challenges. Traditional focus group methods must be adapted to meet two specific goals of design research. For the evaluation of an artifact design, exploratory focus groups (EFGs) study the artifact to propose improvements in the design. The results of the evaluation are used to refine the design and the cycle of build and evaluate using EFGs continues until the artifact is released for field test in the application environment. Then, the field test of the design artifact may employ confirmatory focus groups (CFGs) to establish the utility of the artifact in field use. Rigorous investigation of the artifact requires multiple CFGs to be run with opportunities for quantitative and qualitative data collection and analyses across the multiple CFGs. In this chapter, we discuss the adaptation of focus groups to design science research projects. We demonstrate the use of both EFGs and CFGs in a design research doctoral thesis in the health-care field.

10.1 Introduction

The field of information systems has recognized the importance of design science as an opportunity to increase relevance (Venable, 2006). Hevner et al.'s (2004) information system research framework illustrates how both the behavioral and design science research paradigms in information systems follow similar cycles. Behavioral science research identifies a business need and develops and justifies theories that explain or predict phenomena related to this need. Design science research builds and evaluates artifacts that address particular business needs. Behavioral science researchers search for the truth, while design science researchers seek utility (Hevner et al., 2004).

Monica Chiarini Tremblay, Alan R. Hevner, and Donald J. Berndt

A. Hevner, S. Chatterjee, *Design Research in Information Systems*, Integrated Series
in Information Systems 22, DOI 10.1007/978-1-4419-5653-8_10,
© Springer Science+Business Media, LLC 2010

Design science research can be described as having two phases: the development of the artifact and its evaluation (which cycles for refinement of the design). A design researcher not only designs an artifact that provides utility but also provides evidence that this artifact solves a real problem. In fact, evidence-based artifact evaluation is crucial in design science research (Hevner et al., 2004). This requires that the artifact be evaluated within the technical infrastructure of the business environment. Several artifact evaluation methods have been outlined by researchers, including observation, analytics, experiments, testing or descriptive analysis, and more recently action research (Baskerville and Myers, 2004, Cole et al., 2005, Hevner et al., 2004, Iversen et al., 2004, Lindgren et al., 2004).

In this chapter we propose focus groups as an effective technique to be used for the improvement of an artifact design and for the confirmatory proof of its utility in the application field. We begin with a brief description and history of the focus group technique. Next, we outline the focus group methodology and propose adaptations for the evaluation of design artifacts. Finally, as an example, we describe a recently completed research study in which focus groups were used to both refine and evaluate the design science artifact.

10.2 Research Focus Groups

The focus group technique has long been utilized in social research to study ideas in a group setting (Morgan, 1988). A focus group is defined as a moderated discussion among 6–12 people who discuss a topic under the direction of a moderator, whose role is to promote interaction and keep the discussion on the topic of interest (Stewart et al., 2007). The term *focus* in the title refers to the fact that the interview is limited to a small number of issues. The questions in a focus group are open ended but are carefully predetermined. The set of questions or "questioning route" is meant to feel spontaneous but is carefully planned. Usually, the moderator encourages the sharing of ideas and careful attention is paid to understanding the feelings, comments, and thought processes of the participants as they discuss issues (Krueger and Casey, 2000). A typical focus group lasts about 2 h and covers a predetermined range of topics. Multiple focus groups allow for understanding the range of opinions of people across several groups and provide a much more natural environment than personal interviews because people are allowed to interact, which allows them to both influence and be influenced by others (Krueger and Casey, 2000). This is valuable to gain shared understandings but yet allows for individual differences of opinion to be voiced.

Focus groups have been effective both as a self-contained means of collecting data (as a primary research tool) or as a supplement to other methods of research (as a secondary research tool) (Krueger et al. 2000; Morgan 1988). The focus group technique is particularly not only useful as an *exploratory method* when little is known about the phenomenon but also can be used as a *confirmatory method* to test hypotheses (Stewart et al., 2007).

Originally coined "focused" interviews, focus groups were used during World War II by social scientists to explore morale in the US military for the War Department (Krueger and Casey, 2000, Merton and Kendall, 1946, Stewart et al., 2007). Though invented by academics, the focus group technique was mostly ignored by researchers because of the difficulties in demonstrating rigor in analysis and the fear of possible contamination of the interview process. Focus groups were, however, widely embraced by market researchers in the early 1950s. In fact, the use of focus groups continues to grow in the for-profit sector, accounting for 80% of industry-related qualitative research, and firms have been created to solely support all aspects of focus groups (Krueger and Casey, 2000, Stewart et al., 2007, Wellner, 2003).

In the 1980s, academics re-discovered focus groups as an alternative to other qualitative research, such as interviews and participant observation. Focus groups are now one of the most widely used research tools in the social sciences (Stewart et al., 2007). Researchers in both basic and applied behavioral science disciplines have utilized focus groups as a source of primary data. Education, management, sociology, communications, health sciences (particularly by clinicians), organizational behavior, social psychology, political science, policy research, and marketing are some of the disciplines utilizing focus groups. The diversity of the aforementioned fields suggests that focus groups can be effectively designed, fielded, and analyzed from varying perspectives and priorities.

Information systems' researchers have called for a broader variety of available empirical methods to improve relevance of research (Benbasat and Weber, 1996, Galliers, 1991) and we have seen increased attention on the use of focus groups in IS research (Baker and Collier, 2005, Debreceny et al., 2003, Jarvenpaa and Lang, 2005, Manning, 1996, Mantei and Teorey, 1989, Smith et al., 1996, Torkzadeh et al., 2006, Xia and Lee, 2005). Similarly, the software engineering community has suggested a need for a wider availability of empirical methods to improve validity and generalizability of their designs (Basili, 1996, Kontio et al., 2004). Several software engineers have also suggested their use as an evaluation and knowledge elicitation technique (Kontio et al., 2004, LeRouge and Niederman, 2006, Massey and Wallace, 1991, Nielsen, 1997). In the IT industry, focus groups are widely used in human–computer interface usability studies.[1]

We contend that there are several key reasons focus groups are an appropriate evaluation technique for design science research projects (based on Stewart et al. (2007), p. 42):

Flexibility: Focus groups allow for an open format and are flexible enough to handle a wide range of design topics and domains.

---

[1]For example, usability.gov is a U.S. government web site managed by the U.S. Department of Health & Human Services that outlines the use of focus groups in the design of web pages (see http://www.usability.gov/methods/focusgroup.html).

Direct Interaction with Respondents: This allows for the researcher to clarify any questions about the design artifact as well as probing the respondents on certain key design issues.

Large Amounts of Rich Data: The rich data allow deeper understandings, not only on the respondents' reaction and use of the artifact but also on other issues that may be present in a business environment that would impact the design.

Building on Other Respondent's Comments: The group setting allows for the emergence of ideas or opinions that are not usually uncovered in individual interviews. Additionally, causes of disagreement can point to possible problem areas with the proposed artifact.

10.3 Adapting Focus Groups to Design Research

The traditional literature outlines several steps for the conduct and analysis of focus groups. Obviously, given the breadth of usage and contexts for focus groups, each of these steps can be very different depending on the intent of the research. Figure 10.1 summarizes the basic steps that would be applicable for any research-oriented use of focus groups as found in Krueger et al. (2000), Bloor et al. (2001), Stewart et al. (2007), and Morgan (1988). We analyze each step taking into consideration the focal point of this chapter, the use of focus groups for refinement, and evaluation of a design science artifact.

10.3.1 Formulate Research Question or Problem

In order to effectively define and design the focus groups, the research goals must be clearly identified. In design science research if we seek to design an artifact, incrementally improve the design, and evaluate its utility, we are addressing two complementary, yet different research goals. We propose the use of two types of focus groups to achieve these different research goals: (1) *exploratory focus groups* (EFGs) to achieve incremental improvements in artifact design and (2) *confirmatory focus groups* (CFGs) to demonstrate the utility of the design in a field setting. In Fig. 10.2, we illustrate the positioning of the two types of focus groups in the design science research process. As discussed more fully in Hevner (2007), two forms of artifact evaluation are performed in a design research project – the evaluation of the artifact to refine its design in the design science build/evaluate cycle and the field testing of the released artifact in the application environment. We discuss the similarities and differences between EFGs and CFGs in the following focus group steps.

Exploratory focus groups have two roles: (1) the provision of feedback to be utilized for design changes to both the artifact and the focus group script and (2) the refinement of scripts and the identification of the constructs to be utilized in future focus groups. Feedback for improvement of the design of the artifact (Hevner

Fig. 10.1 Focus group steps

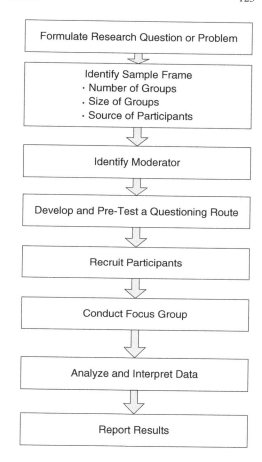

et al., 2004, Hevner, 2007, Markus et al., 2002) is an essential component of design research. Additionally, the questioning scripts can be refined to improve the quality of feedback received in subsequent EFGs. Finally, EFGs can be used to define and consequently refine the coding scheme that will be used for the analysis and interpretation of field testing in CFGs. The number of EFGs run depends on the number of build/evaluate cycles that use focus groups for evaluation. It is important to note that other evaluation methods (e.g., analytic optimization) may be used for early design cycles while focus groups may be used for later cycles of design refinement.

The CFGs are used to demonstrate the utility of the artifact design in the application field. When using focus groups for rigorous research, the unit of analysis will be the focus group and not the individual participants. Thus, it is crucial not to introduce any changes to the interview script and the artifact when multiple CFGs are conducted. This allows for the comparison of the results across CFGs to demonstrate and corroborate proof of utility of the artifact. The number of CFGs run in the

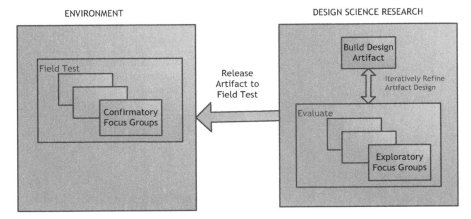

Fig. 10.2 Focus groups in design research

field test depends on the consistency of results across the focus groups and the level of rigor required in the design research project.

10.3.2 Identify Sample Frame

Three decisions are made in this step: (1) number of each type of focus group to run, (2) the desired number of participants in each group, and (3) where to recruit the participants.

10.3.3 Number of Focus Groups

Deciding how many focus groups to run can prove to be quite challenging. Unlike experimentation, there is no power test for the correct sample size. The literature states that focus groups should continue until nothing new is learned (Krueger and Casey, 2000), yet deciding "nothing new" is being learned is a difficult and somewhat arbitrary task. This is especially challenging in design science research. There is always room for improvement of an artifact and certainly a fair amount of subjectivity in interpreting when the design of an artifact is indeed complete. There is certainly a point where we may choose to satisfice in order to move forward. Additionally, there is a need to balance available people and resources, since focus groups can be expensive (most participants receive some sort of compensation) and expert participants may be difficult to find.

In our experience, at the minimum, one pilot focus group, two EFGs, and least two CFGs should be run. This allows for at least two design cycles and enough contrast for field test analysis. Since the unit of analysis is the focus group, it would be difficult to make a compelling argument for the utility of the designed artifact with a smaller number of CFGs.

10.3.4 Number of Participants

Selecting group size has several considerations. It may seem simpler (and less expensive) to run fewer, larger focus groups, since it takes less focus groups to hear from the same number of participants. Yet this could lower "sample size," since there are less groups to compare. Additionally, the dynamics of smaller versus larger groups are different; smaller groups require greater participation from each member and larger groups can lead to "social loafing" (Morgan, 1988). Morgan (1998) suggests a lower boundary of 4 participants and an upper boundary of 12 participants. Depending on the approach taken to demonstrate the artifact to the group, large focus groups (more than six) could be tricky in design research since the subject matter is more complex than traditional focus group topics, for example, a marketing campaign.

10.3.5 Participant Recruitment

The identification of focus group participants is not as statistically rigorous as it would be for survey research. Focus group participants are not randomly selected, but rather are selected based on their characteristics in relation to the topic that is being discussed. In fact, research shows that bringing together groups which are too diverse in relationship to the topic of interests could result in data of insufficient depth (Bloor et al., 2001). For design research the participants should be from a population familiar with the application environment for which the artifact is designed so they can adequately inform the refinement and evaluation of the artifact.

Research is mixed on whether to use pre-existing groups, though for design topics this may be advantageous since the participants have problem solved together and the focus group may approximate a realistic environment (Kitzinger, 1994). Interaction among participants is one of the most important aspects of focus groups. For example, a group of all technical experts may be very different than an expert/non-expert group (Stewart et al., 2007). A design science researcher must consider membership of the focus groups and how it aligns with the research objective early in the participant selection process.

Design researchers should strive to recruit participants that are familiar with the application environment and would be potential users of the proposed artifact. Unfortunately, in many cases such individuals are not easy to find, so plenty of time and effort should be allotted for this task. For instance, it might be possible to conduct the focus group in the evening (most participants will likely work) and offer dinner. Another good approach is to conduct the focus group at a place where the potential participants work, again enticing them with lunch or breakfast. Phone calls and e-mails should be placed at least a month before the focus groups are planned. A few days before the focus groups the participants should be reminded. Researchers should plan for a few participants to not show up, so if the goal is six people, invite eight.

10.3.6 Identify Moderator

Due to the open-ended nature of focus groups, moderation can be complex, especially in social research. Several skills are important when moderating a focus group. Krueger et al. (2000) found the following skills to be highly important: (1) respect for participants, (2) the ability to communicate clearly, both orally and in writing, (3) the ability to listen and the self-discipline to control personal views, and (4) a friendly manner and a sense of humor. For design research, the moderator not only needs to have these skills but also a clear understanding of the technical aspects of the design artifact. In many cases the moderator may be one of the artifact designers. In this case, the moderator has to be very careful not to introduce any personal bias in the presentation of the artifact (we tend to be proud of our work), particularly when conducting an EFG. It may be possible to enlist a second observer to guard against the encroachment of personal views (at least during the initial groups). This is an excellent time to receive good suggestions for improvement of the design and the designer has to be receptive to criticism and suggestions given by the participants, being careful to not justify or defend his work.

10.3.7 Develop and Pre-test a Questioning Route

The questioning route is the agenda for the focus group. In the questioning route you are setting the direction for a group discussion (Stewart et al., 2007) and it should closely align with your research objectives. There should be no more than 12 questions for a 2 h session (Krueger and Casey, 2000, Stewart et al., 2007). Two general principles outlined by Stewart et al. (2007, pg. 61) are to order the questions from the most general to the more specific and to order the topics by the relative importance to the research agenda. Thus, the topics to be discussed are ordered by importance, and within those topics, the questions are ordered from general to specific.

For a designed artifact, this means beginning with a broad explanation of scenarios where the artifact could be utilized, followed by a description of the artifact and how it is to be utilized and finishing with a scenario where focus group participants have the ability to utilize and evaluate the artifact.

For an EFG, the "rolling interview guide" (Stewart et al., 2007) is an excellent approach. With a rolling interview guide, a script is created for the first EFG but is changed for the next EFG, based on the outcome of the previous EFG. One of the advantages of this approach is that it allows for information to unfold over time as you discover more about how people would understand and use the artifact. However, it is imperative that no revisions are made to the interview guide in the CFGs, since continuous change would make comparisons across the focus groups difficult, compromising rigorous interpretation of the results (Stewart et al., 2007).

A promising evaluation approach in design research focus groups (both EFGs and CFGs) is to create a manipulation within the focus group. Participants can be asked to collectively complete a task without the artifact and then again with the artifact. The ensuing discussion should revolve around how the artifact was used and how the completion of the task was altered by its use.

10.3.8 Conduct the Focus Group

Focus group sessions should be fun and stimulating for the participants and moderator (Stewart et al., 2007). The moderator usually greets the participants as they enter and may ask them to fill out demographic information and informed consent forms (e.g., IRB forms). The participants are generally seated in a U-shape arrangement to encourage collaboration (Krueger and Casey, 2000) and allow space for the moderator to demonstrate the artifact. Seating arrangements are also very important. A good approach is to get to know the participants before the questioning route begins, as you greet them when they arrive. The most assertive and expert participant should be seated next to the moderator and the least talkative directly across from the moderator (Krueger and Casey, 2000, Stewart et al., 2007).

Depending on your research protocols, focus groups may be video and/or audio taped. Generally, the participants are told they are being recorded and most institutional review boards require written consent. It is also a good idea to have an observer. The observer will not participate in the focus group, rather will take careful notes, noting in particular any strong reactions, the participants' facial expression, and general tone of any exchange between participants or between the participant and the moderator (Stewart et al., 2007).

Time management is also important when conducting a focus group. A moderator should be able to recognize when all possible issues for a topic have been covered and move on to the next topic. Pilot focus groups can help anticipate and manage the length of focus groups.

Additional guidelines for running focus groups can be found in many excellent texts, such as Krueger and Casey (2000), Stewart et al. (2007), Bloor et al. (2001), and Morgan (1988).

10.3.9 Analyze and Interpret Data

The two design research goals for using focus groups are the incremental improvement of the design of the artifact and the demonstration of the utility of the design. For this reason, we have suggested the different focus group types of EFG and

CFG. While the objectives of the two group types are very different, the methods of analyzing the focus group data from both EFG and CFG can be similar. The interpretation of the focus group discussions has many of the same challenges in demonstrating rigor that all qualitative research encounters share. Several techniques that are used for qualitative data analysis can be considered, carefully selecting those techniques that emphasize the reliability and replicability of the observations and results (Stewart et al., 2007).

One possible approach is template analysis. Unlike a grounded theory approach (Desanctis and Gallupe, 1987), template analysis normally starts with at least a few pre-defined codes which help guide analysis. The first step in template analysis is to create an initial template by exploring the focus group transcripts, academic literature, the researchers' own experiences, anecdotal and informal evidence, and other exploratory research (King, 1998). The contents of the discussions are also examined for the meanings and implications for the research questions. Individual constructs should also be investigated, looking for common themes and variations within the constructs that would provide rich descriptions of the participants' reactions to design features.

In template analysis, the initial template is applied in order to analyze the text but is revised between each EFG session. Once the final template is created after the final EFG, it is used to code the CFG sessions.

10.3.10 Report Results

King (1998) suggests that qualitative results can be reported by creating an account structured around the main themes identified, drawing illustrative examples from each transcript as required. A similar approach can be taken when reporting focus group results. Short quotes are used to aid in the specific points of interpretation and longer passages of quotation are used to give a flavor of the original discussions. Summary tables can be very helpful, displaying both evidence and counter-evidence of the utility of the artifact by focus group. Rich descriptions can further corroborate results by using quotes from the focus group participants.

10.4 A Design Research Example

To illustrate the use of focus groups in a design research project, we discuss a recently completed research project in which an artifact was designed and evaluated in the health-care context. The research investigated issues of data quality in the context of public policy health planning. Three data quality problems are identified and a set of quality metrics are designed to support improved decision making. These metrics aid human decision makers to better understand the quality of the data they have and how to overcome inherent decision-making biases in the presence of potentially incomplete and unreliable information from multiple sources.

10.4.1 Research Context

Like other business organizations, the health-care sector is increasingly becoming an information-driven service (Al-Shorbaji, 2001, Derose and Petitti, 2003, Derose et al., 2002, Friede et al., 1995), particularly for public policy and health planning. In fact, information systems are becoming an integral part of public health decision making. Information acquisition can now be transacted rapidly (Chapman and Elstein, 2000, Maibach and Holtgrave, 1995, U.S., 1995) and from several sources. To improve public health's efficacy and profile, both practitioners and researchers need reliable and timely information to make information-driven or evidence-based decisions (Friede et al., 1995). This study focused on this rich health planning domain, in particular on a set of specific decision-making activities related to community needs assessment.

Figure 10.3 illustrates the research process used to identify potential data quality measures and biases. A field study was conducted (Tremblay et al., 2007) and combined with a review of the literature. Several data quality issues and biases were selected as the focus of the research.

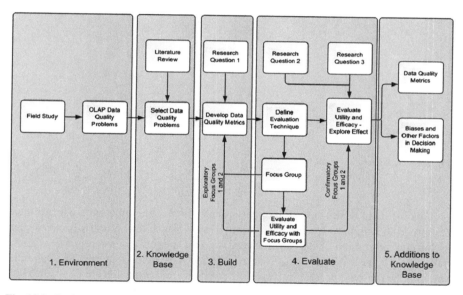

Fig. 10.3 Design research process

10.4.2 Data Quality Metrics Description

Information supply chains (ISC) (Ballou et al., 1998, Ballou and Pazer, 1985, Shankaranarayan et al., 2003) can be complex, multi-step processes that include the collection of raw data from many sources, comprised of intermediate transformations, compositions, and standardizations that ultimately supply the raw data for insightful analysis.

As shown in Fig. 10.4, data quality can be assessed as part of the original data collection process and propagated through transformations and compositions made by the ISC as part of lineage-driven data quality measurement. In contrast, result-driven data quality proceeds from the information product endpoint, with knowledge of the context, and works backward to provide measures that assist decision makers in understanding the uncertainties that account for possible poor decision making due to well-known judgment biases. Result-driven data quality is especially important in an environment where managers and decision makers utilize aggregated data (summary information) retrieved from several data sources in the information supply chain to make tactical decisions.

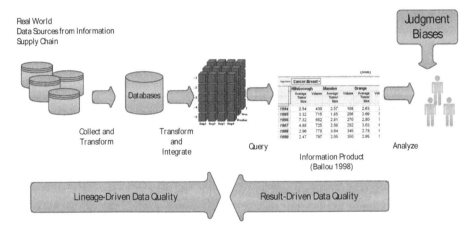

Fig. 10.4   Research landscape

This is true in health care, and in particular in health planning, where health-care resource allocation is often based on summarized data from a myriad of sources such as hospital admissions, vital statistic records, and specific disease registries. These data are utilized to justify investments in services, reduce inequities in treatment, and rank health-care problems to support policy formulation (Berndt et al., 2003).

This project presented methodologies that communicated result-driven data quality (RDQ) information at decision time with simple and comprehensible metrics that can be calculated when the final information product (IP) is created. The decision maker is not involved in the calculation of the metric but considers the metrics as they formulate a context-specific decision. We consider how to present information on the three data quality dimensions for any unique information product in an online analytical processing (OLAP) environment. This project proposed three data quality measures and associated data quality metrics (DQMs) which are summarized in Table 10.1.

Table 10.1 Data Quality Metrics

Data quality problem (Wang and Strong, 1996)	Metric
Completeness: A problem is encountered when combining or aggregating data from multiple sources in the ISC that is missing codes or has codes that do not match other sources of data. This results in data that are not assigned to any of the possible cells in a data cube	*Unallocated data metric* which considers the effects of null values in any of the grouping or filtering variables for *counts* and for *averages*. It proposes a case-based approach for presenting unallocated data to a decision maker, which gives flexibility for the decision maker to consider different "what if" scenarios
Representational consistency: When considering aggregated data or when observing trends, decision makers rely on point estimates, such as an average, which may be biased by noisy data	*Information volatility metric* is a measure of reliability proposed as an addition to OLAP tools when considering aggregated data or when observing trends. Two types of information volatility are defined: intra-cell and inter-cell
Appropriate amount of data: Insensitivity to sample size by decision makers when considering/comparing groupings	*Sample size indicator* is a simple method of drawing the attention of the decision maker in order to mitigate a well-known bias

The data quality metrics are designed and implemented in order to present these metrics in an effective way to decision makers. We considered several alternative evaluation methods and selected the focus group technique as the most appropriate for the research context. The research process in Fig. 10.3 shows the use of both EFGs and CFGs.

10.4.3 Design Research Questions

In order to correctly design the focus group scripts and identify qualified participants the research questions are clearly identified. The research issues for the EFGs are how to improve the design artifact and how to develop a rigorous and comprehensive focus group script and coding schema.

For the CFGs two research questions are formulated:

What are the utilities of the data quality metrics in a realistic field context?

What are the efficacies of the data quality metrics to alter a decision maker's data analytic strategies by eliminating inherent human bias via better understanding of the data?

10.4.4 Identify Sample Frame

A total of five focus groups of 6–12 participants are executed. The first focus group was a pilot to help identify timing issues, refine the questioning route, evaluate the moderator's style, and surface any potential logistical issues. The pilot data were not used further for data analysis.

The following requirements are outlined for the participants of EFGs and CFGs: previous experience with decision making in the health-care field, an advanced college degree, and some training in statistics and decision-making software systems.

10.4.5 Identify Moderator

The moderator is the primary researcher who had some experience in moderating focus groups in both educational and industrial settings. Another researcher serves as an observer to take careful notes and to support the moderator in time keeping.

10.4.6 Develop a Questioning Route

The planning process includes creating a carefully planned script in which all three of the designed metrics are presented to the participants (see Appendix A for a partial script). The research utilizes the "rolling interview guide" (Stewart et al., 2007) for the EFGs. A script is created for the first focus group. Then, based on the outcomes of the first EFG, the guide is revised for use in the second EFG. Based on the outcome of the second EFG, the script, the coding template, and the metrics are revised again. No revisions are made during the execution of the CFGs.

"Vignettes" or story lines are used to create fictitious decision scenarios based on current health-care situations (in recent news reports) and sample health-care data. These data include data from a statewide cancer registry, which has been collecting incidence data since 1981, county data from the US Census Bureau, demographic data from commercial sources, and an internally generated time dimension. The strategy is to present the data with and without the metrics information in order to detect differences in the collective decision-making processes. Thus, we develop an experimental manipulation within the context of a focus group. A PowerPoint presentation is used to describe the vignettes and the metrics. The moderator presents the health-care decision-making context.

Table 10.2 shows examples of the vignettes used in the focus groups

10.4.7 Recruit Participants

Potential participants are identified via personal contacts and phone calls to county public health departments. The potential focus group members are given a brief description of the study and their participation is requested. They are offered dinner after the focus group session. Many of the participants had taken university courses in data warehousing and/or data mining. Several other participants had jobs that

Table 10.2 Example of vignettes

Metric evaluated	Vignette	Decision
Unallocated data metric	Studies have shown that smoking is responsible for most cancers of the larynx, oral cavity and pharynx, esophagus, and bladder. In addition, it is a cause of kidney, pancreatic, cervical, and stomach cancers, as well as acute myeloid leukemia	Is there correlation between smoking and certain types of cancer?
Unallocated data metric	When Hispanics are diagnosed with a certain cancer (fictitious example), they are less likely to receive chemotherapy than non-Hispanics	Is there disparity in care between ethnic groups?
Information volatility metric	Counties neighboring the target county are better at early detection/prevention of breast cancer based on volumes of cases	Examine trend – is this a true claim?
Sample size indicator	Tumor size has been shown to be a good predictor of survival for certain cancers, including breast, lung, and endocrine. Compare average tumor size in the target county to that of neighboring counties	How does the target county compare to other counties?

required use of data analytics (e.g., spreadsheets, business intelligence tools, statistics packages). To illustrate the qualifications of participants in one of the focus groups, Table 10.3 shows the demographic characteristics from one of the focus groups.

10.4.8 Conduct Focus Groups

The focus groups are held in state-of-the-art conference rooms. The participants are seated in a U-shape arrangement to encourage collaboration (Krueger and Casey, 2000) and to allow space for the moderator to demonstrate the design artifacts and PowerPoint presentation. The moderator presents the experimental vignettes and encourages the participants to play the role of a health-care decision maker. In order to analyze the data, the focus group guides the moderator in exploring the health-care data. For example, participants are encouraged to ask the moderator to drill down or roll up data in order to thoroughly understand and compare data for different counties as part of their decision-making process.

The participants are asked to come to consensus on a particular task without the data quality metric. They are then asked to reconsider the decision utilizing the data quality metric. The ensuing discussion revolves around how the data quality metric is used and how the metric affected their decision making. The sessions are recorded and professionally transcribed.

Table 10.3 Sample focus group participants

Gender	Age	Last degree	Current position	Course in statistics?	Years of work experience	Years of health-care experience	Self-reported comfort with data analysis (7-point scale)
M	34	PhD	Health economist	Y	7	6	7
M	51	PhD	Assistant director of measurement and evaluation	Y	28	28	7
F	49	PhD	Researcher	Y	28	28	5
F	35	PhD	Project manager/data analyst/health science specialist	Y	9	9	5
M	56	PhD	Health services researcher	Y	25	20	6
F	31	MA/MPH	Program specialist	Y	8	7	5
F	31	MSPH	Project manager	Y	8	6	7
F	36	PhD	Health economist	Y	NR	3	7

After conducting each of the EFGs, significant changes are made to both the design artifacts (the data quality metrics) and to the focus group scripts and coding templates. The observer helps refine the focus group script used in the EFG. He carefully observes people's understanding of the scenarios, their reaction to the metrics and the flow of the conversation and takes notes. The notes are carefully analyzed and changes are made to the focus group script for the next EFG. For example, the observer noted that the moderator needed to better clarify the goal of research, in particular he needed to give a clearer description of who normally would utilize these types of tools and for what sorts of tasks. Once the CFG begins, no changes are made to the questioning route.

10.4.9 Analyze and Interpret the Data

10.4.9.1 Template Analysis

Template analysis is selected for the interpretation of the focus group discussions. The initial template has a few pre-defined codes which focus on aspects of the data quality metrics. The contents of the focus group discussions are examined for their meanings and their particular implications for the research questions, in our case, changes in data analytic strategies and evidence or counter-evidence of the metrics' usefulness. Individual constructs are investigated, looking for common themes and variations within the constructs that would provide rich descriptions of the participants' reactions to design features and attitudes to decision making with varying levels of data quality as defined by the designed metrics. In addition, several other coding categories are created during coding to explore the entire range of participants' reactions (see Table 10.4 for a partial coding template for the information volatility metric).

Table 10.4 Partial final coding scheme

Construct	Definition
Volatility before	Strategies to deal with volatility prior to receiving metric Interpretation before
Volatility after	Strategies to deal with volatility after receiving metric Interpretation after
Design feature volatility	Mention of the information volatility feature, design improvement suggestion
Speculation	Speculation on data quality problems
Other factors in decision making	Including stakeholder issues

Once the template is completed and agreed upon by the researchers, the transcripts for the first EFG are coded by identifying sections that are relevant and annotating the appropriate codes from the initial template. Cohen's kappa is used to measure inter-rater reliability (Cohen, 1960). The results are then reconciled between coders. The two independent coders discuss the areas of disagreement, stopping when agreement is reached on all higher ordered codes and most of the lower order codes (King 1998). The transcripts are then recoded based on the reconciliation between the two coders.

10.4.10 Report Results

The identified constructs of utility and efficacy are investigated. Utility is defined as "usefulness of the metric" and efficacy as "having the ability to change data analytic strategies." To analyze utility of the metric all passages that are coded as "design feature" are analyzed. Changes in data analytic strategies are evaluated contrasting the passages coded as "before" and "after" for each metric.

For each of the metrics proposed in the study both evidence and counter-evidence of the utility and efficacy of the metrics are presented. The qualitative data are summarized for both utility and efficacy, and then rich descriptions are given using quotes from the focus group participants to corroborate the results.

Table 10.5 is an example of the summary for one of the data quality metrics, information volatility. The results are summarized by focus groups. For this particular metric, the design is improved by adding benchmarking information based on the results from one of the exploratory focus groups. The benchmarking idea came from a participant in the second EFG:

> You (need to) draw a line in the sand and say, this is a problem, this is not. And maybe if it goes over that line, it pops up and says, 'Hey, check this out.'

Table 10.5 Utility of information volatility metric

Focus group	Evidence of utility	Counter-evidence of utility
EFG1	Yes	Difficulty interpreting
EFG2	Yes	Difficulty interpreting
CFG1	Yes – saw several instances where this would be useful in their daily data analysis	None
CFG2	Yes	None

This was corroborated by a remark from a participant on one of the CFGs:

> …benchmarking is a necessary component of it.

Similarly, Table 10.6 shows how the efficacy of the same metric is evaluated. This particular example points out one of the limitations of the use of focus groups. We ran two CFGs to field test the set of design metrics. For the volatility metric, no efficacy data were collected from one of the CFGs. This group was dominated by an individual who rejected the validity of the vignette presented to evaluate the metric. The individual convinced the group to refuse to make a decision. Thus to study this metric, at least one more focus group needs to be run to show stronger evidence.

Table 10.6 Efficacy of information volatility metric

Focus group	Change in data analytic strategies?	Comments/observed changes
EFG1	Yes	
EFG2	Yes	
CFG1	N/A	Rejected task, group disliked low realism of the vignettes, refused to make decision
CFG2	Yes	

10.5 Limitations on the Use of Focus Groups for Design Research

We observed several limitations in the use of focus groups in the evaluation of artifacts. Generalization to a larger population can be difficult for several reasons. The first is due to the convenience nature of focus group recruiting practices. It is particularly difficult to find adequate participants when evaluating artifacts due to the technical nature of the subject which limits the pool of possible participants. Additionally, individual responses cannot be considered because of the interaction between respondents and between respondents and the moderator. A strongly opinionated member may bias the results and discourage other participants from speaking, as we saw in the above example.

Another limitation lies in the difficulty of deciding how many focus groups to run. Unlike experimentation there is no power test for the correct sample size. The focus groups literature states that focus groups should continue until nothing new is learned (Krueger and Casey, 2000), yet deciding whether "nothing new" is being learned is a difficult and somewhat arbitrary task. When considering the design of the artifact, the EFG continuously produced new ideas and suggestions, making the decision to stop and move on to CFG somewhat subjective. Deciding how many CFGs to run is also difficult. In our study the two CFGs found some differing results, thereby highlighting the need for additional CFGs. The choice will most likely be driven by the costs of running focus groups and difficulty in finding additional expert participants.

A very important aspect of conducting focus groups is an effective moderator who is skilled in drawing information from the participants, encourages interaction between participants, and is non-authoritarian and non-judgmental (Stewart et al., 2007). The moderator has to be careful to not bias the results during the focus groups. In our example, the moderator had control of the interface in which the data and metrics were presented to the groups, which certainly led to different results than if the focus group participants had been able to access them directly at their own workstations. However, the goal was to focus the attention of all the participants at the same point to enable common discussion.

10.6 Closing Remarks

The goal of this chapter is to propose focus groups as a useful method for two of the fundamental goals of design science research: refinement of a proposed artifact and demonstration of its utility. We outline how traditional focus group methods can be adapted for these purposes. For the evaluation of an artifact design, *exploratory focus groups* (EFGs) study the artifact to propose improvements in the design, continuing the cycle of build and evaluate until the artifact is released for field test in the application environment. Then, the field test of the design artifact may employ *confirmatory focus groups* (CFGs) to establish the utility of the artifact in field use.

Rigorously designing, planning, selecting participants, conducting, analyzing, and reporting the results of the focus groups have unique concerns as adapted to design science research and we outline several potential approaches for each step in the focus group process. Additionally, the data generated by this methodology are qualitative and we describe a process to capture, code, analyze, and report these data in a rigorous manner.

As we conducted the focus groups, we were encouraged by the emergence of rich ideas and concepts that emerged when using this qualitative technique. The intent of this example research study was the evaluation of the proposed data quality metrics, but several other "user views" of data quality emerged that merited serious consideration and will stimulate further research. The open-ended nature of focus groups allowed for the identification of new artifact ideas, several of which we are currently pursuing.

The focus group technique allowed the researchers to observe data quality in action in actual decision making. One interesting finding, for example, was that though participants were skeptical of the data in the examples (which for the most part was from a real ISC!), they were not skeptical about their own data (data that they utilized in their jobs), perhaps because they have very high ownership of those data and believe their data to be of high quality, even though this is rarely true. We observed that several "irrational" approaches were taken to analyze the data. These included speculating on the reasons for poor data quality without any real evidence (e.g., Hispanics do not go to the doctor as much as other ethnic groups.).

Certainly there are many other avenues to explore in the use of this technique. In every step we outline, there may be diverse approaches that are contingent on the artifact and the application domain. For example, the design of the focus group script will be very different for varying application domains. In our case, we dealt with a decision-making environment in the health-care industry, but another approach may be needed if the context is significantly different (for example, a supply chain bid recommendation agent). In fact, this technique is most appropriate where observational methods can be used for evaluation. Also, template analysis worked well for our study but we undoubtedly can draw from the work of other qualitative researchers for guidance on other ways to analyze transcribed focus groups.

To conclude, we believe that focus groups are a highly relevant and rigorous approach for improving and evaluating design artifacts. However, it is critical that researchers adapt traditional focus group methods to the goals of design science research projects in the forms of exploratory focus groups and confirmatory focus groups. The contributions of this chapter are the explication of how design science focus groups can be performed in order to achieve these research goals and the presentation of an exemplar design science research project that effectively used focus groups for both exploratory and confirmatory evaluations.

References

Al-Shorbaji, N. (2001) Health and Medical Informatics: Technical Chapter, in *Health Information Support, Regional Office for the Eastern Mediterranean, World Health Organization*, Cairo, Egypt.

Baker, T. and D. A. Collier (2005) The Economic Payout Model for Service Guarantees, *Decision Sciences* 36 (2), p. 197.

Ballou, D., R. Wang, H. Pazer, and G. K. Tayi (1998) Modeling information manufacturing systems to determine information product quality, *Management Science* 44 (4), pp. 462–484.

Ballou, D. P. and H. L. Pazer (1985) Modeling data and process quality in multi-input, multi-output information systems, *Management Science* 31 (2), pp. 150–162.

Basili, V. R. (1996) The role of experimentation in software engineering: past, current, and future, in *Proceedings of the 18th International Conference on Software Engineering*, Berlin, Germany, IEEE Computer Society.

Baskerville, R. and M. D. Myers (2004) Special issue on action research in information systems: making is research relevant to practice-foreword, *MIS Quarterly* 28 (3), p. 329.

Benbasat, I. and R. Weber (1996) Research commentary: rethinking "diversity" in information systems research, *Information Systems Research* 7 (4), p. 389.

Berndt, D. J., A. R. Hevner, and J. Studnicki (2003) The CATCH data warehouse: support for community health care decision-making, *Decision Support Systems* 35 (3), p. 367.

Bloor, M., J. Frankland, M. Thomas, and K. Robson (2001) *Focus Groups in Social Research*, Sage, London.

Chapman, G. B. and A. S. Elstein (2000) Cognitive Processes and Biases in Medical Decision Making, in G. B. Chapman and F. A. Sonnenberg (eds.) *Decision Making in Healthcare: Theory, Psychology and Applications*, Cambridge University Press, Cambridge.

Cohen, J. (1960) A coefficient of agreement for nominal scales. *Educational and Psychological Measurement* 20 (1), pp. 37–46.

Cole, R., S. Purao, M. Rossi, and M. k. Sein. (2005) Being proactive: where action research meets design research, in *Twenty-Sixth International Conference on Information Systems*, Las Vegas, 2005.

Debreceny, R., M. Putterill, L.-L. Tung, and A. L. Gilbert (2003) New tools for the determination of e-commerce inhibitors, *Decision Support Systems* 34 (2), p. 177.

Derose, S. F. and D. B. Petitti (2003) Measuring quality of care and performance from a population health care perspective, *Annual Review of Public Health* 24 (1), pp. 363–384.

Derose, S. F., M. A. Schuster, J. E. Fielding, and S. M. Asch (2002) Public health quality measurement: concepts and challenges, *Annual Review of Public Health* 23 (1), pp. 1–21.

Desanctis, G. and R. B. Gallupe (1987) A foundation for the study of group decision support systems, *Management Science* 33 (4), pp. 589–609.

Friede, A., H. L. Blum, and M. McDonald (1995) Public health informatics: how information-age technology can strengthen public health, *Annual Review of Public Health* 16 (1), pp. 239–252.

Galliers, R. D. (1991) Choosing appropriate information systems research approaches: a revised taxonomy, in H. E. Nissen, H. K. Klein, and R. Hirschheim (eds.) *Information Systems Research: Contemporary Approaches and Emergent Traditions*, Elsevier Science Pub., Amsterdam, The Netherlands.

Hevner, A., S. March, J. Park, and S. Ram (2004) Design science research in information systems, *Management Information Systems Quarterly* 28 (1), pp. 75–105.

Hevner, A. R. (2007) A three cycle view of design science research, *Scandinavian Journal of Information Systems* 19 (2), pp. 87–92.

Iversen, J. H., L. Mathiassen, and P. A. Nielsen (2004) Managing risk in software process improvement: an action research approach, *MIS Quarterly* 28 (3), p. 395.

Jarvenpaa, S. L. and K. R. Lang (2005) Managing the paradoxes of mobile technology, *Information Systems Management* 22 (4), p. 7.

King, N. (1998) Template Analysis, in G. Symon and C. Cassell (eds.) *Qualitative Methods and Analysis in Organizational Research*, Sage Publications, London.

Kitzinger, J. (1994) The methodology of Focus groups: the importance of interaction between research participants. *Sociology of Health* 16 (1), pp. 103–121.

Kontio, J., L. Lehtola, and J. Bragge (2004) Using the focus group method in software engineering: obtaining practitioner and user experiences, *International Symposium on Empirical Software Engineering Proceedings of the 2004 International Symposium on Empirical Software Engineering*, IEEE Computer Society, Washington, DC, pp. 271–280.

Krueger, R. A. and M. A. Casey (2000) *Focus Groups: A Practical Guide for Applied Research*, 3rd edn, Sage Publications, Thousand Oaks, CA.

LeRouge, C. and F. Niederman (2006) Information systems and health care Xi: public health knowledge management architecture design: a case study, *Communications of the Association for Information Systems* 18, p. 15.

Lindgren, R., O. Henfridsson, and U. Schultze (2004) Design principles for competence management systems: a synthesis of an action research study, *MIS Quarterly* 28 (3), p. 435.

Maibach, E. and D. R. Holtgrave (1995) Advances in public health communication, *Annual Review of Public Health* 16 (1), pp. 219–238.

Manning, P. K. (1996) Information technology in the police context: the "sailor" phone, *Information Systems Research* 7 (1), p. 52.

Mantei, M. M. and T. J. Teorey (1989) Incorporating behavioral techniques into the systems development, *MIS Quarterly* 13 (3), p. 257.

Markus, M. L., A. Majchrzak, and L. Gasser (2002) A design theory for systems that support emergent knowledge processes, *MIS Quarterly* 26 (3), pp. 179–212.

Massey, A. P. and W. A. Wallace (1991) Focus groups as a knowledge elicitation technique: an exploratory study, *IEEE Transactions on Knowledge and Data Engineering* 3 (2), pp. 193–200.

Merton, R. K. and P. L. Kendall (1946) The focused interview, *The American Journal of Sociology* 51 (6), pp. 541–557.

Morgan, D. L. (1988) *Focus Groups as Qualitative Research*, Sage Publications, Newbury Park, CA.

Nielsen, J. (1997) The use and misuse of focus groups, *IEEE Software* 14 (1), pp. 94–95.

Shankaranarayan, G., M. Ziad, and R. Y. Wang (2003) Managing data quality in dynamic decision environments: an information product approach, *Journal of Database Management* 14 (4), pp. 14–32.

Smith, H. J., S. J. Milberg, and S. J. Burke (1996) Information privacy: measuring individuals' concerns about organizational practices, *MIS Quarterly* 20 (2), p. 167.

Stewart, D. W., P. N. Shamdasani, and D. W. Rook (2007) *Focus Groups: Theory and Practice*, 2nd edn., vol. 20, Sage Publications, Newbury Park, CA.

Torkzadeh, G., J. C.-J. Chang, and G. W. Hansen (2006) Identifying issues in customer relationship management at Merck-Medco, *Decision Support Systems* 42 (2), p. 1116.

Tremblay, M. C., R. Fuller, D. Berndt, and J. Studnicki (2007) Doing more with more information: changing healthcare planning with OLAP tools, *Decision Support Systems* 43 (4), pp. 1305–1320.

U.S. Congress (1995) Bringing Health Care Online: The Role of Information Technologies, Office of Technology Assessment, U.S. Government Printing Office, Washington, DC.

Venable, J. R. (2006) The role of theory and theorizing in design science research, in *DESRIST Conference, Claremont, CA, 2006*.

Wang, R. Y. and D. M. Strong (1996) Beyond accuracy: what data quality means to data consumers, *Journal of Management Information Systems* 12 (4), pp. 5–34.

Wellner, A. S. (2003) The new science of focus groups, *American Demographics* 25 (2), p. 29.

Xia, W. and G. Lee (2005) Complexity of information systems development projects: conceptualization and measurement development, *Journal of Management Information Systems* 22 (1), p. 45.

Chapter 11
Design and Creativity

The intuitive mind is a sacred gift and the rational mind is a faithful servant. We have created a society that honors the servant and has forgotten the gift.

– Albert Einstein

Abraham Maslow once said "The key question isn't 'What fosters creativity?' But it is why in God's name isn't everyone creative? Where was the human potential lost? How was it crippled? I think therefore a good question might be not why do people create? But why do people not create or innovate? We have got to abandon that sense of amazement in the face of creativity, as if it were a miracle if anybody created anything."

Every designer is creative. In the world of software design, we also create artifacts. Where does this creativity come from? What exactly is meant to be creative? In this chapter we explore questions such as these. We also take a brief look at the creativity literature and discuss how information technology tools can help humans become more creative and vice versa.

11.1 Creativity – What Is It?

Creativity typically involves doing something that is novel and the production of some artifact judged by domain experts, in some manner, to be creative and of value. We see creativity manifesting itself in art, in science, and in everyday life.

The potential for enhancing human creativity has been studied by visionaries such as De Bono (1973), whose "lateral thinking" ideas have been widely taught in industry. Couger (1996) in his work cites 22 creativity methods some of which are preparation, incubation, illumination, and verification.

Recently we see synergies in creativity steps with those in engineering design as illustrated in Adams et al. (2003):

- Problem definition – identify need
- Gather information
- Generate ideas – brainstorm and list alternatives

A. Hevner, S. Chatterjee, *Design Research in Information Systems*, Integrated Series in Information Systems 22, DOI 10.1007/978-1-4419-5653-8_11,
© Springer Science+Business Media, LLC 2010

- Modeling – describe how to build
- Feasibility analysis
- Evaluation – compare alternatives
- Decision – select one solution
- Communication – write or present to others
- Implementation

In the past decade, psychologists such as Mihaly Czikszentmihalyi have given as foundation to better understand creativity. Through his two widely cited books (*Creativity*, 1996 and *Finding Flow*, 1997), he posits three key components for understanding creativity:

1. Domain (e.g., mathematics, music) "consists of a set of symbols, rules, and procedures."
2. Field: "The individuals who act as gatekeepers to the domain decide whether a new idea, performance, or product should be included."
3. Individual: Creativity is "when a person has a new idea or sees a new pattern and when this novelty is selected by the appropriate field for inclusion in the relevant domain."

This characterization focuses on the individual but clearly makes creativity a social process. His second contribution is the idea of flow, which is a state of mind in which an individual is performing skilled work at an appropriate level of challenge between anxiety and boredom. Once in the state of flow, they are highly focused and move closer to their goal, often with little awareness of their surrounding. Creative people are often reported to be in a state of flow.

Another notable work is Robert Sternberg's *"The Handbook of Creativity"* (Sternberg 1999). One of the chapters by Nickerson offers 12 steps to teaching creativity:

- Establish purpose and intention
- Build basic skills
- Encourage acquisition of domain-specific knowledge
- Stimulate and reward curiosity and exploration
- Build motivation
- Encourage confidence and risk taking
- Focus on mastery and self-competition
- Promote supportable beliefs
- Provide balance
- Provide opportunities for choice and discovery
- Develop self-management (metacognitive skills)
- Teach techniques and strategies for facilitating creative performance

11.2 Group Creativity

The only constant in this world is change. It could be argued that the basis for much of this change stems from stimulating effects of new ideas and creativity. Most research and writing on creativity has focused on individual creativity with little acknowledgement of group factors that influence the creative process. The lack of attention to group factors in the creativity field is consistent with much evidence in the literature that groups may inhibit intellectual activity or optimal performance. Feeling pressured to come up with consensus (Janis 1982), groups can lower accountability (Karau and Williams 1983) and groups tend to focus on common rather than unique ideas (Strasser et al. 1989). Despite all this, research on minority influence in group contexts has shown that creative thought in other domains is increased as minority views are introduced in a group setting (Nemeth et al. 1992).

The main proponents of group creativity are those who promote teamwork and innovation in organizations (Bennis and Biederman 1997; Osborn 1963). Even though there has been an increasing awareness of the importance of social, cultural, contextual, and organizational factors in creativity, there has thus far been much less systematic focus on the group processes related to creativity. This is a serious problem since increasingly creative achievements require the collaboration of groups or teams (Dunbar 1997).

A decade ago, the general belief was that groups should not be used for creativity due to process loss (Stroebe and Diehl 1994). However, at this time, we know that groups can achieve high levels of creativity and even outperform their best resource in the group. At the information age, it is simply impossible for one person to possess all the necessary knowledge in solving a problem. Reliance on others with a variety of experiences and backgrounds is imperative. In addition, creativity is socially defined (Csikszentmihalyi 1996) and creative ideas should be evaluated and accepted by others as creative ideas in the first place.

It is in light of recent developments in the field of creativity and the need to better understand and maximize group creativity that this is an ongoing and active research field. Researchers have contributed to the creativity domain in terms of both face-to-face group creativity and distributed group creativity. There are indications that electronic groups hold some promise for stimulating higher levels of creativity, especially when the groups are large (Dennis and Williams 2003). There is also evidence that electronic groups do better than face-to-face groups when it is critical to share unique knowledge (Lam and Schaubroek 2000). There is no doubt that there are potential benefits associated with collaboration either in the face-to-face or the electronic means; however, efficient procedures are required to fully benefit from group interaction in promoting creativity.

Convergent thought may have a place in efficiency, but it is unlikely to aid the generation of creative ideas (Hackman 1990). Creativity generally requires novelty, plus appropriateness in solving problems (Amabile 1983). Creativity at the level of idea generation is associated with added flexibility and divergent thinking patterns (Guilford 1950). Flexibility involves thinking in different conceptual categories. However, in the process of group creativity which leads to development of a new product or process or generation of a new way of thinking, there must also be convergent thinking. At some point the group must decide on a course of action and implement the new outcome. This constant sequencing between divergent thinking process and convergent thinking process is the skill that the group members must learn and do well at.

11.3 Conceptual Blockbusting Theory

As part of addressing the efficiency issues associated with group creativity, one should consider the conceptual blockbusting framework (Adams 2001). Adams' perspective is that creativity is not something that creative people possess as an "add-on." Instead he argues that each person has the opportunity to reach his potential by focusing on removing the barriers to their creativity.

Jim Adams has contributed tremendously by identifying and categorizing barriers to creativity. These barriers are identified as conceptual blocks. He categorizes the main blocks as perceptual, emotional, cultural, and intellectual. In the later chapters of his book, he suggests strategies for removing these conceptual blocks.

Perceptional Blocks: These are kinds of mental inflexibility. These are obstacles that prevent the problem solver from clearly perceiving either the problem itself or the information needed to solve the problem. Some of these difficulties include the following:

- Stereotyping – seeing what you expect to see; stereotyped seeing and premature labeling are all common
- Difficulty in isolating the problem
- Tendency to delimit the problem area poorly (imposing too many constraints)
- Inability to see the problem from various viewpoints
- Saturation (mind can only record a limited number of inputs)
- Failure to utilize all sensory inputs (graphical and physical media)

Emotional Blocks: These are barriers that stem from inherent human emotions.

- Fear of taking a risk
- No appetite for chaos is driven by an overriding desire for order
- Judging rather than generating ideas
- Inability to tolerate ambiguity
- Unwillingness to incubate – people often cannot relax ("sleep on it")
- Excessive zeal – having over-motivation to succeed quickly can only see one direction to go (ours)
- Reality versus fantasy
- Of flow and angst

Cultural Blocks: They are acquired by exposure to a set of cultural patterns. Sometimes they get codified into law and are not challenged as society changes. They include the following:

- Taboos
- Fantasy and reflection are waste of time, lazy, and even crazy
- Playfulness is for children only
- Reason and intuition do not help
- Left-handed versus right-handed thinking
- Everybody should be just like me

Environmental Blocks: They primarily stemm from an individual's or group's setting. They include the following:

- Distraction such as phone or e-mail interruptions
- Lack of support to bring ideas into action
- Lack of cooperation and trust among colleagues due to insecurity in job
- Accepting or incorporating criticisms
- Lack of a supporting work environment
- Autocratic boss who only values his own ideas does not reward others
- Inhibiting organizational management styles

Intellectual and Expressive Blocks: These stem partly from lack of domain state-of-the-art knowledge and partly due to weak expressive skills. Examples include the following:

- Individual or group may lack the updated information or even correct information
- Inflexible or inadequate use of intellectual problem-solving strategies
- Formulating problem in incorrect language (e.g., verbal, math, visual)
- Inadequate language skills to express ideas
- Expressive communication across disciplines, admitting ignorance

In his work on creativity, James Adams asserts that removal of creativity blocks contributes to increased creativity. He identifies a variety of blocks such as those elaborated above. Adams' work examines these blocks in relation to an individual. But the idea of conceptual blocks, specifically divergent and convergent thinking patterns, can be applied in relation to groups, namely how would groups deal with conceptual blocks? What strategies must be used in overcoming these blocks? What other factors impact "group" blockbusting when compared to "individual" blockbusting?

11.4 Experiential Learning

Learner-centric education has gained enormous popularity in recent years and institutions of higher education are in the midst of trying to redefine and reinvent their course offerings in a manner that is consistent with this ideal. The experiential learning theory (Kolb and Fry 1975) for many decades has used the principle of the learner as "a creator of learning" rather than the "passive recipient of information." Experiential learning method considers individual student as the focal point for learning while the expert acts as the facilitator to guide this learning process. This method has proved to be very effective in many teaching situations and in particular in teaching "soft skills" in business administration.

David Kolb and Roger Fry developed "the experiential learning model" composed of four elements:

- concrete experience
- observation of and reflection on that experience
- formation of abstract concepts based upon the reflection
- testing the new concepts
- repeating the experience

These four elements are the essence of a spiral of learning that can begin with any one of the four elements, but typically begins with a concrete experience. This model was developed predominantly for use with adult education but has found widespread pedagogical implications in higher education.

11.5 Creativity, Design, and IT

There is growing interest in creativity today and within the scientific community a desire to design and build IT tools that promote, accelerate, and facilitate creativity (Shneiderman 2006). Richard Florida's recent work *The Rise of the Creative Class* (Florida 2002) points out the fact that creativity is critical to economic prosperity and social transformation. Since 2003, there has been a renewed interest on creativity support tools and understanding their design issues. Shneiderman organized a successful NSF workshop (Shneiderman 2006) which brainstormed on what those design requirements should be. One of the outcomes of that workshop is a set of "design principles," sometimes called patterns, to guide the development of new creativity support tools. These principles support exploration and provide an open environment with low threshold, high ceiling, and wide walls to capture many paths and styles that support collaboration. These tools should be simple, easy to navigate, allow reflection, provide iteration capability, and become a design for designers (Support Tools 2005).

The set of "design principles," sometimes called patterns, can guide the development of new creativity support tools (Shneiderman 2006). What distinguishes these

principles from other user interface principles is that they emphasize easy exploration, rapid experimentation and fortuitous combinations that lead to innovations:

1. Support exploration
2. Low threshold, high ceiling, and wide walls
3. Support many paths and many styles
4. Support collaboration
5. Support open interchange
6. Make it as simple as possible – and maybe even simpler
7. Choose black boxes carefully
8. Invent things that you would want to use yourself
9. Balance user suggestions with observation and participatory processes
10. Iterate, iterate, and then iterate again
11. Design for designers
12. Evaluate your tools

Referring back to Maslow's opening quote, why are not more people creative? The
creativity computer science community has been engaged in answering this question
(Greene 2002). Many strongly believe that today we are at the cusp of technology
which can facilitate creative thinking and help produce creative artifacts. But these
tools and technology should be designed well. The design principles are a first set of
guidelines. More recently, Schneiderman has proposed eight tasks that should help
people to be more creative more of the time.

1. Searching: It has been noted that creative people are good at knowing what is
   out there. Collecting what is out there is a first step toward creating something
   novel. The World Wide Web has made search easy and today one can look up
   photos, text, voice, images, videos, music, maps, and works of art by a single
   click on the search engines. This has accelerated the collection of vast amount
   of information. It has also enabled finding consultants or gatekeepers of a field
   when it is time to disseminate your creative work.
2. Visualization: Visualizing data and processes to understand and discover relationships is an essential part of creative work. Drawing mental or concept maps
   of current knowledge helps users organize their knowledge, see relationships,
   and possibly spot what is missing.
3. Relate: Consulting with peers and mentors is important. Today it is facilitated by
   chat, SMS, e-mail, and videoconferencing. Exchange of ideas and bouncing of
   possible alternatives are enabled quite easily with IT tools today.
4. Thinking: Once a problem has been identified, researchers start to work toward
   possible solutions. As mentioned before, "brainstorming" is a necessary activity
   during this phase. Edward de Bono calls this lateral thinking, which he defines
   as "exploring multiple possibilities and approaches instead of pursuing a single
   approach."
5. Exploring: As the solution matures, creative people often need to understand the
   consequence of their decisions and trade-offs. Simulation tools can help here.

Simulations open users minds to possibilities and help answer what-if type of questions.

6. Composition: Tools are very much in use today. The ubiquitous word processor, music editing software such as Cubase or ProTools, graphics composition tools, and slide presentation tools are extremely useful composition tools. New tools should be designed that let users work out their artifacts or performances step by step.

7. Reviewing: Replaying session histories to support reflection is important. The capacity to save previous versions is useful which lets users get back to previous stages.

8. Disseminating: Results are disseminated in the final stage to gain recognition. Users want their work to be part of the searchable collection of resources.

Today, there is active research being conducted within the CS & IT community that is exploring the intersection of information technology, design, and creativity.

11.6 Creativity and Design in the Age of Virtual Worlds

Virtual worlds are computer-maintained environments that provide 3D visual and auditory displays; environments that allow movement and interaction by a human using some control scheme (Singhal and Zyda 1999). Virtual worlds, if designed properly, provide the illusion that the interacting human is "in world" (Bartle 2003). We can create any imaginable environment and we can experience entirely new perspectives and capabilities within it. Virtual worlds originally were built in the mid-1980s as research environments using expensive workstations. By the mid-1990s, commercial videogames began to appear that had better-looking, well-produced worlds. Virtual worlds began to be networked routinely about 1987 (Singhal and Zyda 1999) with that networking providing the extra dimension in the virtual world of other humans with whom one could interact. Early virtual worlds were pretty silent but commercial games today provide at least chat and many voice-over-IP (Chatterjee et al. 2005) capabilities. Games are basically virtual worlds for which a participatory story has been designed, a story whose purpose is to entertain the player. The underlying technology for games and virtual worlds today is basically the same (Zyda, 2007).

The growth rate for virtual world utilization stands at 15% per month with no foreseeable slowdown (Gartner 2008). This is the same with research being carried out in virtual worlds. It is an ever-increasing way for business and governments to use the resources to gather and collate information for their use (Carless 2007). Here we provide brief examples of various uses of virtual worlds in academia and commerce:

- Immersive exhibits in Second Life that allow residents to engage in, experience and respond to information in context, allowing for a deeper understanding of places, situations or circumstances. The UC Davis Virtual Hallucinations facility in Second Life is designed to give visitors a better understanding of schizophrenia by simulating the experience of the visual and aural hallucinations associated with schizophrenia based on interviews with real schizophrenics (Yellowlees and Cook 2006).

- Governments are also beginning to interact in virtual worlds and discussions in terms of governance and law are taking place inside these worlds. Virtual worlds are neither public nor privately owned. It is the people interacting in it that make the world.

- Many companies and organizations now incorporate virtual worlds as a new form of advertizing. There are many advantages to using these methods of commercialization. An example of this would be Apple creating an online store within "Second Life."

- Using virtual worlds gives companies the opportunity to gauge customer reaction and receive feedback. Feedback can be crucial to the development of a project as it will inform the creators exactly what users want.

- Another use of virtual worlds in business is where you can create a gathering place. Many businesses can now be involved in business-to-business commercial activity and will create a specific area within a virtual world to carry out their business. Within this space all relevant information can be held. This can be useful for a variety of reasons. You can conduct business with companies on the other side of the world, so there are no geographical limitations; it can increase company productivity. Knowing that there is an area where help is on hand can aid the employees. Sun Microsystems has created an island in Second Life dedicated for the sole use of their employees. This is a place where people can go and seek help, exchange new ideas, or to advertize a new product.

While still low in numbers, current examples do exist of how virtual worlds are impacting education (Maher 1999; Anderson 2006). Many high schools are taking advantage of virtual worlds, using them to work with other schools or study things and places that otherwise they would never be able to see. Some colleges are accepting the use, creating campuses and providing classes in Second Life (Antonacci and Modaress, 2005). Although very few elementary level educators see the benefits of the revolutionary learning tool, but the possibilities are there for the youngest of students as well. Studying biology? Why not go inside a cell or traverse the DNA highway? Virtual worlds provide these opportunities to students of all ages. A good compilation of educational uses of Second Life can be found at http://sleducation.wikispaces.com/educationaluses.

11.7 Designing Virtual Worlds

How might virtual worlds provide new opportunities for enhancing human creativity? A lot depends on the creativity of the designers. Eventually virtual worlds will permeate into every aspect of life. Virtual worlds and collaborative games hold a great potential for study as laboratories of creativity. The reason for that is that these environments have the potential to be fully instrumented with the actions inside of them recorded for later study and playback. Participants can interact in these environments within the boundaries set by the world/game creators and we can peer at these actions from across the network as both observers and participants.

Bricken (2008) provides insight into how a paradigm shift needs to take place when we are dealing with designing virtual worlds.

- From interface to inclusion: While in the past designers have focused on the interface, a boundary between information environment and person accessing the information (e.g., monitor screen), in virtual world design, the focus should be on inclusion, the ability to get inside the information. An important design consideration stemming from inclusion is that while we interact within a virtual world, we simultaneously inhabit the physical world.
- From mechanism to intuition: Virtual world technology adapts computers to human functioning, rather than training people to cope with interactions based on the computer's mechanism. The task of designing a virtual world then does not rest on helping people interpret what the machine is doing, but on determining the most natural and satisfying behaviors for particular participants and providing tools that augment natural abilities.
- From user to participant: Among software developers, the term user refers to the generic person who, at the end of the programming and interface design process, receives a software application geared to "average" human functioning. Participants are active agents. Sensory coupling requires us to regard each participant as an individual and individuals are highly idiosyncratic.
- From visual to multimodal: Most virtual worlds are 3D, acoustigraphic environments with stereoscopic head-mounted display. These capabilities require designers to consider the issues of sensory load related to individual learning and performance styles.

11.8 Conclusion

All designers need to be creative. Where does that creativity come from? One school of thought says that creativity is innate, i.e., god given. You are either born with it or not. Recent school of thought challenges that notion. The current thinking is that creativity can be fostered and enhanced. With modern information technology, the basic steps of creative thinking can be significantly enhanced. This remains an active research field.

It is still an open question how to measure the extent to which a tool fosters creative thinking? HCI professionals are used to measuring the effectiveness and efficiency of tools, but how do you measure if it supports creativity? Evaluation is difficult because traditional controlled studies are inappropriate and brief case studies are not adequate. To measure creativity, one could look at the various outputs produced. One can comment on the viability of outputs and designs but it is still difficult to get at the quality of solutions. Current thinking is that one would need multi-dimensional long-term case studies to gain deep insights.

Creativity and design go hand in hand. The current activities on what IT can do to enhance creativity will create new tools in the future. That in turn will affect the way we do design. We see an exciting future ahead.

References

Adams, J. (2001) *Conceptual Block-Busting, A Guide to Better Ideas*, 4th edn, Da Capo Press, Cambridge, MA.

Adams, R. S., Turns, J., and Atman, C. (2003) Educating effective engineering designers: The role of reflective practice. *Design Studies* 24, pp. 275–294.

Amabile, T. (1983) *The Social Psychology of Creativity*. Springer-Verlag, New York.

Anderson, T. (2006) An Educator Discovers his Second Life. Virtual Canuck. Accessed at http://terrya.edublogs.org/2006/07/17/an-educator-discovers-his-secondlife/

Antonacci, D. M. and N. Modaress (2005) Second Life: The Educational Possibilities of a Massively Multiplayer Virtual World (MMVW), Educause. URL: http://www2.kumc.edu/tlt/SLEDUCAUSESW2005/SLPresentationOutline.htm

Bartle, R. A. (2003) *Designing Virtual Worlds*, New Riders, Indianapolis, IN.

Ben Shneiderman et al. (2006) Creativity support tools: Report from a U.S. National Science Foundation sponsored workshop. *International Journal of Human Computer Interaction*, 20 (2), pp. 61–77.

Bennis, W. and Biederman, P. W. (1997) *Organizing Genius: The Secrets of Creative Collaboration*, Addison-Wesley, Reading, MA.

Bricken, M. (2008) Virtual Worlds: No Interface to Design – Technical Report R-90-2, University of Washington, Seattle.

Carless, S. (2007) Informa predicts $58.4B game industry in 2007. Gamasutra (Oct. 24, 2005) www.gamasutra.com/php-bin/news_index.php?story=6942 .

Chatterjee, S., T. Abhichandani, B. Tulu, and H. Li (2005) SIP-based enterprise converged network for voice/video over IP: implementation and evaluation of components, *IEEE Journal on Selected Areas in Communications (JSAC)* 23, pp. 1921–1933.

Couger, D. (1996) *Creativity & Innovation in Information Systems Organizations*, Boyd & Fraser, Danvers, MA.

Csikszentmihalyi, M. (1996) *Creativity: Flow and the Psychology of Discovery and Invention*, HarperCollins, New York.

Csikszentmihalyi, M. (1997) *Finding Flow: The Psychology of Finding Engagement with Everyday Life*, Basic Books, New York.

De Bono, E. (1973) *Lateral Thinking: Creativity Step by Step*, Harper, New York.

Dennis, A. R. and M. L. Williams (2003) Electronic Brainstorming: Theory, Research, and Future Directions, in P. Paulus (ed.), *Group Creativity*, Oxford University Press, Oxford.

Dunbar, K. (1997) How Scientists Think: Online Creativity and Conceptual Change in Science, in T. B. Ward, S. M. Smith, and J. Vaid (eds.), *Creative Thought: An Investigation of Conceptual Structures and Processes*, American Psychological Association, Washington D.C., pp. 461–493.

Florida, R. (2002) *The Rise of the Creative Class and How Its Transforming Work, Leisure, Community and Everyday Life*, Basic Books, New York.

Gartner (2008) Virtual Worlds To Have 'Transformational Business Impact', April 2008, http://www.worldsinmotion.biz/2008/08/gartner_virtual_worlds_to_have.php

Guilford, J. P. (1950) Creativity, *American Psychologist* 5, pp. 444–454.

Hackman, J. R. (ed.) (1990) *Groups that Work (and Those that Don't)*, Jossey-Bass, San Francisco.

Janis, Irving L. (1982) *Groupthink: Psychological Studies of Policy Decisions and Fiascoes*, 2nd edn, Houghton Mifflin, New York.

Karau, S. L. and Williams, K. D. (1983) Social Loafing: A meta-analytical review and theoretical integration, *Journal of Personality & Social Psychology* 65, pp. 681–706.

Kolb, D. A. and Fry, R. (1975) Toward an Applied Theory of Experiential Learning, in C. Cooper (ed.) *Theories of Group Process*, John Wiley, London.

Lam, S. S. K. and Schaubroek, J. (2000) Improving group decisions by better pooling information: A comprehensive advantage of group decision support systems, *Journal of Applied Psychology* 85, pp. 565–573.

Maher, M. L. (1999) Designing the virtual campus as a virtual world, Presented at 1999 Conference on Computer support for Collaborative Learning.

Nemeth, C., Mosier, K., and Chiles, C. (1992) When convergent thought improves performance: Majority vs. Minority influence, *Personality & Social Psychology Bulletin* 81, pp. 139–144.

Osborn, A. F. (1963) *Applied Imagination*, 2nd edn, Scribner, New York.

Sharon L. Greene (2002) Characteristics of applications that support creativity. Special issue on creativity IT tools, *Communications of the ACM*, 45 (10).

Singhal, S. and Zyda, M. (1999) *Networked Virtual Environments – Design and Implementation*, ACM Press Books, SIGGRAPH Series, 23 July 1999, ISBN 0-201-32557-8, 315 p.

Sternberg, R. (ed.) (1999) *Handbook of Creativity*, Cambridge University Press, Cambridge, UK.

Strasser, S., Kerr, N. L., and Davis, J. H. (1989) Influence Processes and Consensus Models in Decision-Making Groups, in P. Paulus (ed.), *Psychology of Group Influence*, 2nd edn, Erlbaum, Hillsdale, NJ, pp. 279–326.

Stroebe, W. and Diehl, M. (1994) Why Groups Are Less Effective Than Their Members: On Productivity Loses in Idea-Generating Groups, in W. Stroebe and M. Hewstone (eds.), *European Review of Social Psychology*, Vol. 5, Wiley, London, pp. 271–303.

Support Tools (2005) Workshop Sponsored by the National Science Foundation, June 13–14, 2005, Washington DC. http://www.cs.umd.edu/hcil/CST/

Yellowlees, P. M. and J. N. Cook (2006) Education about hallucinations using an internet virtual reality system: a qualitative survey, *Academic Psychiatry* 30, pp. 534–539.

Zyda, M. (2007) Creating a science of games, *Communications of the ACM*, 50 (7), pp. 27–29.

Chapter 12
A Design Language for Knowledge Management Systems (KMS)

> *Imagination is more important that knowledge. For while*
> *knowledge defines all we currently know and understand,*
> *imagination points to all we might yet discover and create.*

> – Albert Einstein

12.1 Problem Statement

As with all species, humans spend their life in competition. Unlike other organisms, we carry this competitive drive past mere survival and reproduction into the structures of our social and business life. The structures of our business environment revolve around the ability of an organization to obtain long-term competitiveness through the control of rare and valuable resources that have limited substitutability, mobility, and imitability (Barney, 1991, Peteraf, 1993). Knowledge is precisely such a rare and valuable resource and does add greatly to an organization's ability to sustain competitiveness (Alavi and Leidner, 2001, Kogut and Zander, 1992, Argote and Ingram, 2000). The problem all organizations have is to efficiently discover knowledge, create new knowledge, capture it, share it, and use it to gain competitive advantage. They need to develop a system to manage their knowledge: a knowledge management system (KMS).

There is a need for a comprehensive model and a tool that can build on previous research and provide organizations with a better understanding of their unique knowledge flows and how best to leverage the organization's capital to create an efficient and effective KMS. This model needs to consider external inputs, the internal flows of knowledge, and the value of the outputs.

In response to the recognition of knowledge as a resource providing sustainable competitive advantage, there has been extensive research into and development of the nascent discipline of knowledge management. Research efforts have produced conceptualizations of the internal flows of knowledge creation, capture, sharing, and

Robert Judge

A. Hevner, S. Chatterjee, *Design Research in Information Systems*, Integrated Series
in Information Systems 22, DOI 10.1007/978-1-4419-5653-8_12,
© Springer Science+Business Media, LLC 2010

use (Nonaka and Takeuchi, 1995, Rubenstein-Montano et al., 2001, Wiig, 1993, Choo, 1998, Firestone and McElroy, 2003). Several of these models qualify as a white box, connecting enough of the gears to provide some understanding of how knowledge flows through a generic organization.

However, the white box is far from complete. It does not yet help us understand how knowledge flows vary among specific organizations. These models help us understand at a high level how knowledge flows and how we might best manage it. But they fail to provide a means for individual organizations to customize the model of flow to fit their organization as it currently exists and then predict how the flows might change as they grow over time. Each organization faces a unique external environment and scans it for new inputs. Each organization has a unique organizational structure, set of personnel, and information systems infrastructure. And each organization has various forms of barriers to knowledge flow and use. Organizations are also rarely static; they evolve constantly. These factors all affect how efficiently knowledge is used to improve the quality, timeliness, and throughput of solved problems and responses to opportunities. Organizations must be able to strategically determine where and when to invest in an evolving knowledge management system (KMS).

Entrepreneurial and small- to mid-sized enterprises (SMEs) often experience a rapid growth in the need for internally generated knowledge and the external acquisition of knowledge. They experience rapid changes to their organizational structure, growth in the numbers of personnel, and the need for improved information systems infrastructure. They also may have limited access to capital forcing a critical selection process of where to invest for long-term competitiveness. This makes them good candidates for a tool that can help them understand their knowledge flows and how they might be altered over time due to the changes in their internal or external environment.

This research describes and validates a versatile simulation system designed to provide small- to mid-sized enterprises (SMEs) with a means to understand the impact that various barriers and facilitators have on the flow of knowledge given the organization's existing business environment. The initial model of the organization can subsequently be modified and its parameters changed to reflect proposed KMS changes to improve knowledge flows or to reflect the future growth of the company. These subsequent simulations are relevant to an organization's efforts to determine the appropriate strategy (timing and investment) for current and future KMS efforts.

There is no one way to implement a knowledge flow simulation – every company is different. However, this research will use kernel theories (organizational memory (OM), input–process–output (I–P–O), decision execution cycles (DEC), barriers to knowledge, and the cycle of knowledge creation: socialization, externalization, combination, and internalization (SECI)) to establish the requirements for the basic core model needed to represent the primary knowledge flows of a company. The core model will contain constructs representing a process flow concept of knowledge flows (Newman, 2003). The constructs to represent knowledge flows in organizations will be indentified – from competing and complementary theories (Nonaka and Takeuchi, 1995, Firestone and McElroy, 2003, Choo, 1998,

Wiig, 1993). Each construct will then be rigorously defined by theory and characterized computationally by distributions. Simulation will be used to determine how the complexity and turbulence of external inputs to an organization and the configuration of the organization's knowledge processes affect its level of quality, timeliness, and throughput for outputs (solved problems, products, and services).

The research question pursued by this chapter is does the extent and value of knowledge, its linkage, and structural barriers to knowledge flow change as an SME grows? The value in this research is in providing a mechanism for the SME business community to use in evaluating potential strategies when considering or moving forward with the implementation of a KMS. A company that knows the volume, linkage, and structural barriers to knowledge flow can then understand the timing of investments in resources to support an evolving KMS. This research may also prove valuable to those involved in the design of future KMS simulation tools: to create a more effective interface to allow users to capture their corporate knowledge structure and the parameters for factors affecting the flow through that structure. This research and model could also be employed to understand large companies as well. However, SMEs provide an advantage in the simulation because they experience the point where the flow of knowledge through personal contact becomes impacted by growth.

12.2 Concept

The artifact is based on the concept that knowledge is created or acquired and then must flow to others who can apply it in the same or new ways or combine it with other knowledge to create new knowledge. Nonaka (1994) identified four forms of knowledge capture, which in the context of this chapter can be conceptualized as knowledge flows: socialization, externalization, combination, and internalization. This knowledge flow is the key to the artifact model (see Fig. 12.1). The knowledge flows along these pathways as information packets of tacit or explicit information. Socialization is the pathway for tacit information to flow between people. Sometimes this tacit information can be converted to explicit information and flow through the pathway of externalization. Combination occurs when someone is able to take explicit information and add more explicit information to it. Lastly, information that is received as explicit and converted into tacit occurs through internalization. Thus there are several ways that information packets can

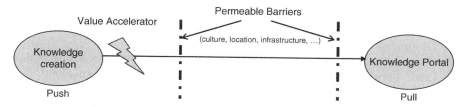

Fig. 12.1 Conceptual model

flow from someone motivated to exchange that knowledge to someone motivated to receive it. Something must induce the flow of knowledge. This chapter assumes a push-pull concept. Push represents the input and capture of created knowledge and the willingness to share it. If there is someone who has the desire for that knowledge, they will pull it toward themselves. The model also represents the fact that there are barriers to the ease with which knowledge flows from those who create and capture it to those who desire it. Examples of barriers that may exist in an organization's flow of knowledge are as follows:

1. Physical: Employees less likely to interact frequently because they are separated by walls, buildings, geography.
2. Too few employees: Few packets of explicit information being entered in a KMS.
3. Employee density: As a company grows, it becomes less likely that each employee will have equal opportunity to interact with every other employee – this in turn will slow the flow of tacit knowledge in the company.
4. Culture and language: Communication of information may be limited by poor ability to understand one another or for cultural reasons that do not encourage sharing for reasons such as loss of power.
5. Lack of motivation to share or use knowledge.
6. Perceived "usefulness": When the users do not receive an adequate amount of relevant information, they will use the system less. When more information packets are present in the system, the users will find it more useful.
7. Information systems infrastructure: Lack of proper KM mechanisms and technologies.
8. Security, and others.

There may also exist "value accelerators" that will improve the ability of an information packet to move through the barrier more readily. Examples of value accelerators are as follows:

1. Linking of packets to other packets: Improving context or broadening to other contexts.
2. Knowledge repositories: Storage of explicit information packets in a readily searchable form.
3. E-mail: It will increase the flow of knowledge among those employees who may not have the chance of meeting face-to-face.
4. Brown bag lunches: Open discussions and storytelling to socialize tacit information.
5. Linking of competence to packets: Providing links to experts who can provide additional details and context related to particular information packets.
6. Expert systems and A.I.: Sophisticated systems that aid the search for key information.
7. Data warehousing and data mining: Providing the tools necessary to consolidate key information and look for unexpected relationships in the information.
8. Communities of practice: Online discussion with others interested and dealing with similar issues – provides for give and take of explicit information.

The permeability of the barriers and the value of the knowledge will determine how effectively the knowledge flows from creator to user. These barriers and value accelerators will vary from organization to organization. The model must allow for the selective inclusion of the relevant barriers and value accelerators and adjustment of their respective parameters.

This research develops a simulation system using the above concepts. The system includes a set of graphical constructs representing the structural characteristics that influence knowledge flow in an organization (see Table 12.1), the capability to simulate the knowledge flows of that structure, and the means to evaluate alternative structures and strategies. The graphical constructs serve a purpose analogous to objects in object-oriented programming and contain methods and parameters. In a given instantiation, the methods determine the context of the construct (object) in the organization's knowledge flows and determine which parameters will be necessary to properly represent it in the simulation.

Table 12.1 Graphical constructs

Permeable Barriers (Physical separation, Cultural, Language, Incentives, Management support, Security, Information infrastructure, etc.)	
Value Accelerators (Linking of packets, Linking of expertise, Communities of practice)	
Portals (Capturing, Adding value, Accessing)	
Knowledge Management Technology Modules (Information packets, Directory of competencies, KB, AI, Expert Systems, OLAP, Data mining, etc.)	
Knowledge Flows (Socialization, Externalization, Combination, and Internalization)	

The process proposed for using such a simulation system entails working with an SME to understand the knowledge flows, barriers, value accelerators, and portals that exist in the company. These constructs will determine the parameters necessary to configure the system's algorithms (percent of tacit versus explicit packets, number of employees, number of packets generated by employees, etc.) and distributions (probability of a useful packet of information being found, impact of the number of employees on socialization, etc.) to properly model the SMEs KMS structural characteristics. A discrete-stochastic simulation, using the model and parameters, will simulate the flow of information packets throughout the organizational structure as modeled. A representative baseline will be developed by adjusting the construct parameters until the flows and usage rates approximate those measured by the organization. This baseline will be stored for comparison to models representing changes to the organizational structure (KM infrastructure, technology and mechanisms, and processes). The comparison of simulations will allow for an understanding of sensitivity of the knowledge flows to changes in the organizational structure and the associated costs/benefits. The organization may then develop a better informed knowledge management strategy.

12.3 Artifact Construction

The simulation constructed to represent the above model concepts was accomplished using iGrafx simulation software and is composed of the following components:

1. Knowledge packet generator

    a. Poisson random number generator
    b. Percent of tacit versus explicit packets
    c. Prioritization of packets (determination of packet value)

2. Barriers

    a. Employee density (socialization pathway)
    b. KMS usefulness (externalization pathway)

3. Value accelerators

    a. Scheduled brown bag meeting (socialization pathway)
    b. E-mail (externalization pathway)
    c. Knowledge repository (externalization pathway)

4. Receiver of knowledge packets

12.4 Knowledge Packet Generator

The knowledge packet generator controls the time between the creation of information packets produced each day. The interarrival time is based on the exponential distribution and adjusted to account for the number of employees. The exponential distribution has repeatedly been found to be a good approximation of the time between arrivals (information packets being generated) (Render et al., 2003). The key assumption associated with the use of an exponential distribution is that the arrivals are independent of one another. Although there may be circumstances where two people generate information packets at the same time because of collaborated content, this is probably rare and not a serious constraint in the use of the exponential distribution. The exponential probability function is

$$P(x) = \frac{1}{\beta} e^{-x/\beta}$$

Table 12.2 The value for β given the number of company employees

Number of employees	Value for β
5	0.5
10	0.3
20	0.2
50	0.15

The mean interarrival time is β (in days) and x is the given service time (in days). β is adjusted each simulation according to the number of employees. Table 12.2 lists the values of β per number of employees in the company for the simulation.

This table is based on the observation that a small company has frequent interactions among its members and with that stimulation of ideas and knowledge. Also, a small company is generally composed of founders who have considerable expertise and inventiveness. Thus a company of five may generate information packets twice per day on average. As the company grows, other employees are brought in for support functions and may not contribute new information as frequently. The time between new packets will decrease because there are more employees; however, the rate of new information generated per person will be less. This reduction in the rate of generating new information per person may also be driven by the new employees being less informed in the technology or having less cognitive capacity to generate knowledge than the initial founding team. The values provided in Table 12.2, and all subsequent tables, are based on limited personal observations and would need to be adjusted based on expert opinion and empirical observations for any specific company to be simulated.

Each information packet is randomly determined to be tacit or explicit and will, respectively, be directed to either the socialization pathway or the externalization pathway of the model. Since there are only two options, the Bernoulli distribution was selected for random assignment. The Bernoulli distribution will assign a given percent of the information packets as either tacit or explicit based on a provided probability of one of these occurring. This probability will change over time as the number of previously generated explicit packets increases. As more explicit packets enter and reside in the KMS, the usefulness of the system will increase because the users will have a greater likelihood of locating valuable packets of information. The percent of tacit and explicit packets will be adjusted in the simulation to increase the probability of explicit packets being created as the volume of existing explicit packets grows. This is accomplished by adjusting the Bernoulli distribution based on Table 12.3.

The last function of the knowledge packet generator is to assign a priority to represent the value of a particular packet just created. Not all packets are created equal. Some have more valuable content that will be desired by one or more people in the company. The normal distribution is used to represent the assignment of priority which has a range of 1–127. It is not unreasonable to assume that in any company, there are some low value and some high value packets, but in general

Table 12.3 Distribution of explicit packets given the number of employees

Number of explicit packets	Percent explicit packets to generate
0–250	0.2
251–500	0.3
501–1000	0.4
1001–2000	0.5
2001+	0.6

most will be somewhere in between in value. The normal distribution should reflect this condition reasonably well.

12.5 Barriers

There are several barriers in this model, two of which will be implemented in the evaluation instantiations described below. One barrier will be placed on the socialization pathway and represents a barrier to information flow caused by employee density. It will be found in all four instantiations. The other barrier, KMS usefulness, will be placed on the externalization pathway in the last two instantiations. The employee density barrier addresses the observation that the communication of ideas flows unimpeded in a small company but less so as the company grows. Although there are many reasons for this, the employee density barrier is concerned with the decrease in flow of tacit packets due to more people. As the employee population increases, there are too many people to meet on a daily basis, which, therefore, decreases the probability of running into the person with the right packet of information. The priority of a packet also plays a role in this barrier. A high priority packet will stimulate a person to tell it to more employees and thus increase the likelihood of the packet getting to the right person. The impact of the barrier in the model represents a delay in the transfer of a packet, which depending on its priority may range from a portion of a day to its never reaching another company employee. This barrier is simulated by the following function:

Delay due to employee density = packet priority × (normally distributed random number selected from between the numbers X and Y) × employee multiplier function

The numbers X and Y are equal to 1 and 3, respectively, in the instantiations evaluated in this chapter, but can be adjusted depending on the variability of desired delays. The employee multiplier function is used to provide a value to calibrate the packet wait time based on the number of employees and is represented in Table 12.4.

The KMS usefulness barrier will be implemented in the externalization pathway. The function used to simulate this barrier has parameters representing the packet

Table 12.4 Employee multiplier table

Number of employees	Multiplier
0–5	0.5
6–10	1.5
11–20	1.5
21–50	2.5
51+	4.0

priority, number of employees, number of explicit packets in the system, and a random generator. The result of this function is a delay attributed to an explicit packet:

KMS barrier delay = priority × (5/#employees) × delay based on number of employees × (normally distributed random number selected from between the numbers X and Y)

Although the priority can range between 1 and 127, for purposes of this function, it is normalized to a range of 1–12 with 12 being the highest priority. The numbers X and Y are equal to 1 and 3, respectively, in the instantiations evaluated in this chapter, but can be adjusted depending on the variability of desired delays. The delay based on the number of employees is represented in Table 12.5. The table is used to increase the delay when there are fewer packets in the system. The users will perceive the KMS to be of low value to them when there are few packets and use it infrequently. This is because the probability of there being a packet the user needs is very low when there are few packets. Therefore, the explicit packets initially entered into the system may be unused for a long period of time until the users see an adequate base of packets to search through and find useful.

Table 12.5 Usefulness delay based on number of packets in the system

Number of packets in the system	Usefulness delay factor
0–100	20
101–250	18
251–600	15
601–1000	12
1001–1500	8
1501–2000	6
2001–5000	3
5001+	1

12.6 Value Accelerators

Just as both the socialization and externalization pathways may have barriers, they may also have various value accelerators. The value accelerators perform the function of increasing an information packets priority. The higher the priority, the more rapidly the packet will pass through any barrier it encounters. There are three value accelerators used in the evaluation section of this chapter: brown bag meetings, e-mail, and knowledge repositories. The brown bag meetings serve as a value accelerator in the socialization pathway by providing a time and place for employees to exchange ideas and build on each others knowledge. This is accomplished in the simulation by a function that increases an existing tacit packet's priority. The brown bag meeting value accelerator is represented by a function which takes into account the existing priority of the packet as well as a randomization component.

Brown bag value accelerator = existing priority × (Normally distributed random number selected from between the numbers X and Y)

The numbers X and Y are equal to 10 and 50, respectively, in the instantiations evaluated in this chapter, but can be adjusted depending on the duration and variability of desired delays.

The e-mail value accelerator increases the value of explicit packets in the externalization pathway by increasing their priority. This has the subsequent effect on movement through barriers as seen above in the brown bag value accelerator. The increase in priority is based on a randomness component plus the number of information packets being sent and viewed. The accelerator assumes that as the email system is used more frequently, the probability of receiving a valuable packet will increase. The e-mail value accelerator is represented in the simulation by the following function:

E-mail value accelerator = existing priority + ((normally distributed random number selected from between the numbers X and Y) × probability of finding a good packet)

The numbers X and Y are equal to 10 and 50, respectively, in the instantiations evaluated in this chapter, but can be adjusted depending on the duration and variability of desired delays. The values used in the simulation of this chapter are found in Table 12.6.

Table 12.6 Probability of receiving a good packet

Number of explicit packets	Probability of receiving a good packet
0–100	0.05
101–250	0.1
251–600	0.2
601–1000	0.3
1001–1500	0.55
1501–2000	0.65
2001–5000	0.85
5001+	0.90

The last value accelerator is the knowledge repository. This value accelerator also operates by increasing the priority of explicit packets. A knowledge repository allows for packets of information to be stored and easily searched. This in turn allows packets to pass from the point and time of creation to an end user more rapidly than by e-mail alone. This effect of the knowledge repository is simulated by the following function:

> Knowledge repository value accelerator = existing priority + ((normally distributed random number selected from between the numbers X and Y) × probability of finding a good packet)

The numbers X and Y are equal to 50 and 100, respectively, in the instantiations evaluated in this chapter, but can be adjusted depending on the duration and variability of desired delays. As is the e-mail value accelerator, the probability of finding a good packet is captured in Table 12.6.

12.7 Receiver of Good Packets

This last function in the simulation gathers statistics on how many packets, either tacit or explicit, were selected and the average length of time they were in the system prior to selection. This function only counts those packets that have a priority higher than 60. This gate can be adjusted for any given simulation. The packets as initially generated receive priorities normally distributed between 1 and 127, so a value of 60 establishes that about 50% of the packets will make it through at some point in time. The percent that ultimately make it through will vary depending on the length of the simulation and more importantly on the number of value accelerators each packet encounters. This follows from the logic that as you add value to your KMS (value accelerators), it will be used more often and thus more packets will be located and used for multiple purposes.

12.8 Evaluation Methodology: SME Model Instantiation Comparisons

The concepts and simulation model developed above will be applied to a theoretical SME environment for the purpose of evaluation. A basic model (see Fig. 12.2) will be developed that can be modified to represent alternative configurations of KMS infrastructure for the SME. The model will be adapted by addition of barriers, value accelerators, and parameter changes to reflect four alternative KM infrastructures for the SME. The artifact will be evaluated by comparing simulations of these separate SME organizational structures of barriers and value accelerators. The four instantiations evaluated in this study are as follows:

(1) *Instantiation #1 – baseline SME organizational structure:* This instantiation will consist of the socialization pathway (tacit packets) with a barrier (employee density) and an externalization pathway (explicit packets) with one value

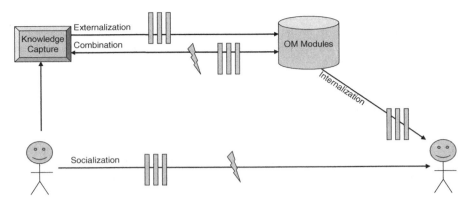

Fig. 12.2 Basic model

accelerator (e-mail). This organizational instantiation represents one of an organization with few initial personnel and a poor KM infrastructure and technologies. It is reflective of a small startup company with few employees and little infrastructure.

(2) *Instantiation #2 – enhanced socialization pathway:* This instantiation builds directly on the preceding one by adding one value accelerator to the socialization pathway. In this situation, the additional value accelerator (brown bag lunches) will represent a means to increase the flow of tacit knowledge by regular open exchanges of knowledge that might not happen by simple meetings in the hallway. This communication helps to promote the flow of knowledge through the employee density barrier found in this instantiation and instantiation #1.

(3) *Instantiation #3 – initial externalization pathway:* This instantiation builds directly on the second instantiation by adding a barrier to the externalization pathway. The barrier is titled "usefulness" and represents that a KM system provides little "usefulness" when the number of explicit information packets available for searching is low. As the number of packets in the system increases, so does the probability of finding a useful packet. The barrier's permeability increases as the number of packets increase.

(4) *Instantiation #4 – enhanced externalization pathway:* This instantiation will build on the third instantiation by adding a value accelerator (knowledge repository) to the externalization pathway. The value accelerator will improve throughput of knowledge packets by allowing for storage and future use. It also adds value by allowing for better categorization to aid in the search for specific information.

Each of the above four instantiations will be simulated 20 times: four categories of company size (5, 10, 20, or 50 employees) times five categories of the number of days (50, 100, 250, 500, and 1000). The results collected by each simulation will be the average time each packet spends in the system and the average number of packets received per person per day for both tacit and explicit packets. These key indicators of the efficiency and usefulness of the system will be plotted to evaluate the effectiveness of the model.

The four instantiations represent a sequential improvement that one might expect to see in an SME over time. The first instantiation represents the baseline and perhaps could be considered a very early stage startup. The second instantiation represents an improvement to the socialization pathway. This difference can be addressed by the following hypotheses:

> *H1a: The value accelerator implemented in instantiation #2 will significantly reduce the average time tacit packets spend in the system over that of instantiation #1.*
>
> *H1b: The value accelerator implemented in instantiation #2 will significantly increase the number of tacit packets received per person per day in the system over that of instantiation #1.*

Instantiation #3 represents the inclusion of a barrier on the externalization pathway to account for low usefulness of a KMS until a critical mass of packets are available for searching and finding valuable information. The fourth instantiation installs a knowledge repository to improve the usefulness of the KMS. This leads to the following hypotheses:

> *H2a: The value accelerator implemented in instantiation #4 will significantly reduce the average time explicit packets spend in the system over that of instantiation #3.*
>
> *H2b: The value accelerator implemented in instantiation #4 will significantly increase the number of explicit packets received per person per day in the system over that of instantiation #3.*

12.9   Results

The data from each simulation was collected in a spreadsheet for analysis and graphing. The data collected for each of the four instantiations was associated with their simulation-specific parameters of the number of employees and the number of days simulated. The key statistics collected for each were (1) the average time until a "tacit" packet reached a user of that packet, (2) the average time until an "explicit" packet reached a user of that packet, (3) the average number of "tacit" packets received by a user each day, and (4) the average number of "explicit" packets received by a user each day. The following figures report this data and are used to validate that the model is operating as instantiated.

The first set of figures (Figs. 12.3, 12.4, 12.5, 12.6, and 12.7) look at the baseline instantiation. This first instantiation, as detailed in the above evaluation section, incorporates an employee density barrier and an e-mail accelerator. The expectation

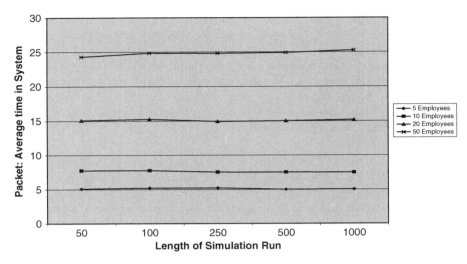

Fig. 12.3 Instantiation #1 – tacit packet average time (days) in system

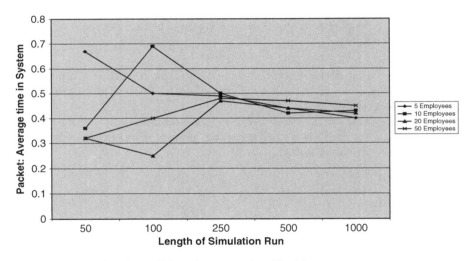

Fig. 12.4 Instantiation #1 – explicit packet average time (days) in system

for such an instantiation is that we would see evidence that the larger the employee population is, the longer the average time a tacit packet takes getting to the user of that packet. This might occur for two primary reasons: (1) as a company brings on more employees, some will be in support roles and not likely to be large contributors of new knowledge, and (2) the original small team, which had a relatively rapid exchange of that sharing, now are spending time managing and working with the new employees and less time exchanging new information. Figure 12.3 shows us

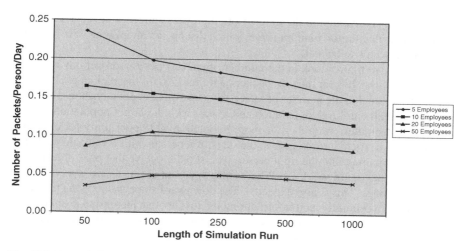

Fig. 12.5 Instantiation # 1 – tacit packets/person/day

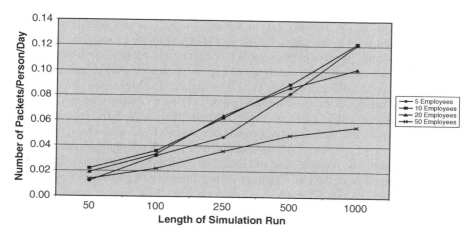

Fig. 12.6 Instantiation #1 – explicit packets/person/day

that our expectations are met. The line for 50 employees shows an average increase of 20 days per packet in the system – about a 400% increase from when there were only 5 employees. The expectation of a longer time through the system was met, but is the difference seen here too excessive or maybe not excessive enough? I believe this may be excessive because as a company grows larger, subgroups form around job responsibilities and the need for similar information. So perhaps a less drastic difference might be more realistic.

Figure 12.4 looks at the impact of this baseline instantiation on the flow of explicit packets. Since this instantiation does not have any barriers to explicit packets flowing through the externalization pathway, we would expect the time spent in the system to be invariant to the number of employees and the number of days simulated. Other than initial random noise, which disappears after about 250 days, this expectation seems to be met.

The next two figures look at the number of packets per person per day received. Figure 12.5 shows this for the tacit packets and Fig. 12.6 for the explicit packets. The expectations are that the number of tacit packets per person per day should be highest with a small employee population and lowest with the larger population. This is because in a smaller group there is more interaction and opportunity for exchange of information. As the group grows, the odds of a person with a valuable packet of information running into the right person who should receive that packet decreases. This is what the figure validates. What is also apparent in this figure is a downward slope for all lines. This is also expected. The downward slope is due to the transition over time from primarily tacit information flow to one of an increasing proportion of explicit packets. Initially there are few explicit packets generated, but as the number of days of simulation increases, more explicit packets enter the system. The more explicit packets in the system, the more interest the users have in looking for those packets, which further encourages the production of explicit packets as all members see this value.

The externalization pathway carries the explicit packets and in instantiation #1 there are no barriers in this pathway. We would expect to see an increase in explicit packets over time. As more explicit packets are accumulated, the "usefulness" of the KMS increases and proportionately more explicit than tacit packets are generated by users. This is validated in Fig. 12.6. This figure also highlights the effects of adding new personnel as the company grows: (1) as a company brings on more employees, some will be in support roles and not likely to be large contributors of new knowledge, and (2) the original small team, which had a given level of sharing and relatively rapid exchange of that sharing, now are spending time managing and working with the new employees and less time exchanging new information. The figure illustrates this effect as a distinctly lower increase in packets per person per day for a company with 50 employees relative to that of the smaller companies.

The next figure looks at the second instantiation, which adds in a value accelerator: brown bag lunches. This accelerator offers a means for a company to improve the flow of tacit packets, which will become more crucial as the company grows. When Fig. 12.3 is compared with Fig. 12.7, it can be seen that the number of days a tacit packet spends in the organization decreases. This comparison validates the expectations of the impact of the value generator in terms of both its effect on the time spent in the system and also on the greater value to a larger company.

Figure 12.8 can be compared with Fig. 12.5 to understand the effect of the brown bag value accelerator on the number of packets received per person per day. This comparison validates, that as expected, the average number packets per person per day increases due to the beneficial impact of the brown bag lunches on facilitating tacit information exchange.

The third instantiation adds the barrier: KMS usefulness. The purpose of this barrier is to reflect the impact perceived usefulness has on actual use of the system. If the users do not perceive the system as useful, because the information desired is

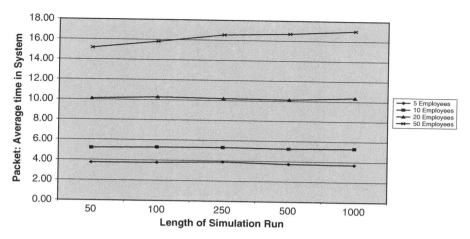

Fig. 12.7   Instantiation #2 – tacit packet average time (days) in system

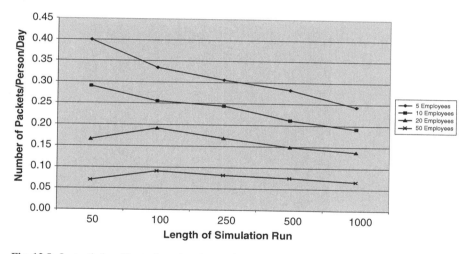

Fig. 12.8   Instantiation #2 – tacit packets/person/day

not available, then they will not use it. The premise of this barrier is that as more explicit packets enter the externalization pathway and build up, the perceived and actual usefulness will increase. Users will have a greater likelihood of locating the information they require in a bigger pool of packets. By adding this barrier, the expectation is that the average time an explicit packet spends in the organization will increase to a point (critical mass) and then begin decreasing as more use of the system occurs. This is validated in Fig. 12.9.

The effect of adding a value generator (knowledge repository) to the externalization pathway occurs in the simulation of the fourth instantiation and is seen in Fig. 12.10. The figure looks similar to Fig. 12.9, but the scale is shifted downward

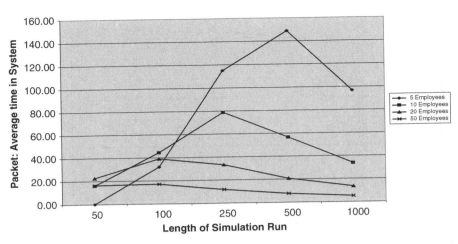

Fig. 12.9 Instantiation #3 – explicit packet average time (days) in system

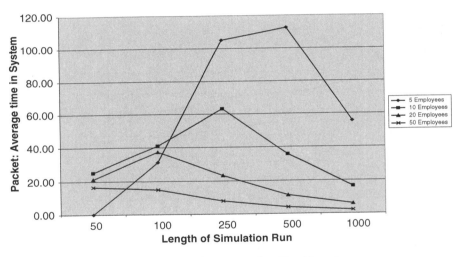

Fig. 12.10 Instantiation # 4 – explicit packet average time (days) in system

representing a faster throughput of packets in the organization. This was expected and validates the externalization pathway for barriers and accelerators (Table 12.7).

12.10 Contribution to Research

The process of developing and validating this artifact identified numerous areas where future research is required:

Table 12.7 Summary of results

Hypothesis	Supported/not supported
H1a: The value accelerator implemented in instantiation #2 will significantly reduce the average time tacit packets spend in the system over that of instantiation #1	Supported
H1b: The value accelerator implemented in instantiation #2 will significantly increase the number of tacit packets received per person per day in the system over that of instantiation #1	Supported
H2a: The value accelerator implemented in instantiation #4 will significantly reduce the average time explicit packets spend in the system over that of instantiation #3	Supported
H2b: The value accelerator implemented in instantiation #4 will significantly increase the number of explicit packets received per person per day in the system over that of instantiation #3	Supported

- How does one measure the number of tacit packets?
- What is the ratio of tacit to explicit packets?
- What factors establish the explicit/tacit ratio or cause it to change?
- What are the real barriers to flow of information and knowledge and what factors define them?
- What are the means to improve the flow of information through barriers and how are these means defined?
- How are all these questions affected by size, age, and industry of the company?

The design itself is an iterative process and as new theory or data on parameters become available the design will be improved. Using the knowledge gained from this study will provide insight into what researchers might look for and what they might see when studying knowledge flows in situ.

This research also provides some support that the organizational structure, number of employees, the type of information packet, and time can be modeled to understand how these variables interact. Future research may provide additional insight into how organizational structure, KM infrastructure, motivators, physical workspace, organizational climate, and actual behaviors work together to produce "usefulness" in a KMS for an SME.

12.11 Conclusion

This model with its four instantiations is an initial attempt to demonstrate that a simplified model of knowledge flows in a company is possible and provides valuable understanding. It points out a means of representing the flow through the use of barriers and value accelerators. Future development of the model needs to address the following:

- Sensitivity analysis of all parameter inputs.
- Validation of distributions used to simulate packet creation, barrier-induced wait time, and probability of finding good packets.
- How cost information can be combined with the model to better analyze strategies for implementation of value accelerators (relevance to the business community).
- Looking at how value accelerators not only alter priority for faster movement through barriers but may also generate new packets themselves (i.e., brown bag lunches provide opportunities to exchange knowledge – but they may also stimulate new knowledge).
- Use of ANOVA to understand the statistical significance of treatments associated with employee population size, time, and other factors on

  - average time for packets moving through the organization and
  - average number of packets received per person per day.

References

Alavi, M. and D. E. Leidner (2001) Review: Knowledge management and knowledge management systems: conceptual foundations and research issues, *MIS Quarterly* 25, p. 107.

Argote, L. and P. Ingram (2000) Knowledge transfer: a basis for competitive advantage in firms, *Organizational Behavior and Human Decision Processes* 82, pp. 150–169.

Barney, J. (1991) Firm resources and sustained competitive advantage, *Journal of Management* 17, p. 99.

Baron, R. and D. Kenny (1986) The moderator-mediator variable distinction in social psychological research: conceptual, strategic, and statistical considerations, *Journal of Personality and Social Psychology* 51 (6), pp. 1173–1182.

Becerra-Fernandez, I. and R. Sabherwal (2001) Organizational knowledge management processes: a contingency perspective, *Journal of MIS* 18 (1), pp. 23–55.

Becerra-Fernandez, I., A. Gonzalez, and R. Sabherwal (2004) *Knowledge Management: Challenges, Solutions, and Technologies,* Pearson Prentice-Hall, Englewood Cliffs, NJ.

Bhattacherjee, A. and G. Premkumar (2004) Understanding changes in belief and attitude toward information technology usage: a theoretical model and longitudinal test, *MIS Quarterly* 28 (2), pp. 229–254.

Bock, G., R. Zmud, Y. Kim, and J. Lee (2004) Behavioral intention formation in knowledge sharing: examining the roles of extrinsic motivators, social-psychological forces, and organizational climate, *MIS Quarterly* 29 (1), pp. 87–111.

Choo, C. W. (1998) *The Knowing Organization: How Organizations Use Information to Construct Meaning, Create Knowledge, and Make Decisions,* Oxford University Press, Oxford.

Davenport, T. H. and L. Prusak (1998) *Working Knowledge,* Harvard Business School Press, Harvard.

Davenport, T., D. Long, and M. Beers (1998) Successful knowledge management projects, *Sloan Management Review* 39 (2), pp. 43–57.

Davis, F. D. (1989) Perceived usefulness, perceived ease of use, and user acceptance of information technology, *MIS Quarterly* 13 (3), pp. 319–340.

Firestone, J. M. and M. W. McElroy (2003) *Key Issues in the New Knowledge Management,* Butterworth-Heinemann, Burlington, MA.

Gefen, D., D. Straub, and M. Boudreau (2000) Structural equation modeling and regression: guidelines for research practice, *Communication of the Association for Information Systems* 4 (7), pp. 1–78.

Hair, J., R. Anderson, R. Tatham, and B. Grablowsky (1979) *Multivariate Data Analysis*, Petroleum Publishing Company.

Holsapple, C. W. and K. D. Joshi (2002) Knowledge management: a threefold framework, *The Information Society* 18, pp. 47–64.

Jennex, M. E. and L. Olfman (2000) Development recommendations for knowledge management/organizational memory systems, *Information Systems Development Conference*, Kristiansand, Norway.

Kenny, D. (2003) Mediation. Retrieved November 22, 2005 from http://davidakenny.net/cm/mediate.htm.

Knapp, E. M. (1998) Knowledge management, *Business and Economic Review* 44 (4), pp. 3–6.

Kogut, B. and U. Zander (1992) *Organization Science* 3, pp. 383–397.

Liebowitz, J. (1999) "Key ingredients to the success of an organization's knowledge management strategy," *Knowledge and Process Management* 6 (1), pp. 37–40.

McEvily, S.K. and B. Chakravarty (2002) "The persistence of knowledge-based advantage: an empirical test for product performance and technological knowledge", *Strategic Management Journal* 23 (4), pp. 285–305.

Mertens, D. (1998) *Research Methods in Education and Psychology: Integrating Diversity with Quantitative and Qualitative Approaches*, Thousand Oaks, Calif, Sage.

Newman, B. (2003) Agents, artifacts, and transformations: The foundations of knowledge flows. In: Holsapple, C. (ed.) *The Knowledge Management Handbook*, Springer, New York. 1, pp. 301–316.

Nonaka, I. (1994) A dynamic theory of organizational knowledge creation, *Organization Science* 5 (1), pp. 14–37.

Nonaka, I. and Takeuchi, H. (1995) *The Knowledge-Creating Company*, Oxford University Press, New York.

Peteraf, M. A. (1993) The cornerstones of competitive advantage: A resource-based view, *Strategic Management Journal*, 14, 179–191.

Poston, R. and C. Speier (2005) Effective use of knowledge management systems: a process model of content ratings and credibility indicators. *MIS Quarterly* 29 (2), pp. 221–244.

Render, B., R. Stair, and N. Balakrishnan (2003) *Managerial Decision Modeling*, Prentice Hall, Upper Saddle River, NJ, USA, pp. 368.

Rich, E. and P. Duchessi (2001) Models for Understanding the Dynamics of Organizational Knowledge in Consulting Firms, Proceeding of the 34th Hawaiian International Conference on System Sciences.

Robson, C. (2002) *Real World Research*, 2nd en, Blackwell Publishing, Cornwall, UK.

Rubenstein-Montano, B., J. Liebowitz, J. Buchwalter, D. McCaw, B. Newman, and K. Rebeck (2001) A systems thinking framework for knowledge management. *Decision Support Systems*, 31, 5–16.

Scott, J. (2000) Facilitating interorganizational learning with information technology, *Journal of Management Information System*, 17 (2), pp. 81–114.

Siemon Website. (October, 2005) Cabling Life Cycles and the Laws of Networking Communications. Retrieved October 14, 2005, from http://www.siemon.com/uk/white_papers/04-03-01_cabling-life.asp

Skyrme, D. and D. Amidon (1997) The knowledge agenda, *Journal of Knowledge Management*, 1 (1), pp. 27–37.

Small Business Statistics. U.S. Small Business Administration. (2004) Retrieved August 4, 2004, from http://www.sbaonline.sba.gov/aboutsba/sbastats.html .

Summary of Small Business Size Standards. U.S. Small Business Administration. (2004) Retrieved August 4, 2004, from http://www.sba.gov/size/summary-whatis.html .

Swartz, N. (2003) The 'wonder years' of knowledge management, *Information Management Journal*, 37 (3), pp. 53.

Takeuchi, H. and I. Nonaka, (1995). *The knowledge Creating Company: How Japanese Companies Create the Dynamics of Innovation*, Oxford University Press, New York, pp. 56–94.

Wiig, K. M. (1993) *Knowledge Management Foundations*, Schema Press Arlington, Tex.

Chapter 13
On Integrating Action Research and Design Research

If we knew what it was we were doing, it would not be called research, would it?

– Albert Einstein

IS research has been criticized for having little influence on practice. One approach to achieving more relevance is to conduct research using appropriate research methods that balance the interests of both researchers and practitioners. This chapter examines the similarities between two methods that address this mandate by adopting a proactive stance to investigating information systems in organizations. These two approaches, action research and design research, both directly intervene in "real-world" domains and effect changes in these domains. We investigate these similarities by examining exemplars of each type of research according to the criteria of the other. Our analysis reveals interesting parallels and similarities between the two suggesting that the two approaches have much to learn from each other. Based on our analysis, we propose ways to facilitate integration of the two approaches that we believe will be useful for both and for IS research in general.

13.1 Introduction

The perceived lack of relevance of IS research for practice has remained a prevalent criticism especially in the last decade or so (Benbasat and Zmud 1999; Dennis 2001; Kock, Gray et al. 2002). The argument is that research must necessarily make a dual contribution to academia and practice. First, the research must add to existing theory in order to make a worthwhile scientific contribution (Davis 1971; Baskerville 2001). Second, the research should assist in solving practical problems of practitioners, problems that are either current or anticipated. Two research methods in the information systems field with this dual orientation are design research (Hevner et al. 2004) and action research (Baskerville and Meyers 2004; Davison et al. 2004). As the IS community becomes more accepting of these diverse research traditions

Sandeep Purao, Matti Rossi and Maung K. Sein

A. Hevner, S. Chatterjee, *Design Research in Information Systems*, Integrated Series
in Information Systems 22, DOI 10.1007/978-1-4419-5653-8_13,
© Springer Science+Business Media, LLC 2010

(Boland and Lyytinen 2004), we need to understand not only how they can be understood within the spectrum of research methods in IS (Mingers and Stowell 1997) but also how the unique strengths of these research methods can be leveraged.

It is the premise of this chapter that design research and action research methods are closely related and can offer unique strengths to the IS research community. However, there has been a separation between the two approaches. This is perhaps attributable to action research having a significant research tradition (Susman and Evered 1978; Baskerville 1999) that design research currently lacks, in spite of significant progress made over the last decade (March and Smith 1995; Purao 2002; Hevner et al. 2004). We believe that the two approaches can significantly inform each other as there is a great degree of similarity and overlap between them, especially since they are both proactive in that they intervene rather than study a phenomenon after the fact (Cole et al. 2005; Järvinen 2007). A growing body of literature is recognizing these cross-fertilization possibilities between AR and DR. Researchers argue for similarity between the two (Järvinen 2007; Lee 2007; Figueiredo and Cunha 2007) as well as caution against fusion (Iivari 2007). Others suggest a middle ground stating that in some situations and contexts, the two may be integrated (Cole et al. 2005; Sein et al. 2007).

To substantiate our argument, we explore the areas of overlap between them, by examining exemplars of each type of research (design research and action research) according to the criteria specified for the other. Through this cross-application of research criteria, we explore implicit assumptions that action and design research approaches may have in common about epistemology, ontology, and, most importantly, axiology (values). Based on the analysis, we propose ways in which each can inform the other and outline a new integrated research approach that exploits the strengths of both of its precursors.

The rest of the chapter is organized as follows. In the next section, we briefly describe the two research approaches, design research and action research, and list the guidelines for each. We then use one research exemplar from each and apply to it the criteria of the other type. In the following section, we discuss implications of our analysis and offer an agenda for an integrated research approach.

13.2 The Research Approaches

13.2.1 Design Research

Design research (DR) consists of activities concerned with the construction and evaluation of technology artifacts to meet organizational needs as well as the development of their associated theories. Consequently, DR is concerned with artificial rather than natural phenomena (March and Smith 1995) and is rooted as a discipline in the sciences of artificial (Simon 1969). Designed physical systems are distinguishable from natural systems by virtue of their teleological causal component; physical systems are designed with fitness of purpose in mind, created to pursue certain ends and evaluated on the basis of conscious selection of alternatives

(Checkland 1981). An information system consists of technology, an associated social setting, and the rich phenomena that emerge from the interaction of the two (Lee 1999). These two research loci, technology and people, are characterized by Hevner et al. (2004) as two major approaches in IS research, behavior science, and design science (or the term used in this chapter, DR). Behavior science is concerned with theories that explain human or organizational behavior; DR is concerned with creating new and innovative artifacts. Thus, DR places axiological emphasis on utility by virtue of the purposeful nature of its phenomena of interest (artifacts). This utility-based goal of DR may at first glance appear to stand in contrast to the goal of behavior research which is truth or understanding. In fact, Hevner et al. (2004) consider these goals as complementary in that truth and understanding inform design and utility informs theory.

However, DR is rooted in pragmatism (see Haack (1976) for a discussion of pragmatism). For the pragmatist, truth and utility are indistinguishable – truth lies in utility. Thus, for DR, the relevance is evaluated by utility provided to the organization and developers. Thus DR must pass both the tests of science and practice (Markus et al. 2002). In other words, DR is not atheoretical tinkering or aimed simply at market acceptance (Purao 2002). It should incorporate theory in the development of the artifact as well as make a theory-building contribution. It should be stressed that the outcome of DR is not only systems. March and Smith (1995) identify four possible design outputs: constructs, models, methods, and instantiations. They further identify two basic activities: build and evaluate. Purao (2002), along with Dasgupta (1996), identifies outcomes that span the spectrum from instantiated artifacts to theoretical contributions. One suggested set of guidelines for conducting and evaluating DR (henceforth, "DR criteria") was proposed by Hevner et al. (2004) and consists of seven elements. These guidelines are summarized in Table 13.1.

Table 13.1   Design research criteria, adapted from (Hevner et al. 2004)

Criterion	Description
1. Design as an artifact	Design research must produce a viable artifact in the form of a construct, a model, a method, or an instantiation
2. Problem relevance	The object of design research is to develop technology-based solutions to important and relevant business problems
3. Design evaluation	The utility, quality, and efficacy of a design artifact must be rigorously demonstrated via well-executed evaluation plans
4. Research contributions	Effective design research must provide clear and verifiable contributions in the areas of the design artifact, design foundations, and/or design methodologies
5. Research rigor	Design research relies upon the application of rigorous methods in both the construction and evaluation of the design artifact
6. Design as a search process	The search for an effective artifact requires utilizing available means to reach desired ends while satisfying laws in the problem environment
7. Communication of research	Design research must be presented effectively to both technology-oriented and management-oriented audiences

13.2.2 Action Research

Action research (AR) is fundamentally a change-oriented approach in which the central assumption is that complex social processes can best be studied by introducing change into these processes and observing their effects (Baskerville 2001). It is a well-established research approach introduced by Kurt Lewin in 1946 to address social system change through action that is at once a means of effecting change and generating knowledge about the change. Within the social science research spectrum, AR occupies a niche defined by focus on practical problems with theoretical relevance (Clark 1972). This unique position allows AR to produce highly relevant results while simultaneously informing theory (Baskerville 1999; Baskerville and Meyers 2004). AR views organizations as a configuration of interacting variables, some of which are highly interdependent; to introduce change into this configuration, one begins with several possible points of intervention and discovers that change may require manipulation of several variables (Clark 1972). Clark, drawing on Leavitt, discusses four salient interacting variables, none of which can be easily controlled for purposes of intervening for organizational change: *tasks*, *technology*, *structure*, and *people*. Each variable may have its own associated change strategies; however due to their high degree of interdependence it is unlikely that any one can be changed without impacting others.

There are several flavors of AR (Baskerville and Meyers 2004) and the epistemological perspective of the action researcher varies depending upon the flavor. The choice is a consequence of the social interventionist perspective of the approach. An action researcher becomes part of the study and interprets the inter-subjective meaning of the observations (Baskerville 1999). Further, the unique nature of each social setting requires consideration of the social values of organization members. Consequently, an idiographic method of enquiry is necessary for AR, i.e., a research approach operationalized through researchers incorporating subjects into their research as collaborators (Baskerville 1999).

Within the field of IS, collaborative mode of AR is strongly advocated (Checkland 1981; Baskerville 2001). Given that the goal of AR is the resolution of a practical problem while simultaneously contributing to scientific theory, a balance between the goal of the researcher (which is by nature epistemological) and that of the sponsor (which is by nature practical) must be maintained for outcome success. AR is, therefore, suited to social situations with which the researcher must be engaged. Researchers must be prepared to react to the research situation and follow it wherever it leads (Checkland 1981).

The description of Susman and Evered (1978) is the most prevalent form of CAR (Baskerville 1999), consisting of a five-phase cyclical process. The first phase, *diagnosing*, is aimed at identifying or defining a problem. The second, *action planning*, involves considering alternative courses of action for solving the problem. The third, *action taking*, consists of selecting a course of action. The fourth, *evaluating*, is aimed at studying consequences of action. The fifth, *specifying learning*, completes the loop by identifying general findings. The five phases are maintained and regulated by the researcher and a client system infrastructure. The infrastructure consists of the research environment and the researcher–client agreement which defines authority for action specification and mutual responsibilities of clients and researchers.

One suggested set of guidelines for conducting and evaluating canonical AR (henceforth, "AR criteria") was proposed by Davison et al. (2004). Their proposed set of criteria for CAR is presented in Table 13.2.

Table 13.2 Canonical action research criteria, adapted from (Davison et al. 2004)

Criterion	Description
1. Principle of researcher–client agreement (RCA)	The RCA provides the basis for mutual commitment and role expectations
2. Principle of cyclical process model (CMP)	The CPM consists of the stages diagnosing, action planning, action taking, evaluating, and specifying learning
3. The principle of theory	Theory must play a central role in action research
4. The principle of change through action	Action and change are indivisible research elements related through intervention focused on producing change
5. The principle of learning through reflection	Considered reflection and learning allow a researcher to make both practical and theoretical contributions

13.3 Cross-Application of Criteria

To examine the similarity between AR and DR, we have applied the AR criteria developed by Davison et al. (2004) to an exemplar DR paper and applied the DR criteria developed by Hevner et al. (2004) to an exemplar AR paper. The exemplars selected for this cross-application were cited by other researchers as high-quality instances of their respective research approach. For the DR exemplar, we chose Markus et al. (2002). This study was reviewed by Hevner et al. (2004) and found to strongly adhere to the guidelines of DR as defined by them. For the AR exemplar, we chose Iverson et al. (2004), which, according to the editors of the September 2004 special issue of *MIS Quarterly*, demonstrates adherence to action research standards and serves as a model for future action research projects (Baskerville and Meyers 2004).

13.3.1 Applying Action Research Criteria to a Design Research Exemplar

The criteria for AR are applied below to the DR exemplar of Markus et al. (2004). This study presents the design and implementation of an IT system called *technology organization and people integration modeler* (TOP modeler) for the support of emergent knowledge process of organizational design.

13.3.1.1 Criterion 1: The Principle of the Researcher–Client Agreement

In the researcher–client agreement (RCA) document, both researchers and clients explicitly agree and commit to the AR approach and the research focus and participant roles are clearly defined. Additionally, the data collection methods, project objectives, and evaluation criteria are explicitly stated. For DR, we do not expect that an explicit agreement necessarily will be present; however, we do expect that motivational factors underlying this principle will be evident.

Although Markus et al. (2002) do not mention the existence of an explicit RCA or discuss details regarding the documentation of data collection methods, objectives, or evaluation criteria, there is evidence of the expected motivational factors that are consistent with this principle. The project was conducted with the active involvement of four companies each of which committed resources in the form of a full-time participant who was dedicated to the project for 3 years.

13.3.1.2 Criterion 2: The Principle of the Cyclical Process Model

The cyclical process model (CPM) is the five-stage model of change of Susman and Evered (1978). According to this principle, the research project should follow the CPM or researchers should justify any deviations from it. Under the CPM, the researcher conducts an independent diagnosis of the organization, plans actions based on that diagnosis, and then implements and evaluates those change actions. Following a change intervention, the researcher reflects on intervention outcomes and makes an explicit decision whether to proceed through an additional change cycle. For DR, we expect a similar iterative lifecycle process to be evident based on the design as a search process criterion of Hevner et al. (2004).

In the development of the TOP modeler, an iterative approach was followed in which functional prototypes were used in authentic use cases of organizational design analysis, rather than mock prototypes in hypothetical scenarios. This allowed Markus et al. (2002) to "intervene directly in the work process and observe which aspects of the system worked and which did not" (p. 196). During an 18-month period, over 70 functional prototypes were evaluated. Reflection was conducted on the outcomes of each prototype evaluation to determine what obstacles were encountered or what questions were raised. In fact, reflection was a specific role of the first author who avoided direct involvement with development, "providing psychological and emotional distance from the project for reflection and identification of lessons learned" (p. 186). However, this distancing is in contrast to the tenets of AR where the participation of the researcher in the intervention is required. Hence, reflection in terms of AR is implicit.

13.3.1.3 Criterion 3: The Principle of Theory

Theory plays a central role in AR, serving as a guide for research activities and as a means of delineating the scope of data collection and analysis (Davison et al.

2004). Theory may be present at the start of a project or develop in a grounded fashion. Typically, changes to theory take place during the reflection stage of AR and lead the project into an additional cycle (Davison et al. 2004). The principle of theory states that the problem domain and setting should be of interest to both the research community and client and that inferred problem causes, change activities, and outcome evaluation must be theory guided. For DR, we expect the same to apply.

Theory played a central role throughout the TOP modeler development process. Using the theoretical framework of Walls et al. (1992) which characterizes IS design theory as consisting of a set of user requirements, a set of system features (or principles for selecting them), and a set of development principles, Markus et al. (2002) first defined the requirements for emergent knowledge processes (EKP) and then developed a kernel theory describing system features and development principles. However, contrary to their expectations, the researchers eventually discovered that the semi-structured decision-making design theories they were using were inapplicable to the problem of organizational design. Consequently, they were forced to re-conceptualize all three aspects of their kernel theory (requirements, features, and development processes). In the end a general design theory for EKPs emerged, which the researchers articulate in detail through a set of six combined design and development principles.

13.3.1.4 Criterion 4: The Principle of Change Through Action

This principle emphasizes the interconnectedness of the concepts of *change* and *action*. Absence of change could imply ineffectiveness of the intervention or the absence of a meaningful problem. Indications of adherence to this principle include motivation of both client and researcher to improve the problem situation, specification of the problem and its hypothetical causes based on diagnosis, and action planning based on these causes. For DR, we expect to see similar evidence of practitioner motivation for change, and change resulting from design outputs. Evidence of change should go beyond mere market acceptance of a design output (Purao 2002) and should reflect the improvement of a previously undesirable problem situation.

This principle is clearly evident in the development of the TOP modeler. First, client motivation, as discussed above, is present. Evidence of behavioral change is apparent at both the individual and organizational levels. Individual level changes include users learning about their organizations, achieving consensus on design issues, reassessing their business strategies, and clarifying business issues. Organizational level changes include the cancellation of the relocation of a plant operation based on weaknesses identified at the target plant as well as the postponement of an international joint venture based on strategic differences uncovered through use of the TOP modeler.

13.3.1.5 Criterion 5: The Principle of Learning Through Reflection

The principle of learning through reflection is a consequence of the dual nature of researcher responsibility to both clients and the research community. Reflection during the cyclical research process is necessary to maintain focus on the practical problems of the clients and their resolution while learning is necessary to advance knowledge toward the goal of making a theoretical contribution. Actions consistent with this principle include researcher-provided progress reports to clients, reflection on outcomes by both researchers and clients, and clear reporting of research activities and outcomes. For DR, we similarly expect evidence of outcome reflection and reporting on research results and implications.

Although Markus et al. (2002) do not explicitly discuss progress reports to clients, it is nonetheless clear that client awareness of TOP modeler development progress was high due to the participative iterative functional prototyping development process utilized. Research outcomes were clearly reported to the research community through (1) the articulation of the existence of an activity area (EKP) that had previously been under-theorized, (2) the demonstration that one process in the general class of EKP can be successfully supported with IT thus facilitating the development of further solutions in this class, (3) the articulation of how features of familiar system types can be effectively integrated to provide support in this domain, (4) the articulation of how development practices need to be modified to meet the needs of EKPs, and (5) setting an agenda for future research through the identification of principles that are subject to empirical validation.

Table 13.3 summarizes the findings from application of the AR criteria to the DR exemplar.

Table 13.3 Application of AR criteria to a DR exemplar

AR criterion	Evidence found in the DR Exemplar
1. The principle of researcher–client agreement (RCA)	No explicit RCA but clear evidence of motivational factors
2. The principle of cyclical process model (CPM)	Iterative design/evaluate process followed
3. The principle of theory	Theory played central role in artifact development and theoretical contribution was made
4. The principle of change through action	Behavioral change evident at both the individual and organizational levels
5. The principle of learning through reflection	No explicit evidence of progress reporting but evidence of strong client engagement; reporting of research outcomes

13.3.2 Applying Design Research Criteria to an Action Research Exemplar

The criteria for DR are applied below to the AR exemplar of Iverson et al. (2004). The research was part of a larger research program and the specific aim of the project was to improve the implementation of software process initiative (SPI) practices.

13.3.2.1 Criterion 1: Design as an Artifact

Although the focus of AR is an organizational change and not the creation of artifacts per se, we expect that intervention in the organizational domain will frequently be associated with the creation of artifacts, which may include outcomes such as documentation of new organizational processes.

Consistent with this definition are the two primary contributions of the exemplar AR study. These contributions were (1) an SPI risk management framework and process and (2) an approach to tailor risk management to specific contexts. These contributions are presented by the researchers as models and methods (similar to March and Smith 1995) in the form of figures and tables that are presented in a generic form and can be tailored to other risk management contexts. However, these were not stated explicitly as artifacts by the authors and hence it is our interpretation that artifacts were created in DR terms.

13.3.2.2 Criterion 2: Problem Relevance

The goal of DR is the solution of organizational problems through the development of technology-based artifacts. As we previously discussed, relevance is a sine qua non of AR. Consequently, one would expect to find clear evidence of problem relevance in an exemplar AR study, and this was the case with the exemplar under investigation.

The research was initiated in the IT department of a large Scandinavian financial institution and was part of a large-scale research program involving four organizations between 1997 and 2000. The aim of the program was to improve the software operation in the participating organizations due to difficulties experienced in achieving satisfactory results in software process improvement initiatives (SPIs). The specific practical problem addressed by the researchers was the question of how risk management can help SPI teams understand and manage their efforts.

13.3.2.3 Criterion 3: Design Evaluation

Measures of effectiveness of design artifacts, such as utility and efficacy, must be rigorously demonstrated via evaluation. For the AR exemplar, we expect to find evidence of evaluation of organizational interventions due to the prominent role played by the evaluation stage in the CPM.

The SPI approach developed in the exemplar AR study was evaluated according to the standard of utility to practitioners. Through several iterations, the SPI framework was utilized by practitioners and refined based on feedback until it reached a stable form that was acknowledged by practitioners as useful. There was no evidence, however, that specific evaluation criteria such as the one suggested by Hevner et al. (2004) or Purao (2002) were applied in a systematic manner to the research outputs.

13.3.2.4 Criterion 4: Research Contributions

DR should provide clear and verifiable contributions in the areas of design artifact, design foundations, and/or design methodologies. For AR, we expect evidence of similar contributions, specifically at the organizational level.

Iverson et al. (2004) discuss several theoretical contributions that result from their study. First, the SPI framework provides a comprehensive, structured understanding of risk areas and resolution strategies. Second, the approach to tailor risk management to specific contexts provided two contributions, a framework for understanding and selecting among the extant approaches to risk management and a process for tailoring risk management to specific contexts that builds on AR literature.

13.3.2.5 Criterion 5: Research Rigor

In both DR and behavioral science research, rigor is based on effective use of the extant knowledge base consisting of theoretical foundations and research methodologies (Hevner et al. 2004). Both DR and AR have their own respective quality criteria, adherence to which is constitutive of rigor. The rigor of the exemplar study is based on adherence to a set of AR criteria based on the canonical criteria of Davison et al. (2004).

Demonstration of this adherence consisted of visibility of the following concepts in the chapter: roles, documentation, control, usefulness, theory, and transfer. A more stringent test of rigor germane to the cross-application of criteria would be to apply the DR criteria as stated by Hevner et al. (2004). This is assessed by application of rigorous methods in the construction and evaluation of the designed artifact. The rigor in the study of Iversen et al. does not apply directly to the artifacts they construct. Instead, they lie in the logic and theoretical premise behind SPI and the collaborative research approach.

13.3.2.6 Criterion 6: Design as a Search Process

Because it is rarely feasible to identify optimal design configurations, the process of designing artifacts is fundamentally cyclical, characterized by a generate test cycle and constrained by available technology and resources to produce a solution in a satisficing manner (Simon 1969). We expect to find a similar search process in AR though the nature of constraints may be different. The cyclical process model of AR is, in fact, fundamentally similar to this DR search process where the tasks *action planning/intervention/evaluate* are analogous to *generate/test*.

This search process was followed by Iversen et al. who performed four cycles of the CPM in which the risk management approach iteratively evolved from the initial prototype. The nature of constraints they encountered appears to be largely resource-based though this is not explicitly acknowledged in the chapter.

13.3.2.7 Criterion 7: Communication of Research

Research results must be communicated to both practitioners and researchers. For DR, sufficient implementation detail must be provided to practitioners to enable the construction of the artifact in a new context and articulation of the theoretical contribution must be provided to researchers. For AR, we similarly expect a high level of detail to be provided to enable the replication of a successful intervention in a similar organizational context.

Iverson et al. presented their results to both audiences through the publication of their research findings in *MIS Quarterly* (Iverson et al. 2004) as well as a book chapter targeting SPI practitioners (Iverson, Mathiassen et al. 2002). In each outlet, the authors were careful to articulate implications for stakeholders, researchers, and practitioners.

Table 13.4 summarizes the findings of the application of the criteria of DR to the AR exemplar.

Table 13.4 Application of DR criteria to an AR exemplar

DR criterion	Evidence found in the AR exemplar
1. Design as an artifact	Instantiation of SPI models and methods (implicit)
2. Problem relevance	Clear evidence of relevance due to high resource commitment by organizations involved
3. Design evaluation	Evaluation based on utility to practitioners
4. Research contributions	Several theoretical contributions present
5. Research rigor	Explicit discussion of adherence to canonical criteria and logic behind SPI
6. Design as a search process	Four CPM cycles executed before the risk management approach was evaluated as stable and usable
7. Communication of research	Results were communicated to both practitioners and researchers

13.4 A Way Forward

Our intent in this chapter was to examine similarities between AR and DR by adopting a novel approach: cross-application of research criteria. Our analysis reveals that the two research approaches indeed share important assumptions regarding ontology, epistemology, and, more importantly, axiology. First, the *ontology* to which both research approaches subscribe assumes that the phenomenon of interest does not remain static through the application of the research process. In the case of AR, the organizational phenomenon undergoes change by virtue of the consultant–researcher engagement with the client to bring about desired changes. In the case of DR, an artifact comes into being through application of the research process. This is seen in the application of DR criterion 6 to AR and the application of AR criterion 1 to DR. Next, the *epistemology* that both research approaches subscribe to assumes a mode of knowing that involves intervening to effect change and reflecting on this intervention. In the case of AR, the intervention occurs in an organizational setting. In the case of DR, the intervention occurs by way of envisioning and constructing an artifact that will bring about the desired change in the organization. This is seen in the application of DR criterion 1 to AR and the application of AR criterion 4 to DR. Finally, the *axiology* that both subscribe to is evident in the manner in which both value the relevance of the research problem and emphasis on practical utility and theoretical knowledge simultaneously. This is seen in the manner in which DR criteria 2 and 3 and AR criterion 5 are applicable to one another.

The arguments above suggest that it may be possible to place AR and DR within a common meta-paradigm, pragmatism. It is intriguing, then, that in the information systems field, canonical expositions of the two research approaches (e.g., Baskerville 2001; Hevner et al. 2004) have taken no note of the other. For example, the process and criteria for design research do not take into account the rich tradition of similar work done on action research. Neither do the process nor do criteria for action research take into consideration writings about search processes and other mechanisms that design researchers use. Below, we suggest three specific possibilities where cross-fertilization of ideas from these two research traditions can lead to a more useful understanding of research approaches, criteria and outcomes.

13.4.1 Adding "Reflection" to Augment Learning from Design Research

One shortcoming in DR is the lack of a clear stage for "reflection" to specify learning. This requires reflecting on the outcomes to understand how they have contributed to the change sought, and why the success or failure is observed in the organizational settings. For DR, this can be especially problematic when the DR project is not carried out in a specific organizational context, for example, in the case of market-based development. The outcome of such a project may result in an artifact, which needs to be shown to have advanced both theoretical and practical knowledge. Current prescriptions about DR research, such as those by Hevner et al. (2004), suggest a useful set of criteria for this purpose, focusing primarily on the evaluation of DR outputs and less on reflection that may provide articulations of what has been learned. The perspective provided by an AR approach can be useful for the latter and may be incorporated as reflection on the outcome of the research process. A specific implementation may include interjecting an AR cycle at the last stage of DR process. Alternatively, a DR project may be framed as an AR project if an organizational problem needs to be solved, and the action involves building a system (to the development of TOP modeler by Markus et al. 2002). In both cases, the two research cycles become intertwined in different ways.

13.4.2 Concretizing Learning from Action Research by Adding "Build"

While canonical AR incorporates a specific learning by reflection stage, the outcomes of AR have been difficult to carry forward without a tangible artifact. Owing in part to this intangible nature, cumulative learning from AR projects has remained a matter of concern. In discussing this problem, Braa, Monteiro et al. (2004) propose that knowledge is shared through networks of organizations and not as an explicit artifact of individual AR projects. (It is revealing that their solution, using networks, was itself through an AR project.) In short, while all AR studies generalize their findings into abstractions and concepts, contributions toward theory building are rare (notable exceptions include the soft systems methodology). One way to concretize or formalize learning is to frame the output of AR as a DR artifact, such as prototypes, frameworks, or models (March and Smith 1995). It can also be argued that the nature of the theoretical contributions from DR is more an embedded artifact, while for AR it is generalizable change processes. In our exemplar, the enhanced SPI is such an artifact. Converting the outcomes of an AR process into an artifact then can serve as the theoretical premise for the next cycle of action research. One specific approach to doing this would involve amplifying the AR *action taking* phase by including the building of a design artifact.

13.4.3 Envisioning an Integrated Research Process

The two possibilities outlined above are indications of the overarching finding based on our analysis: that the "essence" of the two approaches may, indeed, be similar or have much in common. Carrying the idea further would, then, involve a new synthesized research process that would fully integrate the two approaches: design research and action research (see Fig. 13.1). As a preliminary conceptualization, we offer the following four-stage model. The first stage can be problem definition, corresponding to the first step in both, problem definition in DR and diagnosing the problem in AR. In the synthesized approach, this stage would include both perceived problems as a design researcher may conceptualize them or reported problems as an action researcher may start with based on a client engagement. It would be preferred that there is a possible generalizable design solution that can form a basis for a solution for a specific client concern. The second stage is intervention, similar to the "build" stage of DR and a combination of the action planning and action taking stage of AR. The synthesized research process requires both, the construction of an IT

Fig. 13.1 A synthesized
research approach

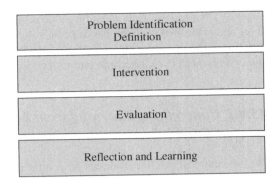

artifact and intervening to change the organization preferably used simultaneously so that the design can accommodate to problems encountered in practice. The third stage is evaluation and incorporates the criteria that are germane to both approaches. The final step would be reflection and learning, which abstracts knowledge to make practical and theoretical contribution to the field.

The proposed research approach would satisfy the call for more relevant information systems research and it can be seen to be in the core of the discipline. Furthermore, the proposed approach clearly distinguishes IS from computer science and organizational science.

We can already see possible instantiations of this integrated approach. Lindgren, Henfridsson et al. (2004) use a canonical action research approach to develop design principles for a competence management system. Their research involved developing prototypes and has the characteristics of a DR approach. It is possible that without cross-fertilization between the two approaches, this research would become part of the AR literature only and remain outside the ken of the DR literature. Clearly, the stress on relevance, problem solving, and intervening to learn are values inherent to both AR and DR. The last point, intervening to learn, also takes a proactive stance to IS research. Not only are we rigorously studying and understanding IS phenomena, we are also stressing relevance at the same time by solving practical problems and constructing reality (Simon 1969). This paradigm has the promise of alleviating a common criticism leveled at academic research that it is carried out in a vacuum and with little influence on practice.

13.5 Conclusions

In this chapter we have analyzed two modes of proactive research: design research and action research. By evaluating a representative example of each by the criteria of the other we have revealed the natural compatibility between these two approaches to scientific inquiry. Furthermore, we showed that the process models of both approaches are similar to a degree that we can form a common process model for them and outlined an integrated approach for combined AR–DR research programs. The contribution of our chapter is thus twofold. First, as these research approaches are compatible, they can inform each other. Especially design research can gain from the more mature body of evaluation and other criteria of performing action research. Second, as both approaches have common starting points and goals, we can perform research in organizations in a manner where we choose between design research and action research only in the stage of the research where we plan the intervention; in other words we can do a late binding of the change action, based on the needs of the situation. Delving deeper into the essences of the two approaches remain on our future research agenda. Specific aspects that need to be examined include their epistemological roots and possible reasons why the two approaches have evolved independently. We believe that our contributions and findings call for further research into possibilities of dynamic co-operation between DR and AR projects.

References

Baskerville, R. (1999) Investigating information systems with action research, *Communications of AIS* 2, pp. 2–31.

Baskerville, R. (2001) Conducting action research: high risk and high reward in theory and practice, *Qualitative Research in IS: Issues and Trends* E. M. Trauth. Hershey, PA, Idea Group.

Baskerville, R. and M. D. Meyers (2004) Special issue on action research in information systems: making is research relevant to practice – forward, *MIS Quarterly* 28 (3), pp. 329–335.

Benbasat, I. and R. W. Zmud (1999) Empirical research in information systems: the practice of relevance, *MIS Quarterly* 23 (1), pp. 3–16.

Boland, R. J. and K. Lyytinen (2004) *Information Systems Research as Design: Identity, Process, and Narrative*, IFIP Working Group 8.2 Conference, Manchester, UK.

Braa, J., E. Monteiro et al. (2004) Networks of action: sustainable health information systems across developing countries. *MIS Quarterly* 28 (3), pp. 337–362.

Checkland, P. (1981) *Systems Thinking Systems Practice*, John Wiley & Sons, New York.

Clark, P. A. (1972) *Action Research and Organizational Change*, Harper & Row, Ltd., London.

Cole, R., S. Purao et al. (2005) *Being Rigorously Relevant: Design Research and Action Research in Information Systems*, ICIS, AIS, Las Vegas, NV.

Dasgupta, S. (1996) *Technology and Creativity*, Oxford University Press, New York, NY.

Davis, M. S. (1971) That's interesting! Towards a phenomenology of sociology and a sociology of phenomenology. *Philosophy of Social Science* 47, pp. 22–43.

Davison, R. M., M. G. Martinsons et al. (2004) Principles of canonical action research, *Information Systems Journal* 14 (1), pp. 65–86.

de Figueiredo, A. and P. de Cunha (2007) Action research and design in information systems: two faces of a single coin, in Kock, N. (ed.), *Information Systems Action Research: An Applied View of Emerging Concepts and Methods*, Springer, Berlin, pp. 61–96.

Dennis, A. (2001) Relevance in information systems research, *Communications of AIS* 6, Article 10.

Haack, S. (1976) The pragmatist theory of truth, *British Journal of Philosophical Science* 27, pp. 231–249.

Hevner, A. R., S. T. March et al. (2004) Design science in information systems research, *MIS Quarterly* 28 (1), pp. 75–105.

Iivari, J. (2007) A paradigmatic analysis of information systems as a design science, *Scandinavian Journal of Information Systems* 19 (2), pp. 39–63.

Iverson, J. H., L. Mathiassen et al. (2002) Risk Management in Process Action Teams, in L. Mathiassen, J. Pries-Heje, and O. Ngwenyama (eds.) *Improving Software Organizations: From Principle to Practice*, Addison Wesley, Upper Saddle River, NJ.

Iverson, J. H., L. Mathiassen et al. (2004) Managing risk in software process improvement: an action research approach. *MIS Quarterly* 28 (3), pp. 395–433.

Järvinen, P. (2007) Action research is similar to design science. *Quality & Quantity* 41, pp. 37–54.

Kock, N., P. Gray et al. (2002) IS research relevance revisited: subtle accomplishment, unfulfilled promise, or serial hypocrisy, *Communications of AIS* 8, Article 23.

Lee, A. (1999) Inaugural editor's comments. *MIS Quarterly* 23 (1), pp. v–xi.

Lee, A. (2007) Action is an artifact: what action research and design science offer to each other, in Kock, N. (ed.), *Information Systems Action Research: An Applied View of Emerging Concepts and Methods*, Springer, Berlin, pp. 43–60.

Lindgren, R., O. Henfridsson et al. (2004) Design principles for competence management systems: a synthesis of an action research study, *MIS Quarterly* 28 (3), pp. 435–472.

March, S. T. and G. F. Smith (1995) Design and natural science research on information technology, *Decision Support Systems* 15 (4), pp. 251–266.

Markus, M. L., A. Majchrzak et al. (2002) A design theory for systems that support emergent knowledge processes, *MIS Quarterly* 26 (3), pp. 179–212.

Mingers, J. and F. Stowell (1997) *Information Systems: An Emerging Discipline?* McGraw-Hill, London.

Purao, S. (2002) *Design Research in the Technology of Information Systems: Truth or Dare*, School of Information Sciences and Technology, The Pennsylvania State University, Pennsylvania, p. 32.

Sein, M. K., M. Rossi, and S. R. Purao (2007) Exploring the limits to the possible: a response to Iivari, *Scandinavian Journal of Information Systems* 19 (2), pp. 105–110.

Simon, H. A. (1969) *The Sciences of the Artificial*, MIT Press, Cambridge, MA.

Susman, G. I. and R. D. Evered (1978) An assessment of the scientific merits of action research, *Administrative Science Quarterly* 23, pp. 582–603.

Walls, J. G., G. R. Widmeyer et al. (1992) Building an information system design theory for vigilant EIS, *Information Systems Research* 3 (1), pp. 36–59.

Chapter 14
Design Science in the Management Disciplines

> *Management is that for which there is no algorithm. Where*
> *there is an algorithm, it's administration.*
>
> – Roger Needham.

Design science and natural science are complementary research paradigms in the management disciplines. Fundamentally the task of management is to develop, articulate, and achieve organizational goals and purposes. Design science research addresses that task by creating novel and effective artifacts that are demonstrated to improve managers' capability to change "existing situations into preferred ones" (Simon (1996), p. 130). Natural science research addresses it by developing theories that provide deep, principled explanations of phenomena, justified by rigorous empirical evidence that managers can use to guide their actions. Designed artifacts have no special dispensation from the laws of nature; however, business organizations and the environments in which they operate are social constructions (Searle, J. R. (1995)). They are themselves *artifacts* designed to achieve human goals, purposes, and intentions, influenced by and operating within the context of emergent and intentional human behavior. Furthermore, natural science explanations of how or why an artifact works or does not work may lag years behind the application of the artifact. If academic research is to make significant contributions to management practice it must utilize the results from each paradigm to guide the other. There is evidence that this integration is beginning to take place in several management disciplines including information systems and organizational science. This paper summarizes and assesses this emerging work.

14.1 Introduction

Design is fundamental to the management disciplines (Simon 1996, Romme 2003, Boland et al. 2008). Managers are engaged in the design and implementation of

Salvatore T. March and Timothy J. Vogus

A. Hevner, S. Chatterjee, *Design Research in Information Systems*, Integrated Series
in Information Systems 22, DOI 10.1007/978-1-4419-5653-8_14,
© Springer Science+Business Media, LLC 2010

business systems aimed at improving organizational performance. A manager's professional responsibility is to transform existing situations into preferred ones, to shape social organizations and economic processes and to create value (Boland et al. 2008).

Yet with the possible exception of management science, academic research in the management disciplines is primarily based on the natural science paradigm. "Organizational phenomena are approached as empirical objects with descriptive properties" (Romme 2003, p. 558), which emerge through natural processes and are governed by the laws of nature. The goal of scientific research is to discover these laws by studying extant organizations, positing theories that explain or predict extant phenomena, and empirically testing those theories. However, organizational phenomena are both emergent and designed. Emergent phenomena occur as designed artifacts are appropriated and engaged in the performance of organizational tasks (Garud et al. 2006). The success of an organization depends on both the design of the organization – its structure, strategies, leadership, incentives, etc. – and the execution of that design by people who exhibit, among other characteristics, free will in moral, ethical, and economic judgments.

Echoing Daft and Lewin (1990), Romme (2003) contends that "the study of organizations needs a design mode ... of engaging in research" as a mechanism to address the "persistent relevancy gap" in organizational studies research (pp. 558–559). Iivari (2007) and Hevner (2007) present a similar view of research in the information systems discipline. Addressing the issue of research relevance Benbasat and Zmud (1999, p. 191) conclude that "our focus should be on how to best design IT artifacts and IS systems to increase their compatibility, usefulness, and ease of use or on how to best manage and support IT or IT-enabled business initiatives." Boland et al. (2008, p. 12) contend that "giving serious attention to Simon's call for recognizing the importance of designing to management is long overdue."

However, natural science and design science are not dichotomous. They are two sides of the same coin. Pragmatist philosophers, for example, argue that truth (justified theory) and utility (artifacts that are effective) are inseparable and that scientific research should be evaluated in light of its practical implications (see, e.g., Aboulafia 1991). Thus science and design represent a "virtuous cycle" in management research (Hevner 2007) with the results of scientific inquiry being "reformulated into (preliminary) design propositions" and the results of design inquiry being "reformulated into hypotheses" that can be tested scientifically (Romme 2003, p. 568).

Natural science and design science, in fact, represent two perspectives on the acquisition and codification of knowledge (March and Smith 1995). Natural science studies "how things are." Design science studies "how things ought to be" (Simon 1996). Design science is artifact-oriented. Its products are assessed against intentional criteria of value or utility (Dunbar and Starbuck 2006). Rather than producing general theoretical knowledge, design science produces and applies knowledge of tasks or situations in order to create effective artifacts. Design problems can be framed in different ways and may have conflicting goals and evaluation criteria. Continual problem finding, framing, and re-evaluation are core activities of design (Rittel and Webber 1973). Research results are perishable (March and Smith 1995). Consequently design as a research paradigm focuses on problem solving and learning by doing (Markus et al. 2002, Järvinen 2007, Daft and Lewin 1990, Argyris et al. 1974, 1985).

Natural science research consists of two activities, discovery and justification (Kaplan 1964). Discovery is the process of generating or proposing scientific claims (e.g., theories). Justification includes activities by which such claims are tested for validity. The discovery process is not well understood. It is fundamentally a creative process of observation and positing explanations. Justification, on the other hand, has been heavily prescribed for by philosophers of science (March and Smith 1995). It makes extensive use of the hypothetico-deductive method in which observational hypotheses deduced from theories are evaluated against norms of truth or explanatory power. Claims must be consistent with observed facts, the ability to predict future observations being a mark of explanatory success (Bechtel 1988). Progress is achieved as new theories provide deeper, more encompassing, and more accurate explanations. Most scientific methodologies used by management researchers are prescriptions for collecting and assessing data in this way (Jenkins 1985, Romme 2003, Iivari 2007).

Parallel to the discovery–justification pair from natural science research, design science research also consists of two activities, build and evaluate (March and Smith 1995). Build is the process of constructing an artifact for a specific purpose and evaluate is the process of determining how well the artifact performs. Analogous to the discovery process in natural science, the build process in design science is a creative process of generating and representing the space of alternative solutions and devising mechanisms for moving from worse to better ones. However, in contrast to the justification process in natural science, the evaluation process in design science is task and situation specific. Significant difficulties result from the fact that the evaluation of an artifact is related to its intended use within a prescribed environment. Thus the evaluation criteria are relative to a particular purpose and environment and to the intended use of an artifact. General problem-solving methods, for example, are applicable to many different problems with performance varying considerably over the domain of application. Thus, not only must an artifact be evaluated but also the evaluation criteria themselves must be determined for the artifact in a particular environment.

Managers are understandably concerned about questions such as "Why do some investments in business systems and organizational structures not result in an improvement in firm performance?" and "What investments will do so?" The first is a theory-based, causal-related question. The second is a design-based, problem-solving question. Each represents a critical class of research questions in the management disciplines. Answering the first question requires an understanding of phenomena that occur at the intersection of markets, industries, organizations, people, and business technologies – the locus of the management disciplines. Researchers addressing it must develop and justify theories that provide deep principled explanations of these phenomena. Such theories must explain what happened, why it happened, and possibly predict what will happen within a given context. This is the focus of much of the research published in the management literature.

While such theories may be strictly explanatory in nature, their relevancy and value are determined by the degree to which they enable managers to design business systems that improve organizational performance (Romme 2003, Dunbar and Starbuck 2006, Alter 2003, Benbasat and Zmud 1999). This is the focus of the second question. Answering it is fundamentally a design task that requires shaping artifacts and events to create an envisioned, more desired future (Boland and Collopy 2004). Researchers addressing it must build and evaluate novel and innovative artifacts that extend the boundaries of management knowledge, addressing important problems heretofore not thought to be amenable to structural approaches (Denning 1997, Sinha and Van de Ven 2005, Vaast and Levina 2006). This is the focus of design science research in the management disciplines.

14.2 Design Concepts

Design is both verb and noun: activity and result, process and product. Design implies purpose and intent (Simon 1996). People design artifacts for specific purposes (Fuller 1992). Those purposes include both aesthetics and accomplishment: form and function, art and tool, beauty and utility. A design (noun) is a conceptualization – an idea, a plan, whose purpose is demonstrated through its implementation and use. A design is evaluated by the degree to which its implementation fulfills that purpose. The evaluation may be primarily subjective as in art and fashion or it may be objective as in structural engineering and mechanical systems or it may be a combination of both as in architecture and management.

Design is considered to be a "wicked problem" when there are (1) conflicting, changing, and ambiguous desired ends; (2) a very large, if not infinite number of design alternatives, at least some of which are unknown; and (3) the consequences of design decisions are difficult or impossible to assess (Rittel and Webber 1973). In such situations creativity, innovation, and imagination are required in all stages of the design process: (1) the conceptualization and visualization of desired goals, (2) the determination of a reasonable set of design alternatives, (3) the development of design evaluation criteria, (4) the assessment of the consequences of design decisions, and (4) the selection of a satisfactory alternative (Simon 1996). Business organizations are designed artifacts whose general purpose is to accomplish the goals of its constituencies. Those goals include maximization of shareholder value, social responsibility, and development of human capital, among many others.

Of course not all organizational design problems are "wicked." To the extent that management can articulate and control the goals and the decision alternatives and predict outcomes of their actions, organizational design problems become more "tame." Such problems are satisfactorily addressed by normal application of best practice – analogous to the practice of "normal science" (Kuhn 1970). It is the wicked organizational problems that are in need of design science research – problems for which managers must balance the goals of various constituencies when developing and implementing organizational designs. Studying such problems requires the type of paradigm shift offered by design science.

Furthermore, design in an organizational context differs from design in the context of physical artifacts. Unlike physical artifacts that obey immutable laws of nature organizations are social constructions (Searle 1995, 2006) that depend upon human behavior and collective intentionality for their success or failure. It is not that business organizations are immune from the laws of nature; but insofar as the components from which organizations are constructed and the environments in which they operate are themselves ideas (Searle 1995), their performance is dependent upon the acceptance and execution of those ideas. The designed artifacts of business organizations are conceptual objects such as incentives, reporting relationships, training, organizational memory, routines and procedures, agreements/contracts, and information systems (Walsh and Ungson 1991, Nelson and Winter 1982, March and Simon 1958, Feldman and Pentland 2003, Benbasat and Zmud 1999). These enable managers to organize, direct, control, and monitor the utilization of the organization's resources (people, machines, products, money, knowledge, etc.).

Organizations are conceptual artifacts – policies, rules, roles, responsibilities, authority, work systems designed to enable and empower people to accomplish tasks and achieve goals. Organization design involves the creation of roles, processes, and formal reporting relationships in an organization. Organizations are designed for specific purposes. These may be explicitly although imperfectly captured in an organization's mission statement or they may be implicitly captured in the culture of the organization. Economists argue that the purpose of a firm is to maximize its long-term value. Of course different stakeholders may ascribe different, multidimensional, and even conflicting criteria to assessing the "value" of the firm.

Information systems and organizational routines (Feldman and Pentland 2003) are among the key components of organizational design as they are extensions of human cognitive capabilities. They are the tools of knowledge work enabling new organizational forms and providing management and decision-making support. For example, incentive structures related to job performance such as achieving sales, product quality, or customer satisfaction goals require information gathering and analysis capabilities. Management of outsourcing and inter-organizational partnerships requires secure information sharing. Identification of problems and opportunities requires the gathering and analysis of "business intelligence" (Simon 1977). More and more frequently business decisions are made based on computer-based analysis and recommendations. Similarly, organizational routines are intended to provide guidance to human action within prescribed organizational contexts. Yet even such artifacts are appropriated and adapted by humans in ways and for purposes that the designers may not have envisioned (Feldman and Pentland 2003).

Thus design must be informed by appropriate theories that explain or predict human behavior; however, these may be insufficient to enable the development and adaptation of effective organizational artifacts. Romme (2003, p. 158) contends that scientific theories may explain "emergent organizational phenomena" related to extant organizational forms and artifacts but they "cannot account for qualitative novelty (Bunge 1979, Ziman 2000)" achieved by human intention, creativity, and innovation in the design and appropriation of such artifacts. That is, science, the process of understanding "what is," may be insufficient for design, the process of understanding "what can be."

Simon (1996) argues that management is a profession and that design differentiates the sciences from the professions. Design as a research paradigm focuses on the construction and evaluation of novel artifacts that enable the solution of important problems for which extant theory and design knowledge are inadequate. It is not "a-theoretical" but "extra-theoretical." It utilizes extant theory and design knowledge but is fundamentally a creative activity in which knowledge is acquired through the building and use of novel problem-solving artifacts, i.e., constructs, models, methods, and instantiations (March and Smith 1995, Hevner et al. 2004). That knowledge must be tested through the evaluation of the produced artifact. Rigorous testing results in a demonstration that the design can be utilized to solve real problems. Designs have no special dispensation from the laws of nature. Hence theoretical research should be utilized to explain why the design works and to specify contingencies upon it. Justification of such theories results in principles that can then become part of the "best practice." However, because organizations and the environments in which they operate are social constructions, such "design theories" are perishable. That is, they are subject to change as the social reality changes. There may, in fact, be no immutable "laws of organizational design" to be discovered and codified.

The importance of design as a mode of research in the management disciplines has been recognized in the academic literature. *Organizational Science* (Dunbar and Starbuck 2006), *Organization Studies* (Jelinek et al. 2008), and *MIS Quarterly* (March and Storey 2008), premier academic journals in their respective disciplines, have recently produced special issues dealing with design science research. All three journals recognize the importance of improving organizational performance, a fundamental goal of design science research and a consequence of theoretical results that guide design practice. In the next section we review the work in organizational studies.

14.3 Design Science Research in Organizational Studies

In the prior sections we have articulated the design science research perspective and have begun to detail its application to management. Organization design research has a prominent place in the history of organizational studies, dating back to the classic works of scholars such as Burns and Stalker (1960), Perrow (1967), Lawrence and Lorsch (1967), and Galbraith (1977). This research operates from the premise that design entails an explicit and intentional effort to improve an organization on specific criteria (Dunbar and Starbuck 2006). In other words, design envisions systems that do not yet exist – either completely new systems or new states of existing systems (Jelinek et al. 2008).

The foundational research on organization design focused primarily on impersonal structural characteristics such as span of control, levels of hierarchy, formalization of rules, and standard operating procedures (Madsen et al. 2006). This body of early organization design research coalesced into structural contingency theory which examined a set of organizational attributes "aligned," "fit," or "congruent" with the current state of a knowable world (Grandori and Furnari 2008). The research on fit entailed matching task environment states with organizational design characteristics and examining the corresponding effects on performance. This work evolved into configurational studies that introduced the idea of equifinality – that a variety of design characteristics might be effective under the same circumstances. Empirical results of studies conducted in the structural contingency tradition (both alignment and configuration studies) were largely equivocal, failing to establish causal links between design characteristics and organizational performance. As a result, further empirical research and design theory development were largely abandoned.

Although this tradition dominated early research studies, there were notable exceptions. Representative of these exceptions, Hedberg et al. (1976) argued for organization designing as an ongoing process performed intuitively by managers, designs themselves being processes that generate dynamic sequences of solutions, which, in turn, trigger new designs. However, this work was primarily case-based or simulation-based and lacked actionable conclusions. In general, design science failed to play a significant role in mainstream organization studies research and attempts to engender a design framework were more "cookbooky" (Simon 1996) and one-off than systematic studies. As a result, the impact of research on management practice was limited (Daft and Lewin 1990).

Recently, however, design science research in organizational studies has enjoyed renewed interest and substance (Boland and Collopy 2004, Dunbar and Starbuck 2006, Jelinek et al. 2008). To articulate the form the renewed interest has taken we first review the essence of the design science mindset applied to organization design. Next, we examine recent empirical work in organization design and highlight how design science concepts have been more fully incorporated into this recent work, most notably, by focusing on design as ongoing process rather than one-off solutions and design as guides for thinking, problem solving, and feeling rather than as solutions in and of themselves. Last, we use recent work on design aesthetics (Barry and Rerup 2006) and the subjective experience of design (e.g., Yoo et al. 2006) to articulate a potential research direction for future work.

A design science perspective on organization design has received recent attention in terms of what constitutes a design approach or mindset. First and foremost, the emerging work in this area emphasizes that successfully designing an organization is necessarily messy, dynamic, iterative, and responsive to ever-changing circumstances such that the design at any particular moment is a temporary arrangement to be revisited, revised, or removed as results become apparent, new needs arise, or better methods emerge (Jelinek et al. 2008). That is, organizational design is essentially a "wicked problem."

This approach is reflected in many of the design-led organizations (e.g., IDEO, Nissan Design, Wolff Olins, etc.) studied by Michlewski (2008). These are characterized by their ability and willingness to embrace discontinuity and open-endedness. Embracing discontinuity and open-endedness is reflected in the assumptions that organization designers make about their organizations and the people who populate them. For example, a design mindset views employees as agents capable of knowledgeable and skilled social action (Dougherty 2008). The implications for organizational design are that design artifacts (structures, policies, procedures, etc.) are seen as operational guides that facilitate action and even improvisation rather than as constraints narrowly channeling and directing thought and action (Dougherty 2008).

Similarly, in a study of the design and redesign of a Pediatric Intensive Care Unit, Madsen et al. (2006) found that the "organizational design" exists at least as much in designers' visions and attitudes as in organizations' formal structures. A design science perspective on organization design is not without structure; however, instead of the formalized and stable structures envisioned by structural contingency theory it entails perishable design principles. These may take the form of (i) simple rules that act to shape and guide employee action and sensemaking (Eisenhardt and Sull 2001), (ii) design propositions that are tailored to specific conditions, contexts, and objectives (e.g., "if condition C is present, to achieve A, do B") (Romme and Endenburg 2006), or (iii) a logic of prescription that states "to achieve outcome O in context C, use intervention type I that operates through generative mechanism M" (Denyer et al. 2008). Developing either general design rules or context-dependent prescriptions implies that there are no immutable "laws of nature" that govern the underlying phenomena – designs are open to revision and updating based on changing conditions (March and Smith 1995).

Some recent work has chosen to bridge the structural contingency theory and design science perspectives more completely by exploring the design science mindset as applied to changes in managerial structures and organizational forms. For example, in their study of redesigning organizational structure at NASA after the Columbia shuttle disaster, Carroll et al. (2006) found a design process that utilized software tools (OrgCon and SimVision) to model assessments of various organization designs (e.g., centralization/decentralization) as a means of supplementing intuitive and experiential-based organization design and for providing a technical grammar, i.e., constructs, for assessing alternatives and otherwise revising designs.

Westerman et al. (2006) similarly advocate a balanced position in their study of organizations developing new lines of business. Their findings lead them to conclude that firms should choose the adaptation mode that best fits their strategic context and capabilities, but should do so in a manner that allows for further exploration and design adaptation. Madsen et al. (2006) provide further evidence of the value of balancing adaptation within a structural contingency theory framework with a design science mindset by showing how a clear managerial vision provides sufficient stability to allow for extreme flexibility, distributed knowledge, and decentralized decision making as well as ongoing evolution of structural characteristics.

Jacobides and Billinger (2006) offer a model of how an organization can use its structure to more fully embrace design thinking. In their study of "Fashion, Inc." the authors examined how the organization "opened itself up" by making its boundaries more permeable (i.e., putting more of the organization into contact with the marketplace) which had the effect of enhancing learning, easing monitoring, and allowing for resources to be more readily redeployed to higher value activities. In sum, the results of this work suggest the importance of balancing an adaptation (i.e., a specific structural change) with processes and a mindset of adaptability (openness to learning and new data). Lastly, Vaast and Levina (2006) illustrate the dangers of ignoring design science in favor of a rigid application of structural contingency thinking. Specifically, they document how a new CIO at ServCo carried out a disastrous redesign of the IT organization by viewing design as static (i.e., failing to adapt once the design was implemented) and matching the redesign to a poor model of the organization's internal environment. Specifically, the CIO, through his redesign, virtually eliminated the historically important socially embedded relationships between IT staff and stakeholders and, even in light of new information that made these problems manifest, remained resistant to adapting the design.

Other recent work has examined organizational design as an ongoing process in which patterns of working create and change designs. In their study of Linux and Wikipedia, Garud et al. (2008), for example, found that design operated as both the medium and the outcome of action. In other words, the "incomplete designs" of these tools blur the line between designer and user and in doing so acts as a trigger for generative engagement. The incompleteness and the engagement it engenders transforms the design and creates new avenues for ongoing engagement which, in turn, attracts a new set of contributors who bring into the fold their own contextualized needs, purposes, and goals and leads to further change and refinement.

Barry and Rerup (2006) similarly argue that effective designs rely as much on processes as solutions and that the designs which remain underspecified and retain tension such that design is viewed as an orienting structure and an action-oriented process are most adaptive. But they carry this argument further by adding that aesthetic experience is the "glue" that can keep an organization together amidst such a world of flux (Barry and Rerup 2006). The architectural firm Gehry Partners further exemplifies the notion of design as process (Boland et al. 2008). Managers are seen as primarily "form givers" charged with fostering a "design gestalt" – a capability that combines ideas, resources, tools, and people into collectives that can create "remarkable artifacts" (Yoo et al. 2006). The design gestalt results from ongoing processes of intense collaboration using representational tools (block models, sketches, and software) to rapidly develop and refine prototypes followed by conscious questioning of the prototype design.

Garud et al. (2006) detail similar practices used by Infosys to create and sustain an organizationally distributed mindset of designing and design as process. Infosys possesses an "asking culture" that entails helping, challenging, and "pragmatic experimentation" (i.e., prototyping) and enables iterative cycles of "experiment, learn, refine, and scale-up" all of which comprise the essence of a "design attitude."

This culture and attitude give rise to formalized forums (PSPD and voice of youth) that provide a safe space for offering dissenting opinions which act to help temper rash design and implementation.

Organization design research that has most fully incorporated a design science perspective also presents some of the most interesting opportunities for future research. For example, Yoo et al.'s (2006) study of Gehry Partners suggests that design may start with creativity and emotion (namely, Gehry's representation of his emotional vision) that acts to mobilize action and engage debate among stakeholders, which refines and reconstitutes the design. This assertion merits further empirical exploration and theoretical development. Specifically, what roles do creativity and emotion play in initiating and sustaining the design process? Moreover, what is the affective experience of designing? Are individuals operating in a manner consistent with design science principles more likely to experience "flow" (Quinn 2005)? Is designing in the manner of operation at Gehry partners likely to generate greater flow, increase engagement, and reduce employee turnover?

In their research on Calder and the constructivists and Learning Lab Denmark (LLD) Barry and Rerup (2006) highlight an additional aspect of design that merits exploration – aesthetics. LLD uses its physical architecture to create an ambiance of warm social enclosures and well-lit, comforting centers that help offset the long Scandinavian winters. The authors contend that aesthetics are profoundly intertwined with design formation such that they guide the design process and govern design reception, use, and revision. This contention deserves further investigation with respect to conceptual artifacts such as organizational structures, policies, and procedures as opposed to physical artifacts such as office configurations. Developing and systematizing design principles based on aesthetic aspects of design and exploring their impact more directly could provide useful insights and likely generate novel prescriptions.

14.4 Conclusions

In his seminal book, *The Sciences of the Artificial*, Simon (1996) observes that "Everyone designs who devises courses of action aimed at changing existing situations into preferred ones" (p. 130). The development, implementation, and use of organizational systems are rooted in changing existing situations into preferred ones. Indeed, management itself can be viewed as a design discipline (Simon 1996, Boland and Collopy 2004). Managers within organizational contexts use incentives, reporting relationships, training, knowledge, agreements, and information technology, among other resources, to define work systems through which organizational goals are accomplished (Alter 2003, Galbraith 1977).

Simon (1996) posits a science of design rooted in (1) utility and statistical decision theory to define the "problem space" and (2) optimization and "satisficing" techniques to search it. The problem space represents "desired situations," "the present situation" and "differences between the desired and the present" (p. 141).

Search techniques represent "actions ... that are likely to remove particular differences between desired and present states" (p. 142). Wicked organizational design problems – those requiring design science research studies, are characterized by significant uncertainty, particularly with respect to objectives and alternatives (Rittel and Webber 1973). Hence, the representation of such design problems and the generation and evaluation of design solutions are the major tasks in design science research.

Challenges for design science research in the management disciplines are to build and evaluate artifacts that enable managers and business professionals to (1) describe desired organizational capabilities and their relationship with present and desired organizational situations and (2) develop actions that enable them to implement organizational capabilities that move the organization toward desired situations. Hence design science research is problem-focused. Initial research in a new problem area typically focuses on constructing "sufficient, and not necessary, actions for attaining goals" (p. 144). These are frequently in the form of prototype artifacts that demonstrate the feasibility of addressing the problem (Markus et al. 2002, Walls et al. 1992, Romme 2003). Subsequent research aims at improving the effectiveness and efficiency of attaining goals or demonstrating the necessity of certain actions, thereby adding to our knowledge of goal attainment (Vaishnavi and Kuechler 2007). Simon (1996) describes the latter as improving the factorization of differences yielding parallel search paths and as improving the allocation of resources applied to such paths.

Design science research is increasingly recognized as an equal companion to behavioral science research in the management disciplines including organizational science (Romme 2003) and information technology (Hevner 2007, Iivari 2007). Contributions of design science research are in the combined novelty and utility of constructed artifacts. These must be demonstrated in the presentation of design science research. Demonstrating that existing business artifacts and theories are or are not adequate for a specified problem is an important step in this process as is comparing the utility of existing artifacts within specific organizational contexts.

Thus, a design science research contribution requires: (1) identification and clear description of a relevant organizational problem, (2) demonstration that no adequate solutions exist in the extant knowledge base, (3) development and presentation of a novel artifact (constructs, models, methods or instantiations) that addresses the problem, (4) rigorous evaluation of the artifact enabling the assessment of its utility, (5) articulation of the value added to the knowledge base and to practice, and (6) explanation of the implications for management practice (Hevner et al. 2004). Echoing Daft and Lewin (1990) and Romme (2003) we contend that this mode of research will indeed have a significant impact on management practice.

References

Aboulafia, M. (1991) *Philosophy, Social Theory, and the Thought of George Herbert Mead* (SUNY Series in Philosophy of the Social Sciences), State University of New York Press.

Alter, S. (October 2003)"18 Reasons Why IT-Reliant Work Systems Should Replace 'The IT Artifact' as the Core Subject Matter of the IS Field," *Communications of the AIS* (12), October 2003, pp. 365-394.

Argyris, C., R. Putnam, and S. Diana McLain (1985) *Action Science,* San Francisco, Jossey-Bass.

Argyris, C. and D. Schön (1974) *Theory in Practice,* San Francisco, Jossey Bass.

Barry, D. and C. Rerup (2006) Going mobile: aesthetic design considerations from calder and the constructivists. *Organization Science* 17 (2), 262–276.

Bechtel, W. (1988) *Philosophy of Science: An Overview for Cognitive Science,* Lawrence Erlbaum, Hillsdale, NJ.

Benbasat, I. and R.W. Zmud (March 1999) Empirical research in information systems: the practice of relevance, *MIS Quarterly* 23 (1), pp. 3–16.

Boland, R. J. and F. Collopy (2004) *Managing as Designing,* Stanford University Press, Palo Alto, CA.

Boland, R. J., F. Collopy, K. Lyytinen, and Y. Yoo (Winter 2008) "Managing as designing: lessons for organization leaders from the design practice of Frank O. Gehry", *Design Issues* 24 (1), pp. 10–25.

Bunge, M. (1979) *Causality and Modern Science,* 3rd rev. ed, Dover Publications, New York.

Burns, T. and G. M. Stalker (1960) *The Management of Innovation,* Oxford University Press, New York.

Carroll, T. N., Gormley, T. J., Bilardo, V. J., Burton, R. M., and K. L. Woodman (2006) Designing a new organization at NASA: an organization design process using simulation. *Organization Science* 17 (2), 202–214.

Daft, R. L. and A. Y. Lewin. (1990) Can organization studies begin to break out of the normal science strait jacket? An editorial essay. *Organization Science,* 1 (1), 1–9.

Denning, P. J. (February 1997) A New Social Contract for Research, *Communications of the ACM* 40 (2), pp. 132–134.

Denyer, D., Tranfield, D., and J. E. van Aken (2008) Developing design propositions through research synthesis, *Organization Studies* 29 (3), 393–413.

Dougherty, D. (2008) Bridging social constraint and social action to design organizations for innovation, *Organization Studies* 29 (3), 415–434.

Dunbar R. L. M. and W. H. Starbuck (March-April 2006) Learning to design organizations and learning from designing them, *Organization Science* 17 (2), pp. 171–178.

Eisenhardt, K. M. and D. N. Sull (2001) Strategy as simple rules, *Harvard Business Review* 79 (1), 106–116.

Feldman, M. S. and B. T. Pentland (2003) Reconceptualizing organizational routines as a source of flexibility and change, *Administrative Science Quarterly* 48 (1), 94–118.

Fuller, R. B. (1992) *Cosmography: A Posthumous Scenario for the Future of Humanity,* Macmillan Publishing Company, New York, NY.

Galbraith, J. R. (1977) *Organization Design,* Reading, MA, Addison-Wesley.

Garud, R., Jain, S., and P. Tuertscher, (2008) Incomplete by design and designing for incompleteness, *Organization Studies* 29 (3), 351–371.

Garud, R., Kumaraswamy, A., and Sambamurthy, V. (March-April 2006) Emergent by design: performance and transformation at infosys technologies, *Organization Science* 17 (2), pp. 277–286.

Grandori, A. and Furnari, S. 2008. A chemistry of organization: combinatory analysis and design, *Organization Studies* 29 (3), 459–485.

Hedberg, B. L. T., Nystrom, P. C., and W. H. Starbuck (1976) Camping on seesaws: prescriptions for a self-designing organization, *Administrative Science Quarterly* 21 (1), 41–65.

Hevner, A. (2007) A three cycle view of design science research, *Scandinavian Journal of Information Systems* 19 (2), pp. 87–92.

Hevner, A., March, S. T., Park, J., and S. Ram (March 2004) Design science research in information systems, *MIS Quarterly* 28(1), pp. 75–105.

Iivari (2007) A paradigmatic analysis of Information Systems as a design science, *Scandinavian Journal of Information Systems* 9 (2), pp. 39–64.

Jacobides, M. G. and S. Billinger (2006) Designing the boundaries of the firm: from "Make, Buy, or Ally" to the dynamic benefits of vertical architecture. *Organization Science* 17 (2), 249–261.

Järvinen, P. (February 2007) Action research is similar to design science, *Quality and Quantity* 41 (1), pp. 37–54.

Jelinek, M. A., Romme, G. L., and R. J. Boland (2008) Introduction to the special issue: organization studies as a science for design: creating collaborative artifacts and research, *Organization Studies* 29 (3), 317–329.

Jenkins, M. A. (1985) Research methodologies and MIS research, in E. Mumford, et al. (eds.) *Research Methodologies in Information Systems*, Elsevier Science Publishers B. V., North Holland, pp. 103–117.

Kaplan, A. (1964) *The Conduct of Inquiry: Methodology for Behavioral Science*, Crowell, San Francisco, CA.

Kuhn, T. S. (1970) *The Structure of Scientific Revolutions*, University of Chicago Press, Chicago, IL.

Lawrence, P. R. and J. W. Lorsch (1967) *Organizations and Environment*, Harvard Business School Press, Boston, MA.

Madsen, P. M., Desai, V. M., Roberts, K. H., and D. Wong (2006) Mitigating hazards through continuing design: the birth and evolution of a pediatric intensive care unit, *Organization Science* 17 (2), 239–248.

March, J. G. and H. A. Simon (1958) *Organizations*, John Wiley & Sons, Inc., New York.

March, S. T. and G. F. Smith (1995) Design and natural science research on information technology, *Decision Support Systems*, 15 (4), pp. 251–266.

March, S. T. and V. Storey (Forthcoming 2008) Design science in the information systems discipline: an introduction to the special issue on design science research, *MIS Quarterly*. (32:4), pp. 725–730.

Markus, M. L., Majchrzak, A., and L. Gasser (September 2002) A design theory for systems that support emergent knowledge processes, *MIS Quarterly* 26 (3), pp. 179–212.

Michlewski, K. (2008) Uncovering design attitude: inside the culture of designers. *Organization Studies* 29 (3), 373–392.

Nelson, R. R. and S. G. Winter (1982) *An Evolutionary Theory of Economic Change*, Harvard University Press, Cambridge, MA.

Perrow, C. (1967) A framework for the comparative analysis of organizations, *American Sociological Review* 32 (2), 194–208.

Quinn, R. W. (2005) Flow in knowledge work: high performance experience in the design of national security technology, *Administrative Science Quarterly* 50, 610–641.

Rittel, H. and W. Melvin (1973) Dilemmas in a general theory of planning, pp. 155–169, *Policy Sciences*, Vol. 4, Elsevier Scientific Publishing Company, Inc., Amsterdam.

Romme, A. G. L. (September-October 2003) Making a difference: organization as design, *Organization Science* 14 (5), pp. 558–573.

Romme, A. G. L. and G. Endenburg (2006) Construction principles and design rules in the case of circular design, *Organization Science* 17 (2), 287–297.

Searle, J. R. (2006) Social ontology: some basic principles, *Anthropological Theory* 6 (1), pp. 12–29.

Searle, J. R. (1995) *The Construction of Social Reality*, Free Press, New York.

Simon, H. A. (1977) *New Science of Management Decision*, Prentice Hall, Reading, PA.

Simon, H. A. (1996) *The Sciences of the Artificial*, 3rd ed., MIT Press, Cambridge, MA.

Sinha, K. K., and A. H. Van de Ven (2005) Designing work within and between organizations, *Organization Science* 16 (4), 389–408.

Vaast, E. and N. Levina (2006) Multiple faces of codification: organizational redesign in an IT organization, *Organization Science* 17 (2), 190–201.

Vaishnavi, V. and W. Kuechler (2007) *Design Science Research Methods and Patterns: Innovating Information and Communication Technology*, Auerbach Publications, Taylor & Francis Group, NY.

Walls, J. G., Widmeyer, G. R., and O. A. El Sawy (March, 1992) Building an information system design theory for vigilant EIS, *Information Systems Research* 3 (1), pp. 36–59.

Walsh, J. P., and G. R. Ungson (1991) Organizational memory, *Academy of Management Review* 16 (1), 57–91.

Westerman, G., McFarlan, F. W., and M. Iansiti (2006) Organization design and effectiveness over the innovation life cycle, *Organization Science* 17 (2), 230–238.

Yoo, Y., Boland, R. J., and K. Lyytinen (2006) From organization design to organization designing, *Organization Science* 17 (2), 215–229.

Ziman, J. (2000) *Real Science: What It Is, and What It Means,* Cambridge University Press, Cambridge, UK.

Chapter 15
Design Science Research in Information Systems: A Critical Realist Approach

It is not what you say, but how you say it.
– A. Putt

Information systems research has serious utilization and relevance problems. To increase IS research utilization and relevance, scholars argue that the dominating behavioral IS research paradigm should be complemented with IS design science research. The most influential IS design science research schools have a strong focus on the IT artifact, in most cases an exclusive focus on the IT artifact. The schools have very little discussions and clarifications regarding underpinning philosophies, but most seem to be based on positivism, traditional realism, or pragmatism. This chapter presents, as a complement to the most influential design science research schools, an alternative approach for IS design science research. The approach builds on the premise that one of the most critical aims of IS design science research is to develop practical knowledge for the design and realization of different classes of IS initiatives, where IS are viewed as socio-technical systems and not just IT artifacts. The underpinning philosophy of the approach is critical realism which has been developed as an alternative to positivism and traditional realism as well as to constructivism (relativism). The developed practical IS design knowledge can be represented in different forms, for example, as heuristic design propositions, design exemplars and patterns, models or frameworks, and stories or narratives. The IS design knowledge can be developed using different methods and techniques. The chapter presents how practical IS design knowledge can be developed as well as the nature of the developed knowledge.

Sven A. Carlsson

A. Hevner, S. Chatterjee, *Design Research in Information Systems*, Integrated Series
in Information Systems 22, DOI 10.1007/978-1-4419-5653-8_15,
© Springer Science+Business Media, LLC 2010

15.1 Introduction

As noted in this book, we have in the last years seen an intensive debate in the information systems (IS) community on the "crisis in the IS field" – see, for example, the debates in journals like *MIS Quarterly* and *Communications of the Association for Information Systems*. Some commentators argue that part of the crisis is related to utilization and relevance problems (Agarwal and Lucas 2005; Hirschheim and Klein 2003): research not addressing relevant issues and research not producing useful and usable results. It seems that too much IS research is "method driven" and/or "theory driven" and not "problem driven." Topics are chosen not because they are important, but because they are amenable to analysis by the ruling "méthode au théorie du jour" – for a similar point but in a different field, see Walt (1999). A theme of this book is that one way to increase IS research utilization and relevance is to produce more IS design science research. As the chapters in this book testify, interesting IS design science research has been produced, but from my perspective two major issues have not been carefully addressed.

First, there is too little discussion about what IS design science research should include and exclude. This is related to the discussion about what the IS discipline ought to be and what ought to be at the core of the IS discipline. When there is a discussion in the IS design science research literature the expressed views stress that IT artifacts and IT design theories should be developed. I have no problems with this, but I think the views are too narrow and they need to be complemented. In fact, Simon's (1988) view on design science shows that it can be more than IT artifacts and IT design theories that the IS field should develop. I will argue that there is a need for IS design science research approaches having a broader view on IS and IS design knowledge.

Second, there is no, or little, discussion about underlying philosophical assumptions in the IS design science research literature. Purao puts it most elegantly: "...the scientific foundations underlying this critical area of the IS field – design research – have remained largely undeveloped. ... Over the years, in spite of important writings about research (e.g., March and Smith 1995), philosophical underpinnings of this form of research have been largely unexplored. Without adequate scientific foundations, research in the technology of information systems (TIS) continues to be a lost child still searching for its scientific home" (Purao 2002). The underlying ontological view an IS design science research framework or approach is built on will ultimately affect how to do IS design science research and what types of outcomes that can be produced. Although current frameworks and approaches to a large extent lack in clearness on underpinning philosophies and ontological views, they seem to be based on positivism, traditional realism, or pragmatism. In behavioral IS research there is an increased and fruitful use of alternative philosophies, for example, the use of constructivism. Consequently, I suggest that it can be fruitful to develop and explore IS design science research frameworks and approaches based on alternative philosophies, that is, frameworks and approaches based on alternative ontologies and epistemologies.

Hence, the aim of this chapter is to present an alternative IS design science research approach. The underpinning philosophy of the approach is critical realism.

The remainder of the chapter is organized as follows: the next section elaborates the above two issues. The section argues for a broader view on IS design science research and for grounding IS design science research in the philosophy of critical realism. A presentation of critical realism follows and this is followed by a presentation of an IS design science research approach based on the philosophy of critical realism. Guiding my work is what I call the idea of the triple hurdle: IS design science research should *meet the criteria of scholarly quality, address practical (professional) issues and problems,* and *generate practical design knowledge.*

15.2 Why an Alternative Information Systems Design Science Research Approach?

Two major IS design science research schools have emerged (El Sawy, O.A., Personal communication, August 2006): (1) the Information Systems Design Theory school (Gregor and Jones 2007; Walls et al. 1992, 2004) and (2) the Design Science Research school (Cao et al. 2006; Hevner et al. 2004; March and Smith 1995; Nunamaker et al. 1990–91). The schools are introduced in Chapter 1. Below I briefly review these schools by primarily focusing on two issues: (1) what is focused in the IS design science research schools and (2) what underlying philosophies – for example, ontological and epistemological views – have the schools. The first issue is related to the discussion on what the IS discipline ought to be and what ought to be at the core of the discipline. The second issue is critical since in all research, including IS design science research, ontology is non-optional (Trigg 2001).

One of the first, if not the first, article on developing IS design theories (ISDT) and IS design knowledge was published in 1992 by Walls et al. (1992). Walls et al. argue that successful construction of ISDT would create an endogenous base for theory in the IS discipline and could be used by scholars to prescribe design products and processes for different classes of IS as they emerged. The authors build on Simon's distinction – natural science and sciences of the artificial – and argue that design is both a *product* and a *process*, which means that a design theory must have two aspects: one that deals with the design product and one that deals with the design process. Using their framework the authors propose an ISDT for the IS-class "vigilant information systems." The components of an IS design theory are summarized in Table 15.1.

Walls et al. use the concept "artifact" quite freely, but in reflecting on their 1992 paper they say "We did not use the current phrase 'IT artifact', but in essence it was that to which we were referring" (Walls et al. 2004). Walls et al.'s work was extended by Gregor and Jones (2007). They extended and clarified Walls et al.'s ISDT and identified eight separate components of design theories: (1) purpose and scope, (2) constructs, (3) principles of form and function, (4) artifact mutability, (5)

Table 15.1 Components of an IS design theory (Walls et al. 1992)

Design product	
1. Meta-requirements	Describes the class of goals to which the theory applies
2. Meta-design	Describes a class of artifacts hypothesized to meet the meta-requirements
3. Kernel theories	Theories from natural or social sciences governing design requirements
4. Testable design product hypotheses	Used to test whether the meta-design hypotheses satisfy the meta-requirements
Design process	
1. Design method	A description of procedure(s) for artifact construction
2. Kernel theories	Theories from natural or social sciences governing design process itself
3. Testable design process hypotheses	Used to verify whether the design hypotheses method results in an artifact which is consistent with the meta-design

testable propositions, (6) justificatory knowledge (kernel theories), (7) principles of implementation, and (8) an expository instantiation.

Building on Simon's work, March and Smith (1995) distinguish between design sciences and natural sciences. The former involves building and evaluating (1) *constructs* which are "concepts with which to characterize phenomenon," (2) *models* that "describe tasks, situations, or artifacts," (3) *methods* as "ways of performing goal-directed activities," and (4) *instantiations* which are "physical implementations intended to perform certain tasks."

Hevner et al. (2004), building on March and Smith, present a design science framework and guidelines for building and evaluating IT artifacts. Hevner et al. expressed their view on what constitutes good – rigorous and relevant – IS design science research in the form of seven guidelines. The authors contend that each of the guidelines should be addressed in some manner for IS design science research to be complete. Guideline one – "design as an artifact" – says "Design-science research must produce a viable artifact in the form of a *construct*, a *model*, a *method*, or an *instantiation*" (Hevner et al. 2004, italics added to indicate similarity with March and Smith's view on the output of design science research). And, the "result of design-science research in IS is, by definition, a purposeful IT artifact created to address an important organizational problem. ... Our [Hevner et al.'s] definition of IT artifacts is both broader and narrower [than other IT artifact definitions] ... It is broader in the sense that we include not only instantiations in our definition of the IT artifact but also the constructs, models, and methods applied in the development and use of information systems. However, it is narrower in the sense that we do not include people or elements of organizations in our definition nor do we explicitly include the process by which such artifacts evolve over time." The Hevner et al. framework is further elaborated in this book.

Regarding what should be included in an IS design research framework, and consequently in IS design theory and IS design knowledge, it is clear that Walls et al., March and Smith, and Hevner et al. focus on the IT artifact. They exclude the non-technological context by excluding people and organizations. Given the schools' focus and what they exclude, the schools might better be named IT design science research schools.

There is a lively debate in the IS community on what constitutes the "IS core" – see, for example, the debate in *Communications of the Association for Information Systems*, especially volume 12 (2003). Benbasat and Zmud (2003) suggest that the core of the IS discipline and IS research should be the IT artifact. I consider this a narrow view on the IS discipline and IS research. Alter (2003) suggests a broader view and argues that the core of the IS discipline should be "work systems." In the IS core debate, Myers (2003) argues for that the IS discipline is nowhere near ready to define an IS core – he argues for open, flexible, and adaptive views. Hence, he argues for broad and emergent views on the IS core. Said Myers: "I believe that diversity is a positive attribute and ensures the continued viability of the field in a rapidly changing environment" (Myers 2003). I agree with Myers. The above IS design science research schools have views more in line with Benbasat and Zmud's view than with Alter's and Myers' views. It should be noted that Walls et al. and Hevner et al. say that IS design theories and frameworks can encompass more than the IT artifact. Furthermore, Hevner et al.'s second design guideline – problem relevance – states "The objective of design-science research is to develop technology-based solutions to important and relevant business problems" (Hevner et al. 2004). It is noteworthy that lists, based on business needs, of current and future critical IS issues, for example, lists published by the Gartner Group, often have "non-technological" issues as the most critical (relevant) and less easy to solve problems like "how to align our business strategy and IT strategy."

My view is that an IS design science research framework or approach should be explicit on what should be produced, for example, design knowledge, artifacts, or artificial IS. I suggest that one of the most critical aims of IS design science research is to develop practical knowledge for the design and realization of "IS initiatives" or to be used in the improvement of the performance of existing IS. By an IS initiative I mean the design and implementation of a solution in a social–technical system where IS (including IT artifacts) are critical means for achieving the desired outcomes of the intervention. My IS initiative view is in line with Alter's (2004) and Agarwal and Lucas' (2005) views. Agarwal and Lucas (2005) argue that IS research to become more relevant needs to have a more macro-oriented focus and should address the transformational impact of information technology and IS, that is, a focus on how information technology and IS can be used to change (transform) an organization or a network of organizations.

The second issue I address is the underpinning philosophies of IS design science research approaches and frameworks. The above-discussed IS design science research schools do not explicitly address ontology, but ontology is non-optional in all research (Fleetwood 2004). Although the above schools do not address underpinning philosophies and ontologies, it is possible to conclude that they are based in positivism, traditional realism, or pragmatism. This conclusion is based on the few philosophical and philosophy of science references used by the authors and that they use concepts like "prove." Hevner et al. explicitly refer to pragmatism and

Cole et al. state that "..DR [Design Research] is rooted in pragmatism" (Cole et al. 2005). Arnott and Pervan (2008) reviewed the DSS discipline, which is a discipline where design science research is central and where a lot of novel artifacts are developed. They found that a fairly large amount of DSS research was design science research (a much higher proportion than for most other IS areas). They also found that DSS research is overwhelmingly dominated by positivism and that 92.3% of the empirical studies in their review were based on positivism.

It is noteworthy that the ISWorld web site on "Design Research in Information Systems" has a section on the "philosophical grounding of design research" (Vaishnavi and Kuechler 2004/5). Unfortunately, the authors mix concepts and definitions and their use of key concepts are inconsistent with what can be found in philosophy of science. For example, they say that "ontological and epistemological viewpoints shift in design research as the project runs through circumscription cycles ... This iteration is similar to but more radical than the hermeneutic processes used in some interpretive research" (ibid.). This means that in IS design science research a researcher's assumptions about how the world is "constructed" and what exists should change during a design science research project. What the authors probably mean is that our knowledge of the world changes which is quite a different matter. They also make what Bhaskar (1975/1978) calls an "epistemic fallacy" in that they transpose what is an ontological matter – concerning what exists – into an epistemological matter of how to develop reliable knowledge about the world. It is interesting to note that the authors make a reference – using Mario Bunge's work – to critical realism: "Bunge (1984) implies that design research is most effective when its practitioners shift between pragmatic and critical realist perspectives, guided by a pragmatic assessment of progress in the design cycle" (Vaishnavi & Kuechler 2004/5). Unfortunately, they do not explore Bunge's view.

To summarize, writings on IS design theory, IS design knowledge, and IS design science research almost never explicitly discuss ontological issues and underpinning philosophies, but most papers (work) seem to be based in positivism, traditional realism, or pragmatism. This is consistent with studies on research in the IS field. The overwhelming majority of research is based in positivism (Chen and Hirschheim 2004). IS research commentators point out weaknesses in positivism, etc., and suggest the use of alternative philosophies, like constructivism. This chapter presents an IS design science research approach based on the philosophy of critical realism, which is an alternative to positivism as well as to constructivism. Critical realism is presented in the next section.

15.3 Critical Realism

Different philosophies of science have different ontological views. Idealists have the view that reality is not mind-independent. Idealism comes in different forms reflecting different views on what is man-created and how it is created. Realists have the view that reality exists independently of our beliefs, thoughts, perceptions, discourses, etc. As for idealism, realism comes in different forms. Today most philosophies of science are based on realism. Bhaskar says that it is not a question of being a realist or not, but what type of realist (Bhaskar 1991).

Critical realism (CR) was developed as an alternative to traditional positivist models of social science and as an alternative to post-approaches and post-theories, e.g., constructivism and structuration theory. The most influential writer on critical realism is Roy Bhaskar. Unfortunately, Bhaskar is an opaque writer, but good summaries of CR are available in Archer et al. (1998), Sayer (2000), Dean et al. (2005), and Chapter 1 in Bhaskar (2002); key concepts and main developments are presented in Hartwig (2007). In Archer et al. (1998) and Lòpez and Potter (2001), chapters focus on different aspects of critical realism, ranging from fundamental philosophical discussions to how statistical analysis can be used in CR-based research.

Critical realism was primarily developed as an answer to the positivist crisis. In 1975 Roy Bhaskar's work "A Realist Theory of Science," with "transcendental realism," was published. In *"Possibility of Naturalism"* Bhaskar (1979/1998) focused the social sciences and developed his "critical naturalism." These two major works present a thorough philosophy of science project and later "critical realism" and "critical naturalism" were merged to "critical realism," a concept also used by Bhaskar. Through the 1980s Bhaskar primarily developed his position through sharpening arguments, etc. The late 1970s and early 1980s also saw a number of other CR scholars publishing influential works, for example, Margaret Archer's *"Social Origins of Educational Systems"* (1979) and Andrew Sayer's *"Method in Social Science"* (1984/1992. Most of CRs early critique was targeting positivism, but later critique is targeting alternatives to positivism, for example, postmodernism and structuration theory. CR is a consistent and all-embracing alternative to positivism and different postmodernistic strands.

Critical realism can be seen as a specific form of realism: "To be a realist is to assert the existence of some disputed kind of entities such as gravitons, equilibria, utility, class relations and so on. To be a scientific realist is to assert that these entities exist independently of our investigation of them. Such entities, *contra* the post modernism of rhetoricians, are not something generated in the discourse used in their investigation. Neither are such entities, *contra* empiricists, restricted to the realm of the observable. To be a *critical* realist is to extend these views into social science" (Fleetwood 2002). CR's manifesto is to recognize the reality of the natural order and the events and discourses of the social world. It holds that "we will only be able to understand – and so change – the social world if we identify the structures at work that generate those events or discourses ... These structures are not spontaneously apparent in the observable pattern of events; they can only be identified through the practical and theoretical work of the social sciences" (Bhaskar 1989). Bhaskar (1978) outlines what he calls three domains: the *real*, the *actual*, and the *empirical* (Table 15.2). The *real* domain consists of underlying structures and mechanisms, and relations; events and behavior; and experiences. The generative mechanisms residing in the real domain exist independently of, but capable of producing, patterns of events. Relations generate behaviors in the social world.

Table 15.2 Ontological assumptions of the critical realist view of science (Bhaskar 1978)

	Domain of real	Domain of actual	Domain of empirical
Mechanisms	X		
Events	X	X	
Experiences	X	X	X

X's indicate the domain of reality in which mechanisms, events, and experiences, respectively, reside, as well as the domains involved for such a residence to be possible.

The domain of the *actual* consists of these events and behaviors. Hence, the actual domain is the domain in which observed events or observed patterns of events occur. The domain of the *empirical* consists of what we experience; hence, it is the domain of experienced events.

Bhaskar argues that "...real structures exist independently of and are often out of phase with the actual patterns of events. Indeed it is only because of the latter we need to perform experiments and only because of the former that we can make sense of our performances of them. Similarly it can be shown to be a condition of the intelligibility of perception that events occur independently of experiences. And experiences are often (epistemically speaking) 'out of phase' with events—e.g. when they are misidentified. It is partly because of this possibility that the scientist needs a scientific education or training. Thus I [Bhaskar] will argue that what I call the domains of the real, the actual and the empirical are distinct" (Bhaskar 1978). Critical realism also argues that the real world is ontologically stratified and differentiated. The real world consists of a plurality of structures and generative mechanisms that generate the events that occur and do not occur. From an epistemological stance, concerning the nature of knowledge claim, the realist approach is non-positivistic which means that values and facts are intertwined and hard to disentangle.

Critical realism is a well-developed philosophy of science, but on the methodological level, it is less well developed. The writings of Layder (1993, 1998, 2005), Kazi (2003), Pawson and Tilley (1997), and Pawson (2006) as well as some of the chapters in Ackroyd and Fleetwood (2000) and Fleetwood and Ackroyd (2004) can serve as guidelines for doing critical realism research. Unfortunately, from an IS design science research perspective, the writings on critical realism have been in the behavioral science paradigm.

Critical realism has influenced a number of disciplines and fields, for example, economics, management, and organization studies. It has until recently been almost invisible in the IS field. CR's potential for IS research has been argued by, for example, Carlsson (2003, 2004, 2009), Dobson (2001), Mingers (2003, 2004), and Mutch (2002). CR-based empirical research can be found in, for example, Morton (2006), Volkoff et al. (2007), Dobson et al. (2007), and De Vaujany (2008). CR has also critical and emancipatory components (Bhaskar 2002). Wilson and Greenhill (2004) and Longshore Smith (2005) address how CR in IS research can work critically and emancipatory. The writings on CR in IS have been focusing on the use of CR in the behavioral science paradigm and not on how it can be used in IS design science research. CR's potential for IS design science has been argued by Carlsson (2006) and Lyytinen (2008). CR-based IS design science can be found in Carlsson et al. (2008) and Hrastinski et al. (2007, forthcoming). In the next section I will present an IS design science research approach underpinned by the philosophy of critical realism.

15.4   A Critical Realist Approach for IS Design Science Research

This section presents and discusses a critical realist approach for IS design science research. I start with discussing what types of IS design knowledge should be produced and for whom. This is followed by a presentation of how IS design knowledge can be developed.

15.4.1   For Whom Should IS Design Science Research Produce Knowledge?

March argues that relevance, rigor, and results are the trifecta of academic IS research and that they are defined by the constituency that comprises and supports the IS discipline. This constituency includes "IS academic researchers, organizations that develop and deploy information technologies (IT), organizations that produce and implement such technologies, IS managers within such organizations and, more and more commonly, general and upper level managers within such organizations" (March 2006, p. 338).

My view is that one of the most important constituent community for the output of IS design science research is IS professionals and managers responsible for IS/IT-supported and IS/IT-enabled processes and activities. This means primarily professionals who plan, manage, govern, design, build, implement, operate, maintain, and evaluate different types of IS/IT initiatives and IS/IT. The design knowledge this community demands include (1) knowledge for developing IT/IS-enabled solutions (including improving previous implemented solutions) that primarily address organizational problems and (2) knowledge for how to implement and integrate the solutions into the context (primarily organizational context). The developed IS design knowledge is to be applied by individuals who have received formal education or a similar training, for example, in the IS field. An IS professional can be defined as a member of a fairly well-defined group who solves real-world IS problems with the help of skills, creativity, and scientific and non-scientific IS design knowledge. (For simplicity I call the problems IS problems although it is more correct to say that someone has defined a problem where one, for one reason or another, has decided to try to solve the problem with an IS initiative).

Another important community is IS education, which means that the knowledge should be useful in different types of IS study programs and IS courses.

Although the primary constituent community works primarily in organizations driven by "utility maximization" (often in terms of profit), it should be noted that critical realism has also critical and emancipatory components (Bhaskar 2002). Wilson and McCormack (2006) show how critical realism can work as a framework to guide appropriate action in emancipatory practice development and realistic evaluation for understanding the outcomes of those actions. The critical and emancipatory issues are far from well addressed in the IS design science research literature. The two major schools discussed above have a clear management perspective and certainly not an emancipatory or critical perspective (Stahl 2008). The emancipatory and critical issues are important. They can, for example, address issues like the development of IT artifacts for increasing democracy or the development of systems development methods for supporting resource-weak stakeholders. I note the importance of emancipatory and critical issues, but leave the issues for further exploration and development.

15.4.2 *What Types of IS Design Knowledge Should IS Design Research Produce?*

As discussed above, there is a lively debate in the IS community on what constitutes the "IS core." In the IS design science research literature this debate has been less lively. It seems that most writings on IS design science research have views in line with Benbasat and Zmud's (2003) view that the core of the IS discipline and IS research should be the IT artifact. As said above, I find the "pure" IT artifact view a too narrow view.

McKay and Marshall (2005, 2007, 2008) argue that IS is a socio-technical discipline and that "design science and the research that builds that body of knowledge must acknowledge that IS is fundamentally about human activity systems which are usually technologically enabled, implying that the context of *design* and *use* is critical, and that research paradigms, practices and activities must embrace such a worldview. (McKay and Marshall 2005, p. 5). Venable (2006) argues that the core of IS design science research is "solution technology invention," where "Solution technologies that are relevant in the IS/IT field include IS development methods, techniques, and tools, IS planning methods, IS management methods, IS/IT security and risk management practices, algorithms for computer processing, such as database processing, and many others, all of which are designed purposefully to address human and organisational problems and all of which must be adapted or redesigned when addressing particular, situated problems." (p. 8)

In line with McKay and Marshall's and Venable's views I suggest that the aim of IS design science research is to develop practical knowledge for the design and realization of "IS initiatives" or to be used in the improvement of the performance of existing IS. The latter is excluded by Hevner et al. (2004), but seems to be critical for practitioners; see, for example, Bendoly and Jacobs (2005) on strategic extension and use of ERP systems. As discussed above, by an IS initiative I mean the design and implementation of an intervention in a socio-technical system where IS (including IT artifacts) are critical means for achieving the desired outcomes of the intervention. My view is that IS design science research should include organizations, people, IS, and IT artifacts. Given some of the current technological and business changes I think such a view is appropriate. For example, many organizations are no longer viewing ERP projects as technical projects, but as major re-organization projects; and the increased use of commercial off-the-shelf (COTS) software and different forms of sourcing requires new relevant, and in part non-IT-artifact, knowledge to be developed. Further, reviewing lists of what IS/IT issues are most critical to organizations I find that most of these are managerial issues and not technological issues (Smith and McKeen 2006). Also, it can be argued that a broader view will become more fruitful as the use of IT moves from connection to immersion and fusion (El Sawy 2003). In immersion IT-based IS are immersed as part of the business environment and cannot be separated from work, processes, and the systemic properties of intra- and inter-organizational processes and relationships. In fusion IT-based IS are fused within the business environment such that business and IT-based IS form a unified fabric. Hence, IT-enabled work and processes are treated as one. Recent studies suggest that business-related IS issues are becoming more and more critical (Zwieg et al. 2006, Luftman et al. 2009). Hence, my view is that IS design science research needs to develop relevant design knowledge for this new "landscape" and not just develop IT artifacts or IT artifact design theories.

IS design science research should develop practical design knowledge to be used to solve classes of IS problems. This means the development of knowledge that can be used in designing and implementing IS initiatives. The knowledge is abstract in the sense that it is not a recipe for designing and implementing a specific IS initiative for a specific organization. A user of the abstract design knowledge, for example, an IS professional, has to "transform" the knowledge to fit the specific problem situation and context. Below I will present, discuss, and illustrate what types of knowledge can be produced and how this knowledge can be produced.

Following Pelz (1978), I distinguish between conceptual and instrumental use of science and research output. The former involves using knowledge for general enlightenment on the subject in question and the latter involves acting on research results in specific and direct ways. Both types are relevant for the IS field, but IS design science research develops primarily knowledge for instrumental use.

Using van Aken's (2004) classification I can distinguish three different types of designs an IS professional makes when designing and implementing an IS initiative: (1) an *object design*, which is the design of the IS initiative (including the design of an IT artifact); (2) a *realization design*, which is the plan for the implementation of the IS initiative; and (3) a *process design*, which is the professional's own plan for the problem-solving cycle and includes the methods and techniques to be used in object and realization design. IS design science research should produce knowledge that can be used by the professionals in the three types of designs, including novel IT artifacts, methodologies, methods and techniques, and socio-technical implementation knowledge. (Although I discuss in terms of an IS professional the different designs are in most cases done by groups/teams of a number of IS professional and often including non-IS professionals like IS users.) Given my broader perspective –

IS intervention in a socio-technical system – than the schools discussed above, it can be argued, based on the IS implementation and IS failure literature, that realization design knowledge is critical and hence should also be developed.

The rationale for developing IS design knowledge to be used in the three types of design is that such knowledge can support practitioners in designing initiatives which will trigger mechanisms which may lead to desired outcomes (recall the discussion above on mechanisms). Figure 15.1 – the realist IS intervention – is adapted from Pawson and Tilley's (1997) model of realist casual explanation: "IS initiative (I)" and "problem situation (P)" have been added. The success of an IS initiative will always be limited by contextual constraints.

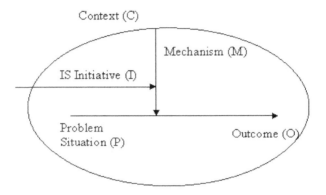

Fig. 15.1 The realist IS intervention

Using my IS design science research approach should lead to evermore detailed answers to the question of *why* and *how* an IS initiative works, for *whom,* and in *what* circumstances. Using the approach means that a researcher attends to how and why an IS initiative has the *potential* to cause a desired change. In this perspective, a researcher works as an experimental scientist, but not according to the logics of traditional experimental research. Since critical realism has an open system view and that it recognizes social systems' complexity the research will generate IS design knowledge being provisional, fallible, incomplete, and extendable.

I do not perceive that IS initiatives "work." It is the actions of the stakeholders making them work, and the causal potential of an IS initiative takes the form of providing the reasons and resources to enable different stakeholders and participants to "make" changes. This means that a researcher seeks to understand *why* and *how* an IS initiative, for example, the implementation of a CRM system, works through understanding the action mechanisms. It also means that a researcher seeks to understand *for whom* and *in what circumstances* (*contexts*) an IS initiative works through the study of contextual conditioning.

Researchers orient their thinking to problem situation (P), IS initiative (I), mechanisms (M), context (C), outcome (O) pattern configurations (PIMCO configurations). A PIMCO configuration is a proposition stating what it is about an IS initiative which works for whom in what circumstances. A refined PIMCO configuration is the finding of an evaluation of an IS initiative. This leads to the development of transferable and cumulative knowledge. Outcome patterns are examined from a "theory-testing" perspective. This means that a researcher tries to understand what the outcomes of an IS initiative are and how the outcomes are produced. Hence, the researcher does not just inspect outcomes in order to see whether an IS initiative works, but analyzes the outcomes to discover whether the conjectured PIMCO configurations are confirmed.

IS design knowledge can be represented in many different forms, for example, algorithmic or heuristic design propositions, design exemplars and patterns, models or frameworks, and stories or narratives. In our IS design science research we have developed IS design knowledge in different forms, for example, as design propositions and frameworks. How this can be done will be presented in the next section.

15.4.3 Developing IS Design Knowledge

IS design science research based on the above is carried out through an IS design science research "cycle" consisting of four major research activities (Fig. 15.2): (1) identify problem situations and desired outcomes, (2) review (kernel) theories and previous research, (3) propose/refine design theory, and (4) test design theory. The figure reveals that IS design science research is not only about doing or designing. An important part of this research approach is to continuously test design theories. This includes testing of theories' applicability, understandability, and actability in practice. Another key characteristic of my IS design science research approach is that one should build on what is already known, i.e., kernel theories and previous research.

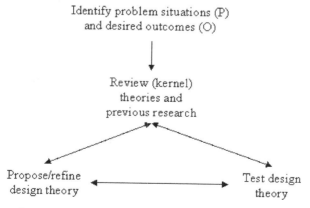

Fig. 15.2 Information systems design science research: development of design theories and design knowledge (based on Carlsson et al. (2008, forthcoming) and Hrastinski et al. (2007, forthcoming))

15.4.3.1 Research Activity: Identify Problem Situations And Desired Outcomes

Design theories and design knowledge aim to support solving practical problems in such a way that desired outcomes are reached. Hence, such theories and knowledge are goal- and outcome-oriented, which means that they should when used increase the likelihood of reaching desired outcomes. Below, three examples of design theories and knowledge and the practical problems that motivated the need for these theories are presented. These design theories and knowledge were developed to guide IS practitioners in how to achieve desired outcomes.

15.4.3.2 Research Activity: Review (Kernel) Theories and Previous Research

Design theories and design knowledge should be enhanced through grounding in previous research. A design theory should be enhanced by continuously "interacting" with what is currently known, that is, grounding in kernel theories and previous research. Gregor (2006) distinguishes five interrelated types of theory: (1) theory for analyzing, (2) theory for explaining, (3) theory for predicting, (4) theory for explaining and predicting, and (5) theory for design and action. Gregor argues that other types of theory can "inform" design theory and that design theory and explanatory and predictive theory are strongly interrelated. van Aken (2005, 2006) maintains that design knowledge in the form of design propositions can be developed through cross-case analyses of previous case studies – see, also, Carlsson et al. (2008, forthcoming), Gregor (2009), and Hrastinski et al. (2007, forthcoming). This means that design knowledge is abstracted from cases. van Aken (2004) refers to this as "extracting case studies" and shows how it has led to a number of useful and actionable design propositions, for example, Kanban Systems and Just-In-Time.

In general, design theories and design knowledge can be enhanced through systematic reviews of previous research. Several scholars (e.g., Pfeffer and Sutton 2006) have argued for the development of evidence-based or evidence-informed management knowledge, including evidence-based design knowledge. In the IS design science research cases presented below, the reviews of previous research were inspired by Pawson's (2006) suggestions on how to conduct systematic reviews to make sense of a heterogeneous body of literature. Such reviews should be driven by PIMCO configurations and should have a specific focus on outcome(s) and how outcome(s) can be produced or enhanced. Using this method for review of relevant literature means that it is possible to move away from the many one-off studies and instead learn from fields such as medicine and policy studies on how to develop evidence-informed IS design knowledge.

15.4.3.3 Research Activity: Propose/Refine Design Theory

When proposing a design theory, for example, in the form of design propositions, it is important to provide "thick descriptions" to aid the reader in understanding the theory, which may support practitioners in translating a theory to specific contexts and situations (van Aken 2005).

A design proposition follows the logic of a technological rule. In the field of IS it may be more appropriate to use the term design proposition instead of technological rule since the latter term may suggest a technical, rather mechanistic approach (Hrastinski et al. 2007) – technological rules are also discussed in Chapter 14. A design proposition can be expressed as follows: In problem situation (P) and context (C), to achieve outcome (O), then design and implement IS initiative (I) (adapted from Bunge 1967). As presented above, the "design and implement IS initiative I" includes three different types of designs: (1) *object design*, (2) *realization design*, and (3) a *process design*. Since a design proposition should be used by practitioners it should be understandable, applicable, and actionable.

A field-tested and grounded design proposition has been tested empirically and is grounded in science. The latter means primarily grounding in results and theories from the behavioral science paradigm. Field-tested and grounded design propositions will in most cases be in the form of heuristics. This is consistent with critical realism's view on causality (Bhaskar 1978, 1998; Groff 2004) and means that the indeterminate nature of a heuristic design proposition makes it impossible to prove its effects conclusively, but it can be tested in context, which in turn can lead to sufficient supporting evidence (Hedström and Swedberg 1998; Groff 2004).

15.4.3.4   Research Activity: Test Design Theory

After having formulated an initial design theory, the next step is empirical tests, which include the selection of appropriate data collection methods (Carlsson 2006). In doing this, it can be examined whether the design theory may be used as support when trying to "change" reality. Based on the results, the outcome may be reflected on and the design theory may be refined. Through multiple studies one can accumulate supporting evidence iteratively and continuously move toward "evidence saturation." We can say that the tests of a design theory go through alpha, beta, and gamma testing. Alpha testing concerns further development by the originator(s) of the design theory. Beta testing concerns further development by other researchers. Gamma testing concerns testing the design theory in practice and includes testing whether practitioners can use it and if the use of the theory leads to the desired outcome(s). To strengthen the validity of design theories, test triangulation may be beneficial, i.e., to combine two or more complementing ways of conducting gamma testing, such as focus groups and field experiments. Further guidance on how to conduct gamma tests are provided by Rosemann and Vessey (2008), who use the term applicability checks to describe this type of testing. They suggest that applicability checks can be made through focus groups, which we have used with appealing results (presented below) – see, also Chapter 10. However, it should be recognized that it can be practically unfeasible to, as suggested by Rosemann and Vessey (2008), gather IS managers to conduct an evaluation. For the future I see a need for a discussion on different techniques for testing design theory and design knowledge and their applicability.

15.4.4 Examples of How to Develop IS Design Theories and Design Knowledge

This section illustrates how my colleagues and I have used the proposed approach when developing three design theories. For each theory, I will briefly describe each of the four research activities. I do so partly not only to illustrate how the approach can be used but also to show that studies based on the approach have been peer reviewed and accepted for publication by the IS community (for more detailed discussion of the design theories, – see Carlsson and Kalling (2006, 2007), Carlsson et al. (forthcoming) and Hrastinski et al. (2007, forthcoming)). Since the studies were done with colleagues I will use "we" instead of "I."

15.4.5 Design Theory #1: Developing a Design Theory for Turning KMS Use into Profit

15.4.5.1 Identify Problems and Desired Outcomes

An underlying assumption of knowledge management (KM), including knowledge management systems (KMS), is that a firm's competitive advantage to a large extent flows from its unique knowledge and how it manages knowledge. Unfortunately, little empirical evidence exists to show that this assumption is true. Even less knowledge on how to manage KMS initiatives to increase financial performance exists (Edwards et al. 2003). This project aims at producing theoretically and empirically grounded KMS design knowledge. The KM/KMS literature is clear on that failures are unacceptably high. The literature suggests also that the field of dreams approach – "if you build it, they will come" – usually fails. The primary cause is the failure to adequately predict and manage the organizational impacts of KM/KMS investments. The project aims at developing a KMS design theory for how to manage KMS investments. Specifically, we focus on how to manage adoption and exploitation of KMS.

A general goal when designing and implementing a KM/KMS initiative is that it should lead to improved performance. The construct "improved performance" forces attention to the dependent variable(s). This research focuses on organizational "net benefits" in terms of financial performance.

15.4.5.2 Review (Kernel) Theories and Previous Research

The review of previous research was inspired by the work of Pawson (2006) and driven by a focus on outcome (profit improvement through KMS use) and how the outcome can be "produced." We tried to identify how KMS management had been used for turning KMS use into profit improvement. The literature on this was very sparse, which meant that we focused not only on success factors and processes but also on failure factors and processes. Underlying kernel theories included primarily knowledge sharing theories, for example, the work of leading KM researchers like Nonaka, Takeuchi, von Krogh, Davenport, Prusak, and Patriotta.

15.4.5.3 Propose/Refine Design Theory

In the multiple case studies conducted for generating the design theory we addressed the research question: Why and how is it that a knowledge sharing initiative works? The design propositions were generated based on a cross-case study (Carlsson and Kalling 2006, 2007). The design propositions were also theoretically grounded, primarily in knowledge sharing theories. The multiple case study was of a KMS initiative in a large multinational firm. The purpose of the KMS initiative was to, through the use of a KMS for knowledge sharing, support production improvement decision making. A KMS, with high information (knowledge) and system quality, to be used for knowledge sharing had been developed and implemented in the firm's plants. Thirty-eight plants were similar enough to be used for a comparative study. A quantitative study of the 38 plants was done. The study addressed (1) whether knowledge sharing had occurred, (2) the effects of sharing on cost items and price, and (3) the effects on profit. After having studied the general links between sharing success and financial performance, certain patterns became evident. In order to study them further, six plants with different degrees of success were singled out for onsite case studies. In this qualitative study we identify a process consisting of three phases: (1) knowledge sharing through the use of the KMS, (2) managing the conversion of knowledge, and (3) improving profit margins. We also identify eight critical success factors and linked them to the different phases. Based on the cross-case study our tentative design theory was generated in the form of nine design propositions for turning KMS use into profit. Examples of design propositions are as follows:

- Design Proposition #2: If you want the sharing initiative to have a positive impact on operations, then link knowledge use to operational decision making and action taking.
- Design Proposition #9: If you want an initiative to have a positive effect on financial performance, then establish, institutionalize, and measure (interlinked) three types of outcomes: employee behaviors, process changes, and financial results.

15.4.5.4 Test Design Theory

One important activity in design theory development is tests. As said above, three types of tests should be performed: alpha, beta, and gamma tests. In this case alpha test has been conducted through applying the generated design propositions on a few numbers of cases. The design propositions have been quite informally tested by practitioners (gamma test). This test has been in the form of presenting the design propositions and having practitioners evaluate the following: (1) Are the design propositions understandable? (2) Are the design propositions actionable? and (3) Is it likely that using the design propositions will result in desired outcomes? Drawing on the test results, the design theory is currently refined. Further testing of the design theory is needed.

15.4.6 Design Theory #2: Developing a Design Theory for Successful Use of e-Learning

15.4.6.1 Identify Problems and Desired Outcomes

In order to succeed with e-learning initiatives, organizations and educational institutions must understand benefits and limitations of different e-learning techniques and methods. An important task for research is to support practitioners by studying the impact of different factors on e-learning effectiveness. Commonly, two basic types of e-learning are compared, i.e., asynchronous and synchronous e-learning. Up till now, e-learning initiatives have mainly relied on asynchronous means for teaching and learning (Hrastinski and Keller 2007). However, recent improvements in technology and increasing bandwidth have led to an increasing popularity of synchronous e-learning. Many practitioners are interested in using e-learning but simply do not know what the benefits and limitations of different approaches are (Hrastinski 2007, forthcoming) and which effects these approaches have on learning outcomes (Cole 2000). However, e-learning use also has organizational implications. Acceptance, i.e., the willingness of teachers and students to use e-learning environments, is a prerequisite for participation (Keller 2007). Thus, this design theory is intended to contribute toward a deeper understanding on a topic where guidance is urgently needed.

15.4.6.2 Review (Kernel) Theories and Previous Research

The review was driven by a focus on outcome, in our case participation, and how outcome can be "produced" (in our case when synchronous and asynchronous communication can be used to enhance participation and learning outcomes in e-learning settings). Underlying kernel theories included technology acceptance models (Venkatesh et al. 2003) and social learning theories that view participation as critical to the learning process (e.g., Vygotsky 1978; Wenger 1998). The cognitive model of media choice (Robert and Dennis 2005) served as an aid in explaining when synchronous or asynchronous communication may be preferred. Furthermore, to focus on the quality of learning outcomes in online education, learning theories describing the prerequisites of deep learning, as opposed to surface learning (e.g., Bloom 1956; Marton et al. 1977), were included among the kernel theories.

15.4.6.3 Propose/Refine Design Theory

In our previous research, the research question of which factors contribute to successful use of e-learning was explored. As a foundation of our design theory, we proposed that acceptance of e-learning environments is a prerequisite for participation in e-learning settings. Participation is, in its turn, a prerequisite of high-quality learning outcomes. The research question was addressed by developing eight design propositions, intended to guide practitioners on the use of e-learning. However, this research activity was revisited many times: The design theory was continuously improved, as lessons were learnt by testing the theory and by analyzing previous research. Examples of design propositions are as follows:

- Design Proposition #5: If you want to enhance "cognitive" participation to provide deep learning, then support asynchronous communication.
- Design Proposition #7: If you want to enhance weak class-wide relations among students, then support "formal" communication.

15.4.6.4 Test Design Theory

One important aspect of design theory development is the empirical test. When having proposed an initial design theory, an empirical gamma test, i.e., a test with practitioner involvement, was conducted. Krueger (1994) argues that focus groups are an appropriate method for evaluating the effect of interventions in social contexts and, thus, seem appropriate for evaluating design propositions by obtaining feedback from experienced practitioners. A brief version of the design propositions was published in a Swedish e-learning magazine. In the article, teachers, managers, administrators, and developers with experience of asynchronous and synchronous e-learning were invited to participate in focus groups to evaluate the design propositions of the theory. Drawing on the results, the design theory was refined.

15.4.7 Design Theory #3: Developing a Design Theory on How to Improve the Capability of IS Integration in M&As

15.4.7.1 Identify Problems and Desired Outcomes

M&As now become a major tool for corporate strategy and an integrated part of many global firm's growth strategy. In a survey by Accenture of 400 corporate executives in the USA and Europe only about 1/3 regarded their last IS integration in a cross-border M&A a "success" (Accenture 2006). IS integration is the third most cited reason for M&As not being able to deliver its expected financial improvements (Rodgers 2005). Yet so, only 16% of companies involve IS management in pre-M&A phases (Accenture 2002).

We asked why firms were adopting this behavior and found that there is simply no management guidance or support building on science and theory available. Thus, our purpose was to develop theoretically grounded knowledge that would assist IS professional dealing with IS integration in M&A. As one part of this outset we addressed the task of improving IS integration from one M&A to the next, which is the design theory presented here.

15.4.7.2 Review (Kernel) Theories and Previous Research

The review was driven by a focus on outcome, in this case improvement of management of IS integration in M&A. The review covered fields like IS (and IT) management, governance and alignment, as well as M&A theory, and the field of organizational learning.

15.4.7.3 Propose/Refine Design Theory

The existing theory explaining how organizations learn, or fail to learn, from one M&A to the next suggested four relationships between organizational learning and IS integration in M&A. These relationships could be restated as design propositions and along with our recommended "thick descriptions" presented to the IS community as an initial design theory. Examples of design propositions are as follows:

- Design Proposition #3: If no reason exists for a heterogeneous IS base, standardization in systems and processes is desirable.
- Design Proposition #4: If the company frequently engages in M&As and needs to develop a strong IS integration capability, using internal IS professionals and not consultants can enhance that capability.

15.4.7.4 Test Design Theory

Testing of the design propositions was made with beta and gamma testing. In the beta testing four researchers with experience from IS in M&A evaluated the propositions for importance, accessibility, and suitability. The gamma testing was made based on the same criteria. Two distinct group of potential users were selected, one with senior IS managers with experience of IS integration in M&A and one of younger IS professionals that had no experience of M&As. In this case it was considered practically unfeasible to collect all high-level IS managers in one place at the same time to participate in focus groups. Instead individual sessions were held which ended out in completed survey forms.

15.5 Conclusion

In this chapter I have presented an IS design science approach. The approach is a complement to the two influential schools. The underpinning philosophy of the approach is critical realism – as noted by Indulska and Recker (2008) there is a lack of approaches having clear ontological and epistemological views. The approach can be seen as part of the changing view on IS design science research noted by Kuechler and Vaishnavi (2008). They say that the "...view of IS design science research as a 'hard' engineering practice is being mitigated in the USA by the increasing influence of European concepts of IS and design in IS; these have traditionally incorporated a greater emphasis on the business environment."

Further theoretical and empirical work is required to enhance and test the approach. Currently, my colleagues and I are using the framework in a number of IS design science research studies. My suggestions make no claims to be the final word in the debate on IS design science research, but research based on the framework could lead to a stream of research that *meets the criteria of scholarly quality, addresses practical (professional) issues and problems*, and *generates practical design knowledge*.

Acknowledgments I would like to thank Omar El Sawy and Pertti Järvinen for a number of valuable design science research discussions over the years. For my ideas I owe a lot to my co-researchers and co-authors Stefan Henningsson, Stefan Hrastinski, and Christina Keller.

References

Accenture (2002). Getting Information Technology Right Is Key to M&A Successes, Accenture.

Accenture (2006) Executives Report that Mergers and Acquisitions Fail to Create Adequate Value, Accenture.

Ackroyd, S. and S. Fleetwood (eds.) (2000) *Realist Perspectives on Management and Organisations*, Routledge, London.

Agarwal, R. and H. C. Lucas (2005) The information systems identity crisis: focusing on high-visibility and high-impact research, *MIS Quarterly* 29 (3), pp. 381–398.

Alter, S. (2003) 18 Reasons why IT-reliant work systems should replace "the IT artifact" as the core subject matter of the IS field, *Communications of the Association for Information Systems*, 12, Article 23.

Alter, S. (2004) Desperately seeking systems thinking in the information systems discipline, in *Proceedings of the Twenty-Fifth International Conference on Information Systems,* Washington, DC, USA, December 12–15, pp. 757–769.

Archer, M. S. (1979) *Social Origins of Educational Systems*, Sage, London.

Archer, M., R. Bhaskar, A. Collier, T. Lawson, and A. Norrie (eds.) (1998) *Critical Realism: Essential Readings*, Routledge, London.

Arnott, D. and G. Pervan (2008) Eight key issues for the decision support systems discipline, *Decision Support Systems* 44, pp. 657–672.

Bendoly, E., and F. R. Jacobs (eds.) (2005) *Strategic ERP Extension and Use*, Stanford Business Books, Stanford, CA.

Benbasat, I. and R. W. Zmud (2003) The identity crisis within the IS discipline: defining and communicating the discipline's core properties, *MIS Quarterly* 27 (2), pp. 183–194.

Bhaskar, R. (1975/1978) *A Realist Theory of Science*, Harvester Press, Sussex.

Bhaskar, R. (1979/1998) *The Possibility of Naturalism*, 3rd edn., Routledge, London.

Bhaskar, R. (1989) *Reclaiming Reality*, Verso, London.

Bhaskar, R. (1991) *Philosophy and the Idea of Freedom*, Basil Blackwell, Oxford.

Bhaskar, R. (2002) *From Science to Emancipation: Alienation and the Actuality of Enlightenment*, Sage, New Delhi.

Bloom, B. S. (1956) *Taxonomy of Educational Objectives: Handbook 1, Cognitive Domain*, Longman, New York.

Bunge, M. (1967) *Scientific Research II: The Search for Truth*, Springer Verlag, Berlin.

Bunge, M. (1984) Philosophical inputs and outputs of technology, in G. Bugliarello and D. Donner (eds.) *History and Philosophy of Technology*, University of Illinois Press, Urbana, IL, pp. 263–281.

Cao, J., J. M. Crews, M. Lin, A. Deokar, J. Burgoon, and J. F. Nunamaker (2006) Interactions between system evaluation and theory testing: a demonstration of the power of a multifaceted approach to information systems research, *Journal of Management Information Systems* 22 (4), pp. 207–235.

Carlsson, S. A. (2003) Advancing information systems evaluation (research): a critical realist approach, *Electronic Journal of Information Systems Evaluation* 6 (2), pp. 11–20.

Carlsson, S. A. (2004) Using critical realism in IS research, in M. E. Whitman and A. B. Woszczynski (eds.), *The Handbook of Information Systems Research*, Idea Group Publishing, Hershey, PA, pp. 323–338.

Carlsson, S. A. (2006) Towards an information systems design research framework: a critical realist perspective, in *Proceedings of the First International Conference on Design Science in Information Systems and Technology (DESRIST 2006)*, Claremont Graduate University, Claremont, CA, February 24–25, pp. 192–212.

Carlsson S. A. (2009) Critical realism, in Y. K. Dwivedi, B. Lal, M. D. Williams, S. L. Schneberger, and M. Wade (eds.) *Handbook of Research on Contemporary Theoretical Models in Information Systems*, IGI Global, Hershey, PA, pp. 57–76

Carlsson, S. A. and T. Kalling (2006) Why is it that a knowledge management initiative works or fails, in *Proceedings of the 14th European Conference on Information Systems*, Gothenburg.

Carlsson, S. A. and T. Kalling (2007) Implementation of a knowledge management initiative: turning kms use into profit, in *Proceedings of the 4th International Conference on Intellectual Capital, Knowledge Management and Organisational Learning (ICICKM)*, University Stellenbosch Business School, Cape Town, South Africa, October 15–16, 2007.

Carlsson S. A., S. Henningsson, S. Hrastinski, and C. Keller (2008) Towards a design science research approach for IS use and management: applications from the areas of knowledge management, E-learning and IS integration, in *Proceedings of the Third International Conference on Design Science Research in Information Systems & Technology* (DESRIST 2008), May 7–9, Atlanta, GA.

Carlsson S.A., S. Henningsson, S. Hrastinski and C. Keller (forthcoming): Socio-technical IS design science research: developing design theory for IS integration management, *Information Systems and e-Business Management*.

Chen, W. and R. Hirschheim (2004) A paradigmatic and methodological examination of information systems research. *Information Systems Journal* 14 (3), pp. 197–235.

Cole, R. A. (2000) Introduction, in R. A. Cole (ed.) *Issues in Web-Based Pedagogy: A Critical Primer*, Greenwood Press, Westport, CT, pp. ix–xx.

Cole, R., S. Purao, M. Rossi, and M. K. Sein (2005) Being proactive: where action research meets design research, in *Proceedings of The Twenty-Sixth International Conference on Information Systems*, Las vegas, NV, December 11–14.

De Vaujany, F.-C. (2008) Capturing reflexivity modes in IS: a critical realist approach, *Information and Organization* 18, pp. 51–71.

Dean, K., J. Joseph, A. and Norrie (2005) Editorial: new essays in critical realism, *New Formations* 56, pp. 7–26.

Dobson, P. J. (2001) The philosophy of critical realism—an opportunity for information systems research, *Information Systems Frontier* 3 (2), pp. 199–201.

Dobson, P., J. Myles, and P. Jackson (2007) Making the case for critical realism: examining the implementation of automated performance management systems, *Information Resources Management Journal* 20 (2), pp. 138–152.

Edwards, J. S., M. Handzic, S. Carlsson, and M. Nissen (2003) Knowledge management research & practice: visions and directions, *Knowledge Management Research & Practice* 1 (1), pp. 49–60.

El Sawy, O. A. (2003) The 3 faces of IS identity: connection, immersion, and fusion, *Communications of the Association for Information Systems*, 12, Article 39.

Fleetwood, S. (2002) Boylan and O'Gorman's causal holism: a critical realist evaluation, *Cambridge Journal of Economics*, 26, pp. 27–45.

Fleetwood, S. (2004) An ontology for organisation and management studies, in S. Fleetwood and S. Ackroyd (eds.) *Critical Realist Applications in Organisation and Management Studies*, Routledge, London, pp. 27–53.

Fleetwood, S. and S. Ackroyd (eds.) (2004) *Critical Realist Applications in Organisation and Management Studies*, Routledge, London.

Gregor, S. (2006) The nature of theory in information systems, *MIS Quarterly* 30 (3), pp. 611–642.

Gregor, S. (2009) Building theory in the sciences of the artificial, in *Proceedings of the Fourth International Conference on Design Science in Information Systems and Technology (DESRIST 2009)*, May 7–8, Malvern, PA.

Gregor, S. and D. Jones (2007) The anatomy of a design theory, *Journal of the Association for Information Systems* 8 (5), pp. 312–335.

Groff, R. (2004) *Critical Realism, Post-positivism and the Possibility of Knowledge*, Routledge, London.

Hartwig, M. (ed.) (2007) *Dictionary of Critical Realism*, Routledge, London.

Hedström, P. and R. Swedberg (1998) Social mechanisms: an introductory essay, in P. Hedström and R. Swedberg (eds.) *Social Mechanisms: An Analytical Approach to Social Theory*, Cambridge University Press, Cambridge, pp. 1–31.

Hevner, A. R., S. T. March, J. Park, and S. Ram (2004) Design science in information systems research, *MIS Quarterly* 28 (1), pp. 75–105.

Hirschheim, R. and H. K. Klein (2003) Crisis in the IS field? A critical reflection on the state of the discipline, *Journal of the Association for Information Systems* 4 (5), pp. 237–293.

Hrastinski, S. (2007) The potential of synchronous communication to enhance participation in online discussions, in *Proceedings of the 28th International Conference on Information Systems*, Montreal.

Hrastinski, S. and C. Keller (2007) Computer-mediated communication in education: a review of recent research, *Educational Media International* 44 (1), pp. 61–77.

Hrastinski, S., C. Keller and S.A. Carlsson (2007) Towards a design theory for synchronous computer-mediated communication in e-learning environments, in *Proceedings of the Second International Conference on Design Science Research in Information Systems & Technology (DESRIST 2007)*, May 13–15, Pasadena, CA, pp. 208–224.

Hrastinski, S., C. Keller, and S.A. Carlsson (forthcoming) Design exemplars for synchronous e-learning: a design theory approach. *Computers & Education.*

Indulska, M. and J. C. Recker (2008) Design science in IS research: a literature analysis, in *Proceedings of the 4th Biennial ANU Workshop on Information Systems Foundation*, Canberra.

Kazi, M. A. F. (2003) *Realist Evaluation in Practice*, Sage, London.

Keller, C. (2007) *Virtual Learning Environments in Higher Education – A Study of User Acceptance*, Dissertation No. 1114, Linköping University, Linköping.

Krueger, R. A. (1994) *Focus Groups: A Practical Guide for Applied Research*, Sage, Thousand Oaks, CA.

Kuechler, W. and V. Vaishnavi (2008) The emergence of design research in information systems in North America, *Journal of Design Research* 7 (1), pp. 1–16.

Layder, D. (1993) *New Strategies in Social Research*, Polity Press, Cambridge, UK.

Layder, D. (1998) *Sociological Practice: Linking Theory and Social Research*, Sage, London.

Layder, D. (2005) *Understanding Social Theory*, 2nd edn, Sage, London.

Longshore Smith, M. (2005) *Overcoming Theory–practice Inconsistencies: Critical Realism and Information Systems Research,* WP134, Department of Information Systems, London School of Economics, London.

Lòpez, J. and G. Potter (eds.) (2001) *After Postmodernism: An Introduction to Critical Realism,* Athlone, London.

Luftman, J., R. Kempaiah, and E. Henrique (2009) Key issues for IT executives, *MIS Quarterly Executive* 8(3), pp. 151–159.

Lyytinen, K. (2008) Design: "shaping in the wild", Key Note Speech at the *Third International Conference on Design Science Research in Information Systems and Technology,* Atlanta, GA.

March, S. T. (2006) Designing design science, in J. L. King and K. Lyytinen (eds.) *Information Systems: The State of the Field,* John Wiley & Sons, Chichester, pp. 338–344.

March, S. T. and G. Smith (1995) Design and natural science research on information technology, *Decision Support Systems* 15 (4), pp. 251–266.

Marton, F., L. O. Dahlgren, L. Svensson, R. and Säljö (1977) *Inlärning och Omvärldsuppfattning: En Bok om den Studerande Människan,* Almqvist & Wiksell, Stockholm.

McKay, J. and P. Marshall (2005) A review of design science in information systems, in *Proceedings of the 16th Australasian Conference on Information Systems,* Sydney, November 29 to December 2, 2005.

McKay, J. and P. Marshall (2007) Science, design, and design science: seeking clarity to move design science research forward in information systems, in *Proceedings of the 18th Australasian Conference on Information Systems Science,* Toowoomba, December 5–7, 2007.

McKay, J. and P. Marshall (2008) Foundation of design science in Information Systems, Sparks working paper, RISO (Research into Information Systems in Organisations), Faculty of Information and Communication Technologies, Swinburne University of Technology, Melbourne, Australia.

Mingers, J. (2003) A critique of statistical modelling from a critical realist perspective, in *Proceedings of the 11th European Conference on Information Systems,* Naples, June 16–21.

Mingers, J. (2004) Re-establishing the real: critical realism and information systems, in J. Mingers and L. Willcocks (eds.) *Social Theory and Philosophy for Information Systems Research,* Wiley, Chichester, pp. 372–406.

Morton, P. (2006) Using critical realism to explain strategic information systems planning, *Journal of Information Theory and Application* 8 (1), pp. 1–20.

Mutch, A. (2002) Actors and networks or agents and structures: towards a realist view of information systems, *Organizations* 9 (3), pp. 477–496.

Myers, M. D. (2003) The IS core—VIII, defining the core properties of the IS discipline: not yet, not now, *Communications of the Association for Information Systems,* 12, Article 38.

Nunamaker, J. F., M. Chen, and T. D. M. Purdin (1990–91) System development in information systems research, *Journal of Management Information Systems* 7 (3), pp. 99–106.

Pawson, R. (2006) *Evidence-Based Policy: A Realist Perspective,* Sage, London.

Pawson, R. and N. Tilley (1997). *Realistic Evaluation,* Sage, London.

Pelz, D. S. (1978) Some expanded perspectives on the use of social science in public policy, in M. Yinger and S. J. Cutler (eds.) *Major Social Issues: A Multidisciplinary View,* Free Press, New York, pp. 346–357.

Pfeffer, J. and R. I. Sutton (2006) *Hard Facts, Dangerous Half-truths & Total Nonsense: Profiting from Evidence-based Management,* Harvard Business School Press, Boston, MA.

Purao, S. (2002) *Design Research in Technology and Information Systems: Truth or Dare,* Unpublished paper, School of Information Sciences and Technology, The Pennsylvania State University, University Park, State College, PA.

Robert, L. P. and A. R. Dennis (2005) Paradox of richness: a cognitive model of media choice, *IEEE Transactions on Professional Communication* 48 (1), pp. 10–21.

Rodgers, M. (2005) Stay hungry, *CIO Magazine.*

Rosemann, M. and I. Vessey (2008) Toward improving the relevance of information systems research to practice: the role of applicability checks, *MIS Quarterly* 32 (1), pp. 1–22.

Sayer, A. (1984/1992) *Method in Social Science: A Realist Approach*, 2nd edn, Routledge, London.

Sayer, A. (2000) *Realism and Social Science,* Sage, London.

Simon, H. A. (1988) *The Sciences of the Artificial*, 2nd edn, MIT Press, Cambridge, MA.

Smith, H. A. and McKeen, J. D. (2006) IT in 2010: the next frontier, *MIS Quarterly Executive* 5 (3), pp. 125–136.

Stahl, B. R. (2008) Design as reification, commodification, and ideology: a critical review of IS design science, in *Proceedings of the 16th European Conference on Information Systems*, Galway.

Trigg, M. (2001) *Understanding Social Science: A Philosophical Introduction to the Social Sciences*, 2nd edn, Blackwell, Malden, MA.

Vaishnavi, V. and W. Kuechler (2004/5) Design Research in Information Systems, January 20, 2004, last updated June 29, 2007, URL: http://www.isworld.org/Researchdesign/drisISworld.htm (Accessed: November 25, 2008).

van Aken, J. E. (2004) Management research based on the paradigm of design sciences: the quest for field-tested and grounded technological rules, *Journal of Management Studies* 41 (2), pp. 219–246.

van Aken, J. E. (2005) Management research as a design science: articulating the research products of mode 2 knowledge production in management, *British Journal of Management* 16 (1), pp. 19–36.

van Aken, J. E. (2006) *The Nature of Organizing Design: Both Like and Unlike Material Object Design,* Working Paper 06.13, Eindhoven Centre for Innovation Studies, Technische Universiteit Eindhoven, The Netherlands.

Venable, J. R. (2006) The role of theory and theorising in design science research, in *Proceedings of the First International Conference on Design Science in Information Systems and Technology (DESRIST 2006)*, pp. 1–18.

Venkatesh, V., M. G. Morris, G. B. Davis, and F. D. Davis (2003) User Acceptance of information technology: toward a unified view, *MIS Quarterly* 27 (3), pp. 425–478.

Volkoff, O., D. M. Strong, and M. B. Elmes (2007) Technological embeddedness and organizational change, *Organization Science*, 18 (5), pp. 832–848.

Vygotsky, L. S. (1978) *Mind in Society: The Development of Higher Psychological Processes,* Harvard University Press, Cambridge, MA.

Walls, J. G., G. R. Widmeyer, and O. A. El Sawy (1992) Building an information systems design theory for vigilant EIS, *Information Systems Research* 3 (1), pp. 36–59.

Walls, J. G., G. R. Widmeyer, and O. A. El Sawy (2004) Assessing information system design theory in perspective: how useful was our 1992 initial rendition? *Journal of Information Technology Theory and Application* 6 (2), pp. 43–58.

Walt, S. M. (1999) Rigor or rigor mortis? Rational choice and security studies, *International Security* 23 (4), pp. 5–48.

Wenger, E. (1998) *Communities of Practice: Learning, Meaning, and Identity,* Cambridge University Press, Cambridge.

Wilson, M. and A. Greenhill (2004) Theory and action for emancipation: elements of a critical realist approach, in B. Kaplan, Truex III, D. P. Wastell, A. T. Wood-Harper, and J. I. DeGross (eds.), *Information Systems Research: Relevant Theory and Informed Practice*, Kluwer, Norwell, MA, pp. 667–675.

Wilson, V. and B. McCormack (2006) Critical realism as emancipatory action: the case for realistic evaluation in practice development, *Nursing Philosophy* 7, pp. 45–47.

Zwieg, P., K. M. Kaiser, C. M. Beath, C. Bullen, K. P. Gallagher, T. Goles, J. Howland, J. C. Simon, P. Abbott, T. Abraham, E. Carmel, R. Evaristo, S. Hawk, M. Lacity, M. Gallivan, S. Kelly, J. G. Mooney, C. Ranganathan, J. W. Rottman, T. Ryan, and R. Wion (2006) The information technology workforce: trends and implications 2005–2008, *MIS Quarterly Executive* 5 (2), pp. 101–108.

Chapter 16
Design of Emerging Digital Services: A Taxonomy

To turn really interesting ideas and fledgling technologies into a company that can continue to innovate for years, it requires a lot of disciplines.

– Steve Jobs

There has been a gigantic shift from a product-based economy to one based on services, specifically digital services. From every indication it is likely to be more than a passing fad and the changes these emerging digital services represent will continue to transform commerce and have yet to reach market saturation. Digital services are being designed for and offered to users, yet very little is known about the design process that goes behind these developments. Is there a science behind designing digital services? By examining 13 leading digital services, we have developed a design taxonomy to be able to classify and contrast digital services. What emerged in the taxonomy were two broad dimensions: a set of fundamental design objectives and a set of fundamental service provider objectives. This chapter concludes with an application of the proposed taxonomy to three leading digital services. We hope that the proposed taxonomy will be useful in understanding the science behind the design of digital services.

16.1 Introduction

There has been a gigantic shift from a product-based economy to one based on services, specifically digital services. This comes as a result of the widespread availability of computers and the pervasive Internet, which together form a digital infrastructure capable of providing digital services in new and different ways. For example, Salesforce.com at the time of the writing has over 900,000 paying subscribers and assiduously claims not to be selling software but a "service" (Salesforce.com 2007). Myspace.com which was founded in 1996 (Alexa Internet 2007) has over 70 million active monthly users (News Corporation 2007) and

Kevin Williams, Samir Chatterjee, and Matti Rossi

A. Hevner, S. Chatterjee, *Design Research in Information Systems*, Integrated Series in Information Systems 22, DOI 10.1007/978-1-4419-5653-8_16,
© Springer Science+Business Media, LLC 2010

is considered one of the most successful social networking sites on the Internet. These are not isolated examples, but represent a major recent trend that from every indication is likely to be more than a passing fad. Moreover, the changes these examples represent will continue to transform commerce and have yet to reach market saturation.

Is there something truly new and different about these digital services, most of which scarcely existed until recently? We claim that the design process for digital services is distinct from previous design genres owing to the dramatic differences in limitations and possibilities of the new digital infrastructures. The whole process of technology acceptance is bound to be different with this new paradigm of ubiquitous digital services (Lyytinen 2004).

While we agree that there are many approaches for examining the differences in digital services we find the field of organizational systematics to be especially useful (McKelvey 1982). McKelvey describes organizational systematics as "science of organizational differences." He continues that "the development of taxonomic theory...is not an outgrowth of sound scientific method in most sciences; it is a prerequisite to such methods." The classification of differences into categories can produce knowledge about the design and design process that may be useful to design researchers.

Thus the development of the taxonomy starts with techniques which are qualitative in nature, since they are based on observation and therefore not initially complete nor entirely conclusive. In this chapter, the development of a classification taxonomy of digital service design serves as a precursor to the scientific study of digital services and in and of itself might not be axiomatic. The motivation of this chapter is to further understand this emerging trend by proposing design taxonomy for the emerging digital services. Using this taxonomy, three successful organizations will be examined to see emerging design patterns. Besides the two previously named examples of Salesforce.com and Myspace.com, the phenomenally successful Itunes.com service will also be profiled using the taxonomy proposed in this chapter. Considering that in a press release Itunes.com announced in April 2007 that after selling more than 3 billion songs, it has "become the largest music retailer in the US." (Apple.com 2007), this is hardly the sign of an insignificant development.

Through this study, we hope to develop a useful method to categorize and classify different types of digital services that will give insight to future designers and guide their design efforts. Clearly, there are some important differences between digital services, existing software products, and non-digital services. While these differences vary from service to service, in developing this taxonomy we hope to see a collection of similarities that will be useful to the field of design science. As far as the authors know the design principles of digital services have not yet been studied.

There has recently been renewed interest in the design science paradigm of research in IS (Walls, Widmeyer et al. 1992; Hevner, March et al. 2004). People have written about what it is (March and Smith 1995), how to evaluate such research (Hevner, March et al. 2004) and also the gap in teaching versus research in systems analysis and design (Bajaj, Batra et al. 2005). ISWorld has also dedicated an entire web site to useful facts and pointers on this research method (ISWorld, 2008). This chapter attempts to fill a void in the design principles that are behind emerging digital services.

The chapter is organized as follows: first we define digital services. In the next section we rationalize the need for the taxonomy that we develop in the following sections. Then, we analyze three popular digital services using the taxonomy and in the final section we draw conclusions and ponder future research considerations.

16.2 Service Versus Digital Service

For the purposes of this chapter "digital services" are services which are obtained and/or arranged through a digital transaction over IP (Internet protocol). To further distinguish between the idea of a service and a digital service it might be helpful to consider the broad definition of a service and compare the differences. In principles of marketing (Kotler 2007), a service is defined as follows:

> Any activity or benefit that one party can give to another, that is essentially intangible and does not result in the ownership of anything. Its production may or may not be tied to a physical product.

The method of delivery being specified as digital is more restrictive than in a normal service since it requires the ability to connect to and use the infrastructure of the IP-based Internet. Human beings cannot participate in digital services unaided by computer technology. This requirement alone sets higher minimum standards than normal services and requires an agreed-upon set of rules to punctuate the interaction.

The digital service may start digitally, but this does not mean that all interactions are limited to be digital. For example, the Amazon.com web site represents a digital service that often includes the delivery of a physical product such as a book but is still in many ways distinctly different from a physical bookstore. This interaction, however, is fast changing as Amazon.com now offers a host of e-books that are digital entities. Often the utility companies that provide water or natural gas in a community are referred to as the "water service" or "gas service" but the service consists of a physical product for which the utility company performs a coordination and delivery of the supply (i.e., water or natural gas). There is a similarity to this utility model in the provision of digital services where the core benefit that the service provider delivers is often the coordination and delivery of a product or ancillary service and may or may not be linked to a physical product.

The tangibility of a digital service is a second difference versus a normal service, but it depends upon the definition of tangibility. Tangibility used to be broadly understood as ability to be perceived by the sense of touch. In this definition the tangible assets were thought of as the hard assets of the organization and therefore were distinct from services. However, with new business models, the legal and financial definitions have changed to the point where tangible assets are those that can be perceived by senses other than touch. A patented method of business can be financially tangible but not a touchable asset. In fact the non-tangible assets are often the key assets of the organization and are accounted for such on the financial statements.

Another difference between digital and non-digital services is the idea of ownership, which is related to the discussion of tangibility above. Ownership indicates possession, but for a digital artifact, the physical possession might not be the same as having full control. Now digital rights and ownership rights have blurred somewhat, making it difficult to know with certainty who owns what and where the rights of one party stop and the other begins. The concept of digital rights is just one area where the provider of a digital service might represent a large number of digital owners in their interactions with other parties. There has been a shift in the legal protections, where software or a business process used not to be patentable and so early software was not patented, but protected with other intellectual property protections such as copyright in the case of Lotus-1-2-3 (Bricklin 2007). Intellectual property protections are especially important for digital services since by their digital nature they are easily reproduced (Cockburn 2007). On one hand it is important to be able to digitally reproduce these services to support scalability, but also to be able to distinguish digital services from those of their competitors. The ability of one organization to protect and differentiate their service from another can take several forms including secrecy, legal protections, name recognition, and other complex interactions between products and services.

The service providers consider the potential needs of their users and meeting these needs is more crucial than the relational interaction between parties. Non-digital services are often based on a personal relationship that is more important than the service being provided. While for digital services, the service provider might never know the service receiver and indeed supra-functional needs (including the emotional, aspirational, cultural and social) are recognized as more important than functional needs (Weightman 2003) and will necessarily be included in the design of the digital service.

In summary the differences between normal services and digital services include the following:

- Being digital, as least for a portion of the interaction
- A different sense of tangible versus intangible
- Often the "digital service" is a coordination or arrangement of something physical
- The idea of ownership is more subtle including digital rights for a certain purpose versus outright ownership
- Consideration of the overall needs in the digital service is more important than the nature of the relationship

16.3 Research Objectives

While software design is a growing and maturing field, digital service design is an emerging and nascent field. We see several digital services being designed and offered to users (see Table 16.1), yet very little is known about the design process that goes behind these developments. It has been argued that innovation is more

Table 16.1 Sample list of digital service providers (Source: Alexa Internet (2007) unless otherwise noted)

Service name	Brief description	Approximate number of users, sales, or measure of size
Amazon.com	Online commerce vendor selling books, CDs, DVDs, and electronics	Sales of $12.2 billion
Ebay.com	International person to person auction site, with products sorted into categories	Sales of $6.8 billion
Apple.com/iTunes	Web site for purchase of music and videos supporting ITunes software	Over 3 billion songs sold and has become the third largest music retailer in the USA (Apple.com 2007)
Salesforce.com	Provides on-demand customer relationship management (CRM) software services to help companies with global customer communication	Over 900,000 paying subscribers (Salesforce.com 2007)
Myspace.com	Social networking site	70 million active monthly users (News Corporation 2007)
YouTube.com	Video sharing web site	Fourth most visited web site on the Internet
Expedia.com	Travel products and services	Sales of $2.3 billion
Facebook.com	Social networking site	Over 15 million active users (Fast Company Staff 2007)
Wikipedia.com	Collaborative encyclopedia	Among the top 10 visited web sites
Secondlife.com	Provides an online society within a 3D world, where users can explore, build, socialize, and participate in their own economy	Over 11 million residents (Secondlife.com 2007)
Craigslist.org	Centralized network of locally organized online communities offering free classified advertisements	More than 5 billion page views per month and 75 million user posting per month (Craigslist.org 2007)
Worldofwarcraft.com	Online role playing game	Over 8.5 million paying online subscribers (Snow 2007)

a result of iterative emergence than design (Van Alstyne and Logan 2007). Our research was guided by the following questions:

- Is there a science behind designing services?
- Are there specific requirements that the developers use?
- What are the metrics and criteria by which such services can be evaluated?
- What makes a digital service successful?
- It is t hese questions that drive our research objectives.

It is important to note that just because one digital service is influential in one way does not mean that all digital services will be the same. For example, Amazon.com has an estimated 14,400 employees and Craigslist.com has a reported 24 employees, even though the estimated "page views" between these two digital services has been quite similar during the past month (Alexa Internet 2007). Thus the metrics for finding a "leading digital service" are a little problematic and if defined too narrowly could exclude a whole host of digital services. Developing a metric for measuring influence is beyond the scope of this chapter, certainly the above list includes what would broadly be considered leading digital services.

16.4 Why Taxonomy?

What is a taxonomy of digital services? It is a classification system so that each digital service can be distinguished from every other digital service of a different type. As McKelvey (1982) suggests, classification is often a prerequisite to the scientific method. This is the point of identity of a type, not of the differences of individual members of the type from one another. This ability to distinguish one digital service from another might prove to be rather difficult as a result of the rapid changes even between different versions of one digital service. The dynamic nature of digital services means that we want to attempt to see elements of the digital services that are transcendent of a particular moment and represent the nature of a certain service. For example, while there have been many versions of Microsoft Windows operating systems, the nature of the Windows versions seem to have followed a certain trajectory. Likewise a new software product containing similarities to another existing product is generally spoken of as being in the same family of applications (i.e., spreadsheets, databases, etc.).

16.5 Grounding of the Taxonomy

We started with classifications of digital services by looking at leading digital services, then we looked for important differences between various services. The idea of "leading digital services" is problematic, since this could mean having a large usage, or being financially successful, or something else. So as the start of the iterative investigations we brainstormed about the digital services we knew about or had a well-known reputation. This ethnographic method is both qualitative and verbal based on observation (Plowman 2003). As a basis for the initial classification areas we started with the "apparent intention" of the designers and their "goals" in the design. The brainstorming took us to the same type of quadrant as bird watching (Stokes 1997), seemingly low on usefulness, but vital as a basis for the development of theory.

During the brainstorming of the differences the two dimensions that appear to emerge from the study of digital services include some fundamental design dimensions and fundamental service provider objectives. The fundamental design dimensions include the ideas of service delivery, service maturity, malleability, and pricing. The fundamental service provider objectives include how the digital service is designed to meet the objectives of business success, technological success, and success of interactions. The expected interactions between these and business objectives are part of the complexity of the taxonomy. Thus, these interaction pathways will provide a matrix for differentiating one digital service from another.

The requirements of a design must "specify the expected services, functions, and features – independent of the implementation" (Henzinger 2007). In Aristole's *Rhetoric*, the combination of artistic and inartistic (or scientific) proofs together formed the design of the speech and these elements need to work together for the speech or other artifact to be successful. This same combination between art and science is one of the issues that make the science of design difficult to isolate. The field of information systems is not alone in this ongoing conflict or integration between science and art, for example, another field which is frequently used as a metaphor for good design is the field of architecture. One of the founding principles is the oft quoted maxim from the roman architect Vitruvius that good architecture has three qualities "commodity, firmness, and delight." (Winograd 1996). The authors seek to identify how these same three qualities could be represented in the field of digital services.

The separation or independence of the implementation from the design means that the implementation needs to be judged on how well the design achieves the functional requirements, but also the extra-functional requirements such as "performance and robustness" and go beyond the basic functional requirements and even achieving Vitruvius' qualities. This combination of art and science makes it possible for the users of the digital service to build a positive long-term relationship which results in attachment of the user to the digital service (Weightman 2003).

16.6 Fundamental Design Dimensions

Through an iterative process of observation and analysis we identified four fundamental design dimensions that we think distinguish one service from the other. That is not to conclude that this is an exhaustive list, but in any iterative approach becomes the starting for the next iteration. These four dimensions are as follows:

- Service delivery
- Service maturity
- Malleability (provider and user)
- Pricing and funding

The above fundamental design dimensions are based on our view that the classical approach of taxonomy (McKelvey 1982) that "three things may be known about any entity – its essence, its definition, and its name." That is, it is possible for two different digital services to be running the exact same software (essence) and serve the same purpose (definition) but have different names and therefore are completely distinct services. These differences should show up as distinct in the taxonomy. This typological approach makes the assumption that artifact implicitly asserts that forms exist (in the Aristotelian sense) and can be known. The idea of "grand strategy" or the overall goal that drives the enterprise (Tow 2003) may be overstating the design of digital services, but we believe that a form or goal must exist that drives the development forward. It may be that the grand strategy is really unfloding as the designers respond to immediate requirements in such a way as not to confound their previous design decisions.

16.6.1 Service Delivery

The service delivery describes how the service is provided and the range of requirements for the consumer of the service to participate at different levels. Some digital services specify minimum requirements to participate in the service offering and others assume that by connecting to their web site the minimum standards have already been achieved. These minimum requirements of the digital service may often vary along a continuum and emerge as follows (see Table 16.2):

Table 16.2 Delivery requirements

Minimum requirements	
High	Specialized hardware or software required (latest versions or certified hardware/software)
Medium	Standard computers with late (past 2 or 3 years) operating system sufficient
Low	Older computers (3+ years) and operating systems work fine, but specified
None	Minimum hardware/software requirements not specified

Examples of the service delivery requirements include the following:

- Network speed or bandwidth
- Hardware (i.e., memory, CPU, disk, satellite dish) requirements
- Software requirements such as browser or helping applications (e.g., Java)
- Identity requirement (e.g., being known by the other party through registration)

These minimum service requirements often refer to the requirements for basic services with additional services possible with higher than the minimum configuration. This distinction between levels of service is an important one as the digital infrastructure makes possible a large range of service levels to different users, including customization to the needs of different service receivers.

Thus another consideration for the dimension of service delivery is the idea of premium or extra services. Furthermore, the malleability of service delivery is a very important part of pricing of customized services (Hagel and Singer, 1999). Highly customized delivery means that the product can be tailored to individual needs according to timeliness, completeness, etc. Low customization means that there are no versions, for example, low bandwidth or premium customers.

16.6.2 Service Maturity

The idea of service maturity is based on three phases of technological adoption (Liddle 2007) where the nature of the interaction changes at each stage, specifically enthusiast, professional, and consumer phases. A fourth level is added to indicate those services that require little or no interaction with the service provider (Henzinger 2007). Thus the four broad levels are enthusiast, professional, consumer, and embedded systems. Table 16.3 summarizes characteristics of each level.

Table 16.3 Four stages of digital service maturity

Development phase	When problems arise	Technical skills required by system users	Overriding goals of phase
Enthusiast	Technical users solve the problems themselves or check with other technical experts or with the system designers	High	Innovation and creativity
Professional/ business	Formal customer service delivery system with occasional interaction with system designers for severe problems	Medium	Value and reliability
Consumer	Eliminated need for interaction with system designers and best practices are built into the system and the customer service delivery systems	Low	Simplicity and trust
Embedded systems	Eliminated the need for interactions with customer service delivery systems. System failures are handled as artifacts of failures of related systems	None	Automation and dependence

At the enthusiast phase the systems are developed by the system designers and used by individuals with knowledge of the design and its limitations.

Technical systems require high technical expertise on the part of the users; generally these systems are developed by techies for techies and are the initial version of the service. The users of these systems often have direct interactions with the system designers. Advanced knowledge to change initial configurations may be required to use this service. Recent early-stage open-source services are good examples of these.

Professional or business systems are where system designers design support systems and tools to reduce the interaction between designers and users. For severe problems there is an often a customer service delivery system that might permit occasional interaction between system designers and users (e.g., Salesforce.com where the provider of the service might need to give best practices for use). The service scalability comes from the homogeneity and little custom training needed for these services.

Consumer users might need training on the advanced functions of the systems, but the designers should have anticipated this and eliminated the need for interactions with system designers and best practices are built into the systems (e.g., Wikipedia.com is so easy to use that very little professional instruction is available).

Embedded systems are "where embedded software is controlling communication, transportation, and medical systems" (Henzinger 2007) and "indeed, the more seamlessly embedded computers and software are integrated into the products and the less often they fail, the less visible they are." Fully automated systems are where the consumers of the service are receiving the benefits without having to interact with the provider at all once the service has been put into place (e.g., electricity is a service that delivers an intangible product).

16.6.3 Malleability

One surprising part of the list of leading digital services as in Table 16.1 is the speed with which these digital services have become so influential in fostering interactions, utilizing technology, and influencing business, for most of these examples were started in the past 10 years. Therefore, a most desirable quality in digital services is clearly the ability to be malleable or to be able to adapt to changing market needs or requirements. Digital services have an apparent advantage in that they can be dynamically and incrementally changed without the need for the users to upgrade their software, since the functionality of the latest code is deployed from the service provider upon use. Therefore one element within the dimension of malleability is the proportion of the digital service that is physical versus digital. As in the above example comparing Amazon.com and Craigslist.org, the former has an inventory and shipping services, while the latter is almost exclusively digital in nature. The requirement to change more than code on the part of the service provider adds to the complexity of making changes. Therefore the overall concept of malleability is a quality of the digital service such that when malleability is high, changes are easier, with less risk and expense.

This variation contributes to the difficulty in making changes and is reflected in the level of malleability for both the service provider and service user. Tables 16.4 and 16.5 characterize the value of each level of malleability which will be used in the taxonomy:

Table 16.4 Dimensions of service provider malleability

Malleability level	Description
High	Changes are easily made to the digital service offerings by the service provider and require no testing
Medium	Changes require changes to more than a few parts of the service and limited testing
Low	Changes are difficult or expensive to implement and require extensive scenario testing
None	Changes require a complete re-write or complete new implementation

Table 16.5 Dimensions of service user malleability

Malleability level	Description
High	The service user is either not impacted by the changes or is positive toward them
Medium	The service user is impacted in their use of the digital service and must make some changes to their user behavior
Low	Changes are difficult or expensive for the service user to consume and may interfere with their continued use of the product unless there are other incentives to remain as a service user
None	The digital service is like a completely new offering and could have been provided by another service provider

This metric is a reflection on the part of the service provider in making changes to their service offering and is probably best measured by the testing required with changes. A good design should reflect the ability to operate at a high level of service provider malleability at least for the anticipated needs of the digital service. It is understandable why design is often cut short in digital services as there are incredible pressures to be early to market which may short circuit appropriate testing and the finding of design flaws. Likewise as the uses of digital services changes, a service with a good initial design might not be appropriate for the changing needs.

However, if digital services are not well designed, there can be significant barriers in addressing future needs or requirements. These barriers are not only on the side of the service provider but also on the part of the service users, since as users become accustomed to new offerings their behavior changes to become dependent on these services and thereby making changes more problematic. The levels of service user malleability are as follows:

This dimension measures the impact on the service user to changes made by the service provider. It is probably best measured by the amount of accommodation necessary on the part of the service user to continue using the existing service. As digital services, it is possible to maintain a compatibility with previous versions and at the same time implement new or customized offering for customers who want them but this may involve extra work on the part of both the service provider and service user.

16.6.4 Pricing and Funding

The value proposition is an important component in digital services, where users pay for the perceived value. User value is based on the concept of user experience (Boztepe 2007) and can be applied just as easily to services as to products. The different approaches to capture revenue range from different methods of pricing to different sources of revenue and different products or services sold. The revenue logic can include both sales revenues and other sources of financing. High initial cost and nearly zero marginal cost characterize the production and dissemination of information-intensive products. Digitally delivered products have unique characteristics of the information products to exploit. For instance, it is possible to use a range of pricing alternatives based on user segments and user-selectable options. Varian (1995) has argued that if the willingness to pay is correlated with some observable characteristics of the consumers, such as demographic profile, then it could be linked to the pricing strategy. One strategy is to bundle goods to sell to a market with heterogeneous willingness to pay. The source of operational funds is an important consideration in the design approach as with different funding types the exigencies of design may change dramatically. For example, if an organization is developing the next killer application, but their operational funds are supplied primarily through bank loans they may experience greater urgency than an organization developing the same type of product but has received a multi-year multimillion dollar research grant. The source of funds can be classified in a broad sense as coming from internal sources and/or external sources. Furthermore, the funds can come directly from customers who use the service (sales revenue), indirect sales not from end users of the service (as in the case of advertising revenue), investors who have equity (shareholders), investors who share in some equity benefit (e.g., venture capitalists), credit (in the form of loans), savings, donations, grants, or subsidies, and taxation.

Generic approaches to revenue logic in the software business have been identified by Rajala et al. (2007) as follows:

- *Licensing*, that is, license sales and royalties as the main source of revenue
- *Revenue sharing* with distribution partners or profit sharing with users
- *Loss-leader pricing*, meaning giving something for less than its value. This is done, for example, in order to increase the customer base for later revenue, or, to support sales of some other part of the product/service offering
- *Media model*, where the revenue is based on advertisement sales either through advertisement in the user interfaces of software or by selling user information for advertisers
- *Effort-, cost-, or value-based pricing*, which is a common approach in customized or tailor-made software solutions and made to order software projects
- *Hybrid models* as various combinations of the above

Let us briefly consider the social networking sites such as myspace.com or facebook.com and the revenue models they use. For example, Facebook.com entered a three year revenue sharing deal with Microsoft for advertising and an agreement to give away 10 million samples with Apple's Itunes.com (Yadav 2006). These sites generally have low startup costs as content is mainly provided by the users themselves. They benefit from the so-called network effect. Most of these sites are successful as they are free to users and rely on advertisers mainly for revenue generation. But we have learned from the dot.com days that value is not click-through or eyeballs but value comes from actual revenues. So beyond advertizing, innovative digital service sites are designing clever ways to monetize their activities. These include (1) revenue sharing in which two sites link each other and any resultant purchase leads to revenue sharing; (2) premium subscription fees that provide above and beyond basic services including privacy protection; (3) corporate sponsorships. Of course the real and albeit value that these social networking sites have is the untapped potential to mine of user data and their activities. Behind each click lies user preferences and when such data can be made available to marketers, a whole new experience to customization starts. Should the service be designed from the beginning to capture all such user data?

16.7 Fundamental Service Provider Objectives

Besides the fundamental design dimensions, we also have come up with three service provider objectives that are part of our taxonomy. They are as follows:

- Business objectives
- Technological objectives
- Interaction objectives

Digital services are offered to users for the benefit of the users, but the service provider is doing so to achieve certain objectives. While all of these objectives are important, often there is a ranking that has a dominating effect on the design of the digital service. The ranking between these factors executes a controlling effect on the design of digital services.

16.7.1 Business Objective

Most service providers do so to be rewarded financially over the long term. With the new digital services, the number of methods to make money have increased and made it possible for digital services to have a number of sources of income instead of simply their customers. The ability to share the profit from a sale with a variety of participants has supplemented the income of digital service provides in such a way that without it, these otherwise marginal services would not have survived.

The business objective is not just about making money but also about building a successful business which includes brand establishment, customer loyalty, and offering superior customer service. The executive function in the organization usually represents this focus but takes input from many quarters. Where the business objective pressures are too intense, promising technological products are canceled.

Some service providers are able to take a very long view of the design objectives as a result of having a large capital base or support of other sources of income which can remove the urgency to be financially secure. Removing this urgency is not always a benefit to the long-term survival of the service provider as the pressure given with the need to be financially viable can help service providers make appropriate decisions more quickly.

Some key questions for the business objectives include the following:

- Can design impact customer acquisition and retention and if so how?
- How does the provider of the system make money to keep their service online?
- How important are service enhancements to their growth and sustenance as a going concern?
- How does the provider of the system differentiate their service from that of competitors?

16.7.2 Technological Objectives

The technological objective describes the level of importance of the choice of technological solutions. A Facebook.com engineer describes how they were able to modify the open-source Mysql database to support the more than 2 million new users per week (Sobel 2007). In this case, the system designers are probably more interested in having a certain technology than consideration of business objective or interaction objectives. Often the focus is on more functionality, bells and whistles, and performance factors. While these are certainly important, there is often conflict between IT and the rest of the organization when choosing the technological direction. In the case where the technology is ranked higher than the business objective, a very good idea might fail to survive without due consideration to business and interaction objectives.

Some questions for the technological objective include the following:

- How much control does the service provider exercise over all components of their technology?
- Where is the product in the life cycle?

16.7.3 Interaction Objectives

By interaction, we mean the human–computer interaction and the experience a user gets while using the service. Many Internet firms have thousands or even millions of users, but if they are focused only about driving traffic to their site, their business model might not make long-term sense. Likewise, without consideration for technological objectives, the web site might appear for a time as trendy and therefore successful in the short term. However, what will the interaction of the consumer of the service be with the service provider and other consumers over a longer term? The designers might not be able to fully understand, articulate, and interpret user needs and so a higher level design does not constrain users to a certain way of interacting with the digital service. "Designers cannot always forecast how users will use products" (Weightman 2003) and vis-à-vis digital services. Many of the social networking sites and their services evolve with seemingly random interactions that then are capitalized as a unique core differentiator.

Principles from the field of product design can be applicable to the design of digital services. Weightman (2003) has suggested that designing for variance involves a modular approach, which has direct applicability to digital services through the use of modular programming techniques (Weightman 2003). Different functional modules can be combined together to synergistically provide digital services which were not conceived of by the service designers. Optimization of the interactions of different modules is often undertaken to improve the overall service quality. Weightman (2003) have suggested that we are moving beyond mass customization to a custom manufacturing realm where "design is too important to leave to designers" and that there needs to be greater collaboration between users and designers.

Some of the questions concerning interaction design include the following:

- How is loyalty encouraged?
- Can customers distinguish between one brand and another?
- Is the digital service easy to learn?
- How does the service provider meet the custom or individual needs of their customers?

16.8 Summary of the Taxonomy

Our taxonomy is presented in Fig. 16.1.

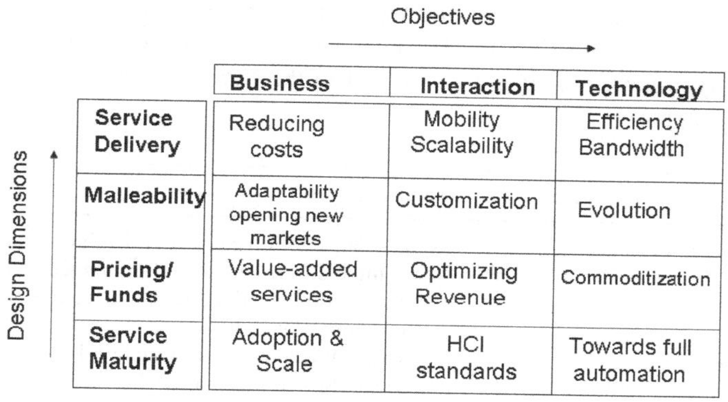

		Objectives	
	Business	**Interaction**	**Technology**
Service Delivery	Reducing costs	Mobility Scalability	Efficiency Bandwidth
Malleability	Adaptability opening new markets	Customization	Evolution
Pricing/ Funds	Value-added services	Optimizing Revenue	Commoditization
Service Maturity	Adoption & Scale	HCI standards	Towards full automation

Design Dimensions

Fig. 16.1 Digital service design taxonomy

A digital service is often a solution to a real-world problem or need but can also be driven by business motivation that there is money to be made in offering such a service. Hence business objectives are important. Since the service is something that is consumed by end users, it is very important to focus on the interaction objectives. How will end user interact with the service implementation? Finally a designer has to develop a set of functions that must be present in the service architecture. Often there is conflict between keeping it simple versus making too many bells and whistles available. Those are hard design trade-offs that one has to make. For example many people cite the success of Google to its very simple web page (Moogridge, 2006).

The diagram shows the four design dimensions that include service delivery, malleability, pricing, and service maturity which then dictates how best to improve the service. Notice that there are dependencies between design objectives and design dimensions as shown by arrows. For example, business objectives are likely going to impact choices of service delivery and pricing functions. Similarly technological objectives will dictate how malleable a service is. Further there could be feedback from pricing and service maturity that could affect the business and technological objectives and as the digital service evolves, fundamental design objectives could change as well.

16.9 Evaluation of the Taxonomy

In this section we briefly apply our taxonomy on three leading digital service companies to further illustrate its usefulness to study the design of these services.

16.9.1 Salesforce.com

Salesforce.com is one of the leading online CRM (customer relationship management) vendors. They currently have over 38,100,000 organizations as customers and provide a broad range of service offerings. The web site claims Salesforce.com is "The Power of an Idea – Not the Power of Software." While this may sound like marketing hype the company's focus is not in the same vane as the tried and true software vendors.

Fundamental design objectives	Salesforce.com
Service delivery	None – "all salesforce.com CRM solutions are delivered as online utilities, upgrades are immediately available with no corresponding hardware requirements" (Salesforce.com 2007)
Service maturity	Professional/business – subscription-based customer service (Salesforce.com 2007)
Malleability (provider and user)	
Service provider	Unknown
Service user	High (Salesforce.com 2007)
Pricing and funding	Premium subscription fees
Fundamental business objectives	
Business objectives	High
Technological objectives	High
Interaction objectives	Low

16.9.2 Myspace.com

Myspace.com is one of the largest social networking sites on the Internet with over 70 million active monthly users (News Corporation 2007).

Fundamental design objectives	Myspace.com
Service delivery	None
Service maturity	Consumer – no customer service phone number
Malleability (provider and user)	
Service provider	Unknown
Service user	High
Pricing and funding	Revenue sharing and corporate sponsorships
Fundamental business objectives	
Business objectives	Low
Technological objectives	High
Interaction objectives	High

16.9.3 Itunes.com

Itunes.com is an Internet provider for the sale of music and videos supporting ITunes software. The cost of each song are a standard price at 99¢ each (USA) and similar prices in other currencies. The following table shows the evaluation of the ITunes.com (also known as Apple.com/ITunes) according to our taxonomy.

Fundamental design objectives	ITunes.com
Service delivery	High – Itunes software required – free download
Service maturity	Consumer
Malleability (provider and user)	
Service provider	Unknown
Service user	High
Pricing and funding	Premium subscription fees
Fundamental business objectives	
Business objectives	High
Technological objectives	High
Interaction objectives	Low

16.10 Future Research Considerations

Platforms that offer digital services are emerging to be an important area of research and study. The design of such systems is not well understood although many of the recent services are flourishing both in terms of subscribers they have and the kind of revenues they are generating. In this chapter, we take the taxonomy approach to illustrate salient design features that apply to these emerging services. This is the first such study as per our knowledge.

In this preliminary attempt, we have identified several key design dimensions and service provider objectives that play an important role in both the success of the service platform as well as the business. We have discussed these dimensions and objectives to provide into what role they play. In the near future, we hope to conduct detailed qualitative interviews and quantitative data collection from digital service companies to map the taxonomy and uncover more interesting facets about their design. The science of design is a nascent field in the field of information systems and it will be very difficult to establish a formula for design when the designers do not know what the goals of their designs will be.

References

Alexa Internet, I. (2007) The Web Information Company. Retrieved December 17, 2007.

Apple.com (2007, July 31) iTunes store tops three billion songs. Retrieved November 27, 2007, from http://www.apple.com/pr/library/2007/07/31itunes.html .

Bajaj, A., D. Batra et al. (2005) Systems analysis and design: should we be researching what we teach? *Communications of AIS* 15, pp. 478–493.

Boztepe, S. (2007) User value: competing theories and models. *International Journal of Design* 1 (2), pp. 55–63.

Bricklin, D. (2007) Why didn't we patent the spreadsheet? Were we stupid? Retrieved November 2, 2007, from http://www.bricklin.com/patenting.htm .

Cockburn, I. (2007) Assessing the value of a patent: things to bear in mind. Retrieved October 30, 2007, from http://www.wipo.int/sme/en/documents/valuing_patents.htm .

Craigslist.org (2007) Craigslist fact sheet. Retrieved December 20, 2007, from http://www.craigslist.org/about/factsheet.html .

Fast Company Staff (2007) Facebook by the numbers. Retrieved December 20, 2007, from http://www.fastcompany.com/magazine/115/open_features-hacker-dropout-ceo-facebook-numbers.html .

Hagel, J. and M. Singer (1999) *Net Worth*, Harvard Business School Press, Boston, MA.

Henzinger, T. and S. Joseph (2007) The discipline of embedded systems design, *IEEE Computer* 40 (10), pp. 32–40.

Hevner, A. R., S. T. March et al. (2004) Design science in information systems research. *MIS Quarterly* 28 (1), pp. 75–105.

Kotler, P. and A. Gary (2007) *Principles of Marketing*, Prentice Hall, Englewood Cliffs, NJ.

Liddle, D. (2007) *Designing Interactions*, The MIT Press, Cambridge, MA.

Lyytinen, K., Y. Youngjin, U. Varshney, M. S. Ackerman, G. Davis, M. Avital, D. Robey, S. Sawyer, and C. Sorensen (2004) Surfing the next wave: design and implementation challenges of ubiquitous computing environments. *Communications of the Association for Information Systems* 13 (Volume 14, 2004), pp. 697–716.

March, S. T. and G. F. Smith (1995) Design and natural science research on information technology. *Decision Support Systems* 15, pp. 251–266.

McKelvey, B. (1982) *Organizational Systematics: Taxonomy, Evolution, Classification*, University of California Press, Berkeley and Los Angeles, CA.

Moggridge, B. (2007) *Designing Interactions*, Massachusetts Institute of Technology, Boston, MA.

News Corporation (2007, July 12) MySpace outperforms all other social networking sites. Retrieved November 12, 2007, from http://www.newscorp.com/news/news_345.html .

Plowman, T. (2003) *Ethnography and Critical Design Practice*, The MIT Press, Cambridge, MA.

Rajala R, J. Nissiläa, and M. Westerlund (2007) Revenue models in the open source software business, in St. Amant K. and B. Still (eds.), *Handbook of Research on Open Source Software: Technological, Economic, and Social Perspectives*, IGI Global, Hershey, PA, pp. 541–554.

Salesforce.com (2007) Customer support: ensuring CRM success. Retrieved December 2007, from http://www.salesforce.com/services-training/customer-support/.

Salesforce.com (2007, September 17) Salesforce.com Dreamforce 2007: financial review. Retrieved November 13, 2007, from http://www.salesforce.com/assets/pdf/investors/Dreamforce_CFO_FINAL.pdf.

Salesforce.com (2007) Salesforce.com enhances enterprise functionality across all applications. Retrieved December 26, 2007, from http://www.salesforce.com/company/news-press/press-releases/2003/02/030210-2.jsp.

Secondlife.com (2007) Second life: economic statistics. Retrieved December 20, 2007, from http://secondlife.com/whatis/economy_stats.php.

Snow, B. (2007) GigaOM top 10 most popular MMOs. Retrieved December 20, 2007, from http://gigaom.com/2007/06/13/top-ten-most-popular-mmos/

Sobel, J. (2007, December 21) The Facebook blog: keeping up. Retrieved December 26, 2007, from http://blog.facebook.com/blog.php?post=7899307130.

Stokes, D. (1997) *Pasteurs Quadrant: Basic Science and Technological Innovation*, Brookings Institution Press, Washington, DC.

Tow, R. (2003) *Strategy, Tactics, and Heuristics for Research*, The MIT Press, Cambridge, MA.

Van Alstyne, G. and R. K. Logan (2007) Designing for emergence and innovation: redesigning design. *Artifact* 1 (2), pp. 120–129.

Varian, H. R. (1995) *Pricing Information Goods*, University of Michigan.

Walls, J. G., G. R. Widmeyer et al. (1992) Building an information system design theory for vigilant EIS. *Information Systems Research* 3 (1), pp. 36–59.

Weightman, D. a. M., Deana (2003) *People are Doing it for Themselves, Designing Pleasurable Products and Interfaces*, ACM, Pittsburgh, PA.

Winograd, T. (1996) *Bringing Design to Software*, ACM Press, New York, NY.

Yadav, S. (2006) Facebook – The complete biography. Retrieved December 20, 2007, from http://mashable.com/2006/08/25/facebook-profile /

Chapter 17
Disseminating Design Science Research

The first ninety percent of the task takes ten percent of the time,
and the last ten percent takes the other ninety percent.

– Ninety-ninety rule of project schedules

17.1 Academic Route – Conference and Journal Papers

As you near the completion of a design science research project, your thoughts are now diverted to what to do next? Every researcher wants to publish their finding to the scientific community and in particular to their peer group. While academic publishing is certainly a preferred outcome of DSR, we would also like to mention that another possible (and lucrative) outcome of DSR is entrepreneurial activity for those who have the mindset. If you have built it, let them come.

As experienced researchers, and editors in the field, we share with the readers the challenges and issues of writing papers for leading conference and journals. In that context, we also briefly discuss getting funds from foundation to support your research. We also discuss the necessary first steps toward commercializing DSR by building a start-up company around the project artifact.

Refereed conference papers and archival journal publications remain the *cache* of the academic world. The mantra "publish or perish" is still true (see Drew and Gray 2008). Particularly in North American universities, getting tenure largely depends on your publication quality. If you are a design science researcher, there are particular issues you have to keep in mind.

Conferences are ideal venues to make your preliminary ideas known and get copyright. They provide excellent venues to network with other well-known researchers as your peer group and conferences are meant to generate feedback and constructive criticism of your research.

Senior scholars often suggest that you take one idea and develop the design and evaluation of it to full extent into a conference paper. It is important to publish your work in peer-reviewed conferences. Generally the reviewers look for certain distinct things in the paper:

A. Hevner, S. Chatterjee, *Design Research in Information Systems*, Integrated Series in Information Systems 22, DOI 10.1007/978-1-4419-5653-8_17,

- Is the idea original?
- Does the researcher know the current literature on the topic?
- Is the problem interesting and relevant?
- Has well-established methodology been followed?
- Is the paper technically sound?
- Is there something novel about the work?
- Is the evaluation, data collection, and analysis proper?
- Does the work have any meaningful contribution?
- Is the presentation and readability good?
- Does the paper fit the theme of the conference?

The above checklist is just a general guideline for researchers when they prepare their paper.

Many novice IS researchers who conduct design research often face a dilemma in choosing which conference to publish their paper. This is not an easy task and within the information system discipline often challenging. All conferences have gained some reputation over the years. People associate certain quality with them. One measure of quality is the acceptance rate. Highest quality conferences can have an acceptance rate of only 10–12%. Moderate conferences have acceptance rates of 33% while the lower quality conferences can have acceptance rate of 50% or higher. It is easy to find out about these measures by communicating with program chairs of conferences. Some people may also cite longevity as a good measure of a conference. If you find a conference that fits your work has been around for 30 years, it is a sign that this is a well-established conference which likely has its followers. But we should point out that design in information system is a fast moving field and every year we see new conferences being announced. Some of these newer conferences may tend to draw the leading researchers.

As we have pointed out in previous chapters, design science research is heavily practiced within disciplines such as engineering, computer science, and software engineering. For several years, the information systems field had stayed away from embracing design science as a valid research method. But since early 2006, it is becoming a recognized method within IS research. Hence some of the leading IS conferences in the past were not suitable venue for DSR. The authors of this book started DESRIST[1] as a definitive conference for design research in IS in 2006. Besides DESRIST, some well-known conferences that publish design research in IS are HICSS, WITS, and ICIS (design track).

It is important to note that a few major associations sponsor conferences. For DSR, the associations that tend to support these conferences are IEEE, ACM, AIS, and IFIP. One should also consider domain-specific conferences within computer science and software engineering that tend to publish design papers.

---

[1] http://desrist.org/

Lastly, we cannot stress enough the importance of good reviews. One can easily measure the quality of a conference from the quality of its reviews. Authors should take note of constructive criticism that reviewers provide and by incorporating the suggested changes, one can significantly improve the quality of their paper.

Once you have worked on a design project, got the preliminary results published in a decent conference, the next step is to conduct more thorough work and publish the final paper in an archival journal. Journal publication is the crown jewel of academia. Journals require a higher level of rigor and may require many cycles of revision.

One question novice researchers often ask "How much different should a journal paper be from a published conference paper?" Our rule of thumb is that the journal paper should have at least 60% new material and results than the last published conference paper. It has to be rigorous and must clearly articulate contribution toward the knowledge base.

17.2 Funding to Support Your Design Research

For researchers working in the academic environment, grants and contracts are a way to support the design research projects. It is a way to recruit graduate students and pay them assistantships and also to build required laboratories with necessary resources. In North America, funding is typically available from three major sources: (1) federal government; (2) private foundations; and (3) corporations. They can differ in their mission and goals. But all of them publish RFPs or CFPs that will detail what they are looking to fund. The first step in preparing a research grant proposal almost always begins by reading the call for proposals.

Adhering to the format as stated in the RFP is very important. Requirements may vary between agencies and from year to year. However a generic proposal format is as follows:

Cover page
Summary/abstract
Understanding of the problem
Technical objectives
Work plan
Related work/background research
Project milestones
Key personnel
Facilities/equipment
Subcontractors/consultants
Prior, current, or pending awards (more for government proposals)
Cost/budget
References
Biographies of key personnel

The budget structure of the proposal could be a determining factor in an application. While the technical merits are clearly important, the proposal's success is also determined by cost. A typical budget includes the following items:

Direct Cost
  Salaries (or summer stipends)
  Fringe benefits
  Equipment
  Materials and supplies
  Travel
  Consultants
  Subcontracts
Indirect Cost
  Facilities and administrative overhead costs (ranges from 49 to 60% depending upon campuses)

Most agencies have a panel or roster of experts who mutually decide the outcome of a grant proposal. If one's proposal has a champion, it is likely to be funded if the reviews are strongly in favor. Hence calling program managers and meeting them at various networking events goes a long way to establish your presence to those who matter.

For IS research, the following are some suggested governmental and corporate agencies that typically fund design and software technology research.

National Science Foundation (NSF) at http://www.nsf.gov
Department of Defense at http://www.defenselink.mil/sites/
National Institutes of Health (NIH) at http://grants.nih.gov/grants/guide/
Department of Homeland Security at http://www.dhs.gov/xres/
National Institutes of Standards and Technology (NIST) at http://www.nist.gov/public_affairs/grants.htm
Ford Foundation at http://www.fordfound.org/grants
Bill & Melinda Gates Foundation at http://www.gatesfoundation.org/Pages/home.aspx
Hewlett Foundation at http://www.hewlett.org/
Robert Wood Johnson Foundation at http://www.rwjf.org/

A comprehensive listing of funding sources and foundations can be obtained by subscribing to http://foundationcenter.org/findfunders/

17.3 Commercializing Your Ideas via Start-Ups

Entrepreneurs turn ideas into business realities. But the journey from a business plan on a piece of paper to a full-fledged profitable company is plagued with challenges and excitement.

A design researcher might have solved a problem and built a prototype artifact. But to take that to the next level of forming start-up companies there are several steps that one has to go through.

Most entrepreneurs need money to hire employees and build the company. Many obtain initial seed funds from friends and family who invest. They are often referred to as "angel investors." It is important to incorporate the company and have lawyers prepare an equity structure for founders so that external money can be raised by selling preferred and common stock shares.

At the early stages finding money is difficult and frustrating process. There are angel investors who can provide small amounts of funds (typically in the range of $100 K–$500 K). But sooner or later, one has to tap into venture capital funds. VCs look at the business idea, management team, and are looking for growth potential and return on investment. Entrepreneurs are asked to submit their plans, and if the VCs like it, are invited to pitch their case. Having patents or copyrights often helps during this negotiation process. After serious negotiations, VCs may invest by acquiring a portion of the company in equity. Else they may turn you down by not funding. VCs are a tough crowd and often take ownership positions by being on the board.

As the company progresses, products and services are launched, it is important to build a brand name while generating revenue. Most companies aspire to become cash flow positive as soon as possible. A typical exit strategy is an initial public offering (IPO), when the company goes public. Or it may be possible that some larger company acquires the smaller start-up. A successful exit usually leaves the founder and entrepreneur a very wealthy person. It is also important to keep in mind that this is not an easy journey at all. High-powered competition often kills great start-ups. In the USA, statistics says that 92 out of every 100 start-ups usually fail or end up dying. For a comprehensive account of how to form start-ups, we refer you to Kaplan (1996) and Henos (1991).

References

Kaplan J. (1996) *Startup: A Silicon Valley Adventure,* Penguin Books USA Inc., 375 Hudson Street, New York, New York 10015, USA.

Henos M. (1991) The Road to Venture Financing: Guidelines for Entrepreneurs, R&D Strategist Magazine, Summer 1991 (access URL http://www.alliancetechventures.com/dynamic/road_to_venture.php5)

Drew, D. E. and P. Gray (2008) What They Didn't Teach You in Graduate School, The Chronicle of Higher Education (Paperback, 2008).

Chapter 18
Design Science Research: Looking to the Future

The best way to predict the future is to invent it.

– Alan Kay

18.1 Introduction

The previous chapters have taken you through the fundamentals of design science research, the problems, solutions space, design process, frameworks, outputs and artifacts, theories and dissemination of the research results. The design science research paradigm is highly relevant to information systems (IS) research because it directly addresses two of the key issues of the discipline: the central, albeit controversial, role of the IT artifact in IS research (Weber 1987; Orlikowski and Iacono 2001; Benbasat and Zmud 2003) and the lack of professional relevance of IS research (Benbasat and Zmud 1999; Hirschheim and Klein 2003). Design science, as conceptualized by Simon (1996), supports a pragmatic research paradigm that calls for the creation of innovative artifacts to solve real-world problems. Thus, design science research combines a focus on the IT artifact with a high priority on relevance in the application domain.

The last few years has been particularly exciting for the IS design science community as there have been a steady increase in discussions, papers, projects, and conference themes and tracks that surround design science research. The momentum behind the research method is gathering and there is now increased recognition within the larger IS community of the rigor and relevance of this science.

How will these trends continue in the future? Predicting the future is not easy and we do not intend to do that. However, we can discuss four possible trends that are likely going to happen in one way or another. We have discussed some of these ideas throughout the book but put a futuristic lens in the presentation that follows.

A. Hevner, S. Chatterjee, *Design Research in Information Systems*, Integrated Series in Information Systems 22, DOI 10.1007/978-1-4419-5653-8_18,
© Springer Science+Business Media, LLC 2010

18.2 Trend 1: Growing Number of IS Scholars Will Use Design as a Research Method

As information technology itself evolves, we find ourselves in unchartered territories. Those wicked problems emerge everyday. Solving those problems through the creation of IT-based artifacts will be necessary. We predict a large number of future IS scholars will be conducting such type of work.

Scholars will use design as the central research method and their labor will be fundamentally driven by trying to solve the problem. Knowledge will be used and new knowledge will be created in the process of building and evaluating the artifact. Hence the build–evaluate cycles that have been presented in the book will come in handy. These scholars are driven by proving utility and efficacy of their solution as opposed to forming hypothesis and proving facts or truths. Innovative thinking along with creativity will largely drive what they do. The novelty of the solution is equally compelling to them.

The domain knowledge of the problem will be very important to the success of such efforts. Technical grounding in the subject matter, making sure that relevant research literature has been covered, and having a laboratory environment to build and break artifacts will be crucial toward achieving success.

If this trend turns out to be true, then the IS community will be well positioned to contribute toward fundamental wicked problem solving. It will become a reference discipline from which other related disciplines can borrow.

18.3 Trend 2: Growing Number of Scholars Will Research Design

There will be a set of researchers who will conduct descriptive research by studying design and designers. Their driver is to understand what process designers follow when they encounter a design problem. A case study approach is well suited to do this study. Some of the techniques presented in this book will come in handy to do that.

This camp of researchers are interested to learn from successful design as well as why certain designs fail. They are after what Vesuvius stated as form, elegance, and beauty in designed artifacts. This is an important contribution as this eventually could become a body of knowledge from which theory can be built. They deal with more meta-level problems. They are conducting pattern recognition in the sense when a problem is presented; they may help identify a certain pattern in design and could potentially solve the problem. The domain of their work tends to be more organizational and socio-technical in nature.

There are other disciplines that study design patterns and designers. One question to ponder is that what do IS scholars bring to the table? To distinguish their work, it will be important to scope the domain of study to IS problems and software development design issues. Will design process embraced in industrial design easily lend itself to software service design? Are there patterns that readily apply to design problems in IS?

18.4 Trend 3: A Small but Steady Number of Scholars Will Study Design Theory

Theories epitomize scientific knowledge. They are often considered the crown jewels in the discovery process. But in this book we have stated that the jury is still out about design theory with respect to two issues: (1) Is theory a necessary type of output artifact in DSR? and (2) Is design theory possible?

We anticipate that in the future, we will continue to see breakthroughs happening in study of design theory. But it is important to realize that any design theory when built should be applicable to design practitioners. They should include normative statements that describe for a particular class of problems, if one adopts a certain design solution, one can expect to get a certain outcome.

The work done by this scholar community is driven by the need to understand why certain designs work? The theory should have predictive capability and should be generalizable across the class of problems.

18.5 Trend 4: An Uptake Is Expected in These Three IT Application Area Thereby Creating a Surge in the Need for Design Researchers

Information technology has been a major driver and key enabler toward a global information society. IT has affected every major industry sector from telecommunications, education, supply-chain systems, transportation, railways, airlines, entertainment, banking, trading, and others. There are other sectors that continue to embrace IT to help them grow and achieve their goals. In this section, we discuss three industry verticals that are showing signs of uptake in the next decade. Of course in a fast-changing economic situation, there is never any guarantee that these sectors will continue to grow. But based on 2009 data, we can expect the following three verticals to prosper for the coming decade. They are health-care sector, green technologies for climate, and collaboration and social networking area.

18.5.1 Health Care and IT

In 2005, a report published in the *Journal of the American Medical Association* found that as many as 98,000 Americans die each year because of medical errors (Weingart, 2005). In that same year, more people died due to medical errors than from Alzheimer's, HIV, automobile fatalities, suicide, homicide, or hypertension. An Institute of Medicine study published in 2000 estimates that medical errors cost the nation about \$37.6 billion each year; about \$17 billion of those costs are associated with preventable errors.

The need for reform stems from long-standing problems in our health system, and the central role of information technology derives from an ever-expanding body of research and experience that attests to its merit in addressing these problems. Despite the fact that the United States spends more on health care than any other country, both in absolute numbers and on a per capita basis, the health status of Americans ranks relatively low when compared with that of people in other developed nations. Moreover, the general discrepancy between expenditures and health status indicators in the United States masks significant differentials among segments of the population, based on socio-economic, geographic, cultural, ethnic, and other factors. Hence, we continue to suffer from inequities in access to health care, inefficiencies in the delivery of care, escalating costs, and the prevalence of adverse lifestyles that exacerbate these problems.

Health IT is about bringing safety and efficiency to the health-care system. Patients seeking treatment have enough to worry about; if one can alleviate the fear that an error will occur, one needs to try to do that. A secure, uniform, interoperable system that works for patients and providers will save time, stress, and money. The digital age has transformed virtually every other sector of the economy; it is time to bring the tremendous benefits of technology to the health-care system.

A number of promising technologies are being designed and implemented within the health-care industry. Electronic medical records (EMRs) will replace the paper-based charts and are shown to reduce medical errors (IOM 2003; Harrison et al. 2007). These EMR systems will be all interconnected via a national health information network (NHIN) that will aggregate case data to a national database that can then be analyzed by data mining experts and epidemiology researchers to mine for trends in emerging diseases. Regional health interoperability exchanges need to be designed and built to connect various systems together. Health IT systems that warn against drug interactions, e-prescription systems, telemedicine systems (Tulu et al., 2007), and clinical decision support systems (Bates et al., 2003) can all lead to an error-free health-care system that provides higher quality.

The design challenges in health-care IT systems stem from the fact that there are multiple stakeholders whose interests have to be met. There are physicians who often are not willing to learn or adopt such systems. There are payers (Medicare, Medicaid, insurance companies, and HMOs) who need to review billing claims. The drug manufacturers need access to clinical data while medical device OEMs also need to view data. Finally there are the patients (you and me) who would like to control our own medical data in a secured manner. Hence there is active research being conducted on personal health records (PHRs) and HIPAA compliance.

18.5.2 Green Technology and Green IT

Environmental scientists point out that global warming is a serious threat. Greenhouse emission is the major cause of global warming. There is worldwide activity to control climate change and produce clean energy. A carbon footprint is a measure of the impact our activities have on the environment, and in particular climate change (Carbon Footprint 2009). It relates to the amount of greenhouse gases produced in our day-to-day lives through burning fossil fuels for electricity, heating, and transportation. The carbon footprint is a measurement of all greenhouse gases we individually produce and has units of tonnes (or kilograms) of carbon dioxide equivalent. All activity is geared to lower our carbon footprint.

A carbon footprint is made up of the sum of two parts, the primary footprint (shown by the darker slices of the pie chart) and the secondary footprint (shown as the lighter slices) (Fig. 18.1).

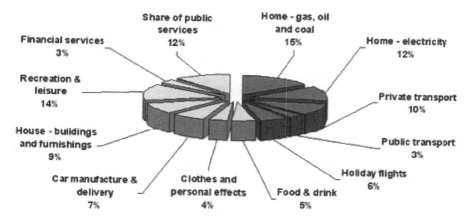

Fig. 18.1 Main elements which make up the total of a typical person's carbon footprint in the developed world

1. The *primary footprint* is a measure of our direct emissions of CO_2 from the burning of fossil fuels including domestic energy consumption and transportation (e.g., car and plane). We have direct control of these.
2. The *secondary footprint* is a measure of the indirect CO_2 emissions from the whole life cycle of products we use – those associated with their manufacture and eventual breakdown. To put it very simply, the more we buy the more emissions will be caused on our behalf.

Renewable energy is clean, safe, and inexhaustible but it is also vastly underused. Switching to green energy is one of the easiest and quickest ways to reduce your carbon footprint. If we switch to renewable energy it is most likely to be coming from wind power or hydroelectric power. Other sources include solar power and wave and tidal energy. There are also other largely untapped sources such as biomass, landfill gas energy, and combined heat and power (known as chp). It is also possible to install solar water heating and small wind turbines on to your own house.

18.5.3 Green Computing

Green computing is the study and practice of using computing resources efficiently (Green Computing, 2009). The primary objective of such a program is to account for the triple bottom line, an expanded spectrum of values and criteria for measuring organizational (and societal) success. The goals are similar to green chemistry; reduce the use of hazardous materials, maximize energy efficiency during the product's lifetime, and promote recyclability or biodegradability of defunct products and factory waste.

Modern IT systems rely upon a complicated mix of people, networks, and hardware; as such, a green computing initiative must be systemic in nature and address increasingly sophisticated problems. Elements of such a solution may comprise items such as end user satisfaction, management restructuring, regulatory compliance, disposal of electronic waste, telecommuting, virtualization of server resources, energy use, thin client solutions, and return on investment (ROI). The imperative for companies to take control of their power consumption, for technology and more generally, therefore remains acute.

Some areas where designers can create or improve new technologies for green computing are the following:

Algorithmic efficiency: The efficiency of algorithms has an impact on the amount of computer resources required for any given computing function and there are many efficient trade-offs in writing programs. As computers have become more numerous and the cost of hardware has declined relative to the cost of energy, the energy efficiency and environmental impact of computing systems and programs have received increased attention.

Computer virtualization: This refers to the abstraction of computer resources, such as the process of running two or more logical computer systems on one set of physical hardware. With virtualization, a system administrator could combine several physical systems into virtual machines on one single, powerful system, thereby unplugging the original hardware and reducing power and cooling consumption. Several commercial companies and open-source projects now offer software packages to enable a transition to virtual computing. Intel Corporation and AMD have also built proprietary virtualization enhancements to the x86 instruction set into each of their CPU product lines, in order to facilitate virtualized computing.

Telecommuting: Teleconferencing and telepresence technologies are often implemented in green computing initiatives. The advantages are many; increased worker satisfaction, reduction of greenhouse gas emissions related to travel, and increased profit margins as a result of lower overhead costs for office space, heat, lighting, etc. The savings are significant; the average annual energy consumption for US office buildings is over 23 kWh per square foot, with heat, air conditioning, and lighting accounting for 70% of all energy consumed.

The McKinsey report offers a concise statement of the issue of green IT: "The rapidly growing carbon footprint associated with information and communications technologies, including laptops and PCs, data centers and computing networks, mobile phones, and telecommunications networks, could make them among the biggest greenhouse gas emitters by 2020. However, our research also suggests that there are opportunities to use these technologies to make the world economy more energy and carbon efficient."

18.5.4 Collaboration, Web 2.0, and Social Technologies

When the World Wide Web first started, it was mainly web sites that provided one-way information to clients. The content and the sites were created by techies who knew HTML and other associated tools. But over time, the web evolved into a two-way information highway where any average user could also post, blog, write, and share content using very easy-to-use tools. A plethora of tools that are mostly available free exists today. Among the most popular tools are blogs, wikis, RSS feed, mashups, voice over IP, and instant messaging services, podcasting, video services such as YouTube, and several social networking sites (such as Facebook and Twitter).

As the Internet became a global platform for business, it also transformed the way people collaborate across countries and time zones. Designers today work cooperatively to design cars, engines, products, and design new IT solutions. Companies have distributed teams that operate out of different countries. These distributed teams are using various technologies such as real-time videoconferencing, VoIP, shared presentations, project management tools, mindmapping tools, web presenting tools, screen sharing and remote control. This in turn encourages global awareness, creativity, innovation, critical thinking, and collaboration. It is transforming the way we learn, get news, share our photos and videos, plan our travel, or look for entertainment. Web 2.0 along with social networking sites can help us achieve healthy living, be better prepared for tomorrow's challenging tasks, and become knowledgeable citizens for the 21st century workforce.

In the beginning we have mentioned that it is foolish to predict. Yet we will end the book with a prediction. *The future will require more designers and design science researchers.* This is something on which we are willing to bet!

References

Bates D. W. et al. (2003) Ten commandments for effective clinical decision support: making the practice of evidence-based medicine a reality, *Journal of the American Medical Informatics Association* 10, pp. 523–530.

Benbasat, I. and R. Zmud (2003) The identity crisis within the IS discipline: defining and communicating the discipline's core properties, *MIS Quarterly* 27 (2), pp. 183–194.

Benbasat, I. and R. Zmud (1999) Empirical research in information systems: the question of relevance, *MIS Quarterly* 23 (1), pp. 3–16.

Carbon Footprint (2009) Home of Carbon Management at http://www.carbonfootprint.com/ (visited June 18, 2009).

Green Computing (2009) At Wikipedia available at http://en.wikipedia.org/wiki/Green_computing (last accessed on June 18, 2009).

Harrison, M. I., R. Koppel, and S. Bar-Lev (2007) Unintended consequences of information technologies in health care – an interactive sociotechnical analysis, *Journal of the American Medical Informatics Association* 14 (5), pp. 542–549.

Hirschheim, R. and H. Klein (2003) Crisis in the IS field? A critical reflection on the state of the discipline, *Journal of the AIS* 4 (5), pp. 237–293.

IOM (2003) Key Capabilities of an Electronic Health Record System, Letter Report, Committee on Data Standards for Patient Safety, Institute of Medicine.

Orlikowski, W. and C. Iacono (2001) Research commentary: desperately seeking the 'IT' in IT research: a call for theorizing the IT artifact, *Information Systems Research* 12, pp. 121–134.

Tulu, B., S. Chatterjee, and M. Maheshwari (2007) Telemedicine taxonomy: a classification tool, *Telemedicine and e-Health* 13 (3), pp. 349–358.

Web 2.0 Tutorial (2009) Available at http://www.ala.org/ala/mgrps/divs/rusa/sections/mars/marssection/marscomm/usac/usac_programs/usac_web2.pdf (last accessed on June 19, 2009).

Weber, R. (1987) Towards a theory of artifacts: a paradigmatic base for information systems research, *Journal of Information Systems* 1 (1), pp. 3–20.

Weingart, S. N. (2005) How many deaths are due to medical errors? *Journal of the American Medical Association* 284, pp. 2187–2187.

Appendix A

RESEARCH ESSAY

DESIGN SCIENCE IN INFORMATION SYSTEMS RESEARCH[1]

By: Alan R. Hevner
Information Systems and Decision
Sciences
College of Business Administration
University of South Florida
Tampa, FL 33620
U.S.A.
ahevner@coba.usf.edu

Salvatore T. March
Own Graduate School of Management
Vanderbilt University
Nashville, TN 37203
U.S.A.
Sal.March@owen.vanderbilt.edu

Jinsoo Park
College of Business Administration
Korea University
Seoul, 136-701
KOREA
jinsoo.park@acm.org

Sudha Ram
Management Information Systems
Eller College of Business and Public
Administration
University of Arizona
Tucson, AZ 85721
U.S.A.
ram@bpa.arizona.edu

Abstract

Two paradigms characterize much of the research in the Information Systems discipline: behavioral science and design science. The behavioral-science paradigm seeks to develop and verify theories that explain or predict human or organizational behavior. The design-science paradigm seeks to extend the boundaries of human and organizational capabilities by creating new and innovative artifacts. Both paradigms are foundational to the IS discipline, positioned as it is at the confluence of people, organizations, and technology. Our objective is to describe the performance of design-science research in Information Systems via a concise conceptual framework and clear guidelines for understanding, executing, and evaluating the research. In the design-science paradigm, knowledge and understanding of a problem domain and its solution are achieved in the building and application of the designed artifact. Three recent exemplars in the research literature are used to demonstrate the application

---

[1]Allen S. Lee was the accepting senior editor for this paper.

A. Hevner, S. Chatterjee, *Design Research in Information Systems*, Integrated Series in Information Systems 22, DOI 10.1007/978-1-4419-5653-8,
© 2004, Regents of the University of Minnesota. Used with permission.

of these guidelines. We conclude with an analysis of the challenges of performing high-quality design-science research in the context of the broader IS community.

Keywords: Information Systems research methodologies, design science, design artifact, business environment, technology infrastructure, search strategies, experimental methods, creativity

Introduction

Information systems are implemented within an organization for the purpose of improving the effectiveness and efficiency of that organization. Capabilities of the information system and characteristics of the organization, its work systems, its people, and its development and implementation methodologies together determine the extent to which that purpose is achieved (Silver et al. 1995). It is incumbent upon researchers in the Information Systems (IS) discipline to "further knowledge that aids in the productive application of information technology to human organizations and their management" (ISR 2002, inside front cover) and to develop and communicate "knowledge concerning both the management of information technology and the use of information technology for managerial and organizational purposes" (Zmud 1997).

We argue that acquiring such knowledge involves two complementary but distinct paradigms, behavioral science and design science (March and Smith 1995). The behavioral-science paradigm has its roots in natural science research methods. It seeks to develop and justify theories (i.e., principles and laws) that explain or predict organizational and human phenomena surrounding the analysis, design, implementation, management, and use of information systems. Such theories ultimately inform researchers and practitioners of the interactions among people, technology, and organizations that must be managed if an information system is to achieve its stated purpose, namely improving the effective-

ness and efficiency of an organization. These theories impact and are impacted by design decisions made with respect to the system development methodology used and the functional capabilities, information contents, and human interfaces implemented within the information system.

The design-science paradigm has its roots in engineering and the sciences of the artificial (Simon 1996). It is fundamentally a problem-solving paradigm. It seeks to create innovations that define the ideas, practices, technical capabilities, and products through which the analysis, design, implementation, management, and use of information systems can be effectively and efficiently accomplished (Denning 1997; Tsichritzis 1998). Such artifacts are not exempt from natural laws or behavioral theories. To the contrary, their creation relies on existing *kernel theories* that are applied, tested, modified, and extended through the experience, creativity, intuition, and problem solving capabilities of the researcher (Markus et al. 2002; Walls et al. 1992).

The importance of design is well recognized in the IS literature (Glass 1999; Winograd 1996, 1998). Benbasat and Zmud (1999, p. 5) argue that the relevance of IS research is directly related to its applicability in design, stating that the implications of empirical IS research should be "implementable,...synthesize an existing body of research, ...[or] stimulate critical thinking" among IS practitioners. However, designing useful artifacts is complex due to the need for creative advances in domain areas in which existing theory is often insufficient. "As technical knowledge grows, IT is applied to new application areas that were not previously believed to be amenable to IT support" (Markus et al. 2002, p. 180). The resultant IT artifacts extend the boundaries of human problem solving and organizational capabilities by providing intellectual as well as computational tools. Theories regarding their application and impact will follow their development and use.

Here, we argue, is an opportunity for IS research to make significant contributions by engaging the complementary research cycle between design-science and behavioral-science to address fundamental problems faced in the productive application of information technology. Technology and behavior are not dichotomous in an information system. They are inseparable (Lee 2000). They are similarly inseparable in IS research. Philosophically these arguments draw from the pragmatists (Aboulafia 1991) who argue that truth (justified theory) and utility (artifacts that are effective) are two sides of the same coin and that scientific research should be evaluated in light of its practical implications.

The realm of IS research is at the confluence of people, organizations, and technology (Davis and Olson 1985; Lee 1999). IT artifacts are broadly defined as *constructs* (vocabulary and symbols), *models* (abstractions and representations), *methods* (algorithms and practices), and *instantiations* (implemented and prototype systems). These are concrete prescriptions that enable IT researchers and practitioners to understand and address the problems inherent in developing and successfully implementing information systems within organizations (March and Smith 1995; Nunamaker et al. 1991a). As illustrations, Markus et al. (2002) and Walls et al. (1992) present design-science research aimed at developing executive information systems (EISs) and systems to support emerging knowledge processes (EKPs), respectively, within the context of "IS design theories." Such theories prescribe "effective *development practices*" (methods) and "a type of *system solution*" (instantiation) for "a particular class of *user requirements*" (models) (Markus et al. 2002, p. 180). Such prescriptive theories must be evaluated with respect to the utility provided for the class of problems addressed.

An IT artifact, implemented in an organizational context, is often the object of study in IS behavioral-science research. Theories seek to predict or explain phenomena that occur with respect to the artifact's use (intention to use), perceived usefulness, and impact on individuals and organizations (net benefits) depending on system, service, and information quality (DeLone and McLean 1992, 2003; Seddon 1997). Much of this behavioral research has focused on one class of

artifact, the instantiation (system), although other research efforts have also focused on the evaluation of constructs (e.g., Batra et al. 1990; Bodart et al. 2001; Geerts and McCarthy 2002; Kim and March 1995) and methods (e.g., Marakas and Elam 1998; Sinha and Vessey 1999). Relatively little behavioral research has focused on evaluating models, a major focus of research in the management science literature.

Design science, as the other side of the IS research cycle, creates and evaluates IT artifacts intended to solve identified organizational problems. Such artifacts are represented in a structured form that may vary from software, formal logic, and rigorous mathematics to informal natural language descriptions. A mathematical basis for design allows many types of quantitative evaluations of an IT artifact, including optimization proofs, analytical simulation, and quantitative comparisons with alternative designs. The further evaluation of a new artifact in a given organizational context affords the opportunity to apply empirical and qualitative methods. The rich phenomena that emerge from the interaction of people, organizations, and technology may need to be qualitatively assessed to yield an understanding of the phenomena adequate for theory development or problem solving (Klein and Meyers 1999). As field studies enable behavioral-science researchers to understand organizational phenomena in context, the process of constructing and exercising innovative IT artifacts enable design-science researchers to understand the problem addressed by the artifact and the feasibility of their approach to its solution (Nunamaker et al. 1991a).

The primary goal of this paper is to inform the community of IS researchers and practitioners of how to conduct, evaluate, and present design-science research. We do so by describing the boundaries of design science within the IS discipline via a conceptual framework for understanding information systems research and by developing a set of guidelines for conducting and evaluating good design-science research. We focus primarily on technology-based design although we note with interest the current exploration of organizations, policies, and work practices as designed artifacts (Boland 2002). Following Klein and Myers (1999) treatise on the conduct and evaluation of interpretive research in IS, we use the proposed guidelines to assess recent exemplar papers published in the IS literature in order to illustrate how authors, reviewers, and editors can apply them consistently. We conclude with an analysis of the challenges of performing high-quality design-science research and a call for synergistic efforts between behavioral-science and design-science researchers.

A Framework for IS Research ■

Information systems and the organizations they support are complex, artificial, and purposefully designed. They are composed of people, structures, technologies, and work systems (Alter 2003; Bunge 1985; Simon 1996). Much of the work performed by IS practitioners, and managers in general (Boland 2002), deals with design—the purposeful organization of resources to accomplish a goal. Figure 1 illustrates the essential alignments between business and information technology strategies and between organizational and information systems infrastructures (Henderson and Venkatraman 1993). The effective transition of strategy into infrastructure requires extensive design activity on both sides of the figure—organizational design to create an effective organizational infrastructure and information systems design to create an effective information system infrastructure.

These are interdependent design activities that are central to the IS discipline. Hence, IS research must address the interplay among business strategy, IT strategy, organizational infrastructure, and IS infrastructure. This interplay is becoming more crucial as information technologies are seen as enablers of business strategy and organizational infrastructure (Kalakota and Robinson 2001; Orlikowski and Barley 2001). Available and emerging IT capabilities are a significant factor in determining the strategies that guide an organization. Cutting-edge information systems allow

organizations to engage new forms and new structures—to change the ways they "do business" (Drucker 1988, 1991; Orlikowski 2000). Our subsequent discussion of design science will be limited to the activities of building the IS infrastructure within the business organization. Issues of strategy, alignment, and organizational infrastructure design are outside the scope of this paper.

To achieve a true understanding of and appreciation for design science as an IS research paradigm, an important dichotomy must be faced. Design is both a process (set of activities) and a product (artifact)—a verb and a noun (Walls et al. 1992). It describes the world as acted upon (*processes*) and the world as sensed (*artifacts*). This Platonic view of design supports a problem-solving paradigm that continuously shifts perspective between design processes and designed artifacts for the same complex problem. The design process is a sequence of expert activities that produces an innovative product (i.e., the design artifact). The evaluation of the artifact then provides feedback information and a better understanding of the problem in order to improve both the quality of the product and the design process. This build-and-evaluate loop is typically iterated a number of times before the final design artifact is generated (Markus et al. 2002). During this creative process, the design-science researcher must be cognizant of evolving both the design process and the design artifact as part of the research.

March and Smith (1995) identify two design processes and four design artifacts produced by design-science research in IS. The two processes are *build* and *evaluate*. The artifacts are *constructs*, *models*, *methods*, and *instantiations*. Purposeful artifacts are built to address heretofore unsolved problems. They are evaluated with respect to the utility provided in solving those problems. Constructs provide the language in which problems and solutions are defined and communicated (Schön 1983). Models use constructs to represent a real world situation—the design problem and its solution space (Simon 1996). Models aid problem and solution understanding and frequently represent the connection

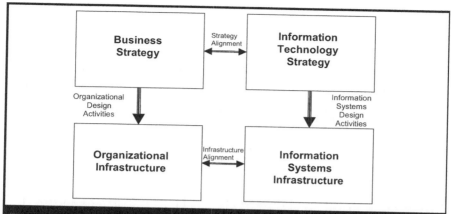

Figure 1. Organizational Design and Information Systems Design Activities (Adapted from J. Henderson and N. Venkatraman, "Strategic Alignment: Leveraging Information Technology for Transforming Organizations," *IBM Systems Journal* (32:1), 1993.)

between problem and solution components enabling exploration of the effects of design decisions and changes in the real world. Methods define processes. They provide guidance on how to solve problems, that is, how to search the solution space. These can range from formal, mathematical algorithms that explicitly define the search process to informal, textual descriptions of "best practice" approaches, or some combination. Instantiations show that constructs, models, or methods can be implemented in a working system. They demonstrate feasibility, enabling concrete assessment of an artifact's suitability to its intended purpose. They also enable researchers to learn about the real world, how the artifact affects it, and how users appropriate it.

Figure 2 presents our conceptual framework for understanding, executing, and evaluating IS research combining behavioral-science and design-science paradigms. We use this framework to position and compare these paradigms.

The environment defines the problem space (Simon 1996) in which reside the phenomena of interest. For IS research, it is composed of people, (business) organizations, and their existing or planned technologies (Silver et al. 1995). In it are the goals, tasks, problems, and opportunities that define business needs as they are perceived by people within the organization. Such perceptions are shaped by the roles, capabilities, and characteristics of people within the organization. Business needs are assessed and evaluated within the context of organizational strategies, structure, culture, and existing business processes. They are positioned relative to existing technology infrastructure, applications, communication architectures, and development capabilities. Together these define the business need or "problem" as perceived by the researcher. Framing research activities to address business needs assures research relevance.

Given such an articulated business need, IS research is conducted in two complementary phases. Behavioral science addresses research through the *development* and *justification* of theories that explain or predict phenomena related to the identified business need. Design science addresses research through the *building* and *evaluation* of artifacts designed to meet the iden-

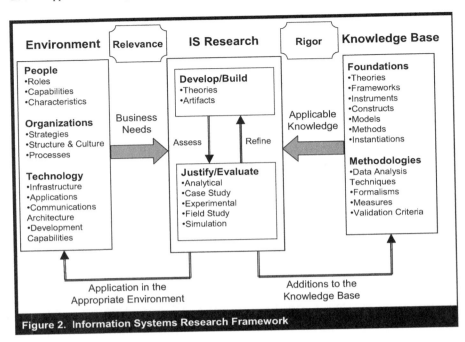

Figure 2. Information Systems Research Framework

tified business need. The goal of behavioral-science research is truth.[2] The goal of design-science research is utility. As argued above, our position is that truth and utility are inseparable. Truth informs design and utility informs theory. An artifact may have utility because of some as yet undiscovered truth. A theory may yet to be developed to the point where its truth can be incorporated into design. In both cases, research assessment via the justify/evaluate activities can result in the identification of weaknesses in the theory or

artifact and the need to refine and reassess. The refinement and reassessment process is typically described in future research directions.

The knowledge base provides the raw materials from and through which IS research is accomplished. The knowledge base is composed of foundations and methodologies. Prior IS research and results from reference disciplines provide foundational theories, frameworks, instruments, constructs, models, methods, and instantiations used in the develop/build phase of a research study. Methodologies provide guidelines used in the justify/evaluate phase. Rigor is achieved by appropriately applying existing foundations and methodologies. In behavioral science, methodologies are typically rooted in data collection and empirical analysis techniques. In design science, computational and mathematical methods are

---

[2]Theories posed in behavioral science are principled explanations of phenomena. We recognize that such theories are approximations and are subject to numerous assumptions and conditions. However, they are evaluated against the norms of truth or explanatory power and are valued only as the claims they make are borne out in reality.

primarily used to evaluate the quality and effectiveness of artifacts; however, empirical techniques may also be employed.

The contributions of behavioral science and design science in IS research are assessed as they are applied to the business need in an appropriate environment and as they add to the content of the knowledge base for further research and practice. A justified theory that is not useful for the environment contributes as little to the IS literature as an artifact that solves a nonexistent problem.

One issue that must be addressed in design-science research is differentiating routine design or system building from design research. The difference is in the nature of the problems and solutions. Routine design is the application of existing knowledge to organizational problems, such as constructing a financial or marketing information system using best practice artifacts (constructs, models, methods, and instantiations) existing in the knowledge base. On the other hand, design-science research addresses important unsolved problems in unique or innovative ways or solved problems in more effective or efficient ways. The key differentiator between routine design and design research is the clear identification of a contribution to the archival knowledge base of foundations and methodologies.

In the early stages of a discipline or with significant changes in the environment, each new artifact created for that discipline or environment is "an experiment" that "poses a question to nature" (Newell and Simon 1976, p 114). Existing knowledge is used where appropriate; however, often the requisite knowledge is nonexistent (Markus et al. 2002). Reliance on creativity and trial-and-error search are characteristic of such research efforts. As design-science research results are codified in the knowledge base, they become best practice. System building is then the routine application of the knowledge base to known problems.

Design activities are endemic in many professions. In particular, the engineering profession has produced a considerable literature on design (Dym 1994; Pahl and Beitz 1996; Petroski 1996). Within the IS discipline, many design activities have been extensively studied, formalized, and become normal or routine.   Design-science research in IS addresses what are considered to be *wicked problems* (Brooks 1987, 1996; Rittel and Webber 1984).   That is, those problems characterized by

- unstable requirements and constraints based upon ill-defined environmental contexts

- complex interactions among subcomponents of the problem and its solution

- inherent flexibility to change design processes as well as design artifacts (i.e., malleable processes and artifacts)

- a critical dependence upon human cognitive abilities (e.g., creativity) to produce effective solutions

- a critical dependence upon human social abilities (e.g., teamwork) to produce effective solutions

As a result, we agree with Simon (1996) that a theory of design in information systems, of necessity, is in a constant state of scientific revolution (Kuhn 1996). Technological advances are the result of innovative, creative design science processes. If not capricious, they are at least arbitrary (Brooks 1987) with respect to business needs and existing knowledge. Innovations, such as database management systems, high-level languages, personal computers, software components, intelligent agents, object technology, the Internet, and the World Wide Web, have had dramatic and at times unintended impacts on the way in which information systems are conceived, designed, implemented, and managed.   Consequently the guidelines we present below are, of necessity, adaptive and process-oriented.

Guidelines for Design Science in Information Systems Research ▪▪▪▪▪▪▪▪▪▪

As discussed above, design science is inherently a problem solving process. The fundamental principle of design-science research from which our seven guidelines are derived is that knowledge and understanding of a design problem and its solution are acquired in the building and application of an artifact. That is, design-science research requires the creation of an innovative, purposeful artifact (Guideline 1) for a specified problem domain (Guideline 2). Because the artifact is *purposeful*, it must yield utility for the specified problem. Hence, thorough evaluation of the artifact is crucial (Guideline 3). Novelty is similarly crucial since the artifact must be *innovative*, solving a heretofore unsolved problem or solving a known problem in a more effective or efficient manner (Guideline 4). In this way, design-science research is differentiated from the practice of design. The artifact itself must be rigorously defined, formally represented, coherent, and internally consistent (Guideline 5). The process by which it is created, and often the artifact itself, incorporates or enables a search process whereby a problem space is constructed and a mechanism posed or enacted to find an effective solution (Guideline 6). Finally, the results of the design-science research must be communicated effectively (Guideline 7) both to a technical audience (researchers who will extend them and practitioners who will implement them) and to a managerial audience (researchers who will study them in context and practitioners who will decide if they should be implemented within their organizations).

Our purpose for establishing these seven guidelines is to assist researchers, reviewers, editors, and readers to understand the requirements for effective design-science research. Following Klein and Myers (1999), we advise against mandatory or rote use of the guidelines. Researchers, reviewers, and editors must use their creative skills and judgment to determine when, where, and how to apply each of the guidelines in a specific research project. However, we contend that each of these guidelines should be addressed in some manner for design-science research to be complete. How well the research satisfies the intent of each of the guidelines is then a matter for the reviewers, editors, and readers to determine.

Table 1 summarizes the seven guidelines. Each is discussed in detail below. In the following section, they are applied to specific exemplar research efforts.

Guideline 1: Design as an Artifact

The result of design-science research in IS is, by definition, a purposeful IT artifact created to address an important organizational problem. It must be described effectively, enabling its implementation and application in an appropriate domain.

Orlikowski and Iacono (2001) call the IT artifact the "core subject matter" of the IS field. Although they articulate multiple definitions of the term *IT artifact*, many of which include components of the organization and people involved in the use of a computer-based artifact, they emphasize the importance of "those bundles of cultural properties packaged in some socially recognizable form such as hardware and software" (p. 121), i.e., the IT artifact as an instantiation. Weber (1987) argues that theories of long-lived artifacts (instantiations) and their representations (Weber 2003) are fundamental to the IS discipline. Such theories must explain how artifacts are created and adapted to their changing environments and underlying technologies.

Our definition of IT artifacts is both broader and narrower then those articulated above. It is broader in the sense that we include not only instantiations in our definition of the IT artifact but also the constructs, models, and methods applied in the development and use of information systems. However, it is narrower in the sense that we do not include people or elements of organizations in our definition nor do we explicitly include the process by which such artifacts evolve

Table 1. Design-Science Research Guidelines

Guideline	Description
Guideline 1: Design as an Artifact	Design-science research must produce a viable artifact in the form of a construct, a model, a method, or an instantiation.
Guideline 2: Problem Relevance	The objective of design-science research is to develop technology-based solutions to important and relevant business problems.
Guideline 3: Design Evaluation	The utility, quality, and efficacy of a design artifact must be rigorously demonstrated via well-executed evaluation methods.
Guideline 4: Research Contributions	Effective design-science research must provide clear and verifiable contributions in the areas of the design artifact, design foundations, and/or design methodologies.
Guideline 5: Research Rigor	Design-science research relies upon the application of rigorous methods in both the construction and evaluation of the design artifact.
Guideline 6: Design as a Search Process	The search for an effective artifact requires utilizing available means to reach desired ends while satisfying laws in the problem environment.
Guideline 7: Communication of Research	Design-science research must be presented effectively both to technology-oriented as well as management-oriented audiences.

over time. We conceive of IT artifacts not as independent of people or the organizational and social contexts in which they are used but as interdependent and coequal with them in meeting business needs. We acknowledge that perceptions and fit with an organization are crucial to the successful development and implementation of an information system. We argue, however, that the capabilities of the constructs, models, methods, and instantiations are equally crucial and that design-science research efforts are necessary for their creation.

Furthermore, artifacts constructed in design-science research are rarely full-grown information systems that are used in practice. Instead, artifacts are innovations that define the ideas, practices, technical capabilities, and products through which the analysis, design, implementation, and use of information systems can be effectively and efficiently accomplished (Denning 1997; Tsichritzis 1998). This definition of the artifact is consistent with the concept of IS design theory as used by Walls et al. (1992) and Markus et al. (2002) where the theory addresses both the process of design and the designed product.

More precisely, constructs provide the vocabulary and symbols used to define problems and solutions. They have a significant impact on the way in which tasks and problems are conceived (Boland 2002; Schön 1983). They enable the construction of models or representations of the problem domain. Representation has a profound impact on design work. The field of mathematics was revolutionized, for example, with the constructs defined by Arabic numbers, zero, and place notation. The search for an effective problem representation is crucial to finding an effective design solution (Weber 2003). Simon (1996, p. 132) states, "solving a problem simply means representing it so as to make the solution transparent."

The entity-relationship model (Chen 1976), for example, is a set of constructs for representing the semantics of data. It has had a profound impact on the way in which systems analysis and database design are executed and the way in which information systems are represented and developed. Furthermore, these constructs have been used to build models of specific business situations that have been generalized into patterns for application in similar domains (Purao et al. 2003). Methods for building such models have also been the subject of considerable research (Halpin 2001; McCarthy 1982; Parsons and Wand 2000; Storey et al. 1997).

Artifact instantiation demonstrates feasibility both of the design process and of the designed product. Design-science research in IT often addresses problems related to some aspect of the *design* of an information system. Hence, the instantiations produced may be in the form of intellectual or software tools aimed at improving the process of information system development. Constructing a system instantiation that automates a process demonstrates that the process can, in fact, be automated. It provides "proof by construction" (Nunamaker 1991a). The critical nature of design-science research in IS lies in the identification of as yet undeveloped capabilities needed to expand IS into new realms "not previously believed amenable to IT support" (Markus et al. 2002, p. 180). Such a result is significant IS research only if there is a serious question about the ability to construct such an artifact, there is uncertainty about its ability to perform appropriately, and the automated task is important to the IS community. TOP Modeler (Markus et al. 2002), for example, is a tool that instantiates methods for the development of information systems that support "emergent knowledge processes." Construction of such a prototype artifact in a research setting or in a single organizational setting is only a first step toward its deployment, but we argue that it is a necessary one. As an exemplar of design-science research (see below), this research resulted in a commercial product that "has been used in over two dozen 'real use' situations" (p. 187).

To illustrate further, prior to the construction of the first expert system (instantiation), it was not clear if such a system *could* be constructed. It was not clear how to describe or represent it, or how well it would perform. Once feasibility was demonstrated by constructing an expert system in a selected domain, constructs and models were developed and subsequent research in expert systems focused on demonstrating significant improvements in the product or process (methods) of construction (Tam 1990; Trice and Davis 1993). Similar examples exist in requirements determination (Bell 1993; Bhargava et al. 1998), individual and group decision support systems (Aiken et al. 1991; Basu and Blanning 1994), database design and integration (Dey et al. 1998; Dey et al. 1999; Storey et al. 1997), and workflow analysis (Basu and Blanning 2000), to name a few important areas of IS design-science research.

Guideline 2: Problem Relevance

The objective of research in information systems is to acquire knowledge and understanding that enable the development and implementation of technology-based solutions to heretofore unsolved and important business problems. Behavioral science approaches this goal through the development and justification of theories explaining or predicting phenomena that occur. Design science approaches this goal through the construction of innovative artifacts aimed at changing the phenomena that occur. Each must inform and challenge the other. For example, the technology acceptance model provides a theory that explains and predicts the acceptance of information technologies within organizations (Venkatesh 2000). This theory challenges design-science researchers to create artifacts that enable organizations to overcome the acceptance problems predicted. We argue that a combination of technology-based artifacts (e.g., system conceptualizations and representations, practices, technical capabilities, interfaces, etc.), organization-based artifacts (e.g., structures, compensation, reporting relationships, social systems, etc.), and people-based artifacts (e.g., training, consensus building, etc.) are necessary to address such issues.

Formally, a problem can be defined as the differences between a goal state and the current state of a system. Problem solving can be defined as a search process (see Guideline 6) using actions to reduce or eliminate the differences (Simon 1996). These definitions imply an environment that imposes goal criteria as well as constraints upon a system. Business organizations are goal-oriented entities existing in an economic and social setting. Economic theory often portrays the goals of business organizations as being related to profit (utility) maximization. Hence, business problems and opportunities often relate to increasing revenue or decreasing cost through the design of effective business processes. The design of organizational and inter-organizational information systems plays a major role in enabling effective business processes to achieve these goals.

The relevance of any design-science research effort is with respect to a constituent community. For IS researchers, that constituent community is the practitioners who plan, manage, design, implement, operate, and evaluate information systems and those who plan, manage, design, implement, operate, and evaluate the technologies that enable their development and implementation. To be relevant to this community, research must address the problems faced and the opportunities afforded by the interaction of people, organizations, and information technology. Organizations spend billions of dollars annually on IT, only too often to conclude that those dollars were wasted (Keil 1995; Keil et al. 1998; Keil and Robey 1999). This community would welcome effective artifacts that enable such problems to be addressed—constructs by which to think about them, models by which to represent and explore them, methods by which to analyze or optimize them, and instantiations that demonstrate how to affect them.

Guideline 3: Design Evaluation

The utility, quality, and efficacy of a design artifact must be rigorously demonstrated via well-executed evaluation methods. Evaluation is a crucial component of the research process. The business environment establishes the requirements upon which the evaluation of the artifact is based. This environment includes the technical infrastructure which itself is incrementally built by the implementation of new IT artifacts. Thus, evaluation includes the integration of the artifact within the technical infrastructure of the business environment.

As in the justification of a behavioral science theory, evaluation of a designed IT artifact requires the definition of appropriate metrics and possibly the gathering and analysis of appropriate data. IT artifacts can be evaluated in terms of functionality, completeness, consistency, accuracy, performance, reliability, usability, fit with the organization, and other relevant quality attributes. When analytical metrics are appropriate, designed artifacts may be mathematically evaluated. As two examples, distributed database design algorithms can be evaluated using expected operating cost or average response time for a given characterization of information processing requirements (Johansson et al. 2003) and search algorithms can be evaluated using information retrieval metrics such as precision and recall (Salton 1988).

Because design is inherently an iterative and incremental activity, the evaluation phase provides essential feedback to the construction phase as to the quality of the design process and the design product under development. A design artifact is complete and effective when it satisfies the requirements and constraints of the problem it was meant to solve. Design-science research efforts may begin with simplified conceptualizations and representations of problems. As available technology or organizational environments change, assumptions made in prior research may become invalid. Johansson (2000), for example, demonstrated that network latency is a major component in the response-time performance of distributed databases. Prior research in distributed database design ignored latency because it assumed a low-bandwidth network where latency is negligible. In a high-bandwidth network, however, latency can account for over 90

Table 2. Design Evaluation Methods	
1. Observational	Case Study: Study artifact in depth in business environment
	Field Study: Monitor use of artifact in multiple projects
2. Analytical	Static Analysis: Examine structure of artifact for static qualities (e.g., complexity)
	Architecture Analysis: Study fit of artifact into technical IS architecture
	Optimization: Demonstrate inherent optimal properties of artifact or provide optimality bounds on artifact behavior
	Dynamic Analysis: Study artifact in use for dynamic qualities (e.g., performance)
3. Experimental	Controlled Experiment: Study artifact in controlled environment for qualities (e.g., usability)
	Simulation – Execute artifact with artificial data
4. Testing	Functional (Black Box) Testing: Execute artifact interfaces to discover failures and identify defects
	Structural (White Box) Testing: Perform coverage testing of some metric (e.g., execution paths) in the artifact implementation
5. Descriptive	Informed Argument: Use information from the knowledge base (e.g., relevant research) to build a convincing argument for the artifact's utility
	Scenarios: Construct detailed scenarios around the artifact to demonstrate its utility

percent of the response time. Johansson et al. (2003) extended prior distributed database design research by developing a model that includes network latency and the effects of parallel processing on response time.

The evaluation of designed artifacts typically uses methodologies available in the knowledge base. These are summarized in Table 2. The selection of evaluation methods must be matched appropriately with the designed artifact and the selected evaluation metrics. For example, descriptive methods of evaluation should only be used for especially innovative artifacts for which other forms of evaluation may not be feasible. The goodness and efficacy of an artifact can be rigorously demonstrated via well-selected evaluation methods (Basili 1996; Kleindorfer et al. 1998; Zelkowitz and Wallace 1998).

Design, in all of its realizations (e.g., architecture, landscaping, art, music), has style. Given the problem and solution requirements, sufficient degrees of freedom remain to express a variety of forms and functions in the artifact that are aesthetically pleasing to both the designer and the user. Good designers bring an element of style to their work (Norman 1988). Thus, we posit that design evaluation should include an assessment of the artifact's style.

The measurement of style lies in the realm of human perception and taste. In other words, we know good style when we see it. While difficult to define, style in IS design is widely recognized and appreciated (Kernighan and Plauger 1978; Winograd 1996). Gelernter (1998) terms the essence of style in IS design *machine beauty*. He describes it as a marriage between simplicity and power that drives innovation in science and technology. Simon (1996) also notes the importance of style in the design process. The ability to creatively vary the design process, within the limits of satisfactory constraints, challenges and adds value to designers who participate in the process.

Guideline 4: Research Contributions

Effective design-science research must provide clear contributions in the areas of the design artifact, design construction knowledge (i.e., foundations), and/or design evaluation knowledge (i.e., methodologies). The ultimate assessment for any research is, "What are the new and interesting contributions?" Design-science research holds the potential for three types of research contributions based on the novelty, generality, and significance of the designed artifact. One or more of these contributions must be found in a given research project.

1. *The Design Artifact.* Most often, the contribution of design-science research is the artifact itself. The artifact must enable the solution of heretofore unsolved problems. It may extend the knowledge base (see below) or apply existing knowledge in new and innovative ways. As shown in Figure 2 by the left-facing arrow at the bottom of the figure from IS Research to the Environment, exercising the artifact in the environment produces significant value to the constituent IS community. System development methodologies, design tools, and prototype systems (e.g., GDSS, expert systems) are examples of such artifacts.

2. *Foundations.* The creative development of novel, appropriately evaluated constructs, models, methods, or instantiations that extend and improve the existing foundations in the design-science knowledge base are also important contributions. The right-facing arrow at the bottom of the figure from IS Research to the Knowledge Base in Figure 2 indicates these contributions.   Modeling

formalisms, ontologies (Wand and Weber 1993, 1995; Weber 1997), problem and solution representations, design algorithms (Storey et al. 1997), and innovative information systems (Aiken 1991; Markus et al. 2002; Walls et al. 1992) are examples of such artifacts.

3. *Methodologies.* Finally, the creative development and use of evaluation methods (e.g., experimental, analytical, observational, testing, and descriptive) and new evaluation metrics provide design-science research contributions.   Measures and evaluation metrics in particular are crucial components of design-science research. The right-facing arrow at the bottom of the figure from IS Research to the Knowledge Base in Figure 2 also indicates these contributions. TAM, for example, presents a framework for predicting and explaining why a particular information system will or will not be accepted in a given organizational setting (Venkatesh 2000). Although TAM is posed as a behavioral theory, it also provides metrics by which a designed information system or implementation process can be evaluated. Its implications for design itself are as yet unexplored.

Criteria for assessing contribution focus on *representational fidelity* and *implementability*. Artifacts must accurately represent the business and technology environments used in the research, information systems themselves being models of the business. These artifacts must be "implementable," hence the importance of instantiating design science artifacts. Beyond these, however, the research must demonstrate a clear contribution to the business environment, solving an important, previously unsolved problem.

Guideline 5: Research Rigor

Rigor addresses the way in which research is conducted. Design-science research requires the application of rigorous methods in both the construction and evaluation of the designed artifact. In behavioral-science research, rigor is often assessed by adherence to appropriate data collection and analysis techniques. Over-emphasis on rigor in behavioral IS research has often resulted in a corresponding lowering of relevance (Lee 1999).

Design-science research often relies on mathematical formalism to describe the specified and constructed artifact. However, the environments in which IT artifacts must perform and the artifacts themselves may defy excessive formalism. Or, in an attempt to be mathematically rigorous, important parts of the problem may be abstracted or "assumed away." In particular, with respect to the construction activity, rigor must be assessed with respect to the applicability and generalizability of the artifact. Again, an overemphasis on rigor can lessen relevance. We argue, along with behavioral IS researchers (Applegate 1999), that it is possible and necessary for all IS research paradigms to be both rigorous and relevant.

In both design-science and behavioral-science research, rigor is derived from the effective use of the knowledge base—theoretical foundations and research methodologies. Success is predicated on the researcher's skilled selection of appropriate techniques to develop or construct a theory or artifact and the selection of appropriate means to justify the theory or evaluate the artifact.

Claims about artifacts are typically dependent upon performance metrics. Even formal mathematical proofs rely on evaluation criteria against which the performance of an artifact can be measured. Design-science researchers must constantly assess the appropriateness of their metrics and the construction of effective metrics is an important part of design-science research.

Furthermore, designed artifacts are often components of a human-machine problem-solving system. For such artifacts, knowledge of behavioral theories and empirical work are necessary to construct and evaluate such artifacts. Constructs, models, methods, and instantiations must be exercised within appropriate environments. Appropriate subject groups must be obtained for such studies. Issues that are addressed include

comparability, subject selection, training, time, and tasks. Methods for this type of evaluation are not unlike those for justifying or testing behavioral theories. However, the principal aim is to determine how well an artifact works, not to theorize about or prove anything about why the artifact works. This is where design-science and behavioral-science researchers must complement one another. Because design-science artifacts are often the "machine" part of the human-machine system constituting an information system, it is imperative to understand why an artifact works or does not work to enable new artifacts to be constructed that exploit the former and avoid the latter.

Guideline 6: Design as a Search Process

Design science is inherently iterative. The search for the best, or optimal, design is often intractable for realistic information systems problems. Heuristic search strategies produce feasible, good designs that can be implemented in the business environment. Simon (1996) describes the nature of the design process as a Generate/Test Cycle (Figure 3).

Design is essentially a search process to discover an effective solution to a problem. Problem solving can be viewed as utilizing available means to reach desired ends while satisfying laws existing in the environment (Simon 1996). Abstraction and representation of appropriate means, ends, and laws are crucial components of design-science research. These factors are problem and environment dependent and invariably involve creativity and innovation. Means are the set of actions and resources available to construct a solution. Ends represent goals and constraints on the solution. Laws are uncontrollable forces in the environment. Effective design requires knowledge of both the application domain (e.g., requirements and constraints) and the solution domain (e.g., technical and organizational).

Design-science research often simplifies a problem by explicitly representing only a subset of the

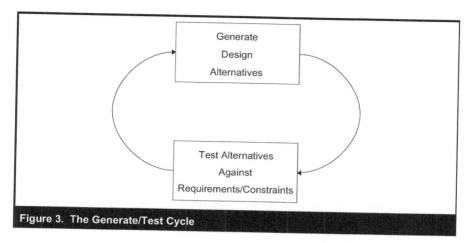

Figure 3. The Generate/Test Cycle

relevant means, ends, and laws or by decomposing a problem into simpler subproblems. Such simplifications and decompositions may not be realistic enough to have a significant impact on practice but may represent a starting point. Progress is made iteratively as the scope of the design problem is expanded. As means, ends, and laws are refined and made more realistic, the design artifact becomes more relevant and valuable. The means, ends, and laws for IS design problems can often be represented using the tools of mathematics and operations research. Means are represented by decision variables whose values constitute an implementable design solution. Ends are represented using a utility function and constraints that can be expressed in terms of decision variables and constants. Laws are represented by the values of constants used in the utility function and constraints.

The set of possible design solutions for any problem is specified as all possible means that satisfy all end conditions consistent with identified laws. When these can be formulated appropriately and posed mathematically, standard operations research techniques can be used to determine an optimal solution for the specified end conditions. Given the wicked nature of many information system design problems, however, it

may not be possible to determine, let alone explicitly describe, the relevant means, ends, or laws (Vessey and Glass 1998). Even when it is possible to do so, the sheer size and complexity of the solution space will often render the problem computationally infeasible. For example, to build a "reliable, secure, and responsive information systems infrastructure," one of the key issues faced by IS managers (Brancheau et al. 1996), a designer would need to represent all possible infrastructures (means), determine their utility and constraints (ends), and specify all cost and benefit constants (laws). Clearly such an approach is infeasible. However, this does not mean that design-science research is inappropriate for such a problem.

In such situations, the search is for satisfactory solutions, i.e., *satisficing* (Simon 1996), without explicitly specifying all possible solutions. The design task involves the creation, utilization, and assessment of heuristic search strategies. That is, constructing an artifact that "works" well for the specified class of problems. Although its construction is based on prior theory and existing design knowledge, it may or may not be entirely clear why it works or the extent of its generalizability; it simply qualifies as "credentialed knowledge" (Meehl 1986, p. 311). While it is important to understand why an artifact works, the critical nature of design in IS makes it important to first establish that it *does* work and to characterize the environments in which it works, even if we cannot completely explain *why* it works. This enables IS practitioners to take advantage of the artifact to improve practice and provides a context for additional research aimed at more fully explicating the resultant phenomena. Markus et al. (2002), for example, describe their search process in terms of iteratively identifying deficiencies in constructed prototype software systems and creatively developing solutions to address them.

The use of heuristics to find "good" design solutions opens the question of how goodness is measured. Different problem representations may provide varying techniques for measuring how good a solution is. One approach is to prove or demonstrate that a heuristic design solution is always within close proximity of an optimal solution. Another is to compare produced solutions with those constructed by expert human designers for the same problem situation.

Guideline 7: Communication of Research

Design-science research must be presented both to technology-oriented as well as management-oriented audiences. Technology-oriented audiences need sufficient detail to enable the described artifact to be constructed (implemented) and used within an appropriate organizational context. This enables practitioners to take advantage of the benefits offered by the artifact and it enables researchers to build a cumulative knowledge base for further extension and evaluation. It is also important for such audiences to understand the processes by which the artifact was constructed and evaluated. This establishes repeatability of the research project and builds the knowledge base for further research extensions by design-science researchers in IS.

Management-oriented audiences need sufficient detail to determine if the organizational resources should be committed to constructing (or purchasing) and using the artifact within their specific organizational context. Zmud (1997) suggests that presentation of design-science research for a managerial audience requires an emphasis not on the inherent nature of the artifact itself, but on the knowledge required to effectively apply the artifact "within specific contexts for individual or organizational gain" (p. ix). That is, the emphasis must be on the importance of the problem and the novelty and effectiveness of the solution approach realized in the artifact. While we agree with this statement, we note that it may be necessary to describe the artifact in some detail to enable managers to appreciate its nature and understand its application. Presenting that detail in concise, well-organized appendices, as advised by Zmud, is an appropriate communication mechanism for such an audience.

Application of the Design Science Research Guidelines

To illustrate the application of the design-science guidelines to IS research, we have selected three exemplar articles for analysis from three different IS journals, one from *Decision Support Systems*, one from *Information Systems Research*, and one from *MIS Quarterly*. Each has strengths and weaknesses when viewed through the lens of the above guidelines. Our goal is not to perform a critical evaluation of the quality of the research contributions, but rather to illuminate the design-science guidelines. The articles are

*   Gavish and Gerdes (1998), which develops techniques for implementing anonymity in Group Decision Support Systems (GDSS) environments

*   Aalst and Kumar (2003), which proposes a design for an *eXchangeable Routing Language* (XRL) to support electronic commerce workflows among trading partners

- Markus, Majchrzak, and Gasser (2002), which proposes a design theory for the development of information systems built to support emergent knowledge processes

The fundamental questions for design-science research are, "What utility does the new artifact provide?" and "What demonstrates that utility?" Evidence must be presented to address these two questions. That is the essence of design science. Contribution arises from utility. If existing artifacts are adequate, then design-science research that creates a new artifact is unnecessary (it is irrelevant). If the new artifact does not map adequately to the real world (rigor), it cannot provide utility. If the artifact does not solve the problem (search, implementability), it has no utility. If utility is not demonstrated (evaluation), then there is no basis upon which to accept the claims that it provides any contribution (contribution). Furthermore, if the problem, the artifact, and its utility are not presented in a manner such that the implications for research and practice are clear, then publication in the IS literature is not appropriate (communication).

The Design and Implementation of Anonymity in GDSS: Gavish and Gerdes

The study of group decision support systems (GDSS) has been and remains one of the most visible and successful research streams in the IS field. The use of information technology to effectively support meetings of groups of different sizes over time and space is a real problem that challenges all business organizations. Recent GDSS literature surveys demonstrate the large numbers of GDSS research papers published in the IS field and, more importantly, the wide variety of research paradigms applied to GDSS research (e.g., Dennis and Wixom 2001; Fjermestad and Hiltz 1998; Nunamaker et al. 1996). However, only a small number of GDSS papers can be considered to make true design-science research contributions. Most assume the introduction of a new information technology or process in the

GDSS environment and then study the individual, group, or organizational implications using a behavioral-science research paradigm. Several such GDSS papers have appeared in *MIS Quarterly* (e.g., Dickson et al. 1993; Gallupe et al. 1988; Jarvenpaa et al. 1988; Sengupta and Te'eni 1993).

The central role of design science in GDSS is clearly recognized in the early foundation papers of the field. The University of Arizona Electronic Meeting System group, for example, states the need for both *developmental* and *empirical* research agendas (Dennis et al. 1988; Nunamaker et al. 1991b). Developmental, or design-science, research is called for in the areas of process structures and support and task structures and support. Process structure and support technologies and methods are generic to all GDSS environments and tasks. Technologies and methods for distributed communications, group memory, decision-making methods, and anonymity are a few of the critical design issues for GDSS process support needed in any task domain. Task structure and support are specific to the problem domain under consideration by the group (e.g., medical decision making, software development). Task support includes the design of new technologies and methods for managing and analyzing task-related information and using that information to make specific, task-related decisions.

The issue of anonymity has been studied extensively in GDSS environments. Behavioral research studies have shown both positive and negative impacts on group interactions. On the positive side, GDSS participants can express their views freely without fear of embarrassment or reprisal. However, anonymity can encourage free-riding and antisocial behaviors. While the pros and cons of anonymity in GDSS are much researched, there has been a noticeable lack of research on the design of techniques for implementing anonymity in GDSS environments. Gavish and Gerdes (1998) address this issue by designing five basic mechanisms to provide GDSS procedural anonymity.

Problem Relevance

The amount of interest and research on anonymity issues in GDSS testifies to its relevance. Field studies and surveys clearly indicate that participants rank anonymity as a highly desired attribute in the GDSS system. Many individuals state that they would refuse to participate in or trust the results of a GDSS meeting without a satisfactory level of assured anonymity (Fjermestad and Hiltz 1998).

Research Rigor

Gavish and Gerdes base their GDSS anonymity designs on past research in the fields of cryptography and secure network communication protocols (e.g., Chaum 1981; Schneier 1996). These research areas have a long history of formal, rigorous results that have been applied to the design of many practical security and privacy mechanisms. Appendix A of the exemplar paper provides a set of formal proofs that the claims made by the authors for the anonymity designs are correct and draw their validity from the knowledge base of this past research.

Design as a Search Process

The authors motivate their design science research by identifying three basic types of anonymity in a GDSS system: *environmental*, *content*, and *procedural*. After a definition and brief discussion of each type, they focus on the design of mechanisms for procedural anonymity; the ability of the GDSS system to hide the source of any message. This is a very difficult requirement because standard network protocols typically attach source information in headers to support reliable transmission protocols. Thus, GDSS systems must modify standard communication protocols and include additional transmission procedures to ensure required levels of anonymity.

The design-science process employed by the authors is to state the desired procedural anonymity attributes of the GDSS system and then to

design mechanisms to satisfy the system requirements for anonymity. Proposed designs are presented and anonymity claims are proved to be correct. A thorough discussion of the costs and benefits of the proposed anonymity mechanisms is provided in Section 4 of the paper.

Design as an Artifact

The authors design a GDSS system architecture that provides a rigorous level of procedural anonymity. Five mechanisms are employed to ensure participant anonymity:

- All messages are encrypted with a unique session key

- The sender's header information is removed from all messages

- All messages are re-encrypted upon retransmission from any GDSS server

- Transmission order of messages is randomized

- Artificial messages are introduced to thwart traffic analysis

The procedures and communication protocols that implement these mechanisms in a GDSS system are the artifacts of this research.

Design Evaluation

The evaluation consists of two reported activities. First, in Appendix A, each mechanism is proved to correctly provide the claimed anonymity benefits. Formal proof methods are used to validate the effectiveness of the designed mechanisms. Second, Section 4 presents a thorough cost-benefit analysis. It is shown that the operational costs of supporting the proposed anonymity mechanisms can be quite significant. In addition, the communication protocols to implement the mechanisms add considerable complexity to the system. Thus, the authors recommend that a cost-benefit justification be performed before determining the level of anonymity to implement for a GDSS meeting.

The authors do not claim to have implemented the proposed anonymity mechanisms in a prototype or actual GDSS system. Thus, an instantiation of the designed artifact remains to be evaluated in an operational GDSS environment.

Research Contributions

The design-science contributions of this research are the proposed anonymity mechanisms as the design artifacts and the evaluation results in the form of formal proofs and cost-benefit analyses. These contributions advance our understanding of how best to provide participant anonymity in GDSS meetings.

Research Communication

Although the presentation of this research is aimed at an audience familiar with network system concepts such as encryption and communication protocols, the paper also contains important, useful information for a managerial audience. Managers should have a good understanding of the implications of anonymity in GDSS meetings. This understanding must include an appreciation of the costs of providing desired levels of participant anonymity. While the authors provide a thorough discussion of cost-benefit tradeoffs toward the end of the paper, the paper would be more accessible to a managerial audience if it included a stronger motivation up front on the important implications of anonymity in GDSS system development and operations.

A Workflow Language for Inter-organizational Processes: Aalst and Kumar

Workflow models are an effective means for describing, analyzing, implementing, and managing business processes. Workflow management systems are becoming integral components of many commercial enterprise-wide information systems (Leymann and Roller 2000). Standards for workflow semantics and syntax (i.e., workflow languages) and workflow architectures are promulgated by the Workflow Management Coalition (WfMC 2000). While workflow models have been used for many years to manage intra-organizational business processes, there is now a great demand for effective tools to model inter-organization processes across heterogeneous and distributed environments, such as those found in electronic commerce and complex supply chains (Kumar and Zhao 2002).

Aalst and Kumar (2003) investigate the problem of exchanging business process information across multiple organizations in an automated manner. They design an eXchangable Routing Language (XRL) to capture workflow models that are then embedded in eXtensible Markup Language (XML) for electronic transmission to all participants in an interorganizational business process. The design of XRL is based upon Petri nets, which provide a formal basis for analyzing the correctness and performance of the workflows, as well as supporting the extensibility of the language. The authors develop a workflow management architecture and a prototype implementation to evaluate XRL in a proof of concept.

Problem Relevance

Interorganizational electronic commerce is growing rapidly and is projected to soon exceed one trillion dollars annually (eMarketer 2002). A multitude of electronic commerce solutions are being proposed (e.g., ebXML, UDDI, RosettaNet) to enable businesses to execute transactions in standardized, open environments. While XML has been widely accepted as a protocol for exchanging business data, there is still no clear standard for exchanging business process information (e.g., workflow models). This is the very relevant problem addressed by this research.

Research Rigor

Research on workflow modeling has long been based on rigorous mathematical techniques such as Markov chains, queueing networks, and Petri nets (Aalst and Hee 2002). In this paper, Petri nets provide the underlying semantics for XRL. These formal semantics allow for powerful analysis techniques (e.g., correctness, performance) to be applied to the designed workflow models. Such formalisms also enable the development of automated tools to manipulate and analyze complex workflow designs. Each language construct in XRL has an equivalent Petri-net representation presented in the paper. The language is extensible in that adding a new construct simply requires defining its Petri-net representation and adding its syntax to the XRL. Thus, this research draws from a clearly defined and tested base of modeling literature and knowledge.

Design as a Search Process

XRL is designed in the paper by performing a thorough analysis of business process requirements and identifying features provided by leading commercial workflow management systems. Using the terminology from the paper, workflows traverse routes through available tasks (i.e., business services) in the electronic business environment. The basic routing constructs of XRL define the specific control flow of the business process. The authors build 13 basic constructs into XRL: Task, Sequence, Any_sequence, Choice, Condition, Parallel_sync, Parallel_no_sync, Parallel_part_sync, Wait_all, Wait_any, While_do, Stop, and Terminate. They show the Petri-net representation of each construct. Thus, the fundamental control flow structures of sequence, decision, iteration, and concurrency are supported in XRL.

The authors demonstrate the capabilities of XRL in several examples. However, they are careful not to claim that XRL is *complete* in the formal sense that all possible business processes can be modeled in XRL. The search for a complete set of XRL constructs is left for future research.

Design as an Artifact

There are two clearly identifiable artifacts produced in this research. First, the workflow language XRL is designed. XRL is based on Petri-net formalisms and described in XML syntax. Interorganizational business processes are specified via XRL for execution in a distributed, heterogeneous environment.

The second research artifact is the XRL/flower workflow management architecture in which XRL-described processes are executed. The XRL routing scheme is parsed by an XML parser and stored as an XML data structure. This structure is read into a Petri-net engine which determines the next step of the business process and informs the next task provider via an e-mail message. Results of each task are sent back to the engine which then executes the next step in the process until completion. The paper presents a prototype implementation of the XRL/flower architecture as a proof of concept (Aalst and Kumar 2003).

Another artifact of this research is a workflow verification tool named *Wolfan* that verifies the *soundness* of business process workflows. Soundness of a workflow requires that the workflow terminates, no Petri-net tokens are left behind upon termination, and there are no dead tasks in the workflow. This verification tool is described more completely in a different paper (Aalst 1999).

Design Evaluation

The authors evaluate the XRL and XRL/flower designs in several important ways:

- XRL is compared and contrasted with languages in existing commercial workflow systems and research prototypes. The majority of these languages are proprietary and difficult to adapt to *ad hoc* business process design.

- The fit of XRL with proposed standards is studied. In particular, the *Interoperability Wf-*

XML Binding standard (WfMC 2000) does not at this time include the specification of control flow and, thus, is not suitable for inter-organizational workflows. Electronic commerce standards (e.g., RosettaNet) provide some level of control flow specification for predefined business activities, but do not readily allow the *ad hoc* specification of business processes.

• A research prototype of XRL/flower has been implemented and several of the user interface screens are presented. The screens demonstrate a mail-order routing schema case study.

• The Petri-net foundation of XRL allows the authors to claim the XRL workflows can be verified for correctness and performance. XRL is extensible since new constructs can be added to the language based on their translation to underlying Petri-net representations. However, as discussed above, the authors do not make a formal claim for the representational completeness of XRL.

Research Contributions

The clear contributions of this research are the design artifacts—XRL (a workflow language), XRL/flower (a workflow architecture and its implemented prototype system), and Wolfan (a Petri-net verification engine). Another interesting contribution is the extension of XRL in its ability to describe and transmit routing schemas (e.g., control flow information) to support interorganizational electronic commerce.

Research Communication

This paper provides clear information to both technical and managerial audiences. The presentation, while primarily technical with XML coding and Petri-net diagrams throughout, motivates a managerial audience with a strong introduction on risks and benefits of applying interorganizational workflows to electronic commerce applications.

Information Systems Design for Emergent Knowledge Processes: Markus, Majchrzak, and Gasser

Despite decades of research and development efforts, effective methods for developing information systems that meet the information requirements of upper management remain elusive. Early approaches used a "waterfall" approach where requirements were defined and validated prior to initiating design efforts which, in turn, were completed prior to implementation (Royce 1998). Prototyping approaches emerged next, followed by numerous proposals including CASE tool-based approaches, rapid application development, and extreme programming (Kruchten 2000). Walls et al. (1992) propose a framework for a prescriptive information system design theory aimed at enabling designers to construct "more effective information systems" (p. 36). They apply this framework to the design of vigilant executive information systems. The framework establishes a class of user requirements (model of design problems) that are most effectively addressed using a particular type of system solution (instantiation) designed using a prescribed set of development practices (methods). Markus et al. (2002) extend this framework to the development of information systems to support emergent knowledge processes (EKPs)—processes in which structure is "neither possible nor desirable" (p. 182) and where processes are characterized by "*highly unpredictable user types* and work contexts" (p. 183).

Problem Relevance

The relevance and importance of the problem are well demonstrated. Markus et al. describe a class of management activities that they term emergent knowledge processes (EKPs). These include "basic research, new product development, strategic business planning, and organization design" (p. 179). They are characterized by "process emergence, unpredictable user types and use contexts, and distributed expert knowledge" (p. 186). They are crucial to many manufacturing organizations, particularly those in high-tech industries. Such organizations recognize the need to integrate organizational design and information system design with manufacturing operations. They recognize the potential for significant performance improvements offered by such integration. Yet few have realized that potential. Markus et al. argue that this is due to a lack of an adequate design theory and lack of scientifically based tools, noting that existing information system development methodologies focus on structured or semi-structured decision processes and are inadequate for the development of systems to support EKPs. TOP Modeler, the artifact created in this research effort, squarely addresses this problem. Not surprisingly, its development attracted the attention and active participation of several large, high-tech manufacturing organizations including "Hewlett-Packard, General Motors, Digital Equipment Corporation, and Texas Instruments" (p. 186).

Research Rigor

The presented work has theoretical foundations in both IS design theory and organizational design theory. It uses the basic notions of IS design theory presented in Walls et al. (1992) and poses a prescription for designing information systems to support EKPs. Prior research in developing decision support systems, executive information systems, and expert systems serves as a foundation for this work and deficiencies of these approaches for the examined problem type serve as motivation. The knowledge-base constructed within TOP Modeler was formed from a synthesis of socio-technical systems theory and the empirical literature on organizational design knowledge. It was evaluated theoretically using standard metrics from the expert systems literature and empirically using data gathered from numerous electronics manufacturing companies in the United States. Development of TOP Modeler used an "action research paradigm" starting with a "kernel theory" based on prior development methods and theoretical results and iteratively posing and testing artifacts (prototypes) to assess progress toward the desired result. Finally, the artifact was commercialized and "used

in over two dozen 'real use' situations." (p. 187). In summary, this work effectively used theoretical foundations from IS and organizational theory, applied appropriate research methods in developing the artifact, defined and applied appropriate performance measures, and tested the artifact within an appropriate context.

Design as a Search Process

As discussed above, implementation and iteration are central to this research. The authors study prototypes that instantiate posed or newly learned design prescriptions. Their use and impacts were observed, problems identified, solutions posed and implemented, and the cycle was then repeated. These interventions occurred over a period of 18 months within the aforementioned companies as they dealt with organizational design tasks. As a result, not only was the TOP Modeler developed and deployed but prescriptions (methods) in the form of six principles for developing systems to support EKPs were also devised. The extensive experience, creativity, intuition, and problem solving capabilities of the researchers were involved in assessing problems and interpreting the results of deploying various TOP modeler iterations and in constructing improvements to address shortcomings identified.

Design as an Artifact

The TOP Modeler is an implemented software system (instantiation). It is composed of an object-oriented user interface, an object-oriented query generator, and an analysis module built on top of a relational meta-knowledge base that enables access to "pluggable" knowledge bases representing different domains. It also includes tools to support the design and construction of these knowledge bases. The TOP Modeler supports a development process incorporating the six principles for developing systems to support EKPs. As mentioned above, TOP Modeler was commercialized and used in a number of different organizational redesign situations.

Design Evaluation

Evaluation is in the context of organizational design in manufacturing organizations, and is based on observation during the development and deployment of a single artifact, TOP Modeler. No formal evaluation was attempted in the sense of comparison with other artifacts. This is not surprising, nor is it a criticism of this work. There simply are no existing artifacts that address the same problem. However, given that methodologies for developing information systems to support semi-structured management activities are the closest available artifacts, it is appropriate to use them as a comparative measure. In effect, this was accomplished by using principles from these methodologies to inform the initial design of TOP Modeler. The identification of deficiencies in the resultant artifact provides evidence that these artifacts are ill-suited to the task at hand.

Iterative development and deployment within the context of organizational design in manufacturing organizations provide opportunities to observe improvement but do not enable formal evaluation—at each iteration, changes are induced in the organization that cannot be controlled. As mentioned above, the authors have taken a creative and innovative approach that, of necessity, trades off rigor for relevancy. In the initial stages of a discipline, this approach is extremely effective. TOP Modeler demonstrates the feasibility of developing an artifact to support organizational design and EKPs within high-tech manufacturing organizations. "In short, the evidence suggests that TOP Modeler was successful in supporting organizational design" (p. 187) but additional study is required to assess the comparative effectiveness of other possible approaches in this or other contexts. Again, this is not a criticism of this work; rather it is a call for further research in the general class of problems dealing with emergent knowledge processes. As additional research builds on this foundation, formal, rigorous evaluation and comparison with alternative approaches in a variety of contexts become crucial to enable claims of generalizability. As the authors point out, "Only the accumulated weight of empirical evidence will establish the validity" of such claims.

Research Contributions

The design-science contributions of this research are the TOP Modeler software and the design principles. TOP Modeler demonstrates the feasibility of using the design principles to develop an artifact to support EKPs. Because TOP Modeler is the first artifact to address this task, its construction is itself a contribution to design science. Furthermore, because the authors are able to articulate the design principles upon which its construction was based, these serve as hypotheses to be tested by future empirical work. Their applicability to the development of other types of information systems can also be tested. An agenda for addressing such issues is presented. This focuses on validation, evaluation, and the challenges of improvement inherent in the evaluation process.

Research Communication

This work presents two types of artifacts, TOP Modeler (an instantiation) and a set of design principles (method) that address a heretofore unsolved problem dealing with the design of an information system to support EKPs. Recognizing that existing system development methods and instantiations are aimed at structured or semi-structured activities, Markus et al. identify an opportunity to apply information technology in a new and innovative way. Their presentation addresses each of the design guidelines posed above. TOP Modeler exemplifies "proof by construction"—it is feasible to construct an information system to support EKPs. Since it is the first such artifact, its evaluation using formal methods is deferred until future research. Technical details of TOP Modeler are not presented, making it difficult for a technical researcher or practitioner to replicate their work. The uniqueness of the artifacts and the innovation inherent in them are presented so that managerial researchers and IT managers are aware of the new capabilities.

Discussion and Conclusions ■

Philosophical debates on how to conduct IS research (e.g., positivism vs. interpretivism) have been the focus of much recent attention (Klein and Myers 1999; Robey 1996; Weber 2003). The major emphasis of such debates lies in the epistemologies of research, the underlying assumption being that of the natural sciences. That is, somewhere some *truth* exists and somehow that truth can be extracted, explicated, and codified. The behavioral-science paradigm seeks to find "what is true." In contrast, the design-science paradigm seeks to create "what is effective." While it can be argued that utility relies on truth, the discovery of truth may lag the application of its utility. We argue that both design-science and behavioral-science paradigms are needed to ensure the relevance and effectiveness of IS research. Given the artificial nature of organizations and the information systems that support them, the design-science paradigm can play a significant role in resolving the fundamental dilemmas that have plagued IS research: rigor, relevance, discipline boundaries, behavior, and technology (Lee 2000).

Information systems research lies at the intersection of people, organizations, and technology (Silver et al. 1995). It relies on and contributes to cognitive science, organizational theory, management sciences, and computer science. It is both an organizational and a technical discipline that is concerned with the analysis, construction, deployment, use, evaluation, evolution, and management of information system artifacts in organizational settings (Madnick 1992; Orlikowski and Barley 2001).

Within this setting, the design-science research paradigm is proactive with respect to technology. It focuses on creating and evaluating innovative IT artifacts that enable organizations to address important information-related tasks. The behavioral-science research paradigm is reactive with respect to technology in the sense that it takes technology as "given." It focuses on developing and justifying theories that explain and predict phenomena related to the acquisition, implementation, management, and use of such technologies. The dangers of a design-science research paradigm are an overemphasis on the technological artifacts and a failure to maintain an adequate theory base, potentially resulting in well-designed artifacts that are useless in real organizational settings. The dangers of a behavioral-science research paradigm are overemphasis on contextual theories and failure to adequately identify and anticipate technological capabilities, potentially resulting in theories and principles addressing outdated or ineffective technologies. We argue strongly that IS research must be both proactive and reactive with respect to technology. It needs a complete research cycle where design science creates artifacts for specific information problems based on relevant behavioral science theory and behavioral science anticipates and engages the created technology artifacts.

Hence, we reiterate the call made earlier by March et al. (2000) to align IS design-science research with real-world production experience. Results from such industrial experience can be framed in the context of our seven guidelines. These must be assessed not only by IS design-science researchers but also by IS behavioral-science researchers who can validate the organizational problems as well as study and anticipate the impacts of created artifacts. Thus, we encourage collaborative industrial/academic research projects and publications based on such experience. Markus et al. (2002) is an excellent example of such collaboration. Publication of these results will help accelerate the development of domain independent and scalable solutions to large-scale information systems problems within organizations. We recognize that a lag exists between academic research and its adoption in industry. We also recognize the possible *ad hoc* nature of technology-oriented solutions developed in industry. The latter gap can be reduced considerably by developing and framing the industrial solutions based on our proposed guidelines.

It is also important to distinguish between "system building" efforts and design-science research. Guidelines addressing evaluation, contributions, and rigor are especially important in providing this distinction. The underlying formalism required by these guidelines helps researchers to develop representations of IS problems, solutions, and solution processes that clarify the knowledge produced by the research effort.

As we move forward, there exist a number of exciting challenges facing the design-science research community in IS. A few are summarized here.

- There is an inadequate theoretical base upon which to build an engineering discipline of information systems design (Basili 1996). The field is still very young lacking the cumulative theory development found in other engineering and social-science disciplines. It is important to demonstrate the feasibility and utility of such a theoretical base to a managerial audience that must make technology-adoption decisions that can have far-reaching impacts on the organization.

- Insufficient sets of constructs, models, methods, and tools exist for accurately representing the business/technology environment. Highly abstract representations (e.g., analytical mathematical models) are criticized as having no relationship to "real-world" environments. On the other hand, many informal, descriptive IS models lack an underlying theory base. The trade-offs between relevance and rigor are clearly problematic; finding representational techniques with an acceptable balance between the two is very difficult.

- The existing knowledge base is often insufficient for design purposes and designers must rely on intuition, experience, and trial-and-error methods. A constructed artifact embodies the designer's knowledge of the problem and solution. In new and emerging applications of technology, the artifact itself represents an experiment. In its execution, we learn about the nature of the problem, the environment, and the possible solutions—hence, the importance of developing and implementing prototype artifacts (Newell and Simon 1976).

- Design-science research is perishable. Rapid advances in technology can invalidate design-science research results before they are implemented effectively in the business environment or, just as importantly to managers, before adequate payback can be achieved by committing organizational resources to implementing those results. Two examples are the promises made by the artificial intelligence community in the 1980s (Feigenbaum and McCorduck 1983) and the more recent research on object-oriented databases (Chaudhri and Loomis 1998). Just as important to IS researchers, design results can be overtaken by technology before they even appear in the research literature. How much research was published on the Year 2000 problem before it became a non-event?

- Rigorous evaluation methods are extremely difficult to apply in design-science research (Tichy 1998; Zelkowitz and Wallace 1998). For example, the use of a design artifact on a single project may not generalize to different environments (Markus et al. 2002).

We believe that design science will play an increasingly important role in the IS profession. IS managers in particular are actively engaged in design activities—the creation, deployment, evaluation, and improvement of purposeful IT artifacts that enable organizations to achieve their goals. The challenge for design-science researchers in IS is to inform managers of the capabilities and impacts of new IT artifacts.

Much of the research published in *MIS Quarterly* employs the behavioral-science paradigm. It is passive with respect to technology, often ignoring or "under-theorizing" the artifact itself (Orlikowski and Iacono 2001). Its focus is on describing the implications of *technology*—its impact on individuals, groups, and organizations. It regularly includes studies that examine how people employ a technology, report on the benefits and difficulties encountered when a technology is implemented within an organization, or discuss how managers might facilitate the use of a technology. Orman (2002) argues that many of the equivocal results in IS behavioral-science studies can be explained by a failure to differentiate the capabilities and purposes of the studied technology.

Design science is active with respect to technology, engaging in the creation of technological artifacts that impact people and organizations. Its focus is on problem solving but often takes a simplistic view of the people and the organizational contexts in which designed artifacts must function. As stated earlier, the design of an artifact, its formal specification, and an assessment of its utility, often by comparison with competing artifacts, are integral to design-science research. These must be combined with behavioral and organizational theories to develop an understanding of business problems, contexts, solutions, and evaluation approaches adequate to servicing the IS research and practitioner communities. The effective presentation of design-science research in major IS journals, such as *MIS Quarterly*, will be an important step toward integrating the design-science and behavioral-science communities in IS.

Acknowledgements

We would like to thank Allen Lee, Ron Weber, and Gordon Davis who in different ways each contributed to our thinking about design science in the Information Systems profession and encouraged us to pursue this line of research. We would also like to acknowledge the efforts of Rosann Collins who provided insightful comments and perspectives on the nature of the relationship between behavioral-science and design-science research. This work has also benefited from seminars and discussions at Arizona State University, Florida International University, Georgia State University, Michigan State University, Notre Dame University, and The University of Utah. We would particularly like to thank Brian Pentland and Steve Alter for feedback and suggestions they provided on an earlier version of this paper. The comments provided by several anonymous editors and reviewers greatly enhanced the content and presentation of the paper.

References

Aalst, W. "Wolfan: A Petri-Net-Based Workflow Analyzer," *Systems Analysis-Modeling-Simulation* (34:3), 1999, pp. 345-357.

Aalst, W., and Hee, K. *Workflow Management: Models, Methods, and Systems*, The MIT Press, Cambridge, MA, 2002.

Aalst, W., and Kumar, A. "XML-Based Schema Definition for Support of Interorganizational Workflow," *Information Systems Research* (14:1), March 2003, pp. 23-46.

Aboulafia, M. (ed.). *Philosophy, Social Theory, and the Thought of George Herbert Mead* (SUNY Series in Philosophy of the Social Sciences), State University of New York Press, Albany, NY, 1991.

Aiken, M. W., Sheng, O. R. L., and Vogel, D. R. "Integrating Expert Systems with Group Decision Support Systems," *ACM Transactions on Information Systems* (9:1), January 1991, pp. 75-95.

Alter, S. "18 Reasons Why IT-Reliant Work Systems Should Replace 'The IT Artifact' as the Core Subject Matter of the IS Field," *Communications of the AIS* (12), October 2003, pp. 365-394.

Applegate, L. M. "Rigor and Relevance in MIS Research—Introduction," *MIS Quarterly* (23:1), March 1999, pp. 1-2.

Basili, V. "The Role of Experimentation in Software Engineering: Past, Current, and Future," in *Proceedings of the 18th International Conference on Software Engineering*, T. Maibaum and M. Zelkowitz (eds.), Berlin, Germany, March 25-29, 1996, pp. 442-449.

Basu, A., and Blanning, R. W. "A Formal Approach to Workflow Analysis," *Information Systems Research* (11:1), March 2000, pp. 17-36.

Basu, A., and Blanning, R. W. "Metagraphs: A Tool for Modeling Decision Support Systems," *Management Science* (40:12), December 1994, pp. 1579-1600.

Batra, D., Hoffer, J. A., and Bostrom, R. P. "A Comparison of User Performance between the Relational and the Extended Entity Relationship Models in the Discovery Phase of Database Design," *Communications of the ACM* (33:2), February 1990, pp. 126-139.

Bell, D. A. "From Data Properties to Evidence," *IEEE Transactions on Knowledge and Data Engineering* (5:6), December 1993, pp. 965-969.

Benbasat, I., and Zmud, R. W. "Empirical Research in Information Systems: The Practice of Relevance," *MIS Quarterly* (23:1), March 1999, pp. 3-16.

Bhargava, H. K., Krishnan, R., and Piela, P. "On Formal Semantics and Analysis of Typed Modeling Languages: An Analysis of Ascend," *INFORMS Journal on Computing* (10:2), Spring 1998, pp. 189-208.

Bodart, F., Patel, A., Sim, M., and Weber, R. "Should the Optional Property Construct be Used in Conceptual Modeling? A Theory and Three Empirical Tests," *Information Systems Research* (12:4), December 2001, pp. 384-405.

Boland, R. J. "Design in the Punctuation of Management Action" in *Managing as Designing: Creating a Vocabulary for Management Education and Research*, R. Boland (ed.), Frontiers of Management Workshop, Weatherhead School of Management, June 14-15, 2002 (available online at http://design.cwru.edu).

Brancheau, J., Janz, B., and Wetherbe, J. "Key Issues in Information Systems Management: 1994-95 SIM Delphi Results," *MIS Quarterly* (20:2), June 1996, pp. 225-242.

Brooks, F. P., Jr. "The Computer Scientist as Toolsmith II," *Communications of the ACM* (39:3), March 1996, pp. 61-68.

Brooks, F. P., Jr. "No Silver Bullet: Essence and Accidents of Software Engineering," *IEEE Computer* (20:4), April 1987, pp. 10-19.

Bunge, M. A. *Treatise on Basic Philosophy: Volume 7—Epistemology & Methodology III: Philosophy of Science and Technology—Part II: Life Science, Social Science and Technology*, D. Reidel Publishing Company, Boston, MA, 1985.

Chaudhri, A., and Loomis, M. *Object Databases in Practice*, Prentice-Hall, Upper Saddle River, NJ, 1998.

Chaum, D. "Untraceable Electronic Mail, Return Addresses, and Digital Pseudonyms," *Communications of the ACM* (24:2), February 1981, pp. 84-87.

Chen, P. P. S. "The Entity-Relationship Model: Toward a Unified View," *ACM Transactions on Database Systems* (1:1), 1976, pp. 9-36.

Davis, G. B., and Olson, M. H. *Management Information Systems: Conceptual Foundations, Structure and Development* (2nd ed.), McGraw-Hill, New York, 1985.

DeLone, W. H., and McLean, E. R. "The DeLone and McLean Model of Information Systems Success: A Ten-Year Update," *Journal of Management Information Systems* (19:4), Spring 2003, pp. 9-30.

DeLone, W. H., and McLean, E. R. "Information Systems Success: The Quest for the Dependent Variable," *Information Systems Research* (3:1), March 1992, pp. 60-95.

Denning, P. J. "A New Social Contract for Research," *Communications of the ACM* (40:2), February 1997, pp. 132-134.

Dennis, A., George, J., Jessup, L., Nunamaker, J., and Vogel, D. "Information Technology to Support Electronic Meetings," *MIS Quarterly* (12:4), December 1988, pp. 591-624.

Dennis, A., and Wixom, B. "Investigating the Moderators of the Group Support Systems Use with Meta-Analysis," *Journal of Management Information Systems* (18:3), Winter 2001-02, pp. 235-257.

Dey, D., Sarkar, S., and De, P. "A Probabilistic Decision Model for Entity Matching in Heterogeneous Databases," *Management Science* (44:10), October 1998, pp. 1379-1395.

Dey, D., Storey, V. C., and Barron, T. M. "Improving Database Design through the Analysis of Relationships," *ACM Transactions on Database Systems* (24:4), December 1999, pp. 453-486.

Dickson, G., Partridge, J., and Robinson, L. "Exploring Modes of Facilitative Support for GDSS Technology," *MIS Quarterly* (17:2), June 1993, pp. 173-194.

Drucker, P. F. "The Coming of the New Organization," *Harvard Business Review* (66:1), January-February 1988, pp. 45-53.

Drucker, P. F. "The New Productivity Challenge," *Harvard Business Review* (69:6), November-December 1991, pp. 45-53.

Dym, C. L. *Engineering Design*, Cambridge University Press, New York, 1994.

eMarketer. *E-Commerce Trade and B2B Exchanges*, March 2002 (available online at http://www.emarketer.com/products/report.php?ecommerce_trade).

Feigenbaum, E., and McCorduck, P. *The Fifth Generation: Artificial Intelligence and Japan's Computer Challenge to the World*, Addison-Wesley, Inc., Reading, MA, 1983.

Fjermestad, J., and Hiltz, S. R. "An Assessment of Group Support Systems Experimental Research: Methodology and Results," *Journal of Management Information Systems* (15:3), Winter 1998-99, pp. 7-149.

Gallupe, R., DeSanctis, G., and Dickson, G. "Computer-Based Support for Group Problem-Finding: An Experimental Investigation," *MIS Quarterly*, (12:2), June 1988, pp. 277-298.

Gavish, B., and Gerdes, J. "Anonymous Mechanisms in Group Decision Support Systems Communication," *Decision Support Systems* (23:4), October 1998, pp. 297-328.

Geerts, G., and McCarthy, W. E. "An Ontological Analysis of the Primitives of the Extended-REA Enterprise Information Architecture," *The International Journal of Accounting Information Systems* (3:1), 2002, pp. 1-16.

Gelernter, D. *Machine Beauty: Elegance and the Heart of Technology*, Basic Books, New York, 1998.

Glass, R. "On Design," *IEEE Software* (16:2), March/April 1999, pp. 103-104.

Halpin, T. A. *Information Modeling and Relational Databases*, Morgan Kaufmann Publishers, New York, 2001.

Henderson, J., and Venkatraman, N. "Strategic Alignment: Leveraging Information Technology for Transforming Organizations," *IBM Systems Journal* (32:1), 1993.

ISR. Editorial Statement and Policy, *Information Systems Research* (13:4), December 2002.

Jarvenpaa, S., Rao, V., and Huber, G. "Computer Support for Meetings of Groups Working on Unstructured Problems: A Field Experiment," *MIS Quarterly* (12:4), December 1988, pp. 645-666.

Johansson, J. M. "On the Impact of Network Latency on Distributed Systems Design," *Information Technology Management* (1), 2000, pp. 183-194.

Johansson, J. M., March, S. T., and Naumann, J. D. "Modeling Network Latency and Parallel Processing in Distributed Database Design," *Decision Sciences Journal* (34:4), Fall 2003.

Kalakota, R., and Robinson, M. *E-Business 2.0: Roadmap for Success*, Addison-Wesley Pearson Education, Boston, MA, 2001.

Keil, M. "Pulling the Plug: Software Project Management and the Problem of Project Escalation," *MIS Quarterly* (19:4) December 1995, pp. 421-447.

Keil, M., Cule, P. E., Lyytinen, K., and Schmidt, R. C. "A Framework for Identifying Software Project Risks," *Communications of the ACM* (41:11), November 1998, pp. 76-83.

Keil, M., and Robey, D. "Turning Around Troubled Software Projects: An Exploratory Study of the Deescalation of Commitment to Failing Courses of Action," *Journal of Management Information Systems*, (15:4) December 1999, pp. 63-87.

Kernighan, B., and Plauger, P. J. *The Elements of Programming Style* (2nd ed.), McGraw-Hill, New York, 1978.

Kim, Y. G., and March, S. T. "Comparing Data Modeling Formalisms," *Communications of the ACM* (38:6), June 1995, pp. 103-115.

Klein, H. K., and Myers, M. D. "A Set of Principles for Conducting and Evaluating Interpretive Field Studies in Information Systems," *MIS Quarterly* (23:1), March 1999, pp. 67-94.

Kleindorfer, G., O'Neill, L., and Ganeshan, R. "Validation in Simulation: Various Positions in the Philosophy of Science," *Management Science* (44:8), August 1998, pp. 1087-1099.

Kruchten, P. *The Rational Unified Process: An Introduction* (2nd ed.), Addison-Wesley, Inc., Reading, MA, 2000.

Kuhn, T. S. *The Structure of Scientific Revolutions* (3rd ed.), University of Chicago Press, Chicago, IL, 1996.

Kumar, A., and Zhao, J. "Workflow Support for Electronic Commerce Applications," *Decision Support Systems* (32:3), January 2002, pp. 265-278.

Lee, A. "Inaugural Editor's Comments," *MIS Quarterly* (23:1), March 1999, pp. v-xi.

Lee, A. "Systems Thinking, Design Science, and Paradigms: Heeding Three Lessons from the Past to Resolve Three Dilemmas in the

Present to Direct a Trajectory for Future Research in the Information Systems Field," Keynote Address, Eleventh International Conference on Information Management, Taiwan, May 2000 (available online at http://www.people.vcu.edu/~aslee/ICIM-keynote-2000).

Leymann, F., and Roller, D. *Production Workflow: Concepts and Techniques*, Prentice-Hall, Upper Saddle River, NJ, 2000.

Madnick, S. E. "The Challenge: To Be Part of the Solution Instead of Being Part of the Problem," in *Proceedings of the Second Annual Workshop on Information Technology and Systems*, V. Storey and A. Whinston (eds.), Dallas, TX, December 12-13, 1992, pp. 1-9.

Marakas, G. M., and Elam, J. J. "Semantic Structuring in Analyst Acquisition and Representation of Facts in Requirements Analysis," *Information Systems Research* (9:1), March 1998, pp. 37-63.

March, S. T., Hevner, A., and Ram, S. "Research Commentary: An Agenda for Information Technology Research in Heterogeneous and Distributed Environment," *Information Systems Research* (11:4), December 2000, pp. 327-341.

March, S. T., and Smith, G. "Design and Natural Science Research on Information Technology," *Decision Support Systems* (15:4), December 1995, pp. 251-266.

Markus, M. L., Majchrzak, A., and Gasser, L. "A Design Theory for Systems that Support Emergent Knowledge Processes," *MIS Quarterly* (26:3), September, 2002, pp. 179-212.

McCarthy, W. E. "The REA Accounting Model: A Generalized Framework for Accounting Systems in a Shared Data Environment," *The Accounting Review* (58:3), 1982, pp. 554-578.

Meehl, P. E. "What Social Scientists Don't Understand," in *Metatheory in Social Science*, D. W. Fiske and R. A. Shweder (eds.), University of Chicago Press, Chicago, IL, 1986, pp. 315-338.

Newell, A., and Simon, H. "Computer Science as Empirical Inquiry: Symbols and Search," *Communications of the ACM* (19:3), March 1976, pp. 113-126.

Norman, D. *The Design of Everyday Things*, Currency Doubleday, New York, 1988.

Nunamaker, J., Briggs, R., Mittleman, D., Vogel, D., and Balthazard, P. "Lessons from a Dozen Years of Group Support Systems Research: A Discussion of Lab and Field Findings," *Journal of Management Information Systems*, (13:3), Winter 1996-97, pp. 163-207.

Nunamaker, J., Chen, M., and Purdin, T. D. M. "Systems Development in Information Systems Research," *Journal of Management Information Systems* (7:3), Winter 1991a, pp. 89-106.

Nunamaker, J., Dennis, A., Valacich, J., Vogel, D., and George, J. "Electronic Meeting Systems to Support Group Work," *Communications of the ACM*, (34:7), July 1991b, pp. 40-61.

Orlikowski, W. J. "Using Technology and Constituting Structures: A Practice Lens for Studying Technology in Organizations." *Organization Science* (11:4), December 2000, pp. 404-428.

Orlikowski, W. J., and Barley, S. R. "Technology and Institutions: What Can Research on Information Technology and Research on Organizations Learn From Each Other?," *MIS Quarterly* (25:2), June 2001, pp 145-165.

Orlikowski, W. J., and Iacono, C. S. "Research Commentary: Desperately Seeking the 'IT' in IT Research—A Call to Theorizing the IT Artifact," *Information Systems Research* (12:2), June 2001, pp. 121-134.

Orman, L. V. "Electronic Markets, Hierarchies, Hubs, and Intermediaries," *Journal of Information Systems Frontiers* (4:2), 2002, pp. 207-222.

Pahl, G., and Beitz, W. *Engineering Design: A Systematic Approach*, Springer-Verlag, London, 1996.

Parsons, J., and Wand, Y. "Emancipating Instances from the Tyranny of Classes in Information Modeling," *ACM Transactions on Database Systems* (25:2), June 2000, pp. 228-268.

Petroski, H. *Invention by Design: How Engineers Get from Thought to Thing*, Harvard University Press, Cambridge, MA, 1996.

Purao, S., Storey, V. C., and Han, T. D. "Improving Reuse-Based System Design with Learning," *Information Systems Research* (14:3), September 2003, pp. 269-290.

Rittel, H. J., and Webber, M. M. "Planning Problems Are Wicked Problems," in *Developments in Design Methodology*, N. Cross (ed.), John Wiley & Sons, New York, 1984.

Robey, D. "Research Commentary: Diversity in Information Systems Research: Threat, Opportunity, and Responsibility," *Information Systems Research* (7:4), 1996, pp. 400-408.

Royce, W. *Software Project Management: A Unified Framework*, Addison-Wesley, Inc., Reading, MA, 1998.

Salton, G. *Automatic Text Processing: The Transformation, Analysis, and Retrieval of Information by Computer*, Addison-Wesley, Inc., Reading, MA, 1988.

Schneier, B. *Applied Cryptography: Protocols, Algorithms, and Source Code in C* (2nd ed.), John Wiley and Sons, New York, January 1996.

Schön, D. A. *The Reflective Practitioner: How Professionals Think in Action*, Basic Books, New York, 1983.

Seddon, P. B. "A Respecification and Extension of the DeLone and McLean Model of IS Success," *Information Systems Research* (8:3), September 1997, pp. 240-253.

Sengupta, K., and Te'eni, D. "Cognitive Feedback in GDSS: Improving Control and Convergence," *MIS Quarterly* (17:1), March 1993, pp. 87-113.

Silver, M. S., Markus, M. L., and Beath, C. M. "The Information Technology Interaction Model: A Foundation for the MBA Core Course," *MIS Quarterly* (19:3), September 1995, pp. 361-390.

Simon, H. A. *The Sciences of the Artificial* (3rd ed.), MIT Press, Cambridge, MA, 1996.

Sinha, A. P., and Vessey, I. "An Empirical Investigation of Entity-Based and Object-Oriented Data Modeling: A Development Life Cycle Approach," in *Proceedings of the Twentieth International Conference on Information Systems*, P. De and J. I. DeGross (eds.), Charlotte, NC, December 13-15, 1999, pp. 229-244.

Storey, V. C., Chiang, R. H. L., Dey, D., Goldstein, R. C., and Sundaresan, S. "Database Design with Common Sense Business Reasoning and Learning," *ACM Transactions on Database Systems* (22:4), December 1997, pp. 471-512.

Tam, K. Y. "Automated Construction of Knowledge-Bases from Examples," *Information Systems Research* (1:2), June 1990, pp. 144-167.

Tichy, W. "Should Computer Scientists Experiment More?" *IEEE Computer* (31:5), May 1998, pp. 32-40.

Trice, A., and Davis, R. "Heuristics for Reconciling Independent Knowledge Bases," *Information Systems Research* (4:3), September 1993, pp. 262-288.

Tsichritzis, D. "The Dynamics of Innovation," in *Beyond Calculation: The Next Fifty Years of Computing*, P. J. Denning and R. M. Metcalfe (eds.), Copernicus Books, New York, 1998, pp. 259-265.

Venkatesh, V. "Determinants pf Perceived Ease of Use: Integrating Control, Intrinsic Motivation, and Emotion into the Technology Acceptance Model," *Information Systems Research* (11:4), December 2000, pp. 342-365.

Vessey, I., and Glass, R. "Strong Vs. Weak Approaches to Systems Development," *Communications of the ACM* (41:4), April 1998, pp. 99-102.

Walls, J. G., Widmeyer, G. R., and El Sawy, O. A. "Building an Information System Design Theory for Vigilant EIS," *Information Systems Research* (3:1), March 1992, pp. 36-59.

Wand, Y., and Weber, R. "On the Deep Structure of Information Systems," *Information Systems Journal* (5), 1995, pp. 203-233.

Wand, Y., and Weber, R. "On the Ontological Expressiveness of Information Systems Design Analysis and Design Grammars," *Journal of Information Systems* (3:3), 1993, pp. 217-237.

Weber, R. "Editor's Comments: Still Desperately Seeking the IT Artifact," *MIS Quarterly* (27:2), June 2003, pp. iii-xi.

Weber, R. *Ontological Foundations of Information Systems*, Coopers & Lybrand, Brisbane, Australia, 1997.

Weber, R. "Toward a Theory of Artifacts: A Paradigmatic Base for Information Systems Research," *Journal of Information Systems* (1:2), Spring 1987, pp. 3-19.

WfMC. "Workflow Standard—Interoperability Wf-XML Binding," Document Number WFMC-TC-1023, Version 1.0, Workflow Management Coalition, 2000.

Winograd, T. *Bringing Design to Software*, Addison-Wesley, Inc., Reading, MA, 1996.

Winograd, T. "The Design of Interaction," in *Beyond Calculation: The Next 50 Years of Computing*, P. Denning and R. Metcalfe (eds.), Copernicus Books, New York, 1998, pp. 149-162.

Zelkowitz, M., and Wallace, D. "Experimental Models for Validating Technology," *IEEE Computer* (31:5), May 1998, pp. 23-31.

Zmud, R. "Editor's Comments," *MIS Quarterly* (21:2), June 1997, pp. xxi-xxii.

About the Authors

Alan R. Hevner is an Eminent Scholar and Professor in the College of Business Administration at the University of South Florida. He holds the Salomon Brothers/Hidden River Corporate Park Chair of Distributed Technology. His areas of research interest include information systems development, software engineering, distributed database systems, and healthcare information systems. He has published numerous research papers on these topics and has consulted for several Fortune 500 companies. Dr. Hevner received a Ph.D. in Computer Science from Purdue University. He has held faculty positions at the University of Maryland at College Park and the University of Minnesota. Dr. Hevner is a member of ACM, IEEE, AIS, and INFORMS.

Salvatore T. March is the David K. Wilson Professor of Management at the Owen Graduate School of Management, Vanderbilt University. He received a B.S. in Industrial Engineering and M.S. and Ph.D. degrees in Operations Research from Cornell University. His research interests are in information system development, distributed data-base design, and electronic commerce. His research has appeared in journals such as *Communications of the ACM*, *IEEE Transactions on Knowledge and Data Engineering*, and *Information Systems Research*. He served as the Editor-in-Chief of *ACM Computing Surveys* and as an associate editor for *MIS Quarterly*. He is currently a senior editor for *Information Systems Research* and an associate editor for *Decision Sciences Journal*.

Jinsoo Park is an assistant professor of information systems in the College of Business Administration at Korea University. He was formerly on the faculty of the Carlson School of Management at the University of Minnesota. He holds a Ph.D. in MIS from the University of Arizona. His research interests are in the areas of semantic interoperability and metadata management in interorganizational information systems, heterogeneous information resource management and integration, knowledge sharing and coordination, and data modeling. His published research articles appear in *IEEE Computer*, *IEEE Transactions on Knowledge and Data Engineering*, and *Information Systems Frontiers*. He currently serves on the editorial board of *Journal of Database Management*. He is a member of ACM, IEEE, AIS, and INFORMS.

Sudha Ram is the Eller Professor of MIS at the University of Arizona. She received a B.S. in Science from the University of Madras in 1979, PGDM from the Indian Institute of Management, Calcutta in 1981 and a Ph.D. from the University of Illinois at Urbana-Champaign, in 1985. Dr. Ram has published articles in such journals as *Communications of the ACM*, *IEEE Transactions on Knowledge and Data Engineering*, *Information Systems Research*, and *Management Science*. Her research deals with interoperability in heterogeneous databases, semantic modeling, data allocation, and intelligent agents for data management. Her research has been funded by IBM, National Institute of Standards and Technology (NIST), National Science Foundation (NSF), National Aeronautics and Space Administration (NASA), and the Office of Research and Development of the Central Intelligence Agency (CIA).

Appendix B
Exemplar Publications of Design Science Research in Information Systems

The design science research paradigm is poised to take its rightful place as a synergistic and equal partner alongside other research paradigms in the information systems (IS) field. In doing so, it is important to recognize some of the seminal design science research that has appeared in the IS literature up to the time of this text. The following list of exemplar publications, while in no means complete, provides a starting point for exploring some of the most significant design science contributions of the IS field over the past 30 years. The goals of this appendix are to highlight recent thinking on design science theories and research practices and to provide exemplar design science papers to contribute to a greater understanding of design science research in the IS community. Communicating IS design science theories and research practices is essential not only to support acceptance among IS professionals but also to establish the credibility of IS design science research among the larger body of design science researchers in computer science, engineering fields, architecture, the arts, and other design-oriented communities.

These exemplar papers are grouped into categories based on research topics. Volume III in the *SAGE Library in Business & Management* provides a collection of a subset of these exemplar papers (Hevner 2008 – Number 5 in the list below).

Design Science Theory and Practice
1. Gregor, S. and D. Jones (2007) The anatomy of a design theory, *Journal of the AIS* 8 (5), Article 2, pp. 312–335.
2. Hevner, A., S. March, J. Park, and S. Ram (2004) Design science in information systems research, *MIS Quarterly* 28 (1), pp. 75–105.
3. Hevner, A. (2007) A three-cycle view of design science research, *Scandinavian Journal of Information* Systems 19 (2), pp. 87–92.
4. Peffers K., T. Tuunanen, M. A. Rothenberger, and S. Chatterjee (2007-8) A design science research methodology for information systems research, *Journal of Management Information Systems (JMIS)* 24 (3), pp. 45–77.
5. Hevner, A. (Volume Editor) (2008) Design science theories and research practices, in L. Willcocks and A. Lee (eds.) Volume III in the *SAGE Major Currents in Information Systems Series*, SAGE Publications, Inc., Thousand Oaks, CA.
6. Iivari, J. (1991) A paradigmatic analysis of contemporary schools of IS development, *European Journal of Information Systems* 1 (4), pp. 249–272.

7. Iivari, J. (2007) A paradigmatic analysis of information systems as a design science, *Scandinavian Journal of IS* 19 (2), pp. 39–64.
8. March, S. and G. Smith (1995) Design and natural science research on information technology, *Decision Support Systems* 15 (4), pp. 251–266.
9. Markus, M., A. Majchrzak, L. Gasser (2002) A design theory for systems that support emergent knowledge processes, *MIS Quarterly* 26 (3), pp. 179–212.
10. Nunamaker, J., M. Chen, and T. Purdin (1991) Systems development in information systems research, *Journal of Management Information Systems* 7 (3), pp. 89–106.
11. Purao, S., C. Baldwin, A. Hevner, V. Storey, J. Pries-Heje, B. Smith, and Y. Zhu (2008) The sciences of design: observations on an emerging field, *Communications of the AIS*, 23, Article 29, pp. 523–546.
12. Peffers, K., T. Tuunanen, M. Rothenberger, and S. Chatterjee (2008) A design science research methodology for information systems research, *Journal of Management Information Systems*, 24 (3), pp. 45–77.
13. Walls, J., G. Widmeyer, and O. El Sawy (1992) Building an information system design theory for vigilant EIS, *Information Systems Research* 3 (1), pp. 36–59.
14. Weber, R. (1987) Towards a theory of artifacts: a paradigmatic base for information systems research, *Journal of Information Systems* 1 (1), pp. 3–20.

Information Systems Development and Systems Modeling

15. Abdel-Hamid, T. and S. Madnick (1989) Lessons learned from modeling the dynamics of software development, *Communications of the ACM* 32 (12), pp. 1426–1438, 1455.
16. Chidamber, S. and C. Kemerer (1994) A metrics suite for object oriented design, *IEEE Transactions on Software Engineering* 20 (6), 476–493.
17. Freeman, P. and D. Hart (2004) A science of design for software-intensive systems, *Communications of the ACM* 47 (8), pp. 19–21.
18. Hevner, A. and H. Mills (1993) Box structured methods for systems development with objects, *IBM Systems Journal* 32 (2), pp. 232–251.

Information and Data Modeling

19. Chen, P. (1976) The entity-relationship model: toward a unified model of data, *ACM Transactions on Database Systems* 1 (1), pp. 9–36.
20. Parsons, J. and Y. Wand (2000) Emancipating instances from the tyranny of classes in information modeling, *ACM Transactions on Database Systems* 25 (2), pp. 228–268.
21. Ram, S. and V. Khatri (2005) A comprehensive framework for modeling set-based business rules during conceptual database design, *Information Systems*, 30 (2), pp. 89–118.
22. Ram, S. and J. Park (2004) Semantic conflict resolution ontology (SCROL): an ontology for detecting and resolving data and schema-level semantic conflicts, *IEEE Transactions on Knowledge and Data Engineering* 16 (2), pp. 189–202.

23. Wand, Y. and R. Weber (1990) An ontological model of an information system, *IEEE Transactions on Software Engineering* 16 (11), pp. 1282–1292.
24. Wand, Y., V. Storey, and R. Weber, An ontological analysis of the relationship construct in conceptual modeling, *ACM Transactions on Database Systems* 24 (4), pp. 494–528.
25. Wang, R., V. Storey, and C. Firth (1995) a framework for analysis of data quality research, *IEEE Transactions on Knowledge and Data Engineering* 7 (4), pp. 623–640.

Database Systems Design

26. Dey, D. and S. Sarkar (1996) A probabilistic relational model and algebra, *ACM Transactions on Database Systems* 21 (3), pp. 339–369.
27. Ram, S. and S. Narasimhan (1994) Database allocation in a distributed environment: incorporating a concurrency control mechanism and queueing costs, *Management Science* 40 (8), pp. 969–983.
28. Storey, V., R. Chiang, D. Dey, R. Goldstein, and S. Sundaresan, Database design with common sense business reasoning and learning, *ACM Transactions on Database Systems* 22 (4), pp. 471–512.

Knowledge and Information Integration

29. Goh, C., S. Bressan, S. Madnick, and M. Siegel (1999) context interchange: new features and formalisms for the intelligent integration of information, *ACM Transactions on Information Systems* 17 (3), pp. 270–293.
30. Krishnan, R., X. Li, D. Steier, and J. Zhao (2001) On heterogeneous database retrieval: a cognitively-guided approach, *Information Systems Research* 12 (3), pp. 286–303.
31. Mylopoulos, J., A. Borgida, M. Jarke, and M. Koubarakis (1990) Telos: representing knowledge about information systems, *ACM Transactions on Information Systems* 8 (4), pp. 325–362.
32. Park, J. and S. Ram (2004) Information systems interoperability: what lies beneath? *ACM Transactions on Information Systems* 22 (4), pp. 595–632.

Data Warehousing and Mining

33. Berndt, D., A. Hevner, and J. Studnicki (2003) The CATCH data warehouse: support for community health care decision making, *Decision Support Systems* 35, pp. 367–384.
34. Datta, A., D. VanderMeer, and K. Ramamritham (2002) Parallel star join + data indexes: efficient query processing in data warehouses and OLAP, *IEEE Transactions on Knowledge and Data Engineering* 14 (6), pp. 1299–1316.
35. Silberschatz, A. and A. Tuzhilin (1996) What makes patterns interesting in knowledge discovery systems, *IEEE Transactions on Knowledge and Data Engineering*, 8 (6), pp. 970–974.

Network and Telecommunications Systems

36. Chatterjee, S., T. Abhichandani, B. Tulu, and H. Li (2005) SIP-based enterprise converged network for voice/video over IP: implementation and evaluation of components, *IEEE Journal on Selected Areas in Communications*, 23 (10), pp. 1921–1933.

Decision Support Systems

37. Adomavicius, G., R. Shankaranarayanan, S. Sen, and A. Tuzhilin (2005) Incorporating contextual information in recommender systems using a multidimensional approach, *ACM Transactions on Information Systems* 23 (1), pp. 103–145.
38. Basu, A. and R. Blanning (1994) Metagraphs: a tool for modeling decision support systems, *Management Science* 40 (12), pp. 1579–1600.
39. Nunamaker, J., A. Dennis, J. Valacich, D. Vogel, and J. George (1991) Electronic meeting systems, *Communications of the ACM* 34 (7), pp. 40–61.
40. Nunamaker, J., R. Briggs, D. Mittleman, and D. Vogel (1997) Lessons from a dozen years of group support systems research: a discussion of lab and field findings, *Journal of Management Information Systems* 13 (3), pp. 163–207.

Workflow Systems

41. Kumar, A. and J. Zhao (1999) Dynamic routing and operational controls in workflow management systems, *Management Science* 45 (2), pp 253–272.
42. van der Aalst, W. and A. Kumar (2003) XML-based schema definition for support of interorganizational workflow, *Information Systems* Research 14 (1), pp. 23–46.

Electronic Commerce Systems

43. Bapna, R., P. Goes, and A. Gupta (2003) Analysis and design of business-to-consumer online auctions, *Management Science* 49 (1), pp. 85–101.
44. Chen, H., A. Houston, R. Sewell, and B. Schatz (1998) Internet browsing and searching: user evaluations of category map and concept space techniques, *Journal of the American Society for Information Science* 49 (7), pp. 582–603.

Contributors

Donald J. Berndt (dberndt@coba.usf.edu) is an associate professor in the Information Systems and Decision Sciences Department in the College of Business at the University of South Florida. His research interests include data warehousing, knowledge discovery, data mining, and health informatics. Dr. Berndt received a Ph.D. in information systems from the Stern School of Business at New York University. He was a research scientist at Yale University and Scientific Computing Associates, where he participated in the development of commercial versions of the Linda parallel-programming environment. He also developed artificial intelligence applications in academic settings and at Cognitive Systems, Inc. Dr. Berndt is a member of Beta Gamma Sigma, AAAI, ACM, and AIS.

Sven A. Carlsson (Sven_Carlsson@hermes.ics.lu.se) is professor of informatics at School of Economics and Management, Lund University. His current research interests include the use of IS to support management processes, knowledge management, enterprise systems, technochange, design and redesign of e-business processes in electronic value chains, and networks in turbulent and high-velocity environments. He has a keen interest in the use of critical realism in IS research and IS design science research. He has held visiting positions at universities in Europe, Australia, the USA, and Singapore. He is a regional editor for *Knowledge Management Research and Practice*. He has published more than 100 peer-reviewed journal articles, book chapters, and conference papers and his work has appeared in journals like *JMIS, Decision Sciences, Information & Management, International Journal of Technology Management, Knowledge and Process Management, Knowledge Management Research & Practice, Information Systems and e-Business Management*, and *Scandinavian Journal of IS*.

Juhani Iivari (juhani.iivari@oulu.fi) is a professor in information systems at the University of Oulu, Finland. He is a senior editor of *MIS Quarterly* and serves in editorial boards of four other IS journals. His research has broadly focused on theoretical foundations of information systems, design science research in information systems, information systems development methodologies and approaches, organizational analysis, implementation and acceptance of information systems, and the quality of information systems. He has published in journals such as

Communications of the ACM, Data Base, European Journal of Information Systems, Information & Management, Information Systems, Information Systems Journal, Information Systems Research, Journal of Management Information Systems, Journal of Organizational Computing and Electronic Commerce, MIS Quarterly, and *Omega.*

Robert Judge (rjudge@mail.sdsu.edu) holds undergraduate degrees in biology and botany, an MBA, and a PhD in the Management of Information Systems and Technology from Claremont Graduate University. His career spans the semiconductor, aerospace, consumer electronics, and Internet service industries at mid-management and executive levels. He has held functional responsibilities that include materiel, manufacturing, information systems, marketing, project management, and customer support. Throughout the last 20+ years of his career, he has served both San Diego State University and the University of San Diego as an adjunct professor teaching graduate and undergraduate courses in operations, supply chain management, manufacturing planning and control systems, project management, and information systems. His current research interests lie in understanding how barriers to knowledge flow arise as small organizations grow, and also in how knowledge management systems in supply chains can influence innovation and the flow of non-logistical knowledge.

Salvatore T. March (sal.march@owen.vanderbilt.edu) is the David K. Wilson Professor of Management at the Owen Graduate School of Management, Vanderbilt University. He received his B.S., M.S., and Ph.D. degrees in operations research from Cornell University. His primary teaching responsibilities and research interests are in the areas of data representation and analysis formalisms, design as a research paradigm, and information system development tools and methodologies. His research has appeared in journals such as *ACM Computing Surveys, ACM Transactions on Database Systems, Communications of the ACM, IEEE Transactions on Knowledge and Data Engineering, Information Systems Research, MIS Quarterly,* and *The Journal of MIS.* He has served as the editor-in-chief for *ACM Computing Surveys,* senior editor for *Information Systems Research,* and associate editor for *MIS Quarterly.* He is currently an associate editor for *Decision Sciences Journal, Journal of Database Management,* and *Communications of the AIS.*

Sandeep Purao (spurao@ist.psu.edu) is an associate professor of Information Sciences and Technology at Penn State. Prior to joining Penn State, Purao was on the faculty at Georgia State University. Purao's research focuses on the design, evolution, and management of complex techno-organizational systems. His current projects include process-focused composition and monitoring of service-based systems, risk mitigation in large-scale organizational IT integration projects, and investigation of web service standardization processes. Purao's work has been published in journals such as *Communications of the ACM, IEEE Transactions on Systems, Man and Cybernetics-A, ACM Computing Surveys,* and *Information Systems Research*; and conferences such as the International Conference on

Information Systems, IEEE Service-Oriented Computing Conference, and the International Conference on Conceptual Modeling. He currently serves as an associate editor for *MIS Quarterly*. Purao holds a Ph.D. in management information systems from the University of Wisconsin-Milwaukee. He is a member of AIS, ACM, and IEEE.

Matti Rossi (matti.rossi@iki.fi) is a professor of information systems at Helsinki School of Economics. He has worked as research fellow at Erasmus University Rotterdam, visiting assistant professor at Georgia State University, Atlanta, and visiting professor at Claremont Graduate University. He received his Ph.D. in Business Administration from the University of Jyväskylä in 1998. He has been the principal investigator in several major research projects funded by the technological development center of Finland and Academy of Finland. His research papers have appeared in journals such as *CACM, Journal of AIS, Information and Management* and *Information Systems*, and over 30 of them have appeared in conferences such as ICIS, HICSS, and CAiSE.

Maung K. Sein (maung.k.sein@uia.no) is a professor of information systems at University of Agder, Norway. A Ph.D. from Indiana University, he has led a nomadic life having previously served at Georgia State, Florida International, and, Indiana Universities in USA and as an adjunct professor at the University of Bergen in Norway. His research interests have moved on from end-user training and cognitive issues in IS to his current focus on IT and national development, e-government, and proactive research approaches, specifically design research and action research and the relationship between the two. He has published in, among others, *Information Systems Research, MIS Quarterly, Communications of the ACM*, and *Human–Computer Interaction* and has widely presented his research. His editorial board experience includes *MIS Quarterly, MIS Quarterly Executive, Communications of the AIS, e-Service Journal, Electronic Journal of e-Government, IT for Development Journal* and guest-editing special issues of *The Communications of the ACM* and *Scandinavian Journal of Information Systems*. He has chaired and served on the program committees of several conferences. He has conducted workshops and seminars on research methods, particularly focusing on design and action research in several countries around the world.

Monica Chiarini Tremblay (mtremblay68@gmail.com) is an assistant professor at Florida International University in Miami, FL. Her research interests are in the areas of data warehouse, data mining, and business intelligence, particularly in the area of health care. Dr. Tremblay has published papers in *Decision Support Systems, The Journal of Computer Information Systems* and has presented her research at several international conferences. She is currently working as a co-investigator in two veterans administration, health services research, and development funded studies: "Using Knowledge Discovery Strategies to Identify Fall-related Injuries in the VA", and "Using Text Mining to Differentiate Between Post Traumatic Stress Disorder and Mild Traumatic Brain Injury in Operations Iraqi Freedom and

Enduring Freedom Veterans." She teaches business intelligence at both the graduate and undergraduate levels and will introduce a new graduate course in health information management in the spring of 2010. Prior to joining academia, Monica worked for Exxon U.S.A., IBM, and Siemens.

Timothy J. Vogus (timothy.vogus@owen.vanderbilt.edu) is assistant professor of management at the Vanderbilt Owen Graduate School of Management. He received his Ph.D. in management and organizations from the Ross School of Business at the University of Michigan. His research has focused on how micro-level actions build, grow, and sustain organizational capabilities, and how organizations can be designed and structured to foster these actions and capabilities. This research has resulted in theories of two critical capabilities: (1) mindful organizing – the capability to detect and correct emerging errors and other unexpected events and (2) resilience – the capability to achieve desirable outcomes amid adversity, strain, and significant barriers to adaptation or development. His research has been published in both managerial and health services outlets including the *Journal of Organizational Behavior* and *Medical Care*. He is currently a member of the editorial board for *Organization Science*.

Kevin Williams (kevin.williams@cgu.edu) is a Ph.D. student in the School of Information Systems and Technology at Claremont Graduate University, California. He holds a B.S. in business administration and an M.S. in finance (M.B.A.) both from California State University, Long Beach. Since 1991 he has been working with mission critical databases on large UNIX systems, first as an employee and for the past 13 years as an independent consultant for a variety of world-class organizations. He has founded two successful consulting companies Gibraltar Associates, Inc. (1996) and Avalon Consulting Solutions, Inc. (2005).

Index

CPSIA information can be obtained at www.ICGtesting.com
Printed in the USA
LVOW01*0858040115

421433LV00007B/307/P